The Left Side of the Screen

ALSO BY BOB HERZBERG
AND FROM McFARLAND

*Savages and Saints: The Changing Image of
American Indians in Westerns* (2008)

*The FBI and the Movies: A History of the Bureau
on Screen and Behind the Scenes in Hollywood* (2007)

Shooting Scripts: From Pulp Western to Film (2005)

The Left Side of the Screen

Communist and Left-Wing Ideology in Hollywood, 1929–2009

BOB HERZBERG

McFarland & Company, Inc., Publishers
Jefferson, North Carolina, and London

LIBRARY OF CONGRESS CATALOGUING-IN-PUBLICATION DATA

Herzberg, Bob, 1956–
The left side of the screen : Communist and left-wing
ideology in Hollywood, 1929–2009 / Bob Herzberg.
p.   cm.
Includes bibliographical references and index.

ISBN 978-0-7864-4456-4
softcover : 50# alkaline paper ∞

1. Motion picture industry — Political aspects — United States — Los Angeles —
History — 20th century.   2. Screenwriters — Political activity — United States —
History — 20th century.   3. Motion picture producers and directors —
United States — History — 20th century.   4. Motion picture actors and actresses —
Political activity — United States — History — 20th century.
5. Communism and motion pictures — United States.   I. Title.
PN1993.5.U65.H45 2011   791.4309794'94 — dc22   2010053704

BRITISH LIBRARY CATALOGUING DATA ARE AVAILABLE

© 2011 Bob Herzberg. All rights reserved

*No part of this book may be reproduced or transmitted in any form
or by any means, electronic or mechanical, including photocopying
or recording, or by any information storage and retrieval system,
without permission in writing from the publisher.*

Cover image © 2011 Shutterstock

Manufactured in the United States of America

*McFarland & Company, Inc., Publishers
Box 611, Jefferson, North Carolina 28640
www.mcfarlandpub.com*

To Marvin,
the Wild Brother who will remain forever young.
Hope you're having a good time —
wherever you ended up…

Table of Contents

Acknowledgments ix
Introduction 1

I. In the Red (1929–1936)   7
II. The Old Left Hook (1937–1941)   63
III. Bodyguard of Lies (1942–1945)   113
IV. A Revolution from Above (1946–1951)   173
V. Breaking Eggs (1952–1958)   234
VI. Containment (1959–2009)   268

Chapter Notes   279
Bibliography   285
Index   289

Acknowledgments

There are many people to thank for assisting me with this book, so let's cut to the chase.

I'd like to thank the Margaret Herrick Library in Beverly Hills, who provided me with studio correspondence, clipping files, budget analyses, letters, plot synopses and casting sheets from various productions, particularly Paramount films like *The General Died at Dawn*, *The War of the Worlds*, *The Remarkable Andrew* and *The Lawless*, as well as background materials on the long-abandoned MGM film version of Sinclair Lewis' *It Can't Happen Here*. I'd like to specifically thank Linda Harris Mehr, Barbara Hall, and Jenny Romero, as well as the always polite and competent staff at the Special Collections Desk.

Many thanks to Sandra Day Lee and Jonathon Auxier, director and curator, respectively, of the Warner Brothers Archives of the School of Cinematic Arts at the University of Southern California. The always reliable Ned Comstock provided the Philip Dunne papers which contained detailed correspondence, as well as script drafts on such Twentieth Century–Fox films as *Three Brave Men* and *Pinky*. Books like this always need good photographs for readers to look at in case they get tired of my writing, so yet *more* thanks to good ol', hard-working Dollie Banner of Jerry Ohlinger Movie Memorabilia whom I kept *very* busy finding dozens of movie stills for use in this book. On the West Coast, the folks at Larry Edmonds Bookshop on Hollywood Boulevard also earned my gratitude.

And now, I'd like to thank my family and friends who patiently endured my ignoring them through the duration of this project. I know it hasn't been easy to deal with me, but I don't believe in bringing laptops to baby showers.

My love and gratitude to my big sister Rose (mother of Allentown, Pennsylvania, City Councilman Michael Schlossberg and published playwright Rebecca Schlossberg). As a movie buff extraordinaire, Rose had the foresight to hold on to many long out-of-print books on film history which have helped me immeasurably in my research. When I was little, she dragged me to many a film retrospective playing in Manhattan. Instead of gratitude, she was rewarded with complaints that these classic films didn't have any shooting in them. *Schvester*, I hope this makes up for it.

And last but not least, my beautiful Colleen, who has loved me and endured my artistic pretensions for, as of this date, 24 years—13 of them as man and wife. She has proofread my material, praised and criticized it, and contributed her insight into the topic of left-wing artists in Hollywood. I love her for her innate goodness, her unending support, and the fact that she makes the best meat loaf in town—in that order.

In the meantime, I hope you all enjoy this work. I took long enough to write it...

Introduction

In May 2008, Russian Communists called for a boycott of the Steven Spielberg camp escapist adventure *Indiana Jones and the Kingdom of the Crystal Skull*. The Communists objected to the sequence where Soviet troops invade an American military installation and cold-bloodedly massacre all the soldiers guarding it. As reported in the *London Sunday Times* of May 20, they heatedly claimed that no Soviet terrorists were sent to the U.S. in 1957, the period in which the film was set. Instead, they boasted of sending the Sputnik satellite up around that time, an event which, according to these officials, elicited "the admiration of the world."

The Sunday Times quoted the Communist lawmaker Andrei Andreyev, who stated, "It is very disturbing if talented directors want to provoke a new Cold War." Mind you, these words were uttered a mere three months before Russian armies invaded the tiny republic of Georgia on its southern border and angrily rejected the international community's calls to desist. But back in May, Reuters quoted St. Petersburg Communist Party boss Sergei Malinkovich as saying, "Why should we agree to that sort of lie and let the West trick our youth?" He furthermore claimed that Russian youth "will go to the cinema and will be sure that in 1957 we made trouble for the United States and almost started a nuclear war."

This coloring of history by Communists has apparently not changed in over half a century. In his *tête-à-tête* with the *London Times*, Andreyev did not mention that the Sputnik elicited a little more than the admiration of the world; it elicited *fear*, a very real fear that a renegade totalitarian power might have a space platform from which to drop atomic weapons on the nations of the world.

The penchant of Communists to once again slam the United States while ignoring its own bloody history began a little less than a century ago. This bellicose attitude of loudly trumpeting a despot system while tearing down the systems of more successful nations carried into its "entertainment": its films, radio, stage, newspapers and eventually TV. It was a culture of lies and double-speak born in a land already drenched in blood…

In February 1917, the Russian people, fed up with the rule of Czar Nicholas II, instigated a popular revolution which swept the aristocracy from power. A provisional government run by former army officer Alexander Kerensky was inaugurated to do away with archaic Czarist rule and institute democratic reforms all over the country, including cutting back workers' hours from 12 to eight, equal distribution of the land, freedom of the press, freedom of assembly and dozens of other laws to insure the civil rights of Russia's citizens.

However, waiting in the wings was a cadre of professional revolutionaries anxious to do away with the democratic leadership and set up a Communist government with sweeping dictatorial powers over the whole nation. It is hard to believe that this epic historical event, the men who were so much a part of it, and those who perpetuated the Communist way for decades, would actually wield a powerful influence over an industry thousands of miles away, whose output usually dealt, not with the intricacies and contradictions of political systems, but with fantasies of glamour and romance: Hollywood.

The twentieth century corruption of Marx and Engels' original idea of Communism can basically be laid at the feet of two men: Vladimir I. Ulanov, alias Lenin, and Iosef Djughasvili, alias Stalin. It is to these two men overall whom we can thank for the system of lies, corruption and mass murder that would exist from the 1930s through the 1950s; ironically, all through Hollywood's Golden Era. Though Lenin would not institute programs of mass murder, as a leader he openly encouraged the use of banditry and terrorism to perpetuate the Communist system of government. Doing away with the provisional government's reforms, he freely approved of mass detentions without trial, censorship of the press and the suppression of civil liberties to justify the aims of the Revolution. That the man who would follow in his footsteps would take this attitude further in order to justify the mass murders of perceived enemies was only natural.

To those folks in the United States and other democratic nations who only have a vague idea of Soviet oppression, the reading of just a few books on Josef Stalin and those who worked under him would reveal a shocking abuse of power and a system of mass human extermination that even Hitler and the Nazi regime couldn't match in its number of victims. (Not that they didn't try.) In order to perpetuate this horror for decades, a totalitarian system such as this would need its followers, its sycophants, its dysfunctional cheerleaders and, unfortunately, its propagandists. Needless to say, one of the ways to spread the word about Marxism was the movies.

In fact, shortly after the Bolshevik takeover and the consolidation of Soviet power, Lenin proclaimed, "Communists must always consider that of all the arts, the motion picture is the most important." After his own ascension to power, Stalin saw the motion picture as "not only a vital agitprop device for the education and political indoctrination of the workers, but also a fluent channel through which to reach the minds and shape the desires of people everywhere." Now that Stalin had used the sinister phrase "political indoctrination," and insisted on the need to "shape the desires of people everywhere," Sovkino and other government bureaucracies were formed to make sure that the cinematic viewpoint of Soviet artists jibed with the aims of the Revolution.

However, the cheerleaders of Marxism weren't satisfied with promoting the overthrow of capitalism within their own borders. They wanted to export it all over the world, especially to that bastion of capitalist freedoms *and* excesses, the United States.

Since a cinematic treatise on Bolshevism was not considered box office in escapist Hollywood, Communists in charge of exporting the glories of Marxism had to make their propaganda more clever, less blatant, and to fit more snugly within the escapist needs of the standard Hollywood product. Although it is inconceivable that anyone would find a way to justify a system that encourages mass terror and genocide on its people in a Hollywood film, the American Communist Party endeavored to do the task. The fact that they succeeded in painting a portrait of a benign Soviet state and at the same time successfully attack several American sacred cows, is because of the talent, drive and, in some cases, the blind fanaticism of a group of leftist Hollywood actors, producers, directors and screenwriters.

During the Depression, the Broadway theater would become a fertile breeding ground for Marxist playwrights, directors and actors. They used the New York stage to spread the glories of the Marxist way by attacking American institutions. At the time, this was certainly easy. The Depression put thousands of Americans out of work all over the country (with rural areas, usually bastions of right-wing sentiment, hit much harder than the big cities). Broadway Marxists created dramatic works which fed on the anger of a disillusioned public. This rage against the rich, who supposedly were never affected by the Depression, was coupled with the bitterness of those Americans who had fought in World War I — a war seen by many then (as today) as a war fought for the interests of colonial expansion and capitalist exploitation.

Playwrights, directors and actors emerged from this milieu who would have an enormous impact on the films to come out of Hollywood throughout the '30s and '40s: John Howard Lawson, Clifford Odets, Elia Kazan, Harold Clurman, Frances Farmer, John Garfield, character actors J. Edward Bromberg, Morris Carnovsky, Luther Adler, Mady Christians, Lee J. Cobb and a veritable who's who of Hollywood's Golden Years. They were not the pampered stars of the MGM variety, who conveyed a world of upper-crust glamour. They were the products of the urban jungle, with upbringings that were usually poor, working-class, and predominantly Jewish. Their rage, fueled mostly by the vicious anti–Semitism of the times, were a sharp contrast to the Hollywood stars of the 1920s and early '30s. If the Clark Gables and Joan Crawfords of the times had to fight poverty, the Broadway Marxists had to fight not only that, but the religious prejudices of the day. Many of these artists were heroes in their own right, as they sincerely fought the good fight against racial and religious discrimination, worker exploitation, sexism and the spread of fascism.

However, some of them were interested in attacking American institutions within the regimentalist dogma of the Communist Party, with no room for compromise or negotiation with those who disagreed with them. Certainly by their own narrow standards, they rarely, if ever, followed a philosophy of liberation and enlightenment among members of their own group.

In time, some would leave the Party for this very reason. Those Hollywood artists who left the Party included Edward Dmytryk, Elia Kazan, Lee J. Cobb and many others. Over time, they couldn't bring themselves to accept an organization preaching tolerance and inclusion while exercising a ruthless dictatorship of exclusion and intolerance. The "my way or the highway" manner in which the Party's leaders ran their groups, which encouraged free discussions as long they adhered to the Party line, and the shouting down of any member who expressed an original thought, eventually repelled those who only wanted to find a way to genuinely help the downtrodden. Many of the disillusioned testified before HUAC during the Blacklist Years in order to save their careers; some informed because they felt it wrong to remain a Party member while American troops were fighting a war against Communist soldiers in Korea. Either way, whether the informers' motives were opportunistic or sincere, the fact that those artists who did leave would be attacked by the Party for decades afterward was not a surprise. The philosophy of "us against them" never leaves room for compromise.

Nevertheless, the fact that Hollywood studios did endeavor to cover up America's ills was obvious. Though the film industry *was* pressured by the powers-that-be, whether in Washington or elsewhere, to "tone down" their product if it attacked social institutions, Hollywood's film bosses also had to contend with a public that would accept just *so* much social comment as it could stomach. The Mayers, Warners, Zanucks and Goldwyns were certainly well aware that preachy message pictures were box office poison (as, for the most part, they still are today). The Hollywood moguls promoted escapism; glamour, romance, action, and maybe a little violence as long as it was "tasteful." A moral lesson was encouraged as long as it promoted the goodness of humanity and condemned the evils of human vice; that is, a moral that did not emphasize social, political or ethnic divisions of any kind. Racial and religious strife rarely existed in American films of the time, and any implication that the powers-that-be in our society should be replaced by an entirely different system was a fiercely fought taboo. How then would the Marxist screenwriters of the time deal with all this?

The answer was, by elision, avoidance and subtlety. With the establishment of the Production Code in 1930 and its more strict enforcement in 1934, the Christian religious institutions won the day in censoring films showing vice, corruption, sleaze and all forms of social attack on America and its institutions. The Production Code Administration (or PCA) saw the proliferation of sleaze and social discontent on screen as the work of East Coast radicals originally from the Broadway stage; and the Christian-backed group also saw the inclusion of social topics attacking America as the work of Jewish influences seeking to overturn Christian sacred cows and undermine Christian dictates. That the PCA was populated with anti–Semites is undeniable today, as more and more examples of vicious Jew-baiting is revealed in books and documentary films about the organization. It was PCA enforcer Joseph I. Breen who claimed that what was wrong with motion pictures was due to the influence of "Eastern European Jews."*

Will Hays was a former postmaster general for the corrupt Harding administration who took over Hollywood's self-regulatory Motion Picture Producers and Distributors of America in 1930. However, it was the pious Catholic Breen who would use the PCA as an instrument in the spreading of Christian values and the restriction of any other points of view. Communist screenwriters, less interested in promoting any other dogma besides the ideology of Marxism, realized that Hollywood was only interested in films that promoted escape. On the Broadway stage, the characters in plays written by Party playwrights could easily address the audience on the evils of Depression-era America and the exploitative ways of capitalistic excess; but in the mass-produced films of Hollywood, such direct calls for communistic action had to be tempered with restraint.

This book is about the screenwriters, playwrights, directors and actors who strove to present the Communist view in Hollywood films, those who were caught in HUAC's net in the postwar years, and those innocent liberals whose sincere humanist beliefs unfortunately threw them into the same group as those who excused Stalin's madness. The book will go into the various clever and subtle (and sometimes clumsy, crude and blatant) ways that leftist scenarists presented their screenplays before the American public. I'll be putting a common-sense spin on the leftist polemics and now cliché-ridden plots and provide a more realistic historical background for the many factual errors and inaccuracies these works contain.

The work will also go into what was actually happening off screen in the global hotbed of international politics, where social upheavals, revolutions and world war had almost as much to do with the content of Hollywood scripts as the whimsical dictates of any studio head.

The book will examine the works of those liberal stars and directors who collaborated with Communist artists in New York and Hollywood—performers like John Garfield, Canada Lee, Frances Farmer, Paul Robeson, James Edwards and Paul Muni, actors whose politics guided the themes of their films every bit as much as the screenwriters who wrote

---

*Letter from Joseph I. Breen to Rev. Wilfird Parsons, Oct. 10, 1932, in Thomas Doherty, *Hollywood's Censor: Joseph I. Breen & the Production Code Administration*, p. 199.

them and the directors who made them; as well as liberal filmmakers Philip Dunne and ex–Communists (and HUAC-friendly witnesses) Elia Kazan, Edward Dmytryk and Robert Rossen. I will also discuss great men of letters like socialists H.G. Wells, Sinclair Lewis and Graham Greene, Party members Theodore Dreiser and Dorothy Parker, and left-leaning authors Ernest Hemingway and Irwin Shaw.

The work will explore how many of these artists first found their voices lifted in social protest in the world of the New York theater, and quote dialogue from many of their angry yet provocative works; such writers as John Howard Lawson, Albert Maltz, and Clifford Odets would make an impact during Hollywood's Golden Age. It will also follow the theater and film output of those social activist playwrights who came up after them, like Lillian Hellman and Arthur Miller.

This book is *not* the story of the Hollywood Ten, though I do examine the lives and careers of several of them. Nor is it a definitive exploration of the blacklist era, though I mention it at times when discussing the period of the late 1940s and beyond. Other historians have done studies of the Hollywood blacklist in much better detail and depth than I do here. Instead, this work explores the personalities of the men and women I discuss, as well as the background and events that shaped their thinking and solidified their commitment to social protest on- and off-camera.

It would be hard to discuss the period of the 1930s to the 1950s without also discussing the political and social figures of the day who carried an impact, whether directly or indirectly, on the content of Hollywood films. As well as the John Howard Lawsons and Lester Coles, the book also features dictators like Josef Stalin, Adolf Hitler, Francisco Franco, Vladimir Lenin, Fulgencia Batista; gangsters like Albert Anastasia and Emanual "Mendy" Weiss; Comintern agents like Willi Munzenberg and Otto Katz; and anti-fascists like Morris "Two-Gun" Cohen and Muriel Gardiner Buttinger. And what would the content of Hollywood films be without the Harry Cohns, Darryl Zanucks and Jack Warners; or the film community's censorship czar during this period, Joseph I. Breen.

I will quote from FBI files on the individuals mentioned, especially the Bureau's COMPIC files (Communist Infiltration of the Motion Picture Industry); HUAC testimony of those accused of injecting Communism into movie scripts; studio correspondence detailing production background and casting choices, as well as correspondence with the Production Code office; correspondence from government agencies and various religious organizations; film and theater reviews of the projects discussed; film studies by various critics and authors; knowledgeable and impartial histories on the subject of the Soviet Union and the Communist Party; passages from the novels and plays by these artists, some eventually made into films; quotes from various autobiographies by the artists mentioned in this book; and quotes from their interviews with contemporary journalists, as well as latter-day histories of their involvement in the Communist Party.

In the past, many of us confused those wonderful performers and craftsmen who were humanists with those who only sought conflict and confrontation. Indeed, we found it hard to disassociate those who promoted the worthy causes of altruism, racial and religious equality, and international peace from those who belonged to a leftist movement that promoted hatred and terror at any price. By the same token, post–HUAC, we confused those on the right who sincerely strove to liberate those victimized by a tyrannical regime with those who exploited this genuine fear for their own ends.

Soviet foreign minister Vyachalev Molotov once said, "In order to make an omelet, you have to break a few eggs."

In the following pages, we'll see how a motion picture screen in a democracy can be used to portray the causes of both the left and the right, and how they were presented under the heading of entertainment. It's a story of international power politics, Broadway egos, high-wattage Hollywood star power, religious pressure groups, and both left-wing and right-wing cliques struggling for domination, with the spoils being the hearts and minds of the American audience.

In the midst of it all is the still-constant struggle between the message film and the escapist film, and the still-widening gap between making a political statement and providing thrilling entertainment.

Certainly, in a democracy, *all* these voices get their chance to be heard, not only one voice.

And *that's* entertainment...

I

In the Red (1929–1936)

> [The revolutionary movement] seems nothing but grime and stink and sweat and obscene noises and the language of beasts. But surely this is what *history* is. It is not just made by gentlemen and scholars.
> —a letter from a Communist friend to Granville Hicks

By 1929, most Hollywood films were now talking. Two years old since Al Jolson first spoke on screen, the talking film was a new innovation that benefited audiences wishing to be entertained, but did little for the nation's ailing economy (with the exception of making Broadway stars richer with Hollywood money). In 1929, the stock market crashed and the country plunged into its worst economic depression in its history (so far). With millions of Americans out of work, angry people went to the movies for escapism. However, at least one special group of artists wasn't going to let the public off the hook with flashy musicals, screwball comedies, soapy romances or dime-store adventure tales.

"I will always present the Communist position,"[1] said the usually intimidating John Howard Lawson.

How this totalitarian movement became the inspiration, and in so many ways, the very meaning of life itself, to so many of Hollywood's talented artists, is a story in itself. Needless to say, the arrival of the Great Depression seemed to prove, to these artists as well as many non–Communists, that capitalism was a failure.

Yet years before the Communist "experiment" had taken hold in Russia, one particular artist had his own ax to grind with capitalist society; and his origins were not the teeming ghettos of New York where the poor barely scraped by, but the all–American, God-fearing Midwest Bible Belt.

> [I was] envying the rich and wishing that I was famous or a member of a wealthy family, and that I might meet one of the beautiful girls I imagined I saw there and have her fall in love with me and make me rich.[2]

These were the imaginings of a young, wistful Theodore Dreiser as he stood outside a row of opulent mansions in the Midwest in the 1890s. This anecdote from his autobiographical journal of his time as a reporter, *Newspaper Days*, clearly reveals the author's obsession with that part of our society where, according to Dreiser, money meant both physical beauty, entrenched power and unbridled sex. Or as he said earlier in the book, "My body was blazing with the keen sex desire I have mentioned, as well as the desire for material and social supremacy."[3]

Though Dreiser would become a dedicated Communist, with his devotion to Marxism only growing as the years went on, he ultimately became a tragic figure whose hunger for the perceived material and sexual power of the rich was never satisfied. By the time he died in 1945, despite his own fame and notoriety, Dreiser remained the frustrated soul from the God-fearing Midwest gazing at the wealthy in their homes, forever shut out and barred from entering.

He was born Herman Theodore Dreiser in Terre Haute, Indiana, on August 27, 1871, the twelfth of thirteen children sired by the prolific John Paul Dreiser, a German immigrant, strict Baptist and apparently a non-believer in birth control. His mother, Sarah, was a Mennonite who later converted to Roman Catholicism. And though I'm sure there were many fine, well-adjusted people who came from such a union, it was soon evident that young Teddy was not one of them, as his later relations with others, especially the opposite sex, would prove.

He attended Indiana University in 1888 and found himself flunking out by '90. However, life as a year-and-a-half college student had its distractions. Around that time, he had met and married Sara Osbourne White (the same first name as his mom, but without the -h), a young woman from a devout Roman Catholic family. Unfortunately, his marriage to the shy Missouri schoolteacher was on the rocks practically from the moment the young couple was pelted with rice. Apparently, young Teddy had some unusual ideas about fidelity which his bride didn't agree with; such as the revolutionary idea that monogamy should be ignored as much as possible (that is, if you were a *man*). After he flaunted his numerous affairs in her face, a hurt and angered Sara finally separated from the budding journalist in 1914 (some sources say 1918). However, faithful to the tenets of Roman Catholicism, she refused to give him a divorce. And so it was that, despite the dozens of admirers, actresses, budding starlets and God-knows-who-else who shared his bed, Theodore Dreiser remained Sara White's husband until her death as a lonely old woman in 1942. In the intervening years, a frustrated Sara pursued Dreiser for financial support, something the young author was apparently not interested in providing.[4]

By 1919, after a career as a journalist for newspapers in St. Louis and Chicago, he journeyed to New York and started writing stories and autobiographical books, though not with great success. Then one Saturday he was visited in his shabby Greenwich Village flat by a second cousin named Helen Richardson. An actress from Portland, Oregon, she was already married (at sixteen) and separated from another thespian who briefly teamed with her for vaudeville gigs in the Pacific Northwest. Later, the enterprising young actress became the secretary to an officer of the Industrial Finance Corporation of New York. Not losing any time, Helen's role in the firm soon switched to mistress, burning the midnight oil with her paramour while going over the company's books. Impressed with his cousin's youth and vitality, Dreiser was well aware of the situation with her boss.[5] As an author, it only added to his perception that getting ahead in America was based on a combination of monetary and sexual power.

In 1920, Helen was 25, Dreiser 49. She was clearly dazzled by her aging cousin, having already sampled his literary output (after her lover at Industrial Finance recommended she read his work, not realizing he was setting her up with his most serious rival). Helen wanted to go to Hollywood and make it big in the primitive silents of the day, while Dreiser had already submitted his scenarios to several low-budget New York–based film companies. As the son of a German immigrant and a burgeoning leftist, Dreiser had already opposed the Great War as a scourge on mankind initiated by imperialist, capitalist warmongers, and some of his scenario ideas fairly reeked with antiwar messages. Nevertheless, Dreiser and Richardson soon arrived in Los Angeles to pursue their dreams.

Many of the scenario proposals Dreiser sent to the studios had dealt with the stories of poor young men who were falsely accused of crimes they didn't commit, all while his heroes were longing for the better things in life that always seemed to elude them.

Years before, Dreiser had written *The Bulwark* and *Sister Carrie*, both of which were not doing well sales-wise; Hollywood success seemed the quickest way to the riches the struggling novelist had always coveted. Finally snagging a meeting with Jesse Lasky of Famous Players (soon to become Paramount Pictures), the author was plainly told by the mogul that his scenarios were being turned down.

Besides this stinging rejection, Dreiser was aware of another painful reality. After living several months in Los Angeles, it was *Helen* who was the breadwinner in the household, not he. She was earning $7.50 a day as an extra and, as time went on, her pay increased to $12.50 a day.[6] Eventually, Helen was able to get herself a sizable role opposite forgotten silent star Charles Ray and gained the attention of director Jerome Storm. In his diary, Dreiser wryly noted, "She had made so great a hit, that I am slightly jealous." In another entry, he had conceived of a story idea about "a jealous clerk who cannot lose his beauty bride to the movies and finally kills her and himself."[7]

For Dreiser, it was an ironic and frustrating situation. As he continued living with an unmarried Helen Richardson, and after years of rejecting any kind of devotion to one woman, the self-involved author now found himself in the same circumstances as his separated but still legally married spouse, Sara Dreiser. Meanwhile, Helen was making herself available to some powerful men in the movie industry, including "Rudi" (as in Valentino), with whom she worked on the silent *The Four Horsemen of the Apocalypse*.[8] Whether these meetings and get-togethers were about business matters or anything more is not known; what is known is that Dreiser, the hater of commitment, didn't like it.

Meanwhile, perhaps to take his mind off his paranoia about his live-in, Dreiser collected articles about recent crimes of passion and murder (note his all-too disturbingly real scenario about the murders of a movie actress and her lover). Usually the details of these crimes always seemed to have one dominant theme, the murder of a woman by her lover so that his position in society remained secure; and in some cases the woman was murdered so that the killer could romance a rich girl. One such case that stood out from the rest was the murder of a young woman named Grace Brown in Herkimer County in upstate New York.

Authorities in Herkimer discovered the drowned body of Brown next to an overturned rowboat and a man's straw hat floating in Big Moose Lake. An autopsy soon revealed that the dead woman was pregnant. Lawmen interviewed her employer, the owner of a local garment factory, and soon learned that Brown was seeing a young man named Chester Gillette. The son of poor Salvation Army missionaries, Gillette was an itinerant laborer traveling across the country when by chance he ran into a wealthy uncle who, wanting to do right by the family, gave the young man a job in his factory. It was there amidst the clatter of the looms and sewing machines that Gillette met and soon lusted after Grace Brown.

When deputies searched Gillette's flat in a cheap rooming house, they discovered letters from Brown begging the callous young man not to desert her. In the meantime, Gillette was romancing (or more likely doing something more intimate) with the daughters of the local bourgeoisie. In fact, he was arrested by the Herkimer County Sheriff's Department as he was playing tennis with one of his paramours at a resort on Eagle Bay.

At his trial in Herkimer in 1906, Gillette pled innocent to murder. On the witness stand, he explained that he had gone to the lake with Brown carrying a suitcase with a tennis racket and camera case, leaving both on shore. He said he was planning to break it off with Brown, but after he told her this, the distraught young woman jumped into the lake and overturned the boat at the same time. He claimed that he had tried to save her, but she had already drowned. Abandoning the tennis racket, he took his case and walked two miles back to Eagle Bay.

The prosecution, however, debunked all this. For instance, Gillette never satisfactorily explained why he had not immediately summoned help; why he and Brown were traveling to Big Moose Lake in separate train cars; why, if Brown was so suicidal, he did not alert authorities to the danger of her harming herself; and the kicker: If Brown had died from drowning, why did she have all these head bruises consistent with those one would get from being clobbered with a tennis racket?

Then, after Brown's love letters were openly read in court, angry jurors reached a verdict of guilty in five hours. One headline from the long defunct *New York World* cried out: "COURT IN TEARS AS LOVE LETTERS BARE GIRL'S SOUL!"[9] After unsuccessful appeals to the governor, Chester Gillette was executed in 1908.

Having failed to get the original court transcripts from Herkimer County, Dreiser nevertheless started work on the novel he would always be remembered for and that Hollywood would return to through the years (particularly Woody Allen, who would neurotically make several films on the idea, with plot variations, while shamelessly denying that he was stealing Dreiser's work). The proposed title of the mammoth novel (over 800 pages) was *An American Tragedy*, though it was sometimes called *Mirage*. The first title perfectly fit Dreiser's leftist politics; to him, the hunger for riches, social position and the sexual liberties that came with it, were what America *really* was about. Needless to say, Dreiser never acknowledged his own hunger for success in a town where glamour, riches and sex were given to those who were deemed worthy; nor did he really acknowledge his own rage at being rejected as a screenwriter while his young and attractive paramour was paying for the groceries.

When *An American Tragedy* was finally published in 1925, Theodore Dreiser was going to show Hollywood a thing or two about self-interest...

"[A] short, red-headed Irishman, quick to wrath, humorous, articulate in anger, representing not a minority in action, but the action of the American majority — the semi-literate lower middle class...."[10] This was how Harvard intellectual Lincoln Kirstein, in the April-June 1932 issue of the literary journal Hound & Horn, described Warner Brothers' newest headliner. *The Public Enemy* had not only made James Cagney a star, but his screen persona, that of the urban milieu's Last Angry Man, brought the actor a great deal of attention from certain political mavericks who had their own beef with the current economic and social system. However, if the actor was an unlikely celebrity to be embraced by the urban intelligentsia, the star himself, at least in those days, had no problem if said intelligentsia were of a certain leftist political bent.

"Gangsters are really the invention of capitalists," says the gangster-hero of the Broadway play upon which *Doorway to Hell* was based.[11] Written by an angry and short-tempered Communist named Rowland Brown (he had punched out a Fox producer in the early 1930s), the play and subsequent film were symbolic of how Communist artists used the gangster film to highlight the evils of capitalist society. *The Public Enemy* was written by two men of wildly divergent political views. Both John Bright and Kubec Glassmon were

A QUICK WITHDRAWAL. James Cagney pulls a .38 on an unidentified player in the classic *The Public Enemy* (1931). Co-written by Communist Party member John Bright, the film revealed the dark underbelly of Depression-era America.

Chicago writers, but Glassmon was a conservative (according to his partner anyway), and Bright was a rabid Communist. They had known gangsters in Chicago, and the drug store owned by Kubec's father was reportedly used as a hangout by Capone's men. Using their experiences among the hoodlum elite, the two men collaborated on a series of stories about Chicago's uncrowned royalty, the ruthless killers who were the *real* power in the Windy City. The unpublished 38-chapter novel, which was titled *Beer and Blood*, ran over 300 pages. Darryl F. Zanuck bought the novel and brought its authors to Hollywood to do the screenplay.

If Glassmon was indeed a conservative, apparently his viewpoint was muted in the screenplay's early sequences, where Bright's focus on big-city crime and the leeches who populate its environs resulted in a not-so-subtle attack on the free-enterprise system that permitted it to happen. At the time, this system had not only allowed millions to become unemployed and homeless, but also very, very angry.

In his analysis of the Cagney persona, Kirstein also wrote, "No one expresses more in terms of pictorial action, the delights of violence, the overtones of a semi-conscious sadism, the tendency towards destruction, towards anarchy, which is the basis of American sex appeal."[12]

Notice Kirstein's key word "anarchy." In the early 1930s, Cagney and other actors who portrayed the hoodlum on screen became the spokesmen for a generation who were discriminated against and lied to by a society that told them about two cars in a garage and a chicken in every pot. However, despite the catharsis of watching central figure Tommy Powers knock down capitalist conventions and get rich in the process, audiences couldn't help noticing that Warner Brothers also framed their new gangster film with the persistent moral that crime does not pay. In *The Public Enemy*, Cagney's Tommy Powers is constantly trumped by the one man he cannot shove around, his upright big brother Mike (Donald Cook), a veteran of the Great War. To him, his younger sibling's profits are "dirty money" and he tries to better himself within society by getting an education.

However, because of the carnage he had been through in the war, Mike now has a dark side; that is, if we are to look at an earlier draft of the script. At the end, after Tommy's body is dumped on the Powers' doorstep and he falls into the living room at Mike's feet, there is an added scene not in the finished film. As Mrs. Powers is fixing up Tommy's bed (he is supposedly returning home from the hospital) and "singing her Irish song happily," Mike's look of horror is "gradually giving way to a look of fury."[13]

The final camera directions listed in the first draft are telling:

CLOSET
Close up on AN OLD SUITCASE LAYING ON THE FLOOR. Mike's hands come into the shot, open up the suitcase, It is filled with war relics, a German helmet, a Dough boy's [sic] tin hat; a bayonet, etc., and a couple hand grenades. Mike's hands seize the two hand grenades.

LIVING ROOM
Mike comes out of the closet stuffing a hand grenade in each pocket. A look of fierce determination on his face. His brother's fate has turned him into a killer. He jams his hat on his head. Pan with him as he strides across the room. He stops for a moment for a last look at Tom's body, then strides out of the house.[14]

And Mrs. Powers continues singing her song, not realizing, ironically, that she will probably lose *two* sons to gangsters, not one. Wisely, so as not to emphasize the chilling implications of vigilante justice, especially by a war hero, director William Wellman cut this bit from the film. Mike just moves off camera, presumably to tell his Ma upstairs about Tommy's death.

Cagney had become a big star, but the poor Irish kid from the Lower East Side never forgot where he had come from. Taking note of this, Communist screenwriter John Bright was going to put him in with some folks who could use the star's new altruism for their benefit.

At the time, the Soviet Union was the new pet of America's intelligentsia. To admire the "Soviet Experiment" was to be a member of the "in" crowd. In his 1931 autobiography, aging Communist writer Lincoln Steffens, having visited the Soviet Union, famously proclaimed, "I have been over into the future and it works."[15] In conversations with Steffens, no one seemed to have brought up the subject of millions of Russians who weren't going to have a future, thanks to the Marxist experiment, but there was no disputing the old man's enthusiasm. Steffens and his wife, author Ella Winter, spent much of their lives loudly proclaiming the miracles of Bolshevism as they lived in a huge house among the capitalists of beautiful Carmel, in Northern California. It was at this house where they hosted many of Hollywood's radical community, though apparently none of their visitors were famous stars.

All they needed was a famous celebrity to popularize their agenda...

In a 1983 interview with Patrick McGilligan and Ken Mate for *Tender Comrades: A Back Story of the Hollywood Blacklist*, John Bright would take credit for a great deal of Cagney's early success. It was *he* who had suggested to Wellman that the actor switch roles with Eddie Woods so he could play Tommy Powers; it was *he* who insisted that Cagney demand a raise in salary at Warners after just his first film; and it was *he* who introduced the actor to the movers and shakers of Hollywood's Communist Party. In the interview, the Marxist screenwriter expresses contempt for Cagney's wife and his brother William, both of whom he described as "very reactionary."

Bright also claimed, "The Irish crowd in Hollywood were all reactionary. Pat O'Brien, practically Cagney's closest friend, was a fascist, also very anti–Semitic. Another member of that crowd was Leo McCarey, who was also anti–Semitic." Predictably, to Party members like Bright, anyone who was anti–Communist *must* have been either a "reactionary," a "fascist," or "anti–Semitic." However, if one views the films written by Bright in the early 1930s, from *Smart Money* to *The Public Enemy* to *She Done Him Wrong*, one could easily find a non-stop parade of anti–Semitic, anti–Irish, anti–Italian, and anti–black stereotypes. Perhaps it was the free-wheeling, pre–Code tenor of the times that allowed such insults, but Bright never admitted to being called a "reactionary" because of his screenplays (or his apparent bias against the Irish). Nevertheless, the scenarist became friendly with Cagney, and when the actor expressed the desire to meet authors Theodore Dreiser and Lincoln Steffens, it was Bright who personally arranged it. In fact, he admitted that Steffens and Winter "sort of adopted Cagney."[16] With Bright as their point man, the Party quickly moved to take advantage of this personal relationship.

During that time, Cagney and Bright attended a dinner at John's Rendezvous in San Francisco, where the guests included Steffens and Dreiser. From there, they went to a workers' rally at the city's Longshoremen's Amphitheater, where 10,000 union members were to hear speeches from Party functionaries and pro-union advocates. Party chief William Schneidermann arranged for Cagney to prominently sit on the dais, where the Communist press and the audience couldn't possibly miss him. Unfortunately for the actor, he was also within sight of Hearst newspaper photographers.[17]

Jack Warner promptly had both actor and scenarist on the carpet, accusing them of being "Communist dupes," perhaps not realizing that Bright already *was* a Party member. In short order, Bright was kicked out of the studio after slugging Warner executive Darryl F. Zanuck; though his bringing Cagney to Communist functions certainly couldn't have helped his situation at the studio.

However, the mogul's warning didn't stop the actor from contributing to organizations later discovered to be Communist fronts. He sent money to striking cotton workers in the San Joaquin Valley, a move that became public after Sacramento District Attorney Neil McAllister ordered a raid on the city's Party headquarters. Out of all the correspondence now in the D.A.'s hands was a letter from Ella Winter to Caroline Decker, secretary of the Communist-led Cannery & Agriculture Workers Union. "I have Cagney's money again," chirped Mrs. Steffens. She went on to write that the actor "is going to bring up other stars to talk to Stef about Communism."[18]

"FILM ACTOR NAMED IN COAST RED PLOT" screamed the headline of the August 18, 1934, issue of the *New York Times*.[19] This was the last straw. The involvement with the radicals came back to haunt Cagney in 1940 when he testified before Martin Dies' then-kinder, gentler convening of the HUAC in Washington. With his career at stake, Cagney disowned his former friends and claimed that as a kid growing up in a poor neighborhood, he just wanted to help those who were on the bottom. "What the hell did I know about the ebb and flow of political movements?" he cried.[20]

Apparently, he would learn fast. Cagney ducked the bullet in a way his two-fisted screen characters never did, and he would make sure he never found himself in the same kind of situation again. Two years after his testimony, he made the hyper-patriotic *Yankee Doodle Dandy* to put the final nails into the coffin of his radical past.

But the whitewash didn't end there. In his 1976 autobiography, *Cagney by Cagney*, the actor fails to mention even one of his numerous contributions to leftist movements. Predictably, the names John Bright (one of the two writers responsible for his early fame), Lincoln Steffens (whom he had so much wanted to meet) and Ella Winter (who supposedly "adopted" him) are also missing from the book. In fact, the autobiography is merely a series of silly anecdotes about Cagney and his movie pals (especially the "Irish crowd" that John Bright had so much contempt for).

Meanwhile, one of the socially conscious authors Cagney had wanted to meet was going to have his own problems....

In an interview on December 26, 1920, Theodore Dreiser had claimed, "Despite many defects, the movies show more of an advance than do our current books and plays.... Some moving picture directors appear to have more brains and tastes than the authors whose work they interpret."[21] Dreiser's rivals in the literary community saw these remarks as those of a pompous man who despaired the low state of American culture, yet at the same time was blatantly ass-kissing Hollywood's moguls. Little did they realize that in a year's time, the brown-nosing would change to something far different.

The following year, Dreiser was hired to do a series of articles for a short-lived magazine on the arts called *Shadowland*. Titled "Hollywood: Its Morals and Manners," the series was about the working life of an actress (with reams of material provided by the hard-working Helen Richardson). Dreiser went into infinite detail on the long hours of movie actresses; their being forced to pay for their own glamourous wardrobes, as well as makeup and hairstyles, out of their already meager paychecks; the harsh non-union working environment; their waiting for big close-ups that are never shot; and then, as if that weren't enough, Dreiser mentioned the casting couch. Calling attention to male producers' and directors' near-prostitution of "literally hundreds of girls and women,"[22] the piece was noticed by more than the usual readers of *Shadowland*. Though it is interesting here to see Dreiser, the ultimate user of women, trying for a seat on the other side of the aisle, Hollywood moguls had other opinions on the author's belated attempt at muckracking. After the film industry pressured *Photodramatist Magazine* to cancel a planned series of articles by Dreiser, the angry author called the producers "muddle-brained braggarts or fat lechers or both, and all they know is the commercial — not the artistic or creative side of their problem."[23]

So much for movie people "having more brains and taste than the authors whose work they interpret."

Though he had a thin skin that would only get thinner as the years passed, Dreiser nevertheless continued to court the studios. He knew that *An American Tragedy* was the most cinematic of his work, and he never abandoned the hope that it would be filmed. Meanwhile, the bitter author declared the United States "a continuation of old Rome. The Romans knew two things, money-getting and war," and he bemoaned the state of American art that denied an equivalent to Michelangelo, Dante and Shakespeare.[24]

Certainly, in *An American Tragedy*, Dreiser expanded on the theme of America as a moral cesspool where handsome young men are compelled to knock off anyone who stands in their way to riches and affluence (and, of course, the great sex that naturally goes with it). Divided into three "books" within its more than 800 pages, the story has Clyde Griffith (Dreiser kept Gillette's initials), the poor son of religious parents, travel across the country and meet a long-lost relative who is the owner of a factory. Obtaining a job there, he meets Roberta "Bert" Alden, a pretty (but nagging) young woman. Then he meets Sondra Finchley, daughter of privilege, and promptly romances her. Clyde impregnates Roberta, she wants marriage, he takes her out on the lake and, well, you know those old rowboats. Instead of Sondra, Clyde gets the chair, as his religious parents fight to clear his name.

After the novel's publication in December 1925, reviewers praised the work and sales rose sharply. H.G. Wells, another author famous for his leftist politics, proclaimed it "one of the greatest novels of this century."[25] After the novel was bought for $93,000 by Paramount (the same studio that had rejected Dreiser's scenarios), rumors persisted that the director would either be D.W. Griffith or the Soviet Union's Sergei Eisenstein. The latter was then quickly signed to a Paramount contract to adapt the screenplay.

Certainly Eisenstein's connection to the project signaled an interest in the novel and its author from the Soviet Union, since the helmsman couldn't possibly have traveled abroad without government approval. In 1927, Soviet officials invited Dreiser to the tenth anniversary celebration of the Bolshevik revolution. Agreeing with Dreiser's anti–American point of view, the Soviets regarded him as "the outstanding literary intelligence in America." Despite this accolade, however, the Soviet government refused to pay him for the rights to publish his novels in the U.S.S.R. until 1945, the year he died.[26]

Though Eisenstein looked like a good bet to direct the film version of the novel, Paramount never really took the suggestion too seriously. Instead, they basked in the glow of publicity that the famous artiste's involvement would bring the production.

Similarly, other Hollywood artists enamored of the Soviet "experiment" were eager to cement relations with their Bolshevik counterparts. Sovkino, the Soviet film organ, desperately wanted to import the films of Charlie Chaplin, which they viewed as pro-worker and anti-capitalist. However, unlike most left-leaning artists who allowed their works to be "donated" to the great Soviet experiment, Chaplin wanted hard capitalist cash for his films. For all their professed love of the comic's works, Sovkino quickly decided that he wasn't worth the rubles after all.[27]

Shortly after arriving in the United States in May 1930 with his assistant director Grisha Aleksandrov and his cameraman, Eduard Tisse, Eisenstein signed a contract with Paramount. The agreement stipulated that he and his two friends were to receive $900 a week for a six-month development deal; if no agreement could be reached on a suitable topic to film (one that interested Eisenstein that Paramount had final approval of), the deal was null and void at the end of three months. Despite this opportunity, however, Eisenstein was not exactly the most grateful employee. Though praised by the film industry as a genius, the Soviet director heaped contempt on the nation that was welcoming him. The director would later call his new temporary residence "the America of anti–Sovietism, of Prohibition; the imperialist America of Hoover."[28]

Meanwhile, the "imperialists" were rolling out the red (pardon the pun) carpet for Eisenstein and his pals. He spoke at Harvard and Columbia; he spoke to a convention of film industry professionals in Atlantic City; and he made an appearance at Times Square's Cameo Theater for the American premiere of *The Old and the New*, an arty Eisenstein film which extolled the wonders of Soviet collectivization.

In Hollywood, as Paramount executives dithered about what would be the famous helmsman's first Hollywood film, with a mammoth production called *Sutter's Gold* high on the list, Eisenstein and his friends were sampling the film community's far from Communist perks. Repeating what they done in England and France while on their way to the U.S., the three dined in the finest restaurants, drank at the best bars and sampled the ladies of the most notorious brothels. As the studio dragged out the process of choosing an appropriate vehicle for Eisenstein, the auteur and his comrades dreaded returning to the U.S.S.R. so soon if the deal went flat. As author Mandy Merck so aptly wrote in *Hollywood's American Tragedies: Dreiser, Eisenstein, Sternberg, Stevens*, "Four months of their contracted six had already passed and it was now September. The prospect of leaving Hollywood so soon must have weighed heavily on the Russians, who were escaping privation for the first time in thirteen years."

This terror of returning to the Soviet Union revealed the hypocrisy behind Eisenstein's pro–Soviet, anti–American statements. Still, the great director continued the farce, making public comments that were starting to irk his gracious hosts. He claimed that the true tragedy of Dreiser's novel was not "in the murder, but in the tragic path that is pursued by Clyde who is driven by the social system to murder."29

Again, according to Merck, this observation was in full accord with Dreiser's:

> The role of fate in the classical tragedies to which Dreiser alludes is assigned to [Eisenstein's term] "American reality," specifically the nation's class system, the prohibition of abortion, politicized legal institutions and religious fanaticism. From the ambiguous anti-hero of Dreiser's novel, Clyde would be transformed into a victim of American injustice.

According to Budd Schulberg, his father B.P. Schulberg and other Paramount executives quickly saw the incongruity of a Communist director making *Sutter's Gold*, a film based on the man who discovered gold and later died broke. Quickly realizing that Eisenstein would have turned the film into a Marxist version of *Money for Dummies*, Lasky and company pulled the plug on the project. (They sold it to Universal, who almost lost their shirts on the 1936 film version.) Added to this apprehension, the studio was also nervous about the prospect of a Communist director in control of a film that slammed the American legal system (the later Moscow show trials would only emphasize Eisenstein's hypocrisy about any mockery of American law). After four months of listening to Eisenstein's ideas for film proposals, all of which called for either impossibly high budgets or inflammatory subject matter, the studio quietly canceled his contract.

When Josef von Sternberg was signed to do the film version of *An American Tragedy*, he was already known as a hard-driving craftsman from Europe. As a Paramount contract director, he had brought fellow German émigré (and lover) Marlene Dietrich to America and made her world-famous. A fan of the anti-money silent masterpiece, *Greed*, Dreiser had wanted Erich von Stroheim to direct, and was angered by Paramount's refusal to hire him. The writer was also infuriated by Hays Office pressure not to use too much of the novel's anti–Americanism. Seconding this opinion, B.P. Schulberg referred to the Eisenstein-Ivor Novello screenplay as "a monstrous challenge to American society."30

For the film's new director, there was a lot of work to do. In record time, von Sternberg tossed out Eisenstein's adaptation, cut out Book One of the novel, ignored any material from Joseph Kearney's stage version of the book, and did a wonderful job calming already nervous Paramount executives who almost expected a hammer and sickle to be the first thing audiences saw in the picture instead of the usual Paramount mountain. In his memoirs, von Sternberg claimed to have done most of the screenplay "with some help from [poet]

Samuel Hoffenstein."[31] Apparently the studio felt otherwise: To this day, Hoffenstein is the only one who is credited with writing the screenplay.

Angered at the prospect that his left-leaning masterpiece might be leaning the other way, Dreiser made his objections known. Now with Eisenstein back in Russia and far away from Hollywood's prostitutes, the author complained about pressure from the Hays Office to water down the anti-religious tenor of the novel; the book's implication that the need for social status prompted Clyde to murder; and the author's view that Clyde was some sort of tragic hero. (Did Dreiser actually think, "So he just knocked off a pregnant woman, how bad could he be?")

The studio did try to get Dreiser's input. However, the author, doing a little running-around on Helen (the woman who had paid the rent when Dreiser was jobless), had met a new girl and promptly took her to Cuba with him, leaving no forwarding address. Paramount tried to find him and put out official notices in the trades. When Dreiser finally emerged in New Orleans (no one knew what happened to his traveling companion), he denounced Paramount's search as "the usual Hollywood swill and bunk."[32]

The perpetrators of swill and bunk tried to get Hoffenstein to meet with the elusive author. After Dreiser tersely telegrammed the studio that he would meet with Hoffenstein in the Big Easy ("If you can discuss this amicably, otherwise not"[33]), the poet flew all the way to Dreiser's New Orleans hotel, only to find a note stating, "I am leaving New Orleans without seeing you. You will understand, I'm sure."[34]

Knowing full well that he was all alone now that he had lost Eisenstein (and the cult of celebrity that followed in the director's wake), Dreiser condemned the project as "a cheap, tawdry tabloid confession story" and that Hollywood (or "Hooeyland" as the author so creatively called it) would turn *An American Tragedy* into "a Mexican comedy."[35]

The film directed by von Sternberg emphatically does *not* bring Cantinflas to mind. Rather, according to the tagline, it was "Drama that happens around you every day — when the wild life of impetuous youth burns away age-old barriers!" Notice how Paramount's advertising was already removing the more controversial elements of Dreiser's novel (as well as the Eisenstein–Novello screenplay); the film was not going to be "a monstrous challenge to American society," but instead, a tale of "wild, impetuous youth," as if it were a JD film of the late 1950s. The author was right; the film *was* becoming a tabloid story. However, it became a *self-conscious* tabloid story, one that was clearly afraid of getting *too* sleazy. Working fast, the Hays Office removed the word "seduction," watered down any mention of pregnancy and cut out all dialogue having to do with abortion.

Dreiser had flown to Hollywood with Communist producer Hy Kraft to hold discussions with von Sternberg. After the two drafted new scenes that more or less brought the screenplay back to Eisenstein's version, von Sternberg argued for keeping all cinematic options open; in other words, he would approve whatever elements looked good on screen and kept the film moving. Never understanding that films need a fast pace and good visuals to keep the audience interested, not endless speeches, the disgusted Dreiser left Hollywood soon afterwards.

Shortly after the film's general release on August 22, 1931, Dreiser filed an injunction against Paramount to defend its distribution of the film. But at the trial in White Plains, New York, studio attorneys struck back, accusing Dreiser of "cold-blooded plagiarism" by his liberal use of newspaper reports and the late Grace Brown's letters. Soon, other unflattering details about the author came out. For instance, when von Sternberg tried to explain that some of Dreiser's suggestions would be censorable, the author responded with an angry tirade that "denounced censors, as well as religious and patriotic institutions."[36] Studio attorney William T. Powers also claimed that von Sternberg knew Dreiser's novel better than the author (which makes sense since von Sternberg would have to know the book well enough to cut out huge sections of it for the film version).

Paramount trial attorney Humphrey J. Lynch (a former justice of the Supreme Court) cited a particularly ugly detail in Dreiser's writing career that supported the earlier allegation of "cold-blooded plagiarism." Lynch brought up the claim by socialist author Sinclair Lewis that Dreiser had lifted wholesale passages from his wife Dorothy Thompson's articles about a trip they had taken to Moscow (titled *The New Moscow*) and used them for his *Dreiser Looks at Russia* (which, apparently, should have been retitled *Dreiser Looks at Russia with Dorothy Thompson's Eyes*). Nevertheless, it did look like Dreiser used Thompson's descriptions of Moscow social life for his own work. Lynch's ploy did the trick; Dreiser became so visibly angry he had to be admonished by the judge. Unfortunately, no judge or bailiffs were present at a party earlier that year when Lewis refused to take back his accusation that Dreiser stole whole sentences verbatim from Thompson's work. Dreiser slapped the author of *It Can't Happen Here* and *Elmer Gantry* several times before someone finally restrained him.

Dreiser was portrayed by the studio as pompous, pretentious, spiritually bankrupt, an author who couldn't even be original and, worst of all, an America hater (which in essence he was). The court refused the injunction against Paramount, and Dreiser was ordered to pay ten dollars in court costs. The studio with the mountain had won.

On August 5, a few days after the verdict was read, the film opened in New York; it "opened wide" on the 22nd. In Mordaunt Hall's *New York Times* review, the critic seemed to dismiss the early portions of the film and accused Phillips Holmes (as Griffiths) of having a "peculiarly flabby conception of the role." Obviously familiar with the book, Hall nitpicked about von Sternberg's adaptation and especially criticized his wholesale excising of early portions of the novel, claiming that the director had "lost the path of the narrative." However, Hall also wrote that in the trial scene, "Mr. Von Sternberg fires his film with feeling."

It was just a few days since that other trial scene that was also "fired with feeling" ended in White Plains. Dreiser, the left-wing author who wrote a novel that was a blistering attack on America and its legal system, was a defeated man. Certainly, the results of the trial were noted by Hollywood's moguls. With the exception of Dreiser's novel *Jennie Gerhardt*, and Warners' purchase of *Sister Carrie* in 1937 (which would ultimately be purchased by the author's nemesis, Paramount, a few years later), Hollywood kept Theodore Dreiser at arm's length, certainly when compared with other authors whose work they sought to film, like Hemingway, Steinbeck and, yes, even he-who-got-slapped, Sinclair Lewis.

In the years ahead, Dreiser did not grow old gracefully. Paranoid and bitter, his head swimming in an alcoholic haze as he ranted against "Jewish influence" and the evils of America, the author never understood that the term *An American Tragedy* could also mean a human being as well as a system...

"Mr. Parker, do you know what it means to feel like God?" This quote not only perfectly fit the megalomaniac ego of the mad Dr. Moreau in Paramount's 1932 version of *The Island of Dr. Moreau* (titled *Island of Lost Souls*), but the image of the standard H.G. Wells hero: a man using scientific means to eradicate one version of mankind so another more "perfect" version could take its place. Herbert George Wells was not a radical on par with the Communists of New York's Group Theater, nor was he a rabid Marxist of the old Bolshevik school. He was an intellectual who proclaimed a sympathy for the downtrodden.

Ironically, however, his writings conjured up visions of future societies where only the most perfect humans are allowed to exist.

Certainly, his professed sympathy with the working classes started early. Born in Bromley, England in 1866, the son of servants, he was forced to work as an apprentice in a drapery shop, a position he detested. Later, the well-read young man became a chemist's assistant and was eventually accepted into London's Normal School of Science where he studied biology. He was also an assistant teacher at the school, and it was during this time that he started to write. His first book, *The Time Machine*, was published in 1896. For some reason, British reviewers started to refer to Wells' work as "scientific romances," when there was very little about them that was romantic. Boy and girl love stories, it seemed, didn't interest Wells as much as cataclysmic depictions of science gone mad.

Very little physical action occurs in *The Time Machine* be-

ÜBERMENSCH. Charles Laughton (with Hans Steinke behind him) as Dr. Moreau in Paramount's *Island of Lost Souls* (1932). Wells' parable of a scientist attempting to turn animals into humans prefigured Nazi experiments in creating a master race.

sides the hero's journey into the future (it is, after all, barely over a hundred pages), yet Wells does give us an idea of a world where a hierarchy of brutal savages takes over. The Morlocks, cannibalistic monsters who enslave the world's humans and eventually devour them, seemed to be a harbinger of the totalitarian monsters to come in the twentieth century.

Silent versions of Wells' novels had been filmed since 1902 (*The First Men in the Moon* being the most common), yet it was two Hollywood films released within months of each other that set the tone for the Wellsian version of science gone wrong that were made to take advantage of the growing popularity of the horror film. *Island of Lost Souls* was released by Paramount in December 1932, with the film version of Wells' *The Invisible Man* released by Universal in May 1933. Here, in the midst of a worldwide depression, audiences witnessed two men, both brilliant scientists, using science in a quest for power. In *Island of Lost Souls*, Dr. Moreau seeks to replace the human race with a more "perfect" model; in *The Invisible Man*, Jack Griffin seeks to gain power through invisibility. Between the releases of both films, Adolf Hitler became chancellor of Germany and Josef Stalin consolidated his power by having popular rival Sergei Kirov assassinated. Both dictators, guilty of launching violent purges upon their respective populaces so that only a select few would rule, probably would have approved of Moreau's experiments and Griffin's ambitions.

The British, who would ignore the Nazi threat as the years wore on, banned *Island of Lost Souls* outright; it would not be seen by British audiences until the late 1950s. In *Island*, the promise of "progress" and "advancement" given by Moreau to his animal-men is shown to be a lie. Instead of elevation of the great unwashed masses (and in this case, un-housebroken as well), Moreau's "lower beings" revert to murderous savagery, chaos, and finally, the destruction of their utopian paradise. Sped-up advancement (or in this case, evolution) based on questionable scientific methods and dictated by a leader who has no intention of following the rules he lays down to his charges, will result in a bloody revolution. Written two decades before the Soviet takeover of Russia, *The Island of Dr. Moreau* is still considered a classic of science fiction mixed with socio-political themes.

Wells himself would praise *The Invisible Man*'s director James Whale and screenwriter R.C. Sherriff for remaining loyal to his book. Yet he also quibbled with Sherriff's having Griffin go insane due to the effect of his invisibility drug; in the book, Griffin goes mad because of naked greed. To Wells, it was the insatiable desire for materialistic gain that set Griffin off, not a chemical he couldn't control. This was quite different from Robert Louis Stevenson's *Dr. Jekyll and Mr. Hyde* in which a drug *does* take control; in Wells' version, the drug is capitalism.

Yet even the visionary Wells would not realize that the film version of *The Invisible Man* would have its socialist politics replaced by the sexual politics of its openly gay director Whale. The helmsman not only turned Wells' rather pompous novel into a black comedy (though with gruesome deaths), but turned Wells' attack on materialistic greed into a different kind of horror. In the film, Whale gives us a biting comment on straight society's neuroses by giving us expository scenes showing the overreactions to Griffin's self-proclaimed "reign of terror." Radio broadcasts (which would forecast Orson Welles' *War of the Worlds* transmissions) warn of an invisible man on the loose, police are out in full force, and we even see one man nailing boards onto his front door. All the while Griffin is sleeping peacefully in Dr. Kemp's bedroom. Here, Whale implies, proper and sexually repressed English society is clearly panicked by the threat of a naked man running through their town.

Unfortunately, Wells' proclaimed sympathy for the downtrodden masses did not extend to the man himself. Though allegedly expressing hatred for the world's imperialist forces in such classics as *The War of the Worlds*, Wells demonstrated an obviously less than tolerant attitude in some of his other writings.

In the novel *The Invisible Man*, some of Griffin's comments to Dr. Kemp could be seen as the coming madness that would consume him if his creator didn't frame these remarks in such a commonplace, acceptable way. Besides telling Kemp that he worked "like a nigger" to find a cure for his invisibility, Griffin relates his stay in a boarding house run by Polish Jews with ugly comments that further expose the character's naked bigotry. Besides describing the landlord as "an old Polish Jew in a long, gray coat and greasy slippers," Griffin also notes that his Yiddish-speaking stepson has a "thick-lipped bearded face" and that he is tempted to "hit his silly countenance." In his excellent biography of Wells, *The Invisible Man*, author Michael Coren notes, "Griffin, the Invisible man, is nowhere described as a man of heroic or noble principles, but it is surely pertinent that such personal venom is reserved for the landlord and his unfortunate family."

It is not surprising that, in a gesture that reflects the anti–Semitic pogroms of the times, Griffin sets fire to the Jews' house with them still in it. Unfortunately, the Universal film, produced by German-Jewish producer Carl Laemmle, gives us a scene which echoes the author's anti–Semitism perfectly. In a montage of scenes showing the panic that Griffin's reign of terror causes, British citizens Whale and Sherriff give us a scene showing a Hasidic Jew who owns a jewelry shop crying out, "Mama, never mind the plated goods, gimme the diamonds!" as he and his wife hide the store's precious stock.

It was a scene Joseph Goebbels would have approved of.

Wells would cross the line from racial stereotyping into outright bigotry with his 1901 book on the creation of a perfect utopia, *Anticipations*. It must be emphasized that *Anticipations* is not a novel, with the author speaking in the context of some fictional character narrating events for the reader; this is *H.G. Wells* talking as a man who is expressing theories he believes are true.

AM I THAT TRANSPARENT? Claude Rains in his star-making role in *The Invisible Man* (1933). In Wells' novel, materialism is the drug that makes him mad. Unfortunately, both novel and film featured anti–Semitic stereotypes.

In writing of the future creation of a "New Republic," Wells asks how this wonderful utopia will deal with what he blatantly refers to as the "inferior races": "How will we deal with the black? How will we deal with the yellow man? How will we deal with that alleged termite in the civilized woodwork, the Jew?" After further describing the Jewish people in the most despicable terms ("[They are] intensely vulgar in dress and bearing, materialistic in thought and cunning in base and methods"), the author pronounces:

> [As for] those swarms of blacks, and brown, and dirty-white, and yellow people [who do not meet the standards of the New Republic], they will have to go.... So far as they fail to develop sane, vigorous and distinctive personalities for the great world of the future, it is their portion to die out and disappear.

So there it was. It takes little imagination to understand what the author meant when he wrote that the above-mentioned peoples would "have to go." Forty years before Hitler's Final Solution took hold of Europe, the self-appointed champion of the masses was advocating race extermination as a solution to the world's problems in the near future. Taking this into account, Michael Coren noted, "The extent to which Wells echoes the fears and proclivities of more traditional anti–Semites is surprising, considering that he advocated a revolutionary society. His anxieties centered on the alien nature of the change he sometimes observed; alien to his notion of Britain, alien to him. For all his internationalist polemics, Wells remained a parochial figure."

In England alone, particularly among British authors (Graham Greene is a good example), anti–Semitic portrayals in films and literature were more common than one might think, even as war with the Third Reich was on the horizon. In the 1930s, Wells would be only one of the left-wing authors (such as George Bernard Shaw) who would openly declare that none of the defendants in the Moscow Show Trials were tortured into making confessions. Obviously, Wells' self-proclaimed passion for internationalism would not be impeded by the broken fingers and put-out eyes of those in the courtroom docks of Stalin's U.S.S.R. Despite the author's ignorance of Stalin's tyranny, the lionization of Wells would continue from most quarters into the 21st century.

In his 2008 mini-biography of Wells in the Internet Movie Database, Charles R. Keller II of the H.G. Wells Society proudly proclaims, in typical adoring fan fashion, Wells' brave opposition to the Nazis. In reality, however, Wells never once apologized for any of his inflammatory writings or speeches. Whether they actually knew of Wells' bigotry or not, filmmakers on both continents ignored the controversies. As the 1930s progressed, with both Hollywood and England giving us film versions of Wells' books, the world's dictators moved closer to the author's elitist worldview than even he would realize.

Wells was right in that respect. The Morlocks were indeed taking over. What historians continue to ignore to this day, however, is how authors like Wells had so much to do with forming their personalities...

"Throw 'em out. Get those Reds. Throw the dirty Reds out of here. Give it to 'em. Dirty Reds!" These angry lines perfectly symbolize the forces at play in the 1933 Broadway season's new political melodrama *Peace on Earth*, which opened at the Civic Repertory Theater on November 29. The scapegoating of Communists for the nation's ills was definitely a major preoccupation for (surprise!) Communist playwrights, but works like *Peace on Earth* also served as a launching pad for those Party members who later became major Hollywood scenarists. Though co-written by George Sklar, *Peace on Earth* was evidently provided a lot of its bite by his writing partner, a passionate young writer from Brooklyn named Albert Maltz.

Born on October 28, 1908, Maltz graduated from Erasmus Hall High School and later received a Bachelor of Arts at Columbia University where he was also Phi Beta Kappa in 1930. In 1931, he attended the Yale University School of Drama; and while there, he met Sklar, another socially conscious writer, who happened to be working part-time in the college library. It was Sklar who discovered an article about a gangland murder in Cleveland and the young laborer who witnessed the crime. The young worker was arrested and, to conceal the local government's collusion with the Mob, later found hanged, an apparent "suicide." Maltz immediately grasped that the crime could be the basis for an exciting play, as well as an indictment of the System.

When *Merry-Go-Round* debuted at Greenwich Village's Provincetown Playhouse on April 22, 1932, Mayor James Walker was in the process of being indicted on corruption charges. In fact, when the play was moved uptown, his administration attempted to thwart the production by withholding fire department licenses to the theater, as well as other means of bureaucratic harassment. Though the play was *not* inspired by Walker's administration, New Yorkers couldn't help but make a connection between the play's crooked, gangland-bought politicians and their own hedonistic, high-living mayor.

The plot concerns a young bellhop named Ed Martin (played by a young Elisha Cook Jr.) who witnesses a mob rubout. However, instead of being protected as a vital witness, he is arrested for the crime and persecuted by the State. Soon, Martin finds himself in a Kafkaesque nightmare. He is framed by the D.A.'s office, brutally beaten by the police (who at first refuse to take him to a hospital), and finally murdered to save the mayor any scandal on the eve of an election. At the end of the play, the mayor makes a pompous speech about his desire to serve "in the best interests of this great public," while the silhouette of Ed Martin's hanging body is seen in the background. The tableau was a stinging attack on the American legal system. In the early 1930s, with the Depression in full swing and civil liberties being the *last* thing on anyone's mind, the production echoed the socially conscious concerns of the authors rather than the audience (the play only lasted 48 performances). When Universal prepared to film the play, now called *Afraid to Talk*, the playwrights went west to do the adaptation. However, the studio promptly threw it out and instead altered the piece radically (pardon the expression), allowing the framed bellhop to live at the end.

Back in New York, Sklar heard of a new theater company that wanted to "present plays that deal boldly with the economic and social problems that confront all of us today." Charles Walker, the treasurer of the newly formed Theater Union, invited Sklar and Maltz to become members of the group's executive board.

The result of their involvement with the Theater Union was *Peace on Earth*, an antiwar melodrama that indicts a capitalist society where freedom, according to the authors, is only meant for *some* of us. When college professor Peter Owens reluctantly joins his friend in a strike at the docks (the unionized longshoremen refuse to load crates of munitions), the police prevent the two from reading the Declaration of Independence out loud and promptly bust up the strike. The munitions company president, John Andrews, is also a trustee of Peter's college and, predictably, uses pressure on his superiors to stop his involvement with the "Reds." When the dock workers return for another protest, one longshoreman, projecting the authors' own politics, blatantly tells the German ship-loaders, "Fellow workers, we call upon you—strike. Strike against war! You're workers like us! Strike with us. Fight with us. Fight against the bosses. Fight against the wars. The bosses want war because they make money from war. But we don't want war. We say to hell with war. To hell with the bosses. Let them fight their own wars."

In one ironic moment before this speech, especially considering the career of Albert Maltz, one company officer threatens the German workers with blacklisting: "I'll have you blacklisted from every goddamn port from here to Shanghai. You'll never get another job on a ship as long as I live."

After indicting Andrews for turning his textile firm into a factory for the manufacture of munitions, Owens is railroaded for murder and taken away to be executed. Like Ed Martin, he is also destroyed by a capitalist system which values dollars over sense. Needless to say, Maltz and Sklar kept their sights on *American* miscarriages of justice, ignoring the wealth of material they could have used from trials in the Soviet Union. However, unlike Ed Martin or Peter Owens, Stalin's victims weren't allowed to make long speeches indicting the barbaric system that was sending them to their deaths.

Though the play made an impact with those who saw it, some reviewers' criticisms were predictable; Joseph Freeman of the *Daily Worker* called it "a landmark in the American theater."[37] However, the usually incisive Brooks Atkinson was perhaps more to the point when he said the work was "hysterically written" and "a jumbled ill-considered propaganda play."[38] Another voice, this time writing in the Communist publication *New Theater*, had a more complicated take on the play. John Howard Lawson called it "a fine achievement," but predictably, the acidic former playwright still had to nitpick. Cuttingly (and perhaps with more than a little jealousy), Lawson called the third act "muddled" and wrote that the "working class connection to the theme"[39] was totally lost.

If anyone can fault the playwrights for anything, it was in following the Communist playbook perhaps *too* closely and not paying attention to the realities of life on the piers of a big city. Longshoremen weren't as Communistic or anti-war as the authors would like to think. It was good ol' American dough, not world peace, that concerned them. Higher wages, shorter hours, and double the pay for overtime was where they lived. In fact, it was more likely that these men were inspired by those great social engineers Lucky Luciano and Vito Genovese, rather than Karl Marx; it was the Mob, not the masses, that dictated the direction of their union. The collusion between gangland and big-city unions, especially in New York, was a well-known fact. Yet Sklar and Maltz, following ideological leftist lines, ignored an obvious real-life situation in order to make an indictment of "warmongering bosses."

After the run of his 1935 play *The Black Pit* at the Civic Repertory Theater (it lasted 85 performances), Maltz decided to branch out as a writer. Staying away from the stage and now having recently joined the Communist Party, he sold stories to magazines and worked on novels for the next seven years. When he returned to Hollywood in 1942, it would be to collaborate on a verifiable cinema classic. Unlike the debacle of *Afraid to Talk*, *This Gun for Hire* finally helped put Maltz on the Hollywood map as a writer. In those seven years, he grew as an author and also deepened his involvement with the Party on both coasts. He also got to know John Howard Lawson, his former nitpicking critic at *New Theater* magazine, now the Party's powerful "enforcer" and major decision-maker. Unfortunately, the redoubtable Lawson would sometimes treat the talented Maltz as if he were some misguided lackey whose work *still* didn't quite make the grade...

"... Civilization falls away from me. My plight becomes real; the horrors, terrible facts. I feel the terror of the slave mart. The degradation of man bought and sold into slavery."[40] This quote was given to London journalists at the West End opening of Eugene O'Neill's *The Emperor Jones* by the actor playing the lead role. None of the reporters present would have an inkling that this actor would be remembered as one of the most groundbreaking performers of the early twentieth century. At the time, said groundbreaking performer was already internationally known for his deep bass voice, his charisma, his sharp intellect (he could sing in several languages) and his highly charged presence which carried with it a sexual aura that charmed women everywhere. To this day, Paul Robeson is considered an icon, not only for black people, but for anyone who respected human rights. He was a talented performer who apparently could do no wrong and whose principled fight against the racism of his day made him way ahead of his time. Between 1977, the year of his death, and 2009, there would be dozens of books and magazine articles written about him; he would be the subject of a one-man play; his face would appear on a U.S. postage stamp; his songs would be released on CDs and his movies, usually made by low-budget outfits, would be digitally re-mastered on deluxe DVD sets.

However, the many bios on him, some written by African Americans, have an uncomfortably slavish and adoring tone to them. Though justifiably praising Robeson's talent, interest in cultural diversity and especially his defiance against the prejudices of his day, many of these works, unfortunately, omit certain details of Robeson's life which might have revealed a less than perfect icon. Ironically, this one-sided picture of Robeson reminds one of the same kind of one-sided picture the star himself would have of the Soviet Union during his own lifetime. This indeed would be the dilemma that would plague his life in later years: how such a brilliant man could also be so short-sighted. It was a controversy that eventually ruined his life.

Born in 1898 in Princeton, New Jersey, Paul LeRoy Bustill Robeson was the son of a former slave who became a minister. Paul's mother died when he was young and he and his siblings were raised by his highly intelligent father, who instilled in them the need to learn about other cultures besides their own. Paul sang in his father's church, gaining attention with his wonderful bass voice. The experience of singing gospel songs remained with Paul the rest of his life; no matter what stage he performed on, the timbre of his voice always seemed to carry with it the memories of spirituals, of ritual and tradition; imbuing the songs with a dramatic import and emotion that other artists of his day clearly lacked.

At 6'3", Paul was a fullback in high school. His ability to win football games served him well when he earned a scholarship to Rutgers University, only the third black person accepted to the school up to that time. Like another athlete from a persecuted minority, Jim Thorpe, Paul seemed to be a perfect physical specimen; he was a four-letter man, excelling at baseball, basketball, track and field and, of course, football. He was no slouch in the brain department either, holding a Phi Beta Kappa key, being chosen class valedictorian and, as a gangling 17-year-old, delivering a speech to the student body that already preached racial tolerance.

Hoping to be a lawyer and take cases where he would defend other blacks, he moved to Harlem and was accepted at Columbia Law School. In the interim, to make some money while paying for law school, he took acting and singing jobs. At Harlem's YMCA, Paul appeared in *Simon the Cyrenian*, a one-act play about the black man who helped carry Christ's cross. Though the play was situated in the ancient past, the show's director could be seen as a harbinger of Paul's future: Charles S. Gilpin, the premier black actor of the time, was also the star of Eugene O'Neill's recent hit *The Emperor Jones*.

Robeson sang at clubs all over Manhattan and acted in a play called *Taboo*, which eventually continued its production in England (under the title *Voodoo*). For Paul, this experience in England was the first time he encountered people who didn't harbor prejudice and he liked the feeling. It would never occur to him that the British, with their own history of racist colonialism and anti–Semitism, saw Robeson as an international performer, just as they did Josephine Baker. These African-American stars were not British natives, but foreigners not subject to England's traditional treatment of blacks, who, unlike these visiting celebrities, were usually forced to live in miserable slums.

By that time, Paul had already met and married a young black woman named Eslanda. In the years ahead, she would be his constant companion during his many battles with the U.S. government, defending his beliefs and unapologetically praising the Soviet Union. She would also still be with him even as he had passionate affairs with many of his leading ladies.

Upon graduation at Columbia, Paul attained a position with a Manhattan law firm. Unfortunately, the firm might as well have been in Alabama since a white secretary there refused to take dictation from him. We can thank this rather ignorant young woman for Paul Robeson abandoning law and embarking on the show business career he was destined to follow.

After his impressive showing in England, Paul was asked to become a member of Greenwich Village's Provincetown Players, with an already dazzled Eugene O'Neill offering him the lead role in the company's *All God's Chillun Got Wings*. The play was a heavy-breathing melodrama that cast Paul as Jim Harris, a young law student (ideal casting here) whose deranged wife ruins his budding career. However, the play had one little element which made audiences sit up and take notice: Jim's wife was white. Indeed, the ending, which had the white wife on her knees before Jim and kissing his hand, was considered offensive by Broadway audiences; and apparently their outrage was so strong, it supported the play's run from May 15 to October 24, 1924. Predictably, in the 1920s, the play's controversy was racial; however, had this work, with its male-worshipping ending, been performed in 2011, feminists would have stormed the theater and demanded the show's closing. Nevertheless, Paul and the cast were reviled from one side of the racial spectrum by African-American leaders who only saw a black man dominated by a white woman and from the other side by the Ku Klux Klan who openly threatened them (though we assume it must've been hard for them to see the show in those white hoods). Conversely, O'Neill was praised for his "honesty and bravery" by no less a giant of black literature than W.E.B. DuBois. During the brouhaha, the playwright continued his support of his favorite star and, after the show's run, offered him a role previously portrayed by Charles S. Gilpin: the amoral Brutus Jones in *The Emperor Jones*.

Though Gilpin would revive the part twice more in the coming years, film and theater historians forever link the role to Paul Robeson. There were several reason for this, besides the obvious one that Robeson starred in the film version. For instance, landmark performer that he was, Gilpin was already 42 when he first portrayed Brutus Jones; he would be nearly 50 when he essayed the role for the last time for a short run in 1927. On the other hand, the tall, strapping Robeson, already exuding a dangerous sexuality and dynamic stage presence, was 27 when he first essayed the role. Robeson's Brutus Jones could dazzle the women, cut a man's throat and effectively puncture the American dream with his own upside-down version of the Horatio Alger story, going from porter to con man to brutal ruler of an island in short order. His portrayal of the role, combining ruthlessness, charm and unlimited gall, electrified Broadway audiences. Compared to this energetic newcomer, Gilpin's run as the premier black stage performer was clearly over. Bald and much slighter than Robeson, Gilpin held on to his declining career as long as he could. He was ignored by racist Hollywood and forgotten by Broadway audiences; by 1930, the actor was dead at the age of 51.

Eventually, his younger, more charismatic replacement in *The Emperor Jones* was going to take the image of the African-American male farther than it had ever gone before…

"Where [Eric] Bentley got the idea that candor is the hallmark of the true revolutionary is beyond me. The idea that real radicals are obligated to adhere to the rules of disclosure imposed by their oppressors seems too fantastic to merit serious discussion."[41] This was the still-angry voice of an unrepentant John Howard Lawson, not long before his death in 1977. During a 20-year period between the late 1920s and late 1940s he had worked as an American screenwriter. Having made thousands of dollars from "the oppressors," he lived the good life in Hollywood. As the chief "enforcer" of the Hollywood section of the Communist Party, he laid down the law to those members who dared deviate from the Party line; like, for instance, actors, directors or screenwriters who had their own ideas about "the Marxist struggle."

Lawson's son, Jeffrey, recalls his father as

> an aloof and very, very angry and driven man who seldom spoke to me, who was not affectionate, and towards whom I felt fascination and awe, but also fear. He was not a disciplinarian, but he was emotionally distant, filled with a frightening ire, and apparently inwardly afraid to be warm and loving to a child.[42]

Certainly, the leaf didn't fall too far from the family tree; for the elder Lawson's father had quite a bit of emotional baggage of his own to carry throughout his life. Lawson himself would describe him as having "maintained an angry silence about everything connected with his childhood."[43]

Born Simeon Levy, Lawson's father was an itinerant journalist who traveled throughout the west during the 1880s, stopping in New Mexico long enough to start an English-language newspaper. Later, he would be appointed an East Coast representative of Reuters. Having married a wealthy woman, he was saddened when she died of breast cancer when John was five. By then, there were other significant changes in the Levy household, not the least of which was their *name*.

For most of his life, Simeon suffered the stings of America's anti–Semitism and, seeking to end this situation by what he thought were the easiest means, he changed his name and those of his family to Lawson. Abandoning Judaism, he ultimately converted to Christian Science. However, like Bernard Malumed's persecuted Russian Jew in *The Fixer*, Simeon found out the hard way that "whenever a Jew pretends he isn't a Jew, an anti–Semite will always remind him." In *Red Star Over Hollywood*, Ronald and Allis Radosh noted that when Simeon took his family to upstate New York WASP resorts, "arriving by coach with footman and staff, the Lawsons would still be turned away when hotel managers heard his thick Yiddish accent."

The derogatory term for Jews without pride, "self-haters," did not exist in the early part of the twentieth century, yet this was clearly the atmosphere that John and his siblings grew up in. In fact, the combination of a motherless family, religious self-denial and coldness from an emotionally distant father was too much for one of John's brothers. Wendell Lawson, tired of being pressured by his father to go into business and give up being a violinist (shades of Clifford Odets' *Golden Boy*), finally committed suicide.

In subsequent works written by John, the playwright would create vehemently angry portraits of cold-blooded, fanatically capitalist males who hated all emotional entanglements that would distract them from their businesses. His most famous play, later filmed by Hollywood, *Success Story*, carried with it an uncomfortably anti–Semitic stereotype of a Jew scratching and clawing his way up the corporate ladder while ignoring the feelings of those who had once loved him (needless to say, he dies at the end). Written years before Budd Schulberg's Hollywood version of the same character in *What Makes Sammy Run*, the authors' real-life family backgrounds point up the difference between the two works. Lawson's play is the work of a young man who grew to detest his father, a self-hater who denied what he was; the more memorable *What Makes Sammy Run* (despite the unflattering portrayal of its main Jewish protagonist) is the work of a young man who loved his father, a studio head who saw no need to change either his name or his religion.

Lawson was born in New York City on September 25, 1894. Unlike his proletarian characters, he was educated at Williams College, a small, prestigious school in the shadow of Massachusetts' Berkshire Mountains, where he attained a Bachelor of Arts degree. Though nestled in the midst of some idyllic rural scenery, the school's interior was far uglier. There was only "one Negro student" at the school and student fraternities were closed to Jews. This was something young John had to face when he was told they didn't want any Jews writing for the student newspaper.

Moving to New York after service in World War I (where he drove an ambulance in France opposite future author John Dos Passos), Lawson hooked up with the leftist theatrical groups, the New Playwrights and the Group Theater, both of whom would produce his plays. Though his admirers would later see him as a successful Broadway playwright with a unique and startling vision of the world, a quick look at any Broadway website reveals that his plays didn't have runs of more than two months at the most; with some plays running a month, and some barely even a week. Only *Success Story* had lasted over three months, debuting on September 26, 1932, and closing in January 1933. Predictably, it would be the only one of his plays that Hollywood would film.

Lawson's style of playwriting could best be described as bad vaudeville merged with vague anti-capitalism and an obsession with the proletariat (or more likely, what passed for the proletariat since Lawson never actually *was* one). Apparently inspired by Aristophanes, much of his work incorporates choruses, some with music and some without, as these oddball figures comment on the skit-like actions onstage. For instance, *Processional*, dealing with the serious topic of a strike at a West Virginia mining operation, is treated as a vaudeville show, though one that was steeped in the ethnic stereotypes of the day. One of the characters' names is Dago Joe and the play itself is populated by, according to film historian Bernard F. Dick, "slow-witted blacks, whining Jews and comic strip Communists."[44] With this last dig at the Left, it was no wonder that vindictive Party commissar Mike Gold would slam Lawson as a "bourgeois Hamlet" in the pages of the Party journal *New Masses*.

Confused about his radicalism, Lawson responded to Gold in suitably penitent, groveling fashion — the same way future Party commissar Lawson would expect others to act opposite *him* when he took charge. In the late 1920s, Lawson had already gone to Hollywood and worked on several screenplays, most notably answering Cecil B. DeMille's offer to come to MGM and write the screenplay of *Dynamite* in 1928. However, Lawson was infuriated to find that DeMille's mistress, longtime collaborator (or perhaps we should say, long-*suffering* collaborator) Jeanie Macpherson received credit for his words. After Lawson protested to DeMille, the great man grudgingly gave him an "added dialogue" credit. Twenty-five years later, now a right-wing icon who approved the blacklist and denounced Jewish "influence" in Hollywood, DeMille had no problem watching Lawson's fortunes crumble during the McCarthy era.

After Bess Meredyth got credit for his work on MGM's *Our Blushing Brides* in 1930, Lawson fled the film community for the east. When he returned to the movie capital in 1934, his confusion about his commitment to Marxism was gone and he would add his name to several screenplays, including the film version of his own *Success Story* (called *Success at Any Price*). He grew steadily in the Party throughout the 1930s, soon becoming the chief enforcer of Party policy, the ultimate arbiter of all political disputes, and the man who could either praise a loyal member or, if he so desired, damn a wayward member (meaning one who asked too many questions) with his brutally caustic tongue.

"I will present only the Communist position,"[45] he proclaimed during those years. And from 1938 to 1948, his Marxist beliefs now crystal clear to him, he would be in his heyday. Some of the films he worked on would attain classic status. Indeed, until the advent of a better Communist writer (Dalton Trumbo, who would work on more prestigious films), Lawson was top dog of leftist screenwriters. In later years, he would even write a book about screenwriting — though, predictably, a highly biased one.

Yet contentment and gratitude for his success was not the way of John Howard Lawson or the Hollywood Party. When F. Scott Fitzgerald wrote to his daughter Frances about what he saw in Hollywood's Communists, he was obviously speaking from personal experience, having met and debated these people at industry parties. In a letter dated March 15, 1940, the author of *The Great Gatsby* wrote:

The important thing is this: They had best be treated not as people holding a certain set of liberal or conservative opinions but rather as you might treat a set of extremely fanatical Roman Catholics among who you find yourself. It's not that you should not disagree with them — the important thing is that you should not argue with them. The point is that Communism has become an intensely dogmatic and almost mystical religion and whatever you say they have ways of twisting it into shapes which put you in some lower category of mankind ("Fascist." "Liberal," "Trotskyite") and disparage you both intellectually and personally in the process.

Raised by a cold, self-hating father and thinking himself intellectually superior to others, John Howard Lawson had found his calling...

In May of 1933, as the nation continued to spiral into a quagmire of poverty and unemployment, Paul Robeson was at Paramount's studios in Astoria being chased through a jungle set by the ghosts of his various victims. Having performed successfully in *The Emperor Jones* on Broadway and London (there had also been a production in Germany, and even an opera), the actor-singer was now prepared to put his performance on celluloid. For six weeks' work, or until early July, Robeson was paid $15,000 and traveling expenses. However, the actor had stipulated in his contract that the company would not film any scenes below the "Mason-Dixon Line" (or as Malcolm X would wryly define the "Mason-Dixon Line" thirty years later, "Below the Canadian border"). Paul certainly didn't want to add to the economy of the racist South, though certainly the safety of the cast and crew must have also been on his mind. He didn't have anything to worry about; New Rochelle in Westchester, New York, substituted nicely for the Deep South in the chain gang sequence.

THE EMPEROR HAS NEW CLOTHES. Paul Robeson shows off his imperial duds in *The Emperor Jones*. The 1933 film took aim at humanity's greed.

It was an independent production released by United Artists; the company was provided with a low budget of around $250,000.[46] Under the direction of liberal screenwriter Dudley Murphy, and with a screenplay by DuBose Heyward, *The Emperor Jones* turned out to be a cut-down version of O'Neill's play, but even this version would remain controversial.

The story begins with Brutus Jones (Robeson) leaving his girlfriend so he can start his new job as a railroad porter. But before he does, he has time to sing in his church, a scene that must have taken Paul back to his choir roots. Once on the cross-country sleeper, the novice porter is shown the ropes by veteran Jeff (Frank Wilson), who counsels him on how to get bigger tips. However, Jones has his own ideas on how to get ahead. Overhearing two white businessmen planning a secret merger, Jones employs subtle blackmail on one of the executives (asking for employment on a better train) to buy his silence. ("There's more room for *big* men in Georgia," says the executive.) The businessman agrees to Jones' terms, exhibiting a certain admiration for this ambitious black man. For 1933, it is an astonishing scene: A white man is doing "business" with a black man, and actually shows him a certain respect for his guile. Such scenes would never have been shot by the major studios, nor would such an "understanding" between a white man and an ambitious black man be shown under the auspices of Will Hays and Joseph Breen's narrow-minded Production Code Office.

Finding that he doesn't need A. Phillip Randolph to help his standing as a Pullman porter, Jones gets better tips and soon has contempt for the penny ante schemes of his ex-pal Jeff. He says as much to Jeff's former squeeze, the gorgeous Undine (played by the gorgeous Fredi Washington). Unfortunately, after her catfight with another woman over Jones, we don't see Fredi for the rest of the film. In fact, after Dudley Murphy re-shot her scenes with her face covered in extra-dark pancake makeup, we see even less of her. This extra makeup was applied because the filmmakers feared that Ms. Washington's light skin would be seen by audiences as white, implying miscegenation in her love scenes with Robeson.

At a gambling joint in Georgia, Jones runs into the surly Jeff and the two shoot craps for high stakes as the patrons watch anxiously. When Jones accuses his ex-friend of using loaded dice, Jeff pulls out a switchblade knife and during the struggle, Jones turns the weapon on his former pal. Hours after Jones has taken it on the lam, a white police officer arrives and is shocked to see the body of Jeff still lying on the floor as the patrons have their backs to the corpse. This is not only a sign of contempt for the white police authorities, but also so Jones will have time to escape. (During the struggle over the knife, Murphy blunders by showing Jeff's hat fall off in long shot and then fall off *again* in close-up.)

However, it seems that someone *has* informed the law, since Jones is tagged for Jeff's murder. Caught and sent to a Georgia work farm, he is ordered by the sadistic white guard to beat a black youth who passed out from a spell in "the sweat-box." After Jones refuses, he is lashed by the guard, who then rather stupidly turns his back. This gives Jones a chance to smash the guard's head in with a shovel. This scene showing a white man being killed by a black man would, needless to say, be cut to the point of absurdity in Southern theaters. Down South, audiences saw Jones get struck by the guard, the guard turn around, then Jones bending over to reach for something. For all we know he could have been tying his shoe, but immediately after this the other guards are on alert and Jones is running for his life. Is Jones being pursued just because he bent from the waist? This is also the version that PBS broadcast on New York TV in the mid–1970s, which is when I first saw the film. In a later home video version of the film, however, we see Jones reach for a shovel and actually swing it, though director Murphy cunningly keeps the white guard's head out of the frame. This was done more to lessen the violence than for Southern sensibilities. (In films with white characters, when a person is shown smashing another in the back of the head with a blunt instrument, the director *always* cuts to the assailant.)

Escaping on a freighter, Jones takes a job shoveling coal with other black men. When one of them tells him of "one of them nigger islands" that are nothing but trouble, Jones arrogantly replies, "Trouble is my buddy." Trouble may be Jones' buddy, but we've seen how this ambitious fellow treats his friends. Also evident in this brief scene is one of the film's lasting controversies. After escaping to the "trouble" island, the forbidden N word will practically attain a life of its own and run rampant all through the rest of the film.

The island of blacks that Jones energetically swims to is under the thumb of a Papa Doc–like dictator, complete with long black coat and top hat. Besides oppressing his people, this despot also imports illegal goods from crooked white trader Smithers (a cockney Dudley Digges). Though Jones is "bought" by Smithers, it soon becomes obvious that "the property" has no plans to be subservient to any man. "I is the property of *Mr.* Smithers," Jones sarcastically agrees. However, Jones has taught the natives gambling and, through his use of crooked dice, attains enough material goods to start his own importing business, and give Smithers competition — that is, until the British trader is forced to give him a partnership.

When Jones rejects the island leader's authority, the despot orders his captain to fire on him, but amazingly the bullets have no effect. Convincing the rather dim natives that he is charmed (he loaded the captain's gun with blanks) and can only be killed by silver bullets, Jones forces the natives to crown him the island's new leader, and orders the despot's arrest ("Get rid of this bush nigger!"). In a scene that infuriated Southerners, Smithers, the former master, is forced to light Jones' cigarette. (This racism over a simple physical gesture did not change in two decades. In the early 1950s, after Sammy Davis Jr. had just finished a slam-bang, knock-'em-dead number on *The Colgate Comedy Hour*, an impressed Eddie Cantor came onstage to mop the sweat off Davis' forehead with his handkerchief. The Jewish comedian was soon the recipient of both racist and anti–Semitic hate mail. Defiantly, Cantor invited Davis back on the show and, weeks later, outraged audiences saw him take out his handkerchief and mop Sammy's head *again*.)

Jones, now an island ruler, has begun to oppress the natives by sending them brutal tax collectors and demanding strict obedience. Realizing that the natives are ready to revolt, Jones opts to escape with his ill-gotten profits, but he dallies too long and is forced to travel the jungle at night. During the endless trek, with Jones seemingly traveling in circles, he imagines his former victims coming after him. Soon, exhausted beyond endurance, Jones thinks back to the days when he was a good man singing in his church. Returning to his former palace, Jones is killed when the natives riddle him with *silver* bullets. Though Smithers stands over his corpse and mocks his former partner's airs, not only is it obvious that he's out of a job, but the natives have foolishly melted down their silver for useless bullets, giving Jones a strange kind of victory.

The scenes of Robeson strutting about in his "emperor" uniform are, of course, controversial in themselves. Was O'Neill saying that this is what will happen to blacks who are ambitious in a white man's world; or is he saying that power will corrupt anyone regardless of skin color? Throughout this shifting balance of Jones' fortunes throughout the film, it is certainly worth noting his relationship to Smithers during all the mayhem.

All through the film, despite the fact that they would gladly cut each other's throats, of all the people Jones meets, Smithers is probably the one who gets the closest to him — closer even than any *female* character. Despite the trader's original appraisal of Jones as a "black ape" and Jones contemptuously addressing him as "white man," it soon becomes obvious that these two reprobates *understand* each other. Despite the racial condensation, both speak to each other as men, not master and servant — that is, most of the time. For instance, with all the blacks on the island, Jones ignores them completely and takes *Smithers* into his confidence; this includes letting him in on the fact that he stashed the island's tax money under a rock somewhere in the jungle.

When the film was released, United Artists took "nigger" off the soundtrack for black theaters and for showings up north; however, it remained on the soundtrack in Southern theaters where white audiences had no problem with the word.

In answer to the complaints about the N word all through the film, especially from black audiences, Paul Robeson Jr. said in a DVD version of *The Emperor Jones*, "He felt in this white playwright [O'Neill] who's trying to capture the humanity of the black character for once.... He didn't give a damn whether it was racially correct or not."

Certainly, despite the constant racist epithets thrown at both blacks and whites in the film, we also see Jones' humanity. At the beginning, he is an innocent church-going young man who goes out into the world to make it as a Pullman porter. However, the world he goes into is populated by profiteers and crooks. Throughout the film, both blacks and whites are portrayed as dishonest, and no matter where Jones goes (usually for a life of hedonism and profit), he finds corruption. Jeff shows him the ropes, meaning more money; Undine begs Jones' forgiveness only when he threatens to break off the money flow (she leaves him but returns to pick up $40 he threw at her); the black characters in the nightclub and gambling scenes are in a world of loose money and loose women, and a kind of "prestige" is bestowed on the man who has both; Smithers and the island's dictator are also interested in turning a dishonest dollar; even the white businessmen are secretly having a merger to gain unfair advantage over competitors. It soon becomes obvious that the island Jones flees to is also populated by natives who are open to being corrupted. He teaches them gambling, and when one gives him a woman as a prize, he refuses, not out of principles, but because to him women are predatory devourers of his money. ("I'm travelin' light," he declares while leaving two girlfriends fight over him in a nightclub.) Far from being a one-sided racist portrait, the film condemns people of all colors as having the seed of rottenness in them. Its moral is simple and to the point: In order to be a personal and financial success in a capitalist society, or *any* society run on the almighty dollar, one must lose their soul.

Bertold Brecht couldn't have said it any better...

"Patriotism or pacifism? Humanity or luxury?" Smash hit or box office bomb? The last was probably the most pertinent question to money-hungry Hollywood as it once again made a film that attacked the world's money and property demons (as author Joe Adamson had referred sardonically to the nation's upper classes). Certainly, this "most startling picture of the year" was proud of its left-wing pedigree.

The three-act play *The Man Who Reclaimed His Head* opened at New York's Broadhurst Theater on September 8, 1932. Written by leftist playwright Jean Bart, it starred a stage actor (and soon-to-be movie star) named Claude Rains as a victimized little man, Paul Verin, and Jean Arthur as his wife Adele. The show also had a director from whom much would be heard in the distant future, a dedicated Communist activist named Herbert Biberman.

The play lasted a mere 28 days (certainly longer than some of John Howard Lawson's works), and some in the audience had to hear speeches slamming rich warmongers which were enacted with the usual sledgehammer subtlety for which radical playwrights were known.

Despite the play's over-the-top anti-capitalist kitsch and Grand Guignol gruesomeness, its antiwar message appealed to Rains, a battlefield veteran of the First World War. However, within the play's text, Bart described Verin as "uncommonly ugly, a painful ugliness, bordering on the grotesque. The hands and feet disproportionately large. Fan-like ears peer from under a mess of bushy hair. Only the eyes, deep and soulful, seem almost beautiful in the sincerity of their gaze."[47] Buried in this awful makeup, many critics compared Rains to the deformed characters played by Lon Chaney. It was *not* meant as a compliment. Certainly, it must have been hard for Bart's antiwar message to come through when her main spokesman looked like a cross between Dumbo and Mickey Mouse. (A note on the sex of the playwright. The Internet Broadway Database refers to Jean Bart as a *man*. Yet most other sources, including *Universal Horrors* by Tom Weaver and Michael & John Brunas, refer to Bart as the *daughter* of a count.)

While the play was running, Rains had basically gotten along well with Herbert Biberman, but he drew the line on the director's other idiosyncrasies. When Biberman invited Rains and actress-producer Helen Westley to a reception for a visiting Chinese actress, the two performers were shocked when the "actress," instead of discussing the theater, launched into a shrill monologue on the wonders of Bolshevism. "Let's get out of here," Rains whispered to Westley, and soon the two made themselves invisible.[48]

Cut to two years later. After two decades as an actor on the London and Broadway stages, Rains was finally an international star thanks to his performance in Universal's *The Invisible Man*. The actor signed a two-picture contract with the studio. (Even then, Rains was reluctant to be typed as a "horror star" and later rejected participation in the studio's *Bride of Frankenstein*.) However, despite its brief run, Bart's play was bought by Universal, with Rains repeating his stage role. Production commenced on September 17, 1934. The screenplay was by Bart and a young screenwriter whose passion for social activism brought him into the Communist Party: Samuel Ornitz.

Born in New York City on November 15, 1890, 12-year-old "Sammy" made his debut in progressive politics (legend has it) when he made a speech on a soapbox to a crowd at Union Square. Ornitz sincerely wanted to help humanity, especially the poor and racially disenfranchised, so he became a social worker. Feeling the desire to do something more creative with his energies, Ornitz soon turned to writing in order to bring attention to the problems of the poor. By the time he turned 33, Ornitz had written several short stories and became a novelist with the publication of *Haunch, Paunch and Jowl*, a tale of Jewish immigrant life in the early part of the twentieth century. Leaving social work behind, Ornitz went to Hollywood and traveled the circuit from one low-budget production to the next.

An exception to this was RKO's *Thirteen Women*, one of his first screenplays. Someone is found to be killing off a group of women who had once been cliquish college classmates; it is soon revealed that the murders were committed by the lone Asian gal among them. Apparently the murderess had been knocking off the girls because she remembers their snobby, racist treatment of her. Unfortunately, the anti-racist message is somewhat undercut by the fact that the Asian woman is played by lily-white Myrna Loy. Still, it was Ornitz's first attempt to take advantage of those pre–Code years and slam white racism as well as the upper classes. The film also features one of the few appearances made by the tragic Peg Entwhistle just a short time before she threw herself off the top of the HOLLYWOODLAND sign.

In RKO's *Highway to Hell*, Ornitz's screenplay, based on actual events, rips the abusive treatment of inmates a year before the more famous *I Am a Fugitive from a Chain Gang*. The film contains such pre–Code elements as the overheated sweat-box, various whippings and beatings, and an outrageously stereotyped gay inmate (who, predictably, is employed as the cook). The film starred Richard Dix as the tough World War veteran–postwar gangster who must keep his younger inmate brother on the straight and narrow. The film also poked fun at religion in a way that Joseph Breen never would have allowed in just two years; it has a pre–Ming Charles Middleton as a Bible-quoting zealot who obviously doesn't believe his own spiel. However, Ornitz also gives us a respectful portrait of black convicts, who are shown to be far more intelligent and aware of what's going on than their white brethren. With the advent of the Production Code years, such positive portrayals would be rare. Ornitz continued with compassionate depictions of African Americans in the first version of *Imitation of Life* (he contributed to the screenplay).

Universal's *The Man Who Reclaimed His Head* begins as Paul Verin (Claude Rains), soldier of the Great War, is visiting his attorney, Fernand de Marnay (Henry O'Neill), with a hatbox. After Verin shows de Marnay the contents, the lawyer recoils in horror. Instead of the latest Parisian chapeau, the hatbox contains a man's head. How it got there and how Paul got hold of it will be solved by the flashback scenes.

Verin is a poor but happy little man. He does not suffer from a facial deformity (as the play's Paul did), but instead possesses the handicap of being a Frenchman with a British accent. He is married to the lovely but obviously dissatisfied Adele (a blonde Joan Bennett), and they have a little girl named Linette (Juanita Quigley). Verin hates war, but this passionate belief in peace has not been putting food on the table. So when rich newspaper publisher Henri Dumont (an unctuous Lionel Atwill) hires Verin to ghost-write articles for which Dumont would take credit, Adele insists that Paul accept the gig. Thanks to Paul's writings, Dumont is soon the toast of France and is made nationally famous on words that he himself has not written.

However, since Dumont is cursed with the plague called money, and lots of it, he betrays the little pacifist faster than you can say "capitalist scum." Backed by France's wealthy munitions manufacturers, Dumont turns Paul's ghost-written articles into words to incite nationalist hatred which would lead the country into war. ("Each death by his bullets meant a dollar for his fun!" shrieked a particularly laughable tagline.) Broken by this revelation, Verin reluctantly joins the nation's war effort against a militarist Germany.

But on the home front, things are not that rosy either. Dumont has the hots for Verin's lovely young bride and, when Paul returns home, he catches the wealthy warmonger putting the moves on her. Quickly forgetting his pacifism, the enraged little man draws his military sword and takes a little off the top; or "reclaims his head," as the title says.

After hearing Paul's sad tale, the attorney, moved by the little veteran's plight, amazingly decides to take his case without demanding a retainer fee.

The film keeps the anti-capitalist bite of the play, especially in the scene where wealthy industrialists are getting together to literally plan a major European war, the citizenry be damned, so they can increase munitions profits. In another unsubtle scene, as he hurries past a train depot, Verin bumps into a nun, causing him to drop his sword and the Sister to drop her Rosary beads. On the ground, we see the beads lying against the Sword of Vengeance. This bit, obviously not in the play, was added by the antiwar Ornitz. Was he saying that Paul's quest for vengeance against the warmongering capitalists is blessed by the church; or was he saying, more perniciously, that organized religion and mass killing instituted by the rich go hand in hand? Certainly, the latter would be proven in less than two years when the Catholic Church in Spain backed Franco's fascist uprising.

Ultimately, the film was *not* a success, most likely because Universal, in a typical nonbrilliant move, decided to market it as a horror film. Why not, the studio figured. It topbilled the stars of *The Invisible Man* and *Doctor X*; the studio was already famous for its horror product; and the title made no bones about the fact that it meant the act of one man taking another man's head off; all were supposedly the tried-and-true elements of a good old-fashioned, blood-curdling horror show. Despite the film's failure, it certainly brought to light a horror of another kind.

Still, unlike the studio's monster films (like *Frankenstein* and *Dracula*), *The Man Who Reclaimed His Head* would not be re-released to theaters as the nation moved closer to involvement in World War II. However, it *was* re-released in July 1948, a time of relative peace, though turmoil still remained in Eastern Europe where the Communists were solidifying their hold on the captive nations. Samuel Ornitz continued to work on screenplays for several Bs, and he would eventually be given sporadic employment with Republic Pictures.

At the height of the Nazi-Soviet Pact, Ornitz made speeches against America's involvement in the war. According to the FBI file on the Hollywood Anti-Nazi League, of which Ornitz was a member, the Communist screenwriter blatantly called President Roosevelt a "traitor." During a speech he made on November 24, 1940, in Los Angeles, despite his being a Jew, Ornitz actually "praised Hitler."

Yet for all his passionate attacks on the warmongering rich men in *The Man Who Reclaimed His Head*, Ornitz would consistently ignore Stalin's aggression in Eastern Europe in the postwar years. By the time he was called before the House Un-American Activities Committee in 1947, the screenwriter would accuse the senators of Jew-baiting, yet stubbornly deny that there was anti–Semitic persecution in the Soviet Union. "Whenever an imperialistic power was threatened by progressivism," he would say, "anti–Semitism was brought up as a scapegoat."[49] Because of his ability to twist Marxist double-talk into something that sounded noble to Party newcomers, Ornitz was known to his comrades as "the Great Explainer."

But the Great Explainer couldn't talk his way out of being blacklisted in 1947; not that it mattered very much by that time. Ornitz's career was already in trouble even before he met with HUAC. In the early 1940s, his screenplays were basically for low-budget companies like Republic and PRC while Dalton Trumbo was still the star screenwriter at MGM. In 1945, he wrote the screenplay for *China's Little Devils*, an absurd title for an absurd little film about the efforts of Chinese kids to sabotage the Japanese war machine. Here, the man who slammed warmongers now encouraged Chinese children to put themselves in the line of fire to stop the fascist invader; hypocritically admitting, through his screenplay, that there *were* reasons to go to war that had nothing to do with profit.

Ornitz died of cancer in Woodland Hills, California, on March 10, 1957. However, his own suffering might have been exacerbated by something else besides physical pain. Party member Paul Jarrico would later comment:

> Sam Ornitz was a highly educated, very talented man who was better informed than most people.... Of course, later on, he was terribly embarrassed about the role he had played during the Pact. He was very proud of being a Jew, but he kept denying that there was any anti–Semitism in the Soviet Union or Eastern Europe, and he *really* denied it until the evidence became irrefutable. And then he was humiliated because he'd stuck his neck out.... So he had prestige which he put on the line, and brother, he really suffered. He really was angrier than almost anybody I know about the 1956 revelations — he suffered more personally, more deeply himself.[50]

In all that time, he never "reclaimed his head."

On December 20, 1934, Paul and Eslanda Robeson had left London and were on their way to Moscow to hold discussions with Sergei Eisenstein about a film based on the life of Haitian leader Toussaint L'Ouverture. Because there was no direct train route to the Soviet Union, the following day the Robesons had to lay over in a European city and board a second train destined for Moscow.

That city happened to be Berlin.

Accompanied by their friend, British journalist Marie Seton (an admirer of the Soviet

Union, she was the go-between to set up the meeting between Paul and Eisenstein), the Robesons went to their hotel to await their departure on the Moscow-bound train. However, after their arrival, Paul knew immediately that something was wrong; he felt it as soon as he set foot on German soil. He had performed in Berlin almost five years before, both as a singer and as an actor, receiving raves for his performance as Brutus Jones in yet another production of *The Emperor Jones*. But this was not five years ago. This was the end of 1934; the Weimar Republic was gone for good.

After the Robesons and Seton returned to Friedrichstrasse Station to await the train for Moscow, Eslanda left them on the platform to go check the train's schedule. Paul immediately noticed the hostile glares from Germans who didn't see two people merely waiting for a Moscow-bound train, but a black man standing next to a white woman.

The Robesons had already been deeply disturbed by a visit from a Jewish friend who stopped by their hotel room. The man was a shadow of his former self; his eyes had shrunk in their sockets, he was pale; he looked like "a living corpse," Eslanda later wrote in her diary.[51] He spoke of the persecution, the harassment, the pogroms that Jews the world over were all too familiar with. Stunned by this revelation, Paul wondered how such a thing could happen in the same cultured Germany he had visited and enjoyed five short years ago.

Now Paul and Marie Seton stood next to each other on a train platform in a land where racial superiority was the order of the day. Then three storm troopers, alerted to the couple's presence by an angry German woman, approached them "with hatred in their eyes."[52] Seeing what was going to happen, Paul remained calm and merely stepped forward to respond to their approach. Perhaps it was something in Paul's eyes (which is what Paul proudly claimed to a reporter years later), or, more realistically, perhaps it was the sudden realization by the storm troopers that these were foreigners merely passing through and that they would be gone as soon as the train arrived; for whatever reason, the three Nazis moved off and didn't push the issue of Paul's mere presence in Aryan-friendly Berlin. Still, the near-incident deeply disturbed him, especially after hearing what the Robesons' Jewish friend had told them just hours before. Eslanda would later write in her diary that she felt "a terrible feeling of wolves waiting to spring."[53]

In Phillip Hayes Dean's play *Paul Robeson*, presented on Broadway for a limited run in early 1978, James Earl Jones, as Robeson, reenacts this scene. However, what in actuality was a tense moment that never became an open confrontation, in the play becomes a highly implausible example of Robeson's courage. As Jones' Robeson relates to the audience:

> Brown-shirts, Hitler's storm-troopers, were everywhere. Nothing furtive or silent about them.... [Paul turns around. Storm troopers are surrounding him.] I beg your pardon! Who are you? ... Herr Kruger ... You came to do what? ... Well, thank you very much, I don't need an escort to the train. Are these men with you? Would you please tell your friends I don't like people getting behind me. [Storm-troopers curse in German.]
>
> Watch your mouth! Yes, I speak German, but I'm telling you in English, watch your mouth! ... You! No, my wife is not German. As a matter of fact, she's not even white. If it's any of your business, she's Negro.
>
> There's no need to ask her, I just told him. If any of you lay a hand on my wife, I swear I'll kill one of you. Even if you put a bullet in my brain I'll live long enough to get my hands on at least one of you. Preferably you, Herr Kruger ... and I swear I will kill you.

After this "encounter," Paul and Eslanda head for the train. "Don't walk too fast ... I don't want those animals to think they smell fear. [Once in the train.] Turn the light out, but leave the shade up. Until the train pulls out, I want to keep my eye on them."

In reality, according to Seton, "For a long time after the train moved out of Berlin, Paul sat hunched in a corner of the compartment, staring out into the darkness."[54] Not exactly a gutsy stare-down with the SS, was it?

In fact, playwright Dean would have us believe that Paul, in the grand celluloid tradition of swashbuckling heroes of the Errol Flynn mold, stood up to several Nazi storm troopers that "were everywhere," not the three men he actually encountered. He would also have us believe that Paul actually threatened a gun-toting Nazi thug with violent death and somehow managed to walk away alive in the Germany of 1934. Even his threat is straight out of, ironically, the Arnold Schwarzenegger playbook of cartoonish cinema heroism; with the hero saying that not even a bullet in the brain will stop him from taking one of his tormentors with him, a nice trick if he could do it. Also, Dean's retelling removes the presence of Marie Seton and instead substitutes Eslanda, who wasn't there at the time.

Certainly, no one, least of all Dean, had to fabricate examples of Paul's courage. When the Nazis approached, Paul merely stood his ground; he wasn't going to run, and he wasn't going to hide. Obviously, he was perfectly ready to confront these enemies of all humanity, regardless of the fact that he must have been scared as well (something he *didn't* admit to that reporter).

Dean's play, debuting a few days after the second anniversary of Robeson's death, would be the beginning of the whitewash. Paul Robeson, the actor-singer who performed in plays that are never revived today; who sang and acted in low-budget films whose non-existent production values and over-the-top acting make one cringe; the champion of civil rights who supported a totalitarian state; and the long-married husband who hurt his wife by constantly having affairs with other women, was now part of legend.

In the years after his death, Paul Robeson was to become an icon. And as we all know, an icon *never* makes mistakes…

> The first question, in my mind, is whether or not the industry, as an industry, should sponsor a picture of this kind. You will have in mind that it is hardly more than a story portraying the Hitlerization of the United States of America. It is an attempt to bring home to American citizens, through the instrumentality of the screen, that which is transpiring in Germany today.[55]

So wrote Joseph I. Breen to Will Hays at the MPPDA's New York offices on December 18, 1935. Said screenplay was based on a novel written by one of the greatest literary figures of the twentieth century. The son of a Minnesota physician, he had written novels attacking American materialism, particularly the status quo values of his fellow Midwesterners. Incisive, witty, acerbic and socialist, Sinclair Lewis captured the imagination of the 1920s reading public as no American author had (that is, with the exception of Hemingway and F. Scott Fitzgerald). Not surprisingly, at the end of the decade, he would be receive the Nobel Prize for Literature.

Author Michael Meyer, in his informative introduction to Signet's 2005 reissue of *It Can't Happen Here*, wrote:

> His five major novels of the 1920s … were all bestsellers that served to hold a mirror up to the parochialism and provincialism of that decade. A good many Americans winced at their own reflections in those novels, but they eagerly bought Lewis' iconoclastic books, because, however much they flinched at his representations of their middle-class lives, they were finally snugly, if not smugly, comfortable in the economic security that produced their prosperous confidence.

However, neither "economic security" nor "prosperous confidence" would be the bywords for the following decade. In fact, Meyer pointed out that there wasn't much left of the middle-class after the 1929 stock market crash. For any astute commentator of the times, it was hard to make fun of former professionals and business leaders now selling apples on street corners.

Lewis, however, was smart enough to see (and predict) something else. An avid reader of world events, the author realized that when nations were plunged into joblessness and hunger, people would be desperate for a solution, any solution, that would get them on their feet again. One of the reasons for such penetrating insight into the growing menace of totalitarianism was the brilliant woman who had become his second wife. How he met her was a story in itself.

Lewis had been married to the former Grace Livingston Hegger since 1914, but the union was falling apart, much of it due to the author's fondness of the sauce (and I don't mean Tabasco). *Elmer Gantry* had been a bestseller in 1927 (especially in the Bible Belt Midwest). In order to get away from all the hoopla, as well as his increasingly critical wife, the alienated author took a European junket with some friends. Hopping about from Yugoslavia to France to England, and after a side trip to Munich, the scribe finally ended up in Berlin. On July 2, he had written to Grace that he was heading home and asked whether she would join him in Nantucket. However, at a party in the German Foreign Ministry on July 8, he met a news correspondent by the name of Dorothy Thompson. On July 24, he cabled his publisher with this message: "Staying Europe several months more. Please inform Grace."[56]

When he next saw the lonely Grace Lewis 13 months later, he informed her that they were through and that Dorothy was going to be his new wife. Sam Dodsworth himself couldn't have been any colder.

However, as he would soon find out, Dorothy Thompson was no man's idea of a docile woman. Outgoing, aggressive, and highly intelligent, she was the daughter of a Methodist minister from upstate New York. A graduate of Syracuse University where she majored in journalism, Thompson was also an activist with the Buffalo, New York, headquarters of the Woman's Suffrage Party. As one of its leading lights, she soon became a brilliant speaker before upstate crowds, haranguing her audiences to support the rights of women. After a period as a publicity writer in New York, and with little money, she went to Europe, hoping to become a foreign correspondent for a major newspaper. Possessing a natural charm and not afraid to be outspoken, Dorothy talked her way into several reporting jobs. Therefore, while Sinclair Lewis was writing his greatest works during the 1920s, Dorothy was becoming well-known in Europe, holding positions as the Berlin correspondent for the *Philadelphia Ledger* and the *New York Evening Post*, respectively, as well becoming the chief of the Central European Service in Berlin — heady posts for a young woman in the 1920s.

When Lewis met her in the Foreign Ministry of the Weimer Republic in 1927, the author of *Arrowsmith* and *Main Street* fell faster than the stock market did two years later. Like many intellectuals of the time, Thompson was an admirer of the Soviet "experiment," not realizing that a Mad Scientist was already hijacking it. In later years, Thompson would wake up to the madness of the Stalinist regime, but at the time, she wrote to Lewis almost daily, insisting that he come to Moscow.

Because his novels of the 1920s had attacked American mores, particularly its alleged obsession with the almighty dollar, Lewis' works were freely published in the Soviet Union (in other words, without paying a single kopek to any foreign author). In fact, the work of Lewis and other leftist American authors neatly outsold the works of Soviet authors (who were forced to print only tripe approved by the government).

When he departed on the Berlin train on November 29, news of his visit spread to Moscow and, to his great dismay, he was met by representatives of the Soviet Society for Cultural Relations, several of their rubber-stamped hack writers, and, more annoyingly, a brass band. After being asked the purpose of his visit by an anxious Soviet official (who was also hoping he'd make some anti–American remark), Lewis answered simply, "Dorothy." He could see that his answer disappointed the Bolshevik toady. As Lewis biographer Mark Schorer pointed out, "It is probable that the Russians never did understand the quixotic Lewis, and equally probable that he had no interest in understanding them...."

Before he could say "Surrender, Dorothy," Lewis was reluctantly feted by Soviet officials, who were once again celebrating the violent takeover of their country from the czar. Also paying homage to Soviet tyranny was another author known for books that criticized America, though with far more severity and contempt than Lewis' more thoughtful works. After arriving in Moscow, a sick Theodore Dreiser was supposedly cared for in his hotel room by Dorothy Thompson. Dreiser, however, had other things in mind besides being fed chicken soup and hot tea; the 56-year-old author of *Sister Carrie* and *Jennie Gerhardt* still fancied himself a ladies' man and later even claimed that Lewis was jealous of his relationship with Dorothy. However, this rather pathetic fantasy was quickly denied by Ms. Thompson. Predictably, Dreiser would get back at her by allegedly lifting wholesale passages from her book *The New Russia* for his own book on the Soviet capital.

Remaining a Berlin correspondent for many years, Dorothy also had a front-row seat for the rise of Nazism. In the early thirties, she had interviewed Hitler, not liking the look or the sound of him. In her articles published between 1931 and 1935, Dorothy warned Americans about Nazi persecution of the Jews and the numerous concentration camps rapidly being built around the country. Lewis was well aware of the demagoguery of pseudo-fascists like Huey Long and Father Coughlin, but the author also had the benefit of firsthand reportage from the one woman who was in a position to see the madness of National Socialism up close, his new bride, Dorothy Thompson.

Berzelius (Buzz) Windrip, the book's major protagonist, was referred to by Michael Meyer as "a New England version of the dictatorial Kingfish, who ushers in a fascistic regime of suppression, terror and totalitarianism — all draped in red, white and blue bunting." And there lies the danger. Starting as a folksy politician, Windrip soon becomes a racist, Jew-baiting fascist nightmare. He has his own troops of brown shirts (called the "Minute Men") terrorize all who oppose his regime, he strictly censors all media and, predictably, he builds concentration camps for the nation's "inferiors."

Published in October 1935, the novel was a bestseller. Though some critics referred to it as "highbrow" and "different," at least one public figure was far more hostile to Lewis' attack on the New Order.

Shortly after the book's publication, William Randolph Hearst declared, "Whenever you hear a prominent American called a 'Fascist,' you can usually make up your mind that the man is simply a LOYAL AMERICAN WHO STANDS FOR AMERICANISM."[57]

Seeing the phenomenal sales of the novel, MGM decided to film the book within two months of its publication. A screenplay was written by playwright Sidney Howard. Then, mysteriously, on February 15, 1936, Lewis was notified that MGM abandoned the project. There were rumors that the Hays Office banned the film because of "complications" in showing it in foreign markets. The MPPDA denied the charge. However, studio files tell a different story. The Hays Office correspondence detailing its objections to the script, the several drafts of Howard's screenplay that still exist, and even Lewis' vocal defense of his book, all bring to light many of the reasons behind the alleged "complications" dealing with the production's cancellation.

Interestingly, in Breen's December 18 letter to Hays, the censor had basically approved of Howard's script, yet he also gave his superior dire warnings about how foreign markets would react to such a film. That same day, Breen also sent a letter to Louis B. Mayer, saying more or less the same thing, though with one major difference: He did not mention the phrases "the Hitlerization of the United States of America" or "what was transpiring in Germany today."[58]

In another letter to Mayer, dated January 31, 1936, Breen apprised the mogul that the basic story was "acceptable under the provisions of the Production Code, *but the story is enormously dangerous from the standpoint of political censorship, in this country and abroad.*" Then, after again mentioning MPPDA catchphrases like "political censorship" and "industry policy," Breen amends his letter granting script approval with a full nine pages of strenuous objections. In fact, it was soon obvious that the censor was becoming more and more upset as he composed his letter. After citing many instances of "brutality and excessive brutality," "violence and excessive violence," and "general public disorder and rioting,"[59] Breen then lists his complaints in graphic detail.

One of his gripes was a character referring to fascism as "Low wages. Top prices." This line, Breen claimed, "will help the European nations to make up their minds to reject your picture in toto." At another point, Breen cites Windrip's line "I don't guess any presidential candidate ever addressed men in a bread line. *Call me a Socialist. Call me anything!* But never forget I was a friend of labor!"

Breen reaction was not unexpected. He called the above

> a dangerous speech from a standpoint of the national political viewpoint in this country, especially as it is likely, if your picture is produced, that it will be current at the height of the presidential campaign. Indeed, this speech may be interpreted as having a sly reference to the political philosophy of the present incumbent in the White House.

Concerning page 27, scene 26, Breen recommended that Windrip's salute not be "even suggestive" of brownshirt salutes in Nazi Germany. In fact, a major preoccupation of Breen's, *vis-à-vis* the script, were his attempts to tone down the anarchic mayhem of the Minute Men. When an overzealous fascist shouts, "With regular arms issued to every man. May have to rob the Army...," Breen recommended the line's elimination in order to "tone down, wherever possible, the inflammatory tone of the picture." In scene 77, he insisted on the deletion of dialogue where presidential candidate Windrip declares a state of martial law. Also on the censor's list were bitter complaints about the Minute Men's frequent use of blackjacks, whips, brass knuckles, pistols, hand grenades and truncheons, as well as "defenseless people being shot down by machine guns; and the bayonets of the Minute Men should not be shown sticking the backs of persons in the mob."[60]

In fact, Howard's script gives full rein to the Minute Men's imaginative use of practically *anything* to deliver as much pain and suffering to their victims as possible. Besides such examples of their brutality as pushing people down stairs and kicking them after they've been knocked down (as well as resorting to a whole array of kidney punches and head blows), this resourceful SS clone also uses a "steel fishing rod" on one of their victims. At another point, they even lower a helpless man into an oil tank.

On page 48, scene 82, Windrip declares, "Thank God there's still enough American spirit to get up a mob" (the last seven words underlined by Breen). The clearly rattled censor responded, "Please keep in mind that social conditions throughout the world today are seriously upset, and that censor boards are not disposed to look with favor upon scenes of any kind showing mass violence or riots."

It was noted that on page 57, Windrip's deputy refers to foreigners as "potential Communists," and on page 60, Windrip himself refers to his rise to power as the "new American Revolution." Breen insisted on the deletion of both phrases.

However, one particular speech struck the pious censor a little too close to home:

> Please delete the following words from the speech by Father Perfixe: "From Calvary Thy Son prayed to Thee.... He said, 'They know not what they do.' Father, forgive not these men, *but curse them*!" It is hardly likely that a Catholic priest, dying, would give expression to such a thought.[61]

Perhaps, but the Hays Office wanted to demonstrate to the movie industry, as well as the Roosevelt administration, that at least *they* knew what they were doing. Predictably, Breen's nine pages of "suggestions" and "deletions" were so numerous that MGM finally realized how disemboweled their film was going to be. More to the point, MGM officials realized that the studio had taken a bath with another parable about a strongman president, 1933's *Gabriel Over the White House*. Further establishing his studio as having "more stars than there were in the heavens," Mayer didn't need the added headache of crossing swords with the Hays Office, the Roosevelt administration, William Randolph Hearst, the Republicans or a European film market that was then rapidly becoming dominated by fascist nations.

Project cancelled!

One voice, however, wouldn't be stilled, and that was the man who created Buzz Windrip and his Minute Men. In the February 16 issue of the *New York Times*, Sinclair Lewis angrily declared:

> The world is today full of fascist propaganda. The Germans are making one pro-fascist film after another, designed to show that fascism is superior to democracy. The Italians are doing the same. On the other side, the Russians are making films to show that Communism is superior to everything else.
>
> I have yet to see Hollywood and its satellites threaten to ban German, Italian and Russian pictures from the market on this ground. But Mr. Hays actually says that a film cannot be made to show the horrors of Fascism and extolling the advantages of Democracy because Hitler and Mussolini might ban other Hollywood films from their countries if we were so rash.
>
> Democracy is certainly on the defensive when two European dictators without opening their mouths or knowing anything about the issue can shut down an American film causing a loss of $200,000 to the producer. I wrote "It Can't Happen Here," but I begin to think it certainly can.[62]

The following day, the Hays Office issued a statement to the press attacking Lewis' claims as being "full of inaccuracies. If he is quoted correctly, he is simply misinformed." Shortly after this, came a comment from those flattered souls for whom the Minute Men were modeled. Far from "not knowing anything about the issue," the Nazi government called Lewis "a full-blooded Communist" and praised MGM for canceling the project.[63]

To Lewis, who had already pocketed his money from the book's sale to the studio, the whole affair was simply a matter of principle. To the Hays Office, where matters of principle were subject to "alterations, suggestions and further deletions," it was obvious that the agency truly feared a movie that portrayed America as teetering on the edge of violent revolution. Certainly, the powers-that-be had no use for a film depicting an American Gestapo taking over the country; a horror show that unmasked the very real fear among those in charge that the Roosevelt administration, bogged down with trying to pull the country out of the Depression, would soon be overthrown by someone who *really* knew how to make the trains run on time.

In October 1936, Lewis turned *It Can't Happen Here* into a play, co-written by John C. Moffitt. It ran briefly in New York, Los Angeles and other cities, with Lewis himself playing the role of the heroic newspaper editor Doremus Jessup. In its issue of October 28, *The Hollywood Reporter* complained, "It is heavy-handed and unconvincing, crying for far better adaptation and the stiff New York cast mouthing the leaden dialogue made it a boring shadow of a stirring novel."[64]

In later years, Lewis continued to write classic works, though his heyday of the 1920s was clearly behind him. By the time of the Hitler-Stalin Pact in 1939, his marriage to Dorothy was in name only. The bloom had long been off the rose since their first meeting at the German Foreign Ministry in 1927. She had become thoroughly disgusted with his self-destructive alcoholism, a disease which severely affected his creative output as time went on. After years of being the recipient of Lewis' drunken abuse, she finally divorced him on January 2, 1942. During those years, Dorothy had also awakened to the hypocrisy of Communism, expressing her rage at a system that pretended to fight for the downtrodden in America while oppressing them in the Soviet Union.

Lewis died alone in Italy at age 65, his heart attack no doubt brought on by years of alcohol abuse. He would not live to see *It Can't Happen Here* made into several TV dramas in the coming decades. Though his work justifiably continues to be praised and studied as landmarks of American literature, the artist named Sinclair Lewis would also be remembered as one of the first to broadcast to the world what would happen to a free nation once it ceased to cherish that freedom...

"Either a comedy, something light and frivolous, or the story of a Slovak coal miner."[65] This was the great Paul Muni in answer to Jack Warner's question about what project he wanted to do after he finished *The World Changes*. It is interesting to note that Muni supposedly became obsessed with the idea of portraying a miner as early as 1933, before the actor was sent material on the subject of exploited miners from several sources; or at least that's the story in Muni's biography *Actor: The Life and Times of Paul Muni* by Jerome Lawrence. According to Lawrence, Paul had already read up on the subject, including mining laws, strikes and the dangers of working in a pit in the ground for little pay and zero health protection. Paul was an intelligent, well-read man; it was certainly not unusual for him to be interested in such a subject.

In the spring of that year, Paul was starring in the road company of Elmer Rice's *Counsellor at Law*, which he had already done on Broadway, and was performing the play at Pittsburgh's Nixon Theater when he ran into a civil court judge named Michael A. Musmanno. After the barrister told Muni how wonderful his performance was as a lawyer, the actor allegedly replied that he was interested in making a film about coal miners. Paul was already doing more than just reading books on the subject. During the train trip, Muni and his secretary Ruth Finkel (the wife of his friend, playwright–Warner scenarist Abem Finkel) stopped off at a Pennsylvania mining town where Paul questioned the miners about their backgrounds. He and Ruth were even invited to visit several coal miners' homes, where Muni studied their dress and mannerisms.

By coincidence, the judge said, he happened to be writing a book about a case he worked on years before about coal miners. Apparently in 1929, Musmanno prosecuted a case concerning a miner named John Barkowski, who was brutally clubbed to death by three company policemen at a mine in Imperial, Pennsylvania. His book fictionalized the miner's name to Jan Volkanik, but otherwise, he claimed, the book was fact-based. Muni wanted to see the work before it was published so he could use it as a vehicle at Warners.

How true the story is, that is, Muni wanting to do a film about coal miners and coincidentally meeting someone who was also writing about coal miners, is anyone's guess. Jerome Lawrence had met Paul in the mid–1950s when the actor was starring in his and Robert E. Lee's *Inherit the Wind* on Broadway. It was obvious that Lawrence liked and respected Muni, and the bio is rife with stories emphasizing the actor's charm, wit and intelligence. Ultimately, Muni himself didn't have a final say in the writing since he was dead in 1967, and his beloved wife Bella (who was always on the set to "approve" the actor's performances) died in 1971, three years before the book was published. Still, Muni's idea for a film about coal miners, whether it involved using Judge Musamanno's unpublished book or not, was about to be put on the back burner. For in the spring of 1934, yet *another* idea for a film about coal miners was circulating around Warners.

> We have enjoyed very much reading the treatment for *Black Hell* which you were kind enough to let us have on Friday last, and I am hastening to tell you that, in our considered judgment,

THE LAST ANGRY MAN. **Paul Muni as a formerly good-hearted coal miner now agitating for a strike in Warners'** *Black Fury* **(1935). Muni insisted on making the film.**

this treatment suggests no Code difficulty whatever and little material which is reasonably censorable.[66]

This was censorship czar Joseph I. Breen in a letter dated May 7, 1934, to Jack L. Warner. The subject matter was a proposed film about a strike by mine workers and the disaster that followed. Little did Breen know that the material which he claimed would not violate the Production Code or had "little material which is reasonably censorable" would ultimately be banned in several states and, in some countries, not shown on TV until the 1970s.

In June of that year, Mary Virginia Inloes of the George McCall Agency sent Paul Muni a story treatment by a "Charles Logue" called *The Bohunk*. This was according to a letter found in Warners' studio files. Other sources claim that *The Bohunk* was an unproduced play by Harry Irving. Nevertheless, whoever wrote it, the material was apparently based on a Pennsylvania steel workers' strike. In her letter, Ms. Inloe also mentioned that Logue's story was rejected by the Warner story department; "however, at a time when they were not looking for material for you." This might mean that the story arrived in early or mid–1932, *before* Muni's stardom in *I Am a Fugitive from a Chain Gang* (which was released on November 19), and probably *before* the star's alleged meeting with Judge Musamanno. The timeline makes sense since a subsequent letter by studio attorney Roy Obringer, dated June 26, 1934, mentions *Black Hell* "as the basis of your *second* [italics mine] picture...." Apparently, between the release of *Fugitive* and mid–1934, Paul had become a star thanks to the prison film and, while the actor was appearing around the country in *Counsellor at Law*, Warners offered him a contract; only *then* did they start to come up with story ideas for him. Actually, his second picture, which he suggested to Jack Warner, *was* a comedy (*Hi, Nellie*), and next came *Bordertown*.

Therefore, in his June 26 letter, the WB mouthpiece also claimed that

> [y]our needs for story material for the present year have been taken care of and, incidentally, in my opinion, I think it would be wise to state that you note Mr. Logue's story is entitled *Bohunk*, and you believe Mr. Logue should be informed at this time that *Black Hell* is based, in part, on a copyrighted play of the same title, and that you desire to give this information to Mr. Logue to avoid any misunderstanding in the future.[67]

Here, Obringer brings up the dilemma that faced the studio in its plans to have a coal-mining setting as the basis for next Muni film: There were far too many cooks making the same broth. Inevitably, Muni himself bought up the rights to the various properties then being offered on coal miners and then sold them back to Warner Brothers for an added profit.

Paul was a hands-on performer; a man who studied his characters' backgrounds with a tenacity and dedication that was completely opposite that of the pretty-boy matinee idols of the time (or for that matter, *today*). After his signing with Warner Brothers, Paul would perform in screen bios and play some distinguished figures of history, but in his career he also played common men: proletarians, victims of society, minority figures. Paul was never really convincing as a Latino in *Bordertown*, or as a Mexican with Native blood in *Juarez*, or as a black man in *Seven Faces*, or as a Chinese man in *The Good Earth* (Paul himself always thought he was racially miscast). However, he was also likable and charismatic, and you *wanted* to accept him in these roles in much the same way Errol Flynn's handsome looks and sincere performances made you accept him in Westerns despite his having a prairie accent straight from the Outback. Muni *was* a good actor, and his stage performances and film portrayals prove his enormous versatility. And if some of Muni's performances descended into ham, at least the actor kept your eyes on screen even if the material faltered;

for if you went past the over-the-top accent, chances were you saw a complete human being under the phony wigs and bushy beards.

Born on September 25, 1895, in what was then Austria-Hungary (now the Ukraine), Meshelem Meir Weisenfreund emigrated to America with his family in the early part of the twentieth century. He made his stage debut for New York's Yiddish Theater in 1907 and did not appear in an English-language production until 1926. All through his life, Muni would retain the habits and performance style of his Yiddish theater origins. The plays that they performed either went for the heartstrings or the big laugh; the performances themselves were far from subtle, whether comic or serious; and the manner in which they were performed, with backstage script prompters calling out lines to forgetful actors, emphasized their relaxed working habits. Muni was a hard-working performer who researched all his roles, yet he would be plagued by a bad memory for lines most of his life.

Paul was also a liberal actor who was signed to a liberal studio. He was a proud Jew who refused to play Jewish characters on screen, yet he would enthusiastically participate in projects that showed Jews in a positive light, like *The Life of Emile Zola*, which profiled the infamous Dreyfuss affair; or his contribution to Broadway's *We Will Never Die* in 1943, a tribute to the Jews of Europe who were then being massacred; or the play *A Flag Is Born*, which told of the Jews' return to the Land of Israel. In 1940, he portrayed a French-Canadian trapper who fights for the rights of Canada's Natives in *Hudson's Bay*. Paul was also a man who was pro-worker. One sensed, despite the sometimes overdone portrayals, that the actor playing the proletarian was at least sincere in his desire to bring attention to the problems of the working man.

One thing, however, made Paul different from other socially conscious actors of the time: He did not and would not join the Communist Party. A well-read man, he was not fooled by the agenda of Communists who proclaimed their desire to help America's downtrodden and yet ignored the downtrodden in the Soviet Union. At the time he was making the coal mining film, a company release about the cast was sent by producer-scenarist Charles Einfield to *Liberty Magazine* on April 10, 1935. In it, Paul is described as a "serious academic" who was presently "studying Russian, preparatory to making a second trip to Russia (he was there for a month last summer) in which he is terribly interested."[68] Paul was like many artists in the 1930s who were fascinated with Russia before the revelations about persecutions came into the open; however, in his studies, he probably realized something about the country that too many others ignored. Paul wasn't bothered by the Communist writers and actors he worked with in Hollywood (he would play a Soviet partisan in John Howard Lawson's *Counter-Attack* in 1945), but he would stay far away from joining any so-called "peace committees" sponsored by them. Though he was passionately anti-fascist, his name is never mentioned in any file on alleged Communist activity held by the FBI, and that certainly includes their voluminous COMPIC files.

Meanwhile, it was back to the coal mines.

The film's plot revolves around Joe Radek (Muni), a big, happy-go lucky coal miner of unknown Slavic nationality who is everybody's pal. He has bought a little house near the mine on which he hopes to settle down with Anna Novak (Communist actress Karen Morley). However, Anna runs off with company cop Slim Johnson (played sympathetically by the likable William Gargan; interestingly, we never see him again after the beginning of the film). Apparently, according to Warner studio files, earlier versions of the script had Anna pregnant with Slim's child, but Joseph Breen insisted on cutting this out ("The less we have about pregnant girls, the better off the story will be," he wrote).

Stunned and hurt by this rejection, Joe takes to the bottle and is easy prey to the machinations of labor agitator Steve Croner (WB contract player J. Carrol Naish). Though we know that Croner is working for a group that profits from labor unrest, such as the private detective agency that is the villain of the piece, the agitator could easily have been sent by Communists seeking to start trouble. The film never actually states *who* sent Croner. Meanwhile, said crooked detective agency, obviously based on the strike-breaking Pinkerton Detective Agency (for whom Dashiell Hammett had worked), is agitating for a strike so they can be hired to smash the union and use their own scabs to replace fired union members. Johnny Farrell (Joseph Crehan) wants the union to stick together and honor the agreement with their obviously benign and straight-as-an-arrow mine bosses.

Influenced by Croner, and too drunk to care, Joe's ravings at the union meeting sway at least half the membership to strike. The other half, led by Joe's best friend Mike Shemanski (John Qualen, Muni's co-star in *Counsellor at Law*), want to honor the agreement; soon there is a furious split between the two old friends. However, when the strike disintegrates into violence, Croner conveniently disappears and leaves Joe holding the bag for the suffering of the now-fired mine workers. In the interim, the detective agency imports thugs to act as uniformed company policeman.

One night, as three company cops are getting plastered, one of them tries to rape Mike's daughter. Joe and Mike, coming from different directions, stop the attack and start fighting with the cops. Joe is knocked out and Mike is fatally struck with a blackjack by McGee (Barton MacLane), the most brutal of all the company's thuggish policemen. In fact, these psycho deputies are even outfitted in scary black uniforms, as if they were taking fashion tips from the Gestapo.

The miners are locked out of the mines by the owners and their families are forced to live in the hills. Anna returns, now wiser and penitent; but when she tries to visit the hospitalized Joe, he refuses to see her. Ultimately, the workers quit the strike and return to their jobs for starvation wages. Realizing that this will ruin all that the workers have fought for, Joe sneaks into the mine, steals a truckload of dynamite and starts a one-man strike against the mine owners. Though the company tries to starve him out, Joe had already stolen provisions and, using his knowledge of the mine tunnels, is able to sneak out and blow up company buildings at will. Against the mine bosses' wishes, the nation is soon alerted to Joe's battle against abuses and takes up his cause.

When the company cops try to infiltrate the mine, Joe causes an explosion that seals the tunnel he's in, but also traps just one cop with him, the brutal McGee. Knowing full well that McGee had murdered his pal Mike, Joe jumps the thug and the two have a fight which ends when McGee strikes his head on one of the ore-bucket tracks. Here, the dignified actor who would play Benito Juarez and Louis Pasteur handles himself quite well in the action department; his fight scene with MacLane is very convincing. The scene was a proletariat's dream: a worker has a knockdown-dragout fight with a fascistic company policeman and wins handily — though with the help of that rail.

Finally tumbling to the crookedness of the detective agency, the mine owners absolve Joe of all crimes and decide to do right by the mine workers. Dragging McGee to the surface, Joe has made the cop confess to the murder of his friend and is then reunited with the now-loving Anna. The only thing missing at the end of the film was an angelic choir reading the provisions of the new union contract out loud.

In a letter to Jack Warner, dated September 12, 1934, Breen had his usual quibbles about the script's violence:

[G]reat care will have to be exercised to play down "the confusion and vicious brutality" on the part of the Coal and Iron Policemen. The "confusion" will be all right, but the "vicious brutality" will have to be handled with great care. There should be no such action suggested ... wherein the mounted policemen "clubs down" the miner "mercilessly."⁶⁹

Breen also insisted on deleting the fact that McGee uses brass knuckles and that Mike's murder "should not be graphically shown." In the film, director Michael Curtiz certainly did shoot this scene with care. Breen also wanted the removal of scenes in the back room of a café between the company policemen and some underage girls (including a 16-year-old). However, Breen wasn't only concerned with removing graphic violence that might repel an audience (in effect changing scenes of labor unrest to something wholesome enough to be viewed by the entire family); the censor also addressed something far more dangerous than graphic sex and violence:

> Aside and apart from the Code and censorship angles on this story, there is involved the important question of *industry policy*. I respectfully direct your attention to the attached copies of correspondence between Mr. Hays, Mr. Harry Warner, and Mr. J.D. Battle of the National Coal Association.
>
> With a view to protecting ourselves against any valid criticism of the organized forces of the bituminous coal industry, we respectfully suggest that in Scene 61, on pages 26 and 27, you might insert a line, spoken by Mike, to the effect that while the miners may not have ideal working conditions, nevertheless, working conditions of the coal industry have vastly improved and are getting better all the time. The point here is to get a line or two that may establish the fact that the miners have little to complain against, and that Croner is unjust in his criticisms of the employing company.
>
> On this same angle of industry policy, we also suggest that in Farrell's speech in scene 122 on page 62, you also include a line to the effect that working conditions in the bituminous coal fields have greatly improved, and, that while these may not be all the miners would want them to be, they are nevertheless, reasonable working conditions and acceptable to organized labor.⁷⁰

In one of those scenes written as an obvious safety valve against charges of radicalism, we see mine owner John Hendricks (WB contract player Henry O'Neill, who always played benign authority figures) insist that the detective agency *not* use violent methods that would endanger the workers or their families. This scene didn't just happen to find its way into Abem Finkel and Carl Erickson's screenplay; the film was also blessed with an unaccredited co-author named Joseph Breen, who, in his same letter to Warner from September 12, "suggested":

> In Scene 198, page 95, we recommend — again, under the general heading of industry policy — that you have Hendricks, the president of the company, say quite frankly to Jenkins that he is proceeding to employ the strike-breakers very *much against his will,* and have him insist with Jenkins that the police so conduct themselves as to take every possible precaution *against the abuse or mistreatment of the miners....* [I]t will be a serious mistake, in our judgment, if we definitely show the employing company as countenancing, or approving, the brutal treatment of McGee and the others.... [T]he responsibility for it rests with Jenkins and McGee and *not* with the employing company.

And so it was that Joseph Breen and the Production Code office decided to take a hand in the film industry's portrayal of labor strife and insist on playing down the very real issues which were at the heart of most worker grievances. No one had ever accused Breen of being John L. Lewis; however, this correspondence alone almost put him into the category of being a pro-management propagandist who would have delighted the brutal Henry Ford. In a letter from October 9, Breen also insisted that Warners delete the work "cops" in describing the company's thugs and instead use the word "deputies."

Meanwhile, as Breen was playing word games, Warner decided to play a few of his own. By the following spring, the studio head ordered that the film undergo a title change from *Black Hell* to *Black Fury*.

The film was shot in late October to mid–November 1934 and was released in New York on April 10, 1935, and then opened wide on April 25. Director Curtiz was under pressure to finish the film up fast, but producer Robert Lord went to bat for him. Calling the film "difficult to shoot, I mean *physically* difficult to shoot" and saying that most of it consisted of "fights, mob scenes, coal mining scenes, etc.," Lord insisted that Warner go on the set and see the film's difficult shoot for himself. Then the producer ends the letter with a plea to go easy on Curtiz: "I am convinced that we will have a great picture, despite all difficulties, if only you will be a little lenient and not hammer at Mike until you completely discourage him. Please, Jack!"[71] Warner, who probably loved his employees begging to him, apparently acquiesced in this case. Curtiz's sure hand is apparent throughout the film, without any sign of his having been under pressure from above.

In a review from the *San Francisco News* shortly after the film's national release, Claude A. La Belle praised Warners for its "guts," but also noted:

> One wishes that Warner Brothers had dared to come straight out and make it what it really is, conflict between capital and labor. But even a hero has to duck now and then, and so the makers of the story put the onus for the strike on a racketeering organization of strike-breakers.
> Even with this compromise, it is still the first film to come out and deal with something that is truly a part of our present social upheaval.[72]

La Belle wrote that Muni "had never done anything on the screen to touch this. It is a far more subtle performance he gave as the bewildered miner than he gave as the chain gang fugitive or as Scarface," and generally called it "acting of a most superior order."

The *New York Herald Tribune* called the actor "excellent as the Slovak hero, playing with power and conviction."[73] But the review ended by saying that *Black Fury* "is as effective as a compromise picture on such a subject could be." The most important review came from the critic who counted the most. Jack Warner praised the film by calling it "as good a picture as *Fugitive*. It's really great. Everyone present too was thrilled by it."

Yet many folks outside Warners ended up *not* being thrilled by it. *Black Fury* would ultimately be banned in Chicago, Guatemala, pre-fascist Spain, Peru, Venezuela, Trinidad and other countries. The film was also banned outright in Illinois and Maryland, states not exactly known for their coal mining. And Pennsylvania, after a long acrimonious debate between its censorship board and state officials, to its credit, decided to show the film intact. New York, however, wanted to cut out the scene of Mike's murder until Judge Musamanno strenuously fought for its inclusion.

Black Fury was symbolic of the kind of Warner Brothers film that sympathized with the working man, despite the fact that they often stopped short of attacking abuses by corporate interests, and in some cases, even excused them. Made by liberals, the film brought up the issue of workers' rights without the sometimes vehement attacks against the capitalist system that were the bread and butter of most Communist screenwriters. It wasn't capitalism who was the bad guy, the film proclaimed, but a group of psychotic thugs masquerading as a detective agency.

Meanwhile, other fires were being tended to back on the East Coast, far from Hollywood and its waffling compromises. A breeding place of radical politics throughout the 1930s, the New York theater community would soon give us more angry voices to replace those of the departing Albert Maltz and John Howard Lawson. One particular voice would eventually make his own impact in a burgeoning Hollywood....

Though born in Philadelphia on July 18, 1906, Clifford Odets really grew up in the Bronx. The hubbub and hustle of New York City, at the time a hotbed of revolutionary fervor, fed his rages as well as his imagination. Growing up in the shadow of a recent world war, a war many believed was started by ruthless capitalist forces, fueled Odets' anger. Much of this rage would be used by the Group Theater, a place Odets considered a second family, to put on works that attacked the American status quo. Started by Cheryl Crawford, Harold Clurman and Lee Strasberg, the Group Theater portrayed capitalism as a system rife with insurmountable problems that needed to be fixed at once.

Odets started his work with the Group in 1930, but not as a writer. He began his theatrical career as an actor and during the early '30s performed in many of their plays, including the dubiously titled *They All Come to Moscow* (a comedy set at the time of the Purges which, needless to say, didn't mention the Purges). His greatest stage triumph as an actor was his performance as the idealistic Dr. Benjamin in the Pulitzer Prize–winning *Men in White* by Sidney Kingsley, a success which ran for 351 performances. (Another leftist playwright, Kingsley would give us the ultimate theatrical production depicting American poverty up to that time, *Dead End*. By the early 1950s, however, he would be attacking the Soviet Union's tyranny in the stage version of Arthur Koestler's novel *Darkness at Noon*.)

In 1934, Odets joined the Communist Party. Having declared himself politically, the leftist actor now decided to write plays for his new theatrical family. These years were Odets' heyday as a playwright; in the period between 1935 and 1939, he had no less than six plays running on Broadway, a record to this day, and all produced by the Group Theater.

It was the worst years of the Depression, and the Group took full advantage of it to stage the angriest theatrical works up to that time. John (then Jules) Garfield had the greatest of his early stage successes in Odets' *Awake and Sing!* Debuting on February 19, 1935, the domestic drama ran over a year. As New Yorkers witnessed the saga of the Bergers, a Bronx Jewish family scratching and clawing their way to survival in Depression-ridden America, some in the audience might have seen a little bit of themselves. However, within the play itself, Odets mixed anger at the Depression with rage at America and the industrialized nations over the recent world war.

As Grandpa Jacob, a passionate Marxist (played by party member Morris Carnovsky), makes quite clear:

> They are there to remind us of the horrors — under those crosses lie hundreds of thousands of workers and farmers who murdered each other in uniform for the greater glory of capitalism. The new imperialist war will send millions to their death, will bring prosperity to the pockets of the capitalist ... will bring only greater hunger and misery to the masses of workers and farmers. The memories of the last world slaughter are still fresh in our minds.

In his admiring analysis of Odets' work *Clifford Odets*, author Gabriel Miller inaccurately wrote, "Jacob's pronouncements in *Awake and Sing!* are mostly a collection of homespun pieties...."

A few weeks after *Awake and Sing!* opened, on March 26, the Group debuted Odets' *Till the Day I Die*, a work that in many ways was more intriguing than the more famous play that preceded it. Instead of the Depression, the play attacked the savagery of the rising Nazi regime. Set in Berlin in 1935, it featured, among other Group Theater alumni, Elia

Kazan as a Communist agitator and Lee J. Cobb as a Nazi police detective. In this work, the Communists are portrayed, in true sledgehammer fashion, as brave, noble and principled folks struggling to free Germany from the brutality of Nazism. Odets also shows us that German officers are so alienated that they themselves can't stand the Nazi way of life.

The play is full of over-the-top set-pieces. We see a German colonel, disgusted with the system's oppressiveness, suddenly shoot himself in the mouth; there is paranoia from one officer that those in the party will investigate his ancestry and find out that a distant relative was Jewish*; Nazi characters deliver unrealistic speeches about how rotten they think their government is, without apparent fear of discovery; the Communist characters make endless speeches about "the working classes" and "the revolution"; and, in what Odets uses as the ultimate condemnation of the Nazi system, it is heavily implied that two Nazi officers are gay:

> SCHLEGEL: [I]t might be much better for both of us if you weren't graceful with those expressive hands of yours. Flitting around here like a soulful antelope. I'm lonely. I've got no one in the whole world.
> ADOLPH: You've got me, Eric.
> SCHLEGEL: Hitler is lonely too. So is God.

A couple lines later, the Aryan Superman officer reveals his real fear:

> SCHLEGEL: All I need is for them to find out about us and I am through for good. My God, you don't know whom to trust.
> ADOLPH: Trust me.
> SCHLEGEL [examining Adolph's face between his hands]: You? You're as fickle as a girl. You know that song by Hugo Wolf, I wish all your charm was painted. It's written for you and me. Last night I heard a lieder concert. There weren't fifty people in the audience. The country is gripped by fear. Houses are locked day and night.
> ADOLPH: Please...I'm very fond of you.

Then, in a plot point that is chillingly ahead of its time, particularly in a play featuring a young Elia Kazan, there is the ugly theme of informing on one's friends. Only this time, it is Communist Party members informing on each other to their Nazi torturers. Indeed, Ernst (played by Alexander Kellman), the revolutionary who did squeal to the Nazis, is roundly condemned by his former friends. In the play's final over-the-top scene, Ernst begs his comrade Carl (Walter Coy) to end his misery:

> ERNST: Take the gun. Carl, you loved me once. Kill me. One day more and I'll stand there like an idiot and identify prisoners for them. I know so many. In all honor and courage you must pull the trigger! I brought the money. Put it in the fighting fund. Maybe tell a few comrades the truth.

After his so-called friend suggests that he "do it himself," Ernst proclaims, "Brothers will live in the soviets of the world! Yes, a world of security and freedom is waiting for all mankind!"

As one can tell, this optimistic prediction that things will get better for the world didn't exactly come true. It was also hard to accept a never-say-die attitude from a character who then goes backstage and puts a bullet in his skull.

Certainly, in the playwright's more blatantly political works (as in those of Bertold Brecht and other Communist writers), informing on your friends is to be punished with

---

*A sympathetic German embassy official having a Jewish grandmother was a strong plot point in Clare Boothe Luce's later Broadway hit *Margin for Error*.

nothing less than death. Considering Odets' own fawning testimony before the House Un-American Activities Committee in 1952 in which he named names, his having the play's Marxists insist on punishing the informer seems like an act of meaningless brutality on a par with those the playwright reserved for his Nazi characters.

Meanwhile, in another part of the world, far away from Communists, fascists and Broadway playwrights, the most powerful black performer of his time was filming a tribute to British colonialism....

On April 8, 1935, London Films released its production of *Sanders of the River* in England, with American audiences getting a chance to see the film on June 26. The film was based on the novel of the same name by the recently deceased Edgar Wallace. The central character of British High Commissioner R.G. Sanders had appeared in several Wallace books, all set in Africa and, unfortunately, all viewed through the intolerant eyes of the British government.

Zoltan Korda, the brother of director Alexander Korda and a director in his own right (he would direct the pro–Soviet *Counter-Attack* in 1945, with a screenplay by John Howard Lawson), had always wanted to make a film version of one of Wallace's *Sanders* novels. In early 1934, he traveled to Central Africa and shot 160,000 reels of footage, which also consisted of tape-recording the sounds of African people, their music, their speeches, and the rhythm of their dances. He journeyed through Uganda, the Sudan, and the nation that was then called the Belgian Congo, and painstakingly put on film the rituals, the traditions and the daily lives of the tribesmen. Hoping to interest the one man whom the Kordas felt could play the powerful Chief Bosambo, the brothers took their tapes to Paul Robeson. Proclaiming Korda's footage "magnificent," Robeson, a man who had always sought to bring the culture of Africa front and center for the entire world to see, enthusiastically accepted the part. Subsequently, he raved to journalists about the sounds and "syncopations" of the African rhythms on the recordings the Kordas let him keep. Given a chance to bring black African culture to an international audience, his enthusiasm was boundless: "For the first time since I began acting, I feel that I've found my place in the world, that there's something out of my own culture which I can express and help to preserve...."[75]

As it turned out, the film did contain scenes of tribal dances, tribal songs and other examples of African culture, despite the fact that a Congo village was recreated on a Shepperton sound stage. Even the magnificent scenes of African canoes on the river were filmed on the Thames.

Nevertheless, much of this alleged sincerity in depicting African life was bound up in a film that clearly lauded British colonialist policy. How can one think otherwise after just a brief look at one of Edgar Wallace's jungle adventures? In Wallace's own words, our introduction to the high commissioner lets us know right off the bat not only what kind of man Sanders is, but also the character of the man who created him:

> Long before [Sanders] was called upon by the British government to keep a watchful eye upon some quarter of a million cannibal folk, who ten years before had regarded white men as we regard the unicorn.... By Sanders' code, you trusted all natives up to the same point as you trust children.

Now that the author has so kindly informed us that black African tribes are populated by either "cannibals" or "children," he briefly explores Sanders' less than compassionate treatment of them. Throughout the series, Sanders is clearly seen as a martinet who is "prompt to hang" all those who defy his, that is, Britain's authority within their spheres of influence on the continent. Wallace makes no excuses, nor has any pangs of human regret for this stern policy. Instead, he praises Sanders' cruelty as something to use against a people to whom tolerance is considered non-existent: "Hesitation to act, delay in awarding punishment, either of these two things would have been mistaken for weakness amongst a people who had neither power to reason, nor will to excuse, nor any large charity."

From the above words written by a man who was clearly parroting Britain's own racism, we can pretty much assume that Paul Robeson had *not* read the Sanders novels. The actor-singer could only see the great opportunity to present African culture to the world in all its wonder.

He was in for a rude awakening.

In the film, Commissioner R.G. Sanders (Leslie Banks) has his problems. He lords it over the various African tribes in his territory with a combination of toughness and wisdom. He is a "father" to his sometimes rambunctious "children," a "parent" who has only the best interests in his heart for the "infants" in his charge. And it never occurs to any of these "kids," not in this film anyway, to kick Daddy out of the house.

Though he is aided by other white officers of the Crown, Sanders' real ace in the hole is the pliable Chief Bosambo (Robeson). There is, of course, no hiding Robeson's charisma in this film, and the actor effortlessly steals every single scene opposite Banks, who is supposed to be the one we admire. Bosambo is a chief who is pleased to see "the handsome face of your [Sanders'] king." However, Bosambo admires the king's puss *only* when it's on a British sovereign. In this bit, we see what the film *could* have become, with a wise and sardonic black chief like Bosambo constantly trumping the usually stiff-necked British approach to the African tribes. And though we clearly see the twinkle in Paul's eye when he delivers his lines, it's soon quite obvious that it's *Sanders*, not Bosambo, who's supposed to get the audience's respect. Also obvious will be the chief's role *vis-à-vis* his relationship to the commissioner. He's a lackey; a charismatic and charming one as played by Robeson, but a lackey nevertheless. He's a bought and paid-for helper to British imperialist policy.

When Sanders leaves the continent to get married in England, two crooked white traders spread the rumor that he is dead. Now without the Almighty example of English rule on the premises, the tribes revolt. This implies that without no-nonsense British superman Sanders, a.k.a. a strong British presence, on the scene, the continent's blacks will kill each other. When Sanders returns, with Bosambo's help, the "bad" black chief is killed and Sanders' specially anointed black leader is made the head of all the tribes as a reward for keeping the continent *on the beam, old chap*!

After seeing the film, Robeson was clearly disgusted. His dream of a motion picture that touted the magnificent culture of African peoples was replaced, not too gracefully either, by a pro-colonialist message that encouraged subjugation of the tribes. He later claimed in an interview with the *Amsterdam News* that the "imperialist angle"[76] was put into the film in the last five days of shooting—an assertion which was ridiculous. As one can tell from the film's very structure, it was hard to divorce Bosambo's allegiance to Sanders from the rest of the story. So ingrained is this characterization into the fabric of the film that to claim that it was inserted into the picture with only five days of shooting is an absurd accusation. Had Paul listened less to his delightful recordings of African music and speech patterns and actually cracked open *any* of Edgar Wallace's *Sanders* books (which usually had an *of the River* in their titles), he would have discovered that the officer to whom Chief Bosambo gives his allegiance is nothing more than a brute who rules with an arrogant sense of entitlement, an obvious symbol of Great Britain's occupation of Africa.

Predictably, the *London Times* parroted their government's stiff-necked view of black Africans, calling the film "a grand insight into our special English difficulties in the governing of the savage races" and that it respected "British sensibilities and ambitions."[77] Of course, it would be no surprise that this country would have their collective heads in the sand even up to the point when Nazi planes were dropping bombs on them five years later.

This portrayal of Bosambo *was* the Kordas' responsibility, but hardly their fault. Both men were originally Hungarian Jews who emigrated to Britain and found a place there as the finest filmmakers of their new adopted country (though anti–Semitic British authors like Graham Greene would hold them in contempt). They wanted to make more films that showed minorities in a more positive light; and in a classic like *The Thief of Bagdad* they euphemistically show an empowered black man (played by Rex Ingram) lording over the film's hapless white characters. Ingram portrays a genie who is both benign and terrifying; the mystical creature cries "Freedom!" as if he had broken the chains of slavery put on him for centuries. The Kordas were responsible for the production of *Sahara* (1943), which featured a positive characterization of the Sudanese soldier, and they produced and directed the African-set attack on apartheid, *Cry, the Beloved Country* (1951). All these films were meant to generate respect and admiration for their black characters.

However, the Kordas were also now in England, and the two were nothing if not loyal to their new country. In all honesty, they probably thought that they were showing English audiences a "positive" black figure with Bosambo; someone they could like since he was so obviously on their side. Apparently, the future president of Kenya, Jomo Kenyatta, had no problem with the film: The young man played a bit part as one of the many tribesmen. (The film employed working class black men from England, as well as over 250 African tribesmen.) Kenyatta lent his name to the gift of a gold cigarette case which was presented to the Korda brothers by the cast and crew. The Kordas' hearts were usually in the right place; in the years ahead, the brothers would lend their offices to British Intelligence to use to spy on the Nazis when World War II started.

However, the Kordas' star was furious, and would remain so for some time to come. In 1938, Robeson still fumed: "It is the only one of my films that can be shown in Italy and Germany for it shows the Negro as Fascist States desire him — savage and childish."[78]

Worse yet, in late 1935, the film had won the Mussolini Cup for Zoltan Korda at the Venice Film Festival. We assume Korda didn't send Paul Robeson to pick up the award in his place...

By 1936, Clifford Odets was Broadway's most popular playwright. A Hollywood that then valued leftist writers during the height of the Depression soon beckoned. Paramount Pictures, a studio that didn't have the track record of hiring leftist screenwriters as did Warners, signed Odets to write a screenplay with a politically oriented plot (based on an unpublished novel by Charles Booth). The result, released that year, was *The General Died at Dawn* (original title: *Chinese Gold*).

Directed by Lewis Milestone, the film top-billed Paramount's biggest star (and right-wing icon) Gary Cooper as an intrepid, globe-trotting hot-shot named O'Hara. Though the role is written as that of an "adventurer," the heroic Irish-American is actually a mercenary looking to collect funds from poor Chinese peasants to purchase weapons for them to overthrow fascistic warlord General Yang (a star-making performance by Russian-accented

Akim Tamiroff). Also along for the political mishegas are Madeleine Carroll as Judy, the daughter of double-dealing louse Petrie (Porter Hall, in the flower of his double-dealing louse phase); William Frawley (the future Fred Mertz; then a contract player with Paramount) as Brighton, an alcoholic weapons dealer; J.M. Kerrigan as the appropriately named Mr. Leach; and the very British Dudley Digges as Chinese rebel leader Mr. Wu.

Though basically approving of the script, there were still some reservations from the Breen office. In a letter to Paramount executive John Hammell, dated April 18, Breen warned:

> We recommend and urge strongly that before putting this picture into production, you secure the services of a competent authority to advise you with regard to the possible reaction of the Chinese government to this particular story. It is dangerous, in our judgment, to suggest that Wang is a general of the Chinese Army. We think, too, that the Chinese will seriously resent the implication that foreign interests are at work to cheat and grind down the Chinese workmen.
>
> Because of this and a number of other details, we do hope, for your own sakes, that you will get competent advice from the Chinese angle before you begin to shoot.[79]

Basically, as Yang cuts a brutal swath through poor Chinese villages, O'Hara romances the reluctant turncoat Judy, Petrie double-crosses everyone in sight and Brighton quickly drinks up his profits, a game is played where the money belt filled with funds for weapons travels from one person to another throughout the film; or as *New York Times* critic Frank Nugent called it, "a bit of button, button, who's got the money?"[80]

Odets' leftist politics come through quite plainly in one sledgehammer-blunt moment at the beginning of the film which showcases capitalist ignorance to oppression of the masses. When one upper-crust Englishman denigrates the poor Chinese peasants, O'Hara asks the man for a cigarette; when the man replies that he's out, the mercenary socks him on the jaw. After the Englishman indignantly demands to know why he was struck in the face, O'Hara explains that those very same peasants that the man had made fun of are attacked in much the same way by General Yang's thuggish troops. The Englishman is instantly humbled. Of course, had O'Hara done this in the real world, he would have been beaten to a pulp. This "logic" is laughable, but it showed Odets using the clumsiest examples ever to demonstrate capitalist neglect of the world's poor.

Finally, after various shootings, beatings, and assorted acts of warlord terror, the denouement arrives. While searching for the money belt, General Yang is mortally stabbed by Brighton before the general's rather slow-moving bodyguards finally kill the chronically plastered gun dealer. Since Brighton is a capitalist seller of munitions, Odets goes by the Communist playbook and portrays him as a mean, nasty, seedy and perpetually drunken example of human flotsam. Two years later, Communist scenarist Lester Cole would go one better in James Whale's moronically titled *Sinners in Paradise* and portray two capitalist arms manufacturers as murderous thugs.

At the film's climax, O'Hara begs the mortally wounded Yang not to put Judy before a firing squad. Promising that he and Judy will praise the general's greatness to the world after his death, O'Hara finally convinces Yang to order a halt to the execution at the last minute. This would not be British actress Madeleine Carroll's last brush with the work of Communist scenarists. The following year, Walter Wanger cast her as a suffering British heroine caught up in the Spanish Civil War in John Howard Lawson's *Blockade*.

Before he dies, Yang orders his incredibly stupid men to shoot each other to death. It is chillingly staged by Milestone: The helmsman gives us one full close-up of Yang's brainwashed troops pointing .45s at each other and then cuts away before we hear multiple gunshots. Here, more than in any overt platitudes or speeches, Odets and Milestone show us the horrors of totalitarian obedience that robs men of their free will and makes them willingly die for a cruel despot. Had the filmmakers shown us more scenes of horror such as this, *The General Died at Dawn* might have been far more memorable than it was. As it is, the film is mainly remembered for Tamiroff's fascinating portrayal of a fascistic general out to instill his own brand of a New Order on the victimized Chinese.

In fact, Paramount executives instantly saw through Odets' unflattering portrait of a real-life Chinese strongman then very much in the news. In a cable from November 9, the studio apprised Breen:

> *General* opened Manila Tuesday stop Before release we made small cuts eliminating reference to dates and gave prominent publicity that story took place before Ching Kai-shek conquest and establishment Nanking Government stop Made forward before feature that conditions for trade not existing today and that government had freed the nation from oppression and also that story and characters fictitious stop Committee appointed by Chinese Consul headed by president Chinese Chamber of Commerce reviewed picture issued statement Chinese press saying that picture as presented not offensive Chinese....[81]

Nice to know that the Chinese government of 1936 had permanently freed their people from oppression, at least, according to Paramount.

Still, the film did have one other character who was derived from a real person. Reportedly, Odets based his troubleshooting hero O'Hara on larger-than-life mercenary Morris "Two-Gun" Cohen. A Polish Jew who learned to use his fists at an early age in London's poor East End, Cohen eventually emigrated to Canada. He worked as a cowboy on a Saskatchewan ranch, and then, answering the call of patriotism, fought in World War I with the Canadian Railway Troops in Europe. At a time when so many of his people were trapped in poor ghettos all over the continent, Cohen used his considerable skills to aid oppressed peoples by training rebel armies fighting against dictatorial regimes. In Asia, he trained Dr. Sun Yat-sen's troops, ran guns to Chinese warlords and, after Japan

MR. DEEDS IS PACKIN' HEAT. Madeleine Carroll is protected by a gun-totin' Gary Cooper in a publicity still from Clifford Odets' *The General Died at Dawn* (1936). Cooper's two-fisted adventurer was reportedly based on anti-fascist soldier of fortune Morris "Two-Gun" Cohen.

THE WARLORD GIVETH AND THE WARLORD TAKETH AWAY. Gary Cooper (at left) listens as Akim Tamiroff's General Yang (also seated) lays down the law to Porter Hall (right) in *The General Died at Dawn*. Philip Ahn is behind Tamiroff's left shoulder and Hans Fuerberg (in uniform) is behind his right. Odets' general is a ruthless slam at China's *real* supreme warlord, Chiang-Kai Chek.

invaded the Chinese mainland, smuggled weapons to Chinese resistance forces. While fighting with British special operations units, he was captured by the Japanese, but was eventually freed in a prisoner exchange. After the war, his support for rebel forces put him in good stead with China's Communist government and his many dealings with them kept him quite comfortable until his death in 1970.[82]

In his review of *General* on September 3, Frank Nugent remarked that the project had "the literary signature of proletarian playwright Clifford Odets" and that the film had "far less 'social consciousness' than Mr. Odets' admirers will believe…." After calling it "preposterous, hair-raising, and entertaining in equal and generous proportions," the critic accurately noted the presence of Group Theater groupies among the audience:

> At the midnight showing Tuesday there was a voluble faction, seated appropriately in the theater's left-wing, which seemed to find a great deal of the *Waiting for Lefty* spirit in Mr. Odets' first Hollywood effort, particularly in some of the opening scenes. But even the claque quieted down before long; one does not have to be a dramatic crusader in the class struggle to espouse the cause of the suffering Chinese against a fee-fie-fo-fuming war lord. And it is a Chinese war lord who is the target of Mr. Odets' and Gary Cooper's democratic mouthings in *The General Died at Dawn*…. Mr. Odets' script is vigorous and colorful, even if not entirely dedicated to the class struggle….

Nugent, a sober-minded critic (and later screenwriter for John Ford) was not the type to hysterically focus on Odets' Communist leanings or, for that matter, take note of his allegedly Marxist audience, as many right-wingers would have. That Odets' politics were now emphasized in print by writers like the highly intelligent Nugent made it clear that the playwright's fame as a left-wing writer was now undeniable. However, Nugent's review alone could have been seen as a warning to Odets that the type of political material he chose to write, including his characters, their speeches and the usual proletarian environment they moved in, might limit him as a writer. Now that Odets was a Hollywood screenwriter, with an ever-watchful Breen office breathing down his neck, he started to reevaluate not only his choice of material, but his associates as well. One incident that occurred before the release of *General* helped the playwright come to an important decision. In June 1935, Odets was asked by John Howard Lawson to head a delegation from the League of American Writers (identified in FBI files as a Communist organization) to investigate labor conditions in dictator Fulgencia Batista's Cuba. In March of that year, the Batista government had ended a nationwide strike the way dictators usually ended nationwide strikes: with much gunfire and little negotiating. Lawson had painted such a dreadful picture of the situation that, as a socially conscious humanist, Odets couldn't possible refuse. "Officially" appointed chairman of the tongue-twisting American Committee to Investigate Labor and Social Conditions in Cuba, Odets and his "committee" set sail June 29 on the *Oriente*. It was not until they had almost reached Havana that the playwright received a shock. It seemed that party functionary Conrad Komorowski was the real head of the group and that Odets was chosen for the mission only for publicity value. He then discovered that his so-called committee wasn't going to investigate anything, and instead, they were all set up to be arrested by Batista's secret police.

After being detained overnight in "a smoking room" and having their luggage ransacked, Odets and his committee then returned to a heroes' welcome in New York. The publicity value of the trick worked, as Lawson and the Party cynically knew it would.

Odets then wrote a series of articles attacking the conditions in Batista's Cuba and specifically slammed the American government's support of the dictatorship. He even started writing a play about Cuba, but, try as he might, the playwright couldn't get a handle on the island nation or its people. This is revealed through a character he calls "Author" who frankly states to another character than he knows nothing of the country, its people, its culture or traditions. Indeed, how *could* Odets know anything about Cuba or its people when all he saw of it was a ship's dock in Havana and a dingy "smoking room" under police guard?[83]

However, Odets would not officially make public his double-cross by Lawson and the Party until the playwright's testimony before the HUAC many years later. And though he still maintained the image of a good Communist doing the Party's bidding, his exit from the group was on the horizon. He had several plays on Broadway and a successful film to his credit; like many a Communist artist, the temptations of fame and money were starting to turn him. One of those "temptations" was a beautiful blonde-haired, blue-eyed actress of astonishing talent who was indeed hard to resist.

"[She is] not merely a delight to the masculine eye, but an actress of more than usual merit, and Mr. Goldwyn is to be congratulated for having recognized it."[84] In his *New York Times* review of *Come and Get It*, Frank Nugent was not exaggerating. Though most actresses known merely for being delights to the masculine eye have come and gone, the films of Frances Farmer entertain us to this day. She was beautiful, talented, and highly volatile; there were few in Hollywood, even among those Communist artists who *were* blacklisted, who suffered more for their political beliefs; or, for that matter, were condemned with such vehemence. Perhaps this was because Frances Farmer was something John Howard Lawson, Albert Maltz or any of the other "infamous Reds" were not.

She was a woman.

One can count on the fingers of one hand how many major film actresses at the time were as socially committed as Farmer, a brutally frank person who refused to play the game; and "playing the game" sometimes meant being a victimized woman in male-dominated Hollywood.

Frances was born in Seattle on September 19, 1913. She was a junior in high school when she took writing classes with the reportedly radical teacher Belle McKenzie, and then wrote her controversial essay *God Dies*. In this piece, Frances supposedly questioned why God would allow the recent death of a classmate. West Seattle, a town steeped in Christian traditions, was outraged. If one wants to believe William Arnold's book *Shadowlands*, as well as Mel Brooks' pirated film version with Jessica Lange, Frances was told by the religious women of the town that she would "burn in hell." Whether this incident actually happened or not, religion does not come off very well in at least one of Frances' movies, *Ebb Tide* (1937). Lloyd Nolan plays a religious psychopath lording over the island's natives who consider him a god. Farmer was not the film's writer or director, but she couldn't have failed to notice the film's underlying theme of fanaticism being substituted as religion; or how in the late 1930s fascism was being treated as a kind of "religion" in a Europe and Asia rapidly becoming totalitarian.

By 1934, Farmer wanted to experience new surroundings with people who possessed unconventional points of view. At the time, Washington state was a place that liked its scabs. Uncompromisingly right-wing, Washington authorities had no patience for radical movements; and during World War I, had come down hard on the International Workers of the World, otherwise known as the Wobblies. While Frances was still in college, the local Communist newspaper, *The Voice of Action*, sponsored a subscription drive contest to focus attention on student support for a radical labor movement. As an alumni at the University of Washington, she was already a star of the college's drama department and considered a highly intelligent student of journalism. But mixed with her studies were courses of another kind: She was attending Communist lectures and handing out Party pamphlets. Supposedly, with her enthusiastic permission, youthful Party members sold subscriptions to *Voice of Action* in her name. Seeing a good prospect if ever there was one, the Party awarded her a VIP tour of the Soviet Union.

For her anti–Communist mother, as well as her pious neighbors, this was the last straw. For the Seattle section of the Communist Party, it was great propaganda; they were able to get this young woman from God-fearing Washington state to be their salesperson. It was obvious that Party members had little concern with how this would hurt Frances with her family, neighbors or fellow students. Once in the Soviet Union, Frances attended performances of the Moscow Art Theater (strictly censored) and the Bolshoi Ballet. She was also given a tour of quickly cleaned-up factories and suddenly organized collective farms, and even attended a May Day Parade. It was obvious, as it would be in later years when Lillian Hellman and other pro–Soviet celebrities took tours of the U.S.S.R., that her movements were severely restricted to only those places the government approved of. Frances supposedly never saw any hints of famine, police brutality or worker abuse. However, to her credit, she also defended America when Soviet officials heaped scorn upon it.

With her exploits making national news, Paramount quickly signed the young actress around the same time she became acquainted with Broadway's Group Theater. Though everyone seemed to think that *Come and Get It* was Frances' film debut, actually it was her fourth film. There was not much to say about Paramount's *Too Many Parents*, *Border Flight* or *Rhythm on the Range,* the last co-starring Bing Crosby (though its plot seemed to stick to the Communist playbook: People who had money were seen as shallow and phony; and Farmer's heiress had to marry someone for love, not that evil green paper stuff).

However, her loan-out to Goldwyn, *Come and Get It*, based on Edna Ferber's sprawling novel, was right up her alley. The film gave her a dual role, that of a young woman who attracts the love of Edward Arnold's rising young capitalist, and her daughter, who is still an object of youth and desire to Arnold's now-wealthy businessman. Barney Glasgow (Arnold) abandons saloon girl Lotta (Farmer), whom he loves, in order to marry the daughter of a man who could set him up in a lucrative partnership. The film heaps contempt on the machinations that businessmen use to get ahead, especially when they hurt those who cannot forward their careers. In Ferber's eyes, Barney Glascow has allowed money to trump love, and he inevitably suffers for his ambition. Again, Farmer had to have been sharp enough to immediately grasp the film's theme of the personally damaging effects of rampant materialism (at one point, Walter Brennan's Swan calls it "stealing" when Barney and his partner concoct a plan to grab acres of forest and essentially rape the land). It shows in her intelligent and moving performance. One of the few major dramatic film actresses at that time who was also able to sing, and sing well, Frances showed herself to be much more than "a delight to the masculine eye."

After the Goldwyn film, she returned to Paramount for a series of films which euphemistically attacked certain aspects of American society. In her next film for the studio, the underrated *Exclusive*, Frances and Fred MacMurray played reporters on opposing newspapers and Charlie Ruggles played her father, a newspaper veteran. After Ralph Morgan's ruined businessman shoots himself in front of Frances (the camera is on her very convincing reaction), the message is quite clear: American news media that print propaganda and not facts signal a far deeper problem within the system than just the newspaper business. Lloyd Nolan is Charlie Gillette, a scandal sheet editor who's clearly in league with gangsters, and his newspaper is responsible for Morgan's suicide. Cynically fighting fire with fire, MacMurray and Farmer print their own scandalous headline accusing Gillette of murder.

Then comes the most chilling scene in the film. The public on the street, blindly following what the headline reads, becomes an uncon-

THEATER ANGEL. The beautiful Frances Farmer in a 1937 Paramount publicity shot. Her social consciousness as well as her feminism combined to get her in trouble in sexist Hollywood. Though not a Communist, she would suffer more than any Party member for her beliefs.

trollable mob which storms Gillette's newspaper and almost kills him as they chase him into the printing room. He is rescued by the police, but he still has the nerve to ask the officers how much they'll take to release him (implying a corrupt police force in league with the mob).

This cynicism that the American public can become a lynch mob simply because of an inflammatory news headline was a powerful statement under an American screen controlled by the dictates of the Production Code (In the anti-blacklist Western *Silver Lode* [1954], lynch mobs are formed merely because they believe accusations written on a piece of paper delivered by killer Dan Duryea.) Though other films showed mob rule at the time (like *Fury*, *They Won't Forget* and *You Only Live Once*), *Exclusive* was one of the few films which showed the dangerous effects of propaganda sheets pretending to be newspapers. The filmmakers might have had right-wing media mogul William Randolph Hearst in mind. (Hearst, a notorious commie-hater, would have had no use for someone like Frances Farmer.)

Frances was loaned out to RKO in 1937 for *The Toast of New York*, again with Edward Arnold as a crooked super-capitalist, and an up-and-coming Cary Grant as her leading man. At the end, Arnold's manipulation of the stock markets ruins many New York businessmen, until he himself is ruined and finally killed, again with an angry mob rioting at the climax. (There were not too many actresses in those days who could boast of ending so many of their films with scenes of rioting mobs. Frances' films were definitely not built on the same themes as Crawford's or Garbo's!) The message of *The Toast of New York* was clear: The stock markets, to some a symbol of capitalist greed, will inevitably turn on those who at first profit from it. One could almost make a case that the title of the film already implies the theme of financial ruin: *Toast*.

In reviews of Paramount's *Ebb Tide*, critics praised how lovely Frances looked in Technicolor. Shipwrecked on a South Seas island with Ray Milland and Barry Fitzgerald, she also has to deal with Lloyd Nolan's religious zealot island ruler (the actor again playing a pseudo-fascist figure). In the studio's *Ride a Crooked Mile*, Frances and Akim Tamiroff play Russian émigrés. Tamiroff is the leader of an outlaw band made up of ex–Cossacks, apparently one of many who roamed the Old West. Giving us a convincing Russian accent that was probably based on the Soviet officials she had met years ago, Frances also sings in the film. The screenplay apparently appealed to Frances, even if the role wasn't her greatest; the ex–Cossack outlaws are portrayed as decadent symbols of the autocratic czarist regime, not the present Bolshevik one.*

During this busy period, Farmer also found time to do a Broadway play written by the married man she was falling in love with…

In 1937, Clifford Odets gave Broadway audiences *Golden Boy*. Though the story of a young man torn between the violent world of boxing and becoming a concert violinist was clichéd even then (as was Odets' laughable attempt at gritty, street-wise dialogue), the playwright brought to the work his usual savage indictment of a capitalist lifestyle that forces a burgeoning artist to lower his aspirations for the sake of money (though by this time,

---

*Years later, in the Universal B Western *Salome, Where She Danced* (1945), Walter Slezak portrays a garrulous Russian who aids our heroes in the Old West. Towards the end of the film, Albert Dekker's evil Prussian (basically a 19th-century Nazi in everything but name) pressures the *czar* to order Slezak's return. In 1945, when the Soviets were still our allies, this B Western slams the czarist regime, and takes pains not to attack those who were against them.

Odets was skillful enough not to hit us over the head with the message, as John Howard Lawson or Lester Cole would have).

Debuting on November 4, 1937, *Golden Boy* ran a total of 250 performances, making it Odets' most successful play. Not until the 1950-51 Broadway season would he have anything as popular, with the emphatically non-political *The Country Girl* racking up 236 performances at the height of the Blacklist Years.

John (then Jules) Garfield yearned for the lead role of Joe ("Napoleon") Bonaparte, the aspiring musician who becomes a driven fighter in the ring. Constantly preached to by other members of the Group to avoid the materialism of Hollywood and stick to the sheer joy of doing proletarian plays on Broadway for little money, Garfield was shocked to find that Group Theater producer Harold Clurman exercised the privilege of nepotism and gave the plum role to his brother-in-law Luther Adler. So much for the principle of casting roles on merit alone. Instead of Bonaparte, Garfield was given the supporting role of Ziggy, the comical cab driver. That he was bitter at the snub was an understatement. Clurman's cynical casting choice helped push the actor further away from the Group, and when Warner Brothers scouts offered him a contract during the play's run, he took the deal without hesitation.

Garfield was not a star yet, but he wasn't the only talented performer exploited by the Group. Clurman's avowed contempt for the trappings of Hollywood phoniness and glamour while at the same time casting movie stars like Frances, Sylvia Sidney and Franchot Tone to boost the Group's box office, was seen by the New York theater community as hypocrisy.

However, this view was especially shared by the company's most exploited minority. Though many artists in the Group fervently believed in the dream of a Marxist utopia free of bigotry and class distinctions, as far as women were concerned, things couldn't get any more status quo.

As Wendy Smith makes clear in her excellent *Real Life Drama: The Group Theater and America, 1931–1940*:

> The Group's new commercial imperatives weighed more heavily on the female members — on Broadway, an actress in her late twenties was either a star or over the hill — and they resented it. They liked Frances Farmer personally, and they agreed she'd been good as Lorna [in *Golden Boy*], but it was demoralizing to learn that Clurman and Odets were again seeking new female faces, both for *Rocket [to the Moon]* and *The Gentle People*, for which he was considering Sylvia Sidney.

Soon, with the nation's growing optimism during the late 1930s, and the departure of its Hollywood stars, the Group Theater would cease to exist. But in that fall 1937-spring 1938, the company would continue to clean up at the box office with Odets' *Golden Boy*.

Immersed in his Broadway success, Odets married two-time Oscar-winner Luise Rainer. However, the union quickly went on the rocks when he became physically involved with new star Frances, fortuitously cast as *Golden Boy*'s female lead Lorna Moon. Unfortunately, the actress mistook Odets' sexual passion for romantic commitment and thought Odets was going to leave Luise for her. Certainly, if this was the case, Frances underestimated the man who created the cutthroat Bessie Berger and the power-mad General Yang. In fact, in October 1937, Odets sent Frances a telegram that read, "My wife returns from Europe today, and I feel it best for us never to see each other again."[86]

Just as he promised, Odets returned to Luise. However, even after his breakup with Farmer, the playwright continued to cheat on his wife, reportedly carrying on passionate affairs with Hollywood's Fay Wray and Broadway actress Betty Grayson. On May 28, 1938, in the midst of all these affairs, Rainer sent Odets a telegram informing him that she was pregnant. The playwright responded, "Dear Luise: Will wire you Monday because now I don't know what to say. Love, Clifford."[87]

For the star of *The Good Earth* and *The Great Ziegfeld*, this was the last straw.

Shortly after his divorce from Rainer, Odets wrote *Clash By Night*, about a woman's affair with her husband's handsome young best friend. Bordering on soap opera and devoid of any political issues, the play (which lasted just 49 performances) focused on the hurt and pain that the affair brought to its protagonists, a subject Odets was quite familiar with....

In the meantime, events in other parts of the world helped give an odd kind of legitimacy to the Popular Front of the Communist Party. Besides the Depression, the rise of global fascism gave the Leftists of Broadway and Hollywood further ammunition to use against their enemies.

Never before or since has so much suffering inspired so much creativity...

II

The Old Left Hook (1937–1941)

> I think we in the Party are the only people who can afford to tell the truth about anything, because we have a better understanding of what makes the world tick.
> — Alvah Bessie

On July 17, 1936, soldiers of the Spanish Foreign Legion and the Army of Africa rebelled against their nation's Republican government. In what was then known as Spanish North Africa, but would later become Morocco, Spanish forces not only staged a coup against the regime on the mainland, but they ordered mass liquidations of those army personnel who did *not* join the revolt. Though the rebellion was gaining strength in Morocco, it soon became apparent that the rebels would have been soundly defeated by Republican forces— that is, if not for the initiative of one Spanish officer who realized that the uprising needed outside assistance.

And so it was that Generalissimo Francisco Franco made personal appeals to Nazi Germany and fascist Italy for help in overthrowing the legally elected government of Spain. Years later, many would call the Spanish Civil War a dress rehearsal for World War II; in reality, the conflict ran much deeper than that. For if this was indeed a "dress rehearsal," the costumes didn't always match the actors wearing them.

There was certainly no disguising who Francisco Franco was. Though the rebellion was actually started by General Emilio Mola, it was soon obvious who was fast becoming the star of this production. Franco was a man practically weaned on military life. As a young man, he wanted to join the Spanish Navy, just as his father and other men in his family had, but the naval academies were closed by the Loyalists and Francisco instead enlisted in the army, eventually becoming a lieutenant in the Spanish infantry. Through the years, from 1911 to the 1930s, he would be stationed in Spanish North Africa where he fought bandits and guerrillas. He witnessed firsthand the brutality of the Moroccan tribesmen who literally gutted the Spanish soldiers who fell into their hands. After becoming commanding officer of occupation troops, Franco had no problem repaying this barbarity in kind, and it is said that he personally joined his men in decapitating Moroccan guerrillas in several raids. He also ensured that his men were not punished for their brutal behavior among the civilian populace in the Moroccan villages, with some of this behavior including rape and murder.

A lifetime as an officer in an occupation army taught the young man not only how to handle any perceived enemy to his country, but also how to survive the jungle of Spanish politics. He always considered himself a soldier, not a politician, and heaped contempt on the "liberals" who were eventually brought back to power in early 1936. The Spanish officer corps had been chafing under a succession of leftist governments for many years. Still angry over the loss of their "possessions" in the war of 1898, these men saw the glory of Spain fading as the new century wore on, and they tenaciously held on to Morocco as the last vestige of their nation's military power beyond its borders.

When the idea for a rebellion was broached, Franco was, as usual, cautious; but once the guns were fired, his stature in the movement grew as the rebellion gained in strength (and General Mola's plane was later shot down by Republican forces). Rejecting the hysterical ravings of a Hitler, a lifetime of imperialist intrigue had molded Franco's personality early on. He was the military bureaucrat as thug, an unrepentant mass murderer who ordered repressions with no more outward feeling than donning his army tunic.

It is said that during the Moroccan occupation, a Spanish legionnaire, angry over the horrible food served to the men, threw the contents of his plate into the face of Franco, who was making an inspection. This attack prompted the future generalissimo to calmly wipe his face and then issue three orders. The first order was that he had the food improved; the second order confined the legionnaire's company to camp for several weeks; the third order was for the food-tossing legionnaire to be promptly taken away and shot.

Republican ships with crews loyal to the government blockaded the advance of the army of Africa to the mainland, but a week after the rebellion broke out, things would change drastically. France, under the government of socialist premier Leon Blum, at first promised aid to the Republicans, but under pressure from Britain, the French reneged. Ironically, Hitler and Mussolini kept their word, and soon, to the horror of the Republican government, German and Italian ships ferried the army of Africa to the Spanish mainland. With the help of the fascist nations, Spanish troops continued an offensive that would shock the free world, culminating in the sight of Nazi warplanes bombing fleeing civilians in places like the Basque capital of Guernica on April 26, 1937.

Though the western democracies aggressively blockaded any attempts to interfere in the conflict, with Germany and Italy being signatories on a British-initiated non-intervention pact, Hitler and Mussolini simply ignored what their representatives had just signed and continued to supply the rebels.

On September 28, 1936, a full two months after the civil war started, Stalin ordered military assistance to the Republican government. Though Soviet propagandists would later portray this as long overdue help to a struggling nation, recently opened Soviet archives tell a different story. The Soviet Comintern, the international Communist propaganda organ headed by Willi Munzenberg and his right-hand man, NKVD agent Otto Katz, would be instrumental in organizing the Abraham Lincoln Brigade, a group of men from around the world who wanted to fight fascism (including a future member of the Hollywood Ten, Alvah Bessie). They were much romanticized by the Left; few would hear of the Brigade's real-life conflicts with the regular Spanish Republican Army who saw them for what they were, a sometimes sincere, sometimes self-glorifying and definitely naïve group of young men who thought they were fighting for the oppressed. The men of the Loyalist army must have been smirking derisively and shaking their heads at their American, French, British and native Spanish fighters, most of whom refused to submit to the army's military discipline. With the Spanish populace caught in the middle between the forces of the Right and the Left, it soon became obvious that the war had little to do with right and wrong, but a lot to do with power.

Besides the Brigade's badly organized, ragtag group of mercenaries, the "assistance" given by the Soviets didn't exactly help Spain either. Stalin sent dated weaponry; with tanks, ships and guns hardly matching the latest in German military hardware. And for all this so-called assistance, the Soviets purposely denied the Republican government any financial credit on this military support. Instead, with little hesitation, they demanded every peso in the Spanish national treasury as payment for their "support." The Soviets later claimed that their confiscation of Spain's gold was for "safekeeping" in the event that Franco's armies took Madrid. The Russians already had military advisors in the Spanish government and, many years later, these "advisors" would be revealed to be NKVD agents. (Imagine having members of the Gestapo in the British Foreign Office.) In fact, it was soon obvious that the Soviets had no intention of returning Spain's gold reserves whether the Republicans had won or not. This naked thievery was finally proven when, years after Franco's death and after the return to power of a liberal government in Spain, the Soviets still refused to return the country's gold.

Meanwhile, the Hollywood Communist Party would whitewash the intrigues of the Soviets and instead portray the Spanish conflict as "the Peoples' War." Walter Wanger was a liberal producer who was genuinely sincere about making films that spoke out against injustice, but he also employed a screenwriter whose allegiances weren't exactly on the side of the oppressed: that loyal Stalinist, John Howard Lawson.

But first, Wanger went for a writer with a bit more prestige and polish, someone who was already famous as one of Broadway's brightest lights. And so, in 1937, Clifford Odets, already experienced at politically themed adventures thanks to *The General Died at Dawn*, was hired for Wanger's as-yet untitled Spanish Civil War project. The playwright's script was to be called *The River Is Blue*. Whether the river was blue, yellow or mauve, Wanger was ultimately not satisfied with it and felt that Odets needed a collaborator.

Following Harold Clurman's suggestion, the producer put Odets' nemesis Lawson on the project. Odets had "officially" left the party in 1935 (some say 1936), but the playwright never forgot Lawson's double-cross about his role in the Cuban debacle. For whatever reason, Odets didn't cherish the possibility of collaborating with a man whose stridence in everything political usually left all other opinions, no matter how viable, rotting in the dust, and he soon left the project. The playwright turned his attention to the Broadway staging of *Golden Boy* and cheating on his wife with Frances Farmer.

Inevitably, Lawson's dreams of finally doing a screenplay that slammed Franco's fascists hit a roadblock named Joseph Breen. To the censor, Production Code guidelines were specific in their dictates. Under Article 10 entitled National Feelings, the rule stipulated, "The history, institutions, prominent people and citizenry of all nations shall be represented fairly."

With the world rapidly going to hell, following this precept was going to be tough. In fact, it was under this insane rule that Breen and the Catholic Legion of Decency would consider any depiction of the Holocaust as an insult to Nazi Germany's "National Feelings." It was certainly no accident that the anti–Semitic Breen and his equally bigoted minions in the Code office fought like demons to keep Hollywood films from attacking Nazi Germany throughout the 1930s. With Spain's Catholic Church openly backing the Franco rebellion, the Catholic Legion of Decency frowned on a film that would attack their supposedly God-fearing allies. No matter how liberal he was, Wanger could not afford to antagonize the Church.

Breen, who had reluctantly approved Odets' *The River Is Blue*, had serious problems with Lawson's screenplay, now called *Blockade*. (Other titles included *Loves of Jeanne Ney* and *Castles in Spain*.) After declaring that any film depicting the Spanish Civil War was "in

ON THEIR GUARD. Madeleine Carroll is hushed by Henry Fonda in the Spanish Civil War drama *Blockade* (1938). The Walter Wanger production had a screenplay by Party "enforcer" John Howard Lawson, but the filmmakers were forced to remove any reference to the combatants' identities.

our judgment, highly dangerous," the censor stipulated that no attempt be made to "identify any of the combatants with either faction of the Spanish Civil War."[1]

Great. A war film featuring mystery warriors.

Lawson and director William (originally Wilhelm) Dieterle were fans of Eisenstein's *Potemkin* and used it as a blueprint in the shooting of certain scenes. The anti-czarist masterpiece would certainly be a great influence in scenes depicting the actual sea blockade and the sailors' sympathies to the starving people on shore.

Our story begins in the mythical town of Castlemare, somewhere in Spain in the spring of 1936, an interesting time period that was meant to disguise the Spanish military's July rebellion; needless to say, the specification of the date is clumsy, for it fooled no one. Beautiful blonde British shiksa Norma (played by beautiful blonde British shiksa Madeleine Carroll) runs her flivver into the ox-cart of peasants Marco (Henry Fonda) and Luis (Leo Carrillo). As far as appropriate Latino casting was concerned, the actor playing Luis made the cut, but we can only assume that the actor playing Marco was obviously from the Nebraskan part of Spain.

Marco waxes enthusiastically about "the Mother Earth" and Spanish soil as he verbally spars with rich girl Norma. Lawson uses this situation the way a Communist screenwriter would; as the film progresses, rich girl is made to see poor boy's point of view about the suffering of the "people." As Marco and Luis talk endlessly about their wonderful country, it becomes fairly obvious that *something* has to happen soon to jump-start this maudlin

YOUNG REPUBLICANS. Henry Fonda and Leo Carrillo (with unidentified extra in between) as Loyalist guerrillas in *Blockade* (1938). The film made no mention of the real-life war between Franco's Nationalists and the duly elected Republican government.

scene filled with cornball dialogue. Before you can say "Hail, Franco," fascist bombs land on that same Spanish soil Marco had just recently anointed.

Throughout the film, allegiances change fast and spies for one side or the other appear out of the Spanish woodwork. Norma's father Basil (Vladimir Sokoloff), as it turns out, is working for the opposition — whoever that is. However, once Norma sees the suffering of the people, including children being endangered by falling bombs (Marco rescues a baby from a bombed-out apartment building), the rich gal sees the evil in those people of glaringly unidentifiable political allegiance who are taking over the country for blatantly nameless secret forces. And did I also mention they were of unknown origin?

Marco has certainly changed. At first a naïve young man, he joins the "people's fight" and now wears a black uniform identifying himself with the (unnamed) Loyalist forces. His uniform looks too uncomfortably fascist-like for the audience to cheer him as a liberator. However, it's quite possible that the characters' military uniforms were designed with a certain sartorial anonymity in mind. In a letter to Wanger, dated February 22, Breen insisted:

> It might be well for you shooting this picture, not to definitely identify any of the combatants with either faction of the Spanish Civil War. This means that you ought not to definitely identify, by means of uniform or otherwise, those actively participating in the fracas.[2]

Certainly, Dieterle's direction of the "fracas" was good; however, Wanger's production values were not. For with the exception of the crumbling apartment house and a few shots of the blockaded ships headed for the shore, the producer obviously skimped on the budget. As everyone can see, the fascist bombs being dropped from unseen planes are obviously exploding on a large sound stage. The result of this blunder is that it becomes awfully hard for an audience to identify with the oppressed extras of Stage 12.

In a letter to Wanger, dated January 4, 1938, Breen insisted that the victimized Spaniards of the film should suffer a "kinder, gentler" version of oppression: "Scene 403: The shot, showing the road covered with 'maimed and dead bodies,' should not be too realistically gruesome."[3]

"Gruesomeness" aside, by the time of curtain, Marco exposes the fifth columnist working for an unidentified country masquerading as a patriot for unnamed home forces. Told by his (unidentified) superior to find peace, the Nebraskan-accented Spaniard unsubtly faces the cameraman (how'd *he* get into the police station?) and cries:

> Peace? Where can you find it? Our country has been turned into a battlefield. There is no safety for old people and children. Women can't keep their families safe in their houses; they can't be safe in their own fields. Churches, schools and hospitals are targets. It's not war; war is between soldiers. It's murder, murder of innocent people. There's no sense to it. The world can stop it. Where's the conscience of the world?

We presume the conscience of the world was on hiatus — or at least, judging from Lawson's screenplay, incredibly selective. In the years ahead, he and other Communist screenwriters would use the coming of the Second World War to slam capitalist appeasement of the fascist powers; and most of the Hollywood Ten (as well as Lillian Hellman) would write screenplays depicting a world where the western democracies ignored Japanese aggression in China, the growth of fascism in Italy, and the rise of Nazi Germany. These same writers would also blatantly ignore Stalin murdering his own people in the collectivization famine, his slave labor camps and the Moscow show trials.

Predictably, Wanger's film infuriated the nation's Catholic organizations. According to Joseph F. Lamb, state deputy of the New York State Council of the Knights of Columbus:

> Based on a stereotyped plot and a background of scenery that is too obviously synthetic, this picture uses a commendable ideal, Peace, as a Trojan horse for subtle foreign political propaganda.
>
> This picture is historically false and intellectually dishonest. It is a polemic for the Marxist-controlled cause in Spain, which would ruthlessly destroy Christian civilization. Particularly in view of the well-known sympathies of some of those associated with the picture, and of the fact that a definite phase of Marxist strategy is to acquire a controlling influence over the cinema, this red trial balloon should be punctured.[4]

The "puncturing" was only beginning.

After referring to the "governing ghouls" at Madrid and Barcelona (two Loyalist strongholds), the unnamed writer of an editorial in the *Catholic News* of June 18, 1938, noted, "Pope Pius XI again very penetratingly points out that Catholics have an obligation to stay away from motion pictures, not only those which offend Christian morality, but from those which are 'offensive to truth.'" This was the same Pius XI who had recently signed a Concordat with Hitler and Mussolini which effectively bought the Church's silence to any fascist outrage, including the coming Holocaust.

Continuing Joseph Lamb's "Trojan horse" imagery, the *Catholic News* ended its editorial with:

> We expect the defenders of the film will say that it is a great plea and preachment for peace and that it is a great and graphic invective against the bombardment of non-combatants. Again, the Trojan horse is dragged within the walls! It is a plea for peace, but at the Reds' price![5]

After referring to Odets, Lawson, Dieterle and Wanger as "well-known Leftists," the Catholic newspaper, the *Tablet*, claimed that "radicals look upon [the film] as favorable propaganda."[6]

While they were at it, the *Tablet* also decided to moonlight as film critics: "The entertainment value of the picture is poor. The film is stupid, the plot weak, confused and the continuity poor; the acting is only mediocre, the photography leaves much to be desired and the staging is frequently absurd."

Not exactly Frank Nugent, but we get the point.

Still, not all Church officials saw the film as propaganda. In a July 19 letter to Breen, Charles J. Turck, general director of the Board of Christian Education of the Presbyterian Church, wrote:

> I understand that according to many competent picture critics, this is regarded as a very great picture. My information is that the groups that stop the showing of the picture are usually associated with the Catholic Church. These groups identify those who murder civilians in the picture with Franco's army in Spain, the army which the Catholic Church is very desirous to see win the war.[7]

Clearly annoyed by Turck's comments about the Catholic Church, Breen responded on August 4:

> I am not so sure that the critics regarded this picture as a "very great picture." The fact is that it is a rather ordinary spy story of a kind which has been done many times before.
>
> You are correct ... that the groups seeking to prevent the showing of the picture are, for the most part, groups of the members of the Knights of Columbus — and not the Legion of Decency.

Though Breen's defensive letter does have the definite subtext of protesting too much, the censor accurately pointed out that "those exploiting the film are endeavoring to stir up a little controversy in the hope that it will direct greater attention to the picture."[8]

For instance, the Communist Party spread the rumor that Franco tried to have the film destroyed; in reality, it was extremely doubtful the dictator even knew it existed. The film was ultimately banned in twelve countries, including, needless to say, Nazi Germany and fascist Italy.

Despite the fact that the criticisms the Knights and other Catholic organizations were heaping onto the film were absolutely true, especially their claims that the picture presented only the Communist point of view *vis-à-vis* the Spanish Civil War, their opinions about the film's performances is debatable. Besides Fonda's obvious miscasting, his talents were wasted. The moment his character becomes more committed to the fight, the more stiff his acting becomes; instead of moral rectitude, he seems to have a sizable broomstick up the back of his pompous military uniform.

Madeleine Carroll was another story. Playing another heroine with a double-crossing father, as she did in *The General Died at Dawn*, the British actress was more than familiar with leftist film material, and would be cast in another Wanger production the following year, the Hitchcock-directed *Foreign Correspondent*. In *Blockade* her performance is actually better than the stiff-necked Fonda's, but it never pleased the nitpicking Lawson:

> The difficulty related to the performers and especially to Madeleine Carroll's personality and manner as an actress.... [I]t was hard for her to express the woman's feelings.... [I discussed] a scene with her at length and the speech in which she confesses her guilt was rewritten a dozen times.[9]

The speech was rewritten a dozen times because an actress couldn't deliver her dialogue? I'd say this was extremely doubtful on Walter Wanger's usually chintzy budgets and fast shooting schedules. Though Lawson *was* forced to do several drafts of the script, it was at the behest of the Breen Office seeking to remove any attack on the Franco uprising, not because of Madeleine Carroll's alleged difficulties delivering her lines. In fact, not only was Lawson's malicious attack on the actress based on a lie, but she ended up making a sketchily written character far more likable than the scenarist probably intended. Curiously, the strident Lawson was usually reluctant to attack *male* actors, perhaps because a well-deserved punch in the mouth might be in the offing. Though he would write the supposedly pro-feminist *Smash-Up: The Story of a Woman*, Lawson always seemed to reserve some bile towards the actresses who appeared in his films. The following year, he would also sharpen his verbal stylus on Hedy Lamarr, the actress whose presence and sex appeal helped make the Lawson-scripted *Algiers* a popular hit.[10]

Meanwhile, to the endless frustration of Hitler and Mussolini, Franco bided his time in the manner in which he used his army during the civil war. Carefully, almost maddeningly carefully, the generalissimo concentrated on spreading out his forces without relying on a series of decisive battles to break Republican resistance. Instead of a knife thrust at the heart of Republican Spain, the rebels became an encroaching cancer, slowly but tenaciously spreading over the body of the Spanish nation. By this innovative military approach, it was soon obvious that Franco wanted to *prolong* the war, not shorten it. Ultimately, by rejecting the Hitlerian concept of the blitzkrieg, the generalissimo was proven right. Using his army to capture and entrench themselves in conquered territory and then advance *gradually*, Franco guaranteed that little resistance would be left once the rebels attained a final victory in 1939.

The Soviets also wanted to prolong the war, but for different reasons. As long as the Nazis were involved in Spain, Hitler's attention was turned away from the Soviet Union; and as long as Nazi bombers delivered death blows on an unarmed populace, the Red Army, through its NKVD personnel on Spanish soil, were able to get firsthand reports on the effectiveness of German armaments in actual battle. Once this was done, and with Spain's gold reserves now in Soviet hands, all NKVD and Red Army personnel left Spain, followed, with their tails between their legs, by surviving members of the Abraham Lincoln Brigade. Stalin cared nothing for the Spanish people, and even less for the Loyalists who fought Franco's forces.

The lie that the Soviets were aiding the Spanish people was blown out of the water once and for all in August 1939 after the signing of the Nazi-Soviet Pact. Now the Communists were openly allying themselves with the nation that sent their war planes into Spain to bomb its citizens. With absolutely no pangs of regret, and as a gesture of good will to his new allies, Stalin ordered the NKVD to compile lists of all Communist and Republican activists still in Spain and then turn them over to the Gestapo. The Gestapo then turned the lists over to Franco's intelligence forces, who promptly liquidated everyone they could who had once thought that they were fighting a "people's war."

In later years, Lawson would angrily blame the Breen Office, the Catholic Church and even international banks for watering down any impact that *Blockade* would have had on audiences. However, Lawson, who ordered members of the Party to forget their principles and praise the infamous Pact the following year, would never have written a script about the Soviet Union's betrayal of Spain.

Indeed, where *was* the conscience of the world?

In 1913, the manager of an Atlanta pencil factory named Leo Frank was arrested for the murder of 13-year-old employee Mary Phagan. On April 26, the day of the city's Confederate Day Parade, little Mary had left home to go to the pencil factory to pick up her wages. The next day, the night watchman found her bloody body in the factory basement.

After authorities called in Frank, he admitted that he paid Phagan her wages, but couldn't say where she went afterward. However, this honest admission made Frank supposedly the last person to see Phagan alive; and Atlanta lawmen, ignoring the fact that his housekeeper placed him at home having lunch at the time of the murder, promptly tagged him as the chief suspect. Unfortunately, Frank had a few more things which worked against him in the Deep South of 1913: He was from the North, he was college-educated and, the most damning of all, he was a Jew. (He was the head of his local B'nai B'rith chapter.)

State prosecutor Hugh Dorsey sought a grand jury indictment against Frank. Inflaming an already volatile situation, his office quickly spread rumors that Phagan was also sexually assaulted. Despite the fact that Frank provided employment to Atlanta residents, these same employees had no problem claiming that he had made sexual advances to female co-workers.

Prosecutor Dorsey painted a dark picture of Frank as a lecher. At the time, amidst a cult of Southern chivalry, it was considered a hanging offense for African Americans to have any contact with the "flower of white womanhood." Indeed, as Dorsey and the press portrayed Frank as a pervert lusting after teenage Christian girls, the gentile townsfolk, the same ones who were celebrating the glories of a slave state the day Phagan was murdered, had little problem forming into hate mobs demanding "justice."

An African-American janitor named Jim Conley was arrested two days after Frank because he was seen washing blood off his shirt. The janitor even admitted to writing two notes that were found on Phagan's body. Though the police had the notes pointing to him as the murderer, Conley later claimed that Dorsey coached him into saying that Frank admitted to him in the factory's lathe room that he killed Phagan. Continuing this fable, Conley also claimed that Frank paid him to write the notes and to move Phagan's body to the basement.

Amazingly, in the first instance of a Southern white jury using a black man's testimony to convict a white man (and perhaps convincing themselves that it was all right since said white man wasn't a Christian), they found Frank guilty in less than four hours. Meanwhile, outside the courtroom, townsfolk shouted "Hang the Jew!" and one reporter overheard a perspective juror say, "I'm glad they indicted the goddamn Jew. They ought to take him out and lynch him."

After Frank was sentenced to death, Georgia's higher courts rejected his appeals and the U.S. Supreme Court, acting very non-judiciously, voted 7–2 against reopening the case. The defendant's only hope lay in a commutation of his death sentence by Governor Frank Slaton. After the verdict was declared, the atmosphere in town was so tense that state police kept a crowd of five thousand from storming the governor's mansion. Despite this intimidation, however, and unlike most state and local officials involved in the case, Slaton had principles.

A few days after the indictment, the governor wrote movingly of Frank's case, and how it mirrored that of another Jew railroaded by a mob centuries before:

> Two thousand years ago, another governor washed his hands and turned over a Jew to a mob. For two thousand years that governor's name has been accursed. If today another Jew were lying in his grave because I had failed to do my duty, I would all through life find his blood on my hands and would consider myself an assassin through cowardice.[11]

Days after the indictment, Leo Frank found himself in a prison hospital, a victim of an anti–Semitic inmate who had slashed him in the throat. On August 17, 25 men who were laughably described as "sober, intelligent, of established good name and character" broke into the hospital and grabbed Frank. They drove him over a hundred miles to a grove of cottonwoods outside Marietta. It is said that Frank faced his accusers with dignity and calmly proclaimed his innocence before the group hanged him from a tree. Then, those same "sober, intelligent" folks of "established good name and character" took turns posing for pictures beneath Frank's still-swinging body.

The compassionate Frank Slaton did not seek reelection, knowing full well that hate-filled Georgians would never vote for him. Unfortunately, the people elected grand inquisitor Hugh Dorsey instead.

In 1986, the Georgia State Board of Pardons granted Leo Frank a posthumous pardon, not because they thought he was innocent, but because his lynching deprived him of his right to appeal. Though Jim Conley was later revealed beyond a shadow of a doubt to be Mary Phagan's murderer, to this day, the family's descendants still insist on saying that Frank was guilty.

> I have given considerable thought to the problem presented by your proposed picturization of *Death in the Deep South*. My conclusion is that this is a situation highly fraught with danger.... There are so many people involved in the case that it is hard to tell in advance who will be libeled.[12]

So wrote Warner executive Morris Ebenstein to producer Mervyn LeRoy on Christmas Eve, 1936. LeRoy had produced some of the studio's hardest hitting social protest films, including the classic *I Am a Fugitive From a Chain Gang*, which forever changed Georgia's penal system. Now LeRoy was again going to indict the state of Georgia for its flagrant disregard for the due process of law. Based on the novel *Death in the Deep South* by former *Atlanta Journal* reporter Ward Greene, LeRoy's film would be titled *They Won't Forget*. By any name, however, the studio was going to tackle a case whose sinister undertones of anti–Semitism echoed loudly in a year that saw the continued spread of Nazi terror in Germany.

In a letter to Warner executives, dated July 3, Greene wrote:

> Neither *Death in the Deep South* nor *They Won't Forget* is a factual rendition of the Frank case.... I personally covered the Frank case. While I was writing the book I read every bit of testimony in a transcript supplied me, by the way, by Judge Hugh Dorsey, and I checked newspaper accounts of the case to refresh my memory. This was not only to give me a pick of actual facts for the book but to guide me in guarding against libel.

Here, the author attempts to calm the studio's jitters about a libel suit from surviving participants in the trial by pointing out that Judge Roan and Mary Phagan are dead and, surprisingly, "Hugh Dorsey read the book and was not at all offended by it."

Continuing on this theme, Greene explained:

> There is nothing in the picture libelous of Mary Phagan, who is revealed in the actual evidence as a worse little girl than Mary Clay [the script character]. The family is not going to sue on that account. She had — so far as I know — *no* brothers, so they are safe on the score that her brothers are portrayed as actual lynchers. (The actual lynchers were citizens of Marietta, led by

II. The Old Left Hook (1937–1941)

the son of a U.S. "statesman.") I can't for the life of me see anything libelous of Hugh Dorsey in the picture. Griffin [the screenplay's prosecutor character] isn't crooked, he's a politician and God knows Hugh Dorsey *did* ride to glory on the Frank case and *was* elected governor.[13]

Then Greene's justifiable rage comes to the fore when he mentions the bigotry and incompetence that he witnessed up close while covering the case:

> Jack Slaton, accused of taking Jewish gold, should have no quarrel with [the script character of] Governor Mountford. As for the cops and detectives, than the detectives in the Frank trial and all the evidence of planted bloody shirts on Newt Lee, the framed testimony that Frank was a pervert, etc., etc., proves it.... Of course, Atlanta won't like it, but Atlanta doesn't like any publicity that isn't endorsed by the chamber of commerce.

Then Greene chides the studio's attorneys for being

> skittish because of the kickback on [*I Am a Fugitive from a Chain Gang*] but I think they are raising up some silly specters if they anticipate suits or judgement [*sic*] on *They Won't Forget*.... Warners shouldn't have made it in the first place if they didn't expect [it] to be daring.

Greene ended his letter by arguing that if he wasn't going to get on-screen credit, he suggested other more immediate compensation, in bold letters: "CASH."

Unfortunately, Greene's letter didn't calm Warners very much. Ten days later, the studio's legal department sent an emergency telegram from its New York offices to Mervyn LeRoy in Burbank.

> We feel strongly that *They Won't Forget* should carry usual announcement that characters and incidents are fictitious. Stop. This necessary legal protection since several reviews already have attempted to identify picture with Frank case. Stop. Our failure to carry this notice may be construed as acquiescence. Stop. This especially since Greene's book carries similar announcement. Stop. We strongly urge this for legal protection and would appreciate your confirmation immediately.[14]

And sure enough, even before the WB symbol flies at us on the screen, there is a rare disclaimer

READY FOR HER BIG CLOSE-UP. Superstar-in-the-making Lana Turner in her small role as the murder victim in *They Won't Forget* (1937). Based on the real-life murder of Mary Phagan and the lynching of the innocent Leo Frank, the Warners film avoided any mention of anti–Semitism.

announcing that the story, names, characters, incidents, institutions, etc., in said production are fictitious, and that no identification with any actual persons, living or deceased, is intended or should be inferred. This disclaimer was usually seen in small print at the bottom of the technical credits and *always* ignored by audiences; this time Warners put it front and center, so that there would be no doubt that the film couldn't possibly be based on reality.

A viewer might also notice something else strange about the opening credits. *They Won't Forget* is one of the few films which does not give credit to a director. However, since the final title is a large "A Mervyn LeRoy Production," it isn't hard to figure out the identity of the film's mysteriously shy helmsman.

Despite LeRoy's influence, however, it was one of the film's two screenwriters who helped turn the project in the direction of social protest. Indeed, his humble background almost seemed like the plot of an old Warner Brothers film.

Robert Rossen (born Rosen) was born in New York on March 16, 1908. He was the child of Russian-Jewish immigrants who had to scrape to provide for a family on the tough Lower East Side. Surrounded by rundown tenements and rising crime, with good jobs and education denied them by their ethnicity, a Jewish youth generally had one of two directions to go: organized crime or show business. Young Bobby Rosen had no desire to become a two-bit heist man or a thumb-breaker for the mob. Instead, he became a professional boxer, and picked up much background information that would serve him well when he wrote and directed *Body and Soul*. However, like other angry young Jewish men denied a fair shake in early twentieth century America, he became associated with New York's Communist Party, believing in their proclaimed sympathy for the downtrodden. Through them, he was able to write, direct and produce plays which championed the oppressed and criticized the status quo.

Certainly, like many other plays backed by Communists during the Depression, they were angry, passionate, lecturing, and had very short runs. In April 1932 Rossen directed *The Tree*, which featured in its cast the later blacklisted Marc Lawrence and future Warner contract player Barton MacLane. Written by then-leftist Richard Maibaum (who would later write and produce the anti–Communist James Bond films), *The Tree* debuted at the Park Lane Theater on April 12 and lasted a mere seven performances. Set under a tree on "a bleak landscape north of the Mason-Dixon line," the work commented on Southern lynching, a subject more popular dramas avoided. On November 21, 1933, the 49th Street Theater presented Maibaum's *Birthright*, produced and directed by Rossen. Set in "the parlor of Jakob Eisner's house in Charlottenburg, south of Berlin,"[15] the play was one of the first indictments of Nazi Germany on a Broadway stage, beating out by years the anti-fascist works of Clifford Odets, Elmer Rice and Lillian Hellman. However, like the previous play Rossen was involved in, it lasted just seven performances; apparently, audiences at the time were not crazy about seeing a work that attacked the Third Reich.

The third time was the charm. It was by chance that scouts from Warners were in the audience when they saw his failed play *The Body Beautiful*, which lasted a mere four performances. The brothers Warner were always concerned with issues of social justice (as well as making a buck), and at the time the studio openly welcomed Communist or left-leaning writers, directors and actors to their stable. This policy would, of course, change by the late 1940s, but at the time, being angry and discontented with America almost certainly guaranteed an artist employment at the studio. Certainly, these men and women, whether liberal or out-and-out Communists, provided much-needed color and bite to Hollywood's usual dose of pap. A passionate artist and activist like Rossen fit into the studio perfectly.

II. The Old Left Hook (1937–1941)

In 1937, Rossen wrote his first film for the studio, *Marked Women*. Based on New York District Attorney Thomas Dewey's successful prosecution of Mafia boss Lucky Luciano for operating a prostitution ring, the film starred Bette Davis as the trollop who turns state evidence and Humphrey Bogart as the Dewey-like prosecutor. At the end, as he is congratulated by his supporters, it is implied that the D.A. will soon become governor (which is what happened in real life), while the brave woman responsible for the gangster's downfall wanders off into the night fog with her friends, her courage unheralded and unrewarded.

Co-written by Aben Kandel, another leftist writer swooped up from Broadway by Warner scouts (he wrote *Wonder Bar* which starred Al Jolson), *They Won't Forget* turns the judicial system as shown in *Marked Women* upside down. Instead of a decent prosecutor fighting an uphill battle against the mob, in *They Won't Forget* the prosecutor uses another kind of mob to perpetuate an injustice. Still, the results are the same in both films; the prosecutor, whether filled with good intentions or evil ones, is sent to the governor's mansion. However, in the latter film, Rossen and Kandel seem to be saying that abuse of power is rewarded with even *more* power — especially in America.

The film begins (after those take-no-stand disclaimers) with the camera showing a quote on a plaque at the base of Lincoln's statue. Then, to show that the film takes no sides, the camera closes in on a plaque at the base of Robert E. Lee's statue. Ar rise we see a group of Confederate army veterans (including character actor Harry Davenport) in their old uniforms having a dry run for the Confederate Day Parade in their small Southern town (the film doesn't say where). Here, the leftist-Jewish scenarists accurately portray these old men as moldy relics who continue to uphold the glories of a slave state. At one point, Davenport's old man says that if the public forgets the Confederate soldiers, they'll come back out of their graves and make them remember. "They won't forget," he declares, almost as a warning. The scene with these mummies in gray sharply establishes the South (which was still lynching African Americans at the time) as a region filled with backwards, ignorant people whose unapologetic stance *vis-à-vis* the Civil War sets up the disaster to come.

Professor Robert Perry Hale (Edward Norris in one of his few "A" films) is a teacher from the north now teaching girls in the local school. Professor Buxton (E. Alyn Warren) chastises him for still teaching on Memorial Day (at the time, in the north it was called Decoration Day), and when he insults the teacher's "ignorance," the girls laugh at him; all of them, that is, except pretty Mary Clay (future superstar Lana Turner). Mary has a crush on the handsome teacher and is the only one who is on his side.

Later, in Mervyn's LeRoy's able hands, Turner takes what amounts to a star-making stroll through town. With the dark-blonde starlet wearing the tightest of tops, the helmsman makes the most of his protégé's assets. In fact, one wonders why the parade's onlookers are not gawking at Mary instead of the crumbling old men in rebel gray.

In one of the parade vehicles rides Governor Mountford (Paul Everton) and his loving wife (Ann Shoemaker). A wise and astute leader, Mountford notes that the cheers of the crowd could easily turn to jeers under different circumstances. Riding in the car behind them is District Attorney Andrew Griffin (Claude Rains, again playing a villain named Griffin four years after *The Invisible Man*). The D.A. is impatient to capture the governorship, and seeks to capitalize on "one break, something big, something that'll put me right up on top."

Meanwhile, the town's journalists (including a very funny Frank Faylen) are bored stiff because nothing's worth writing about in the sleepy town; even the police are bored. Reporter Bill Brock (Broadway's Allyn Joslyn in his film debut) is just like Griffin: He is also looking for the "big break" story that will put *him* on top.

When Mary Clay's body is found in the school basement by the African-American janitor Tump (Clinton Rosewood), both Griffin and Brock's wishes comes true. The scene where Tump calls the police and is presumably still gazing at the body, is revealing in its dark implications. Tump is clearly based on Jim Conley, Mary Phagan's *real* murderer. However, LeRoy, Rossen and Kandel pack the visuals with a powerful hidden meaning. When Tump makes his call, his fear goes beyond the usual stereotype in movies of the time where a black man finds a dead body. Here, the filmmakers point out something else in Tump's hysteria: a deep-rooted fear beyond all normal proportions. It is the terror of a Southern black man surrounded by whites who would be happy to lynch him for even *looking* at Mary Clay, much less killing her.

Meanwhile, Hale lets out his frustrations about the town and the school to his loyal and beautiful wife Sybil (the tragic Gloria Dickson). Witnesses place Hale at the school at the purported time of Clay's murder. When the law visits him, the cops say it is for "questioning," but it soon becomes obvious that these Southern Keystone Cops have no intention of honoring due process. Sybil is now part of a Kafkaesque nightmare where her husband is accused of murder because of the flimsiest of evidence (remember what Ward Greene said about the Georgian police detectives), as well as vicious rumors and anti-north prejudice. Warners didn't want to rock the boat by also mentioning anti–Semitism.

When Brock and his yellow journalist pals announce to Sybil that her husband has been arrested, she faints. This gives us one of the film's most outrageous scenes: Brock and his reporter pals stepping over Sybil's prone body and searching through the house for more dirt on Hale. Even a female journalist who revives Sybil and gains her trust quickly leaks Sybil's confidential remarks to the scandal sheets. Meanwhile, Mary's brothers (Greene said she had no brothers) are pressing Griffin to get a conviction. Character actor Trevor Bardette shines as Shattuck "Shack" Clay, the most vindictive brother. Even when he and the other brothers give a sympathetic plea to Griffin to prosecute Mary's murderer, the scenarists unmask Shack and his siblings as vengeance-crazed thugs. Shack even pressures Mary's boyfriend, the boastful Joe Turner (an overacting Elisha Cook Jr. with a bad Southern accent) to "avenge" his sister's murder. "'Cause we know how it's gonna end," Shack chillingly intones to his pool-playing friends.

Aided by his cohort Brock, Griffin is fanning the flames of hate in a town of ignorant Southerners still living 70 years in the past. Sybil is forced to hire important (and expensive) attorney Michael Gleason (Otto Kruger) to defend Hale. Throughout the trial scenes, there are breaks in the action by a montage showing a map of the country and radio announcements about the trial with northern news outlets supposedly insisting on playing up "the prejudice angle." In a blatant attempt to show some balance, the studio is showing us anti–Southern hysteria being whipped up in the north. Ever mindful of the Southern box office (one of the reasons African Americans continued to be stereotyped for decades), Warners implied that there was bigotry from the north; however, it didn't wash, since LeRoy, Rossen and Kandel never show us any scenes of northern "hysteria." We do not see scenes set in the north where rocks are thrown at people in cars (both Gleason and an investigator hired by Sybil are attacked that way); nor do we have a yellow journalist from the north on a par with Brock's talent for hate propaganda. In reality, during the Frank case, there wasn't any northern campaign of hate, just journalistic outrage from most quarters over a miscarriage of justice.

Hale is sentenced to death and it is up to Governor Mountford to commute his sentence to life imprisonment. With a mob outside his mansion tossing rocks through their window (in real-life, the governor had 50 state troopers keeping the mobs away), Mountford compassionately commutes his sentence. Tragically, the governor's principled stand indirectly dooms Hale, as Shack and his mob grab the screaming man off the train (reportedly, Leo Frank didn't panic) and take him away. Then LeRoy gives us a shot of a mailbag hanging from a pole that is quickly snatched away by a passing train, so we have a very good idea what happened to Hale.

At the end, the opportunistic Griffin is on the road to the governor's mansion, with Brock as his right-hand man. However, the successful pair are visited by Sybil, who blames them for her husband's death. Oddly, she absolves the mob who "had a reason" for what they did. (And the filmmakers ignore all the picture-taking these "reasonable" men did after the lynching.) Then she indicts, not only the "hatred and prejudice down here," but the hatred and prejudice of "Gleason and his crowd up north." This is a fantastic statement since Gleason is portrayed as a sober-minded man just doing his job and "his crowd up north" is never even seen in the film. Again, to calm Southern sensitivities, the studio is trying to balance the narrative by stating that *both* the north and the south are responsible for the lynching. Like the earlier effort at "fairness," it doesn't wash.

Opening around the country on October 9, the film was a hit with the critics, if not all the nation's audiences. (It was banned from many southern theaters.) Howard Barnes wrote in his *Herald Tribune* review:

> A challenging indictment of bigotry and mob violence has received superb motion picture treatment in *They Won't Forget*. It is based on Ward Greene's novel of sectional prejudice *Death in the Deep South*, which bore striking resemblance to an actual *cause celebre* of perverted justice.[16]

Unfortunately, keeping the issue of anti-Semitism out of their reviews, critics generally followed Barnes' lead and rarely, if ever, brought it up; to them, it was just an instance of "perverted justice." Frank Nugent of the *New York Times* never mentioned anti-Semitism as the root cause of the lynching either, though he *did* say that Greene's book was based on the Leo Frank case.

Crediting LeRoy (presumably as the *producer*, since Barnes didn't know who directed it), the critic proclaimed that

> [i]t considers some ugly aspects of civilized behavior. In form it is a melodramatic tragedy, filled with action, suspense and a burden or terror and despair. In substance, it is an ominous disclosure of the case with which mass passions can supercede democratic processes and human rights.[17]

In fact, at the end of the film, after Sybil has ripped both Griffin and Brock a new one, the two men are ashamed, though not exactly sorry. Then, as the two now-powerful men watch her go from their window, they deliver the film's most chilling lines:

BROCK: Andy, now that it's all over, I wonder if Hale really did it.
GRIFFIN: I wonder...

As in the real-life case, powerful Southerners were ready to send a man to his death when they weren't even sure he was guilty. It would not be Robert Rossen's last screenplay portraying an American political system literally gone mad.

On May 19, 1938, Universal Pictures released a film titled *Sinners in Paradise*. Ordinarily, this project would appear to be just another South Sea island B picture, but for the direction of the studio's formerly number one helmsman, the declining James Whale; and the input of one of the screenwriters, a passionate young radical named Lester Cole.

The FBI's COMPIC (Communist Influence in the Motion Picture Industry) Files contains a quick profile of Cole:

> Vice-president of the Screen Writers Guild, is a member of the League of American Writers. He was one of the signers of the letter of "150," "400," which were part of the struggle between STALIN and TROTSKY for control of the Communist Party. He was a signer of the call for the Fourth Congress of the League of American Writers, which was a supporter of the American Peace Mobilization. He is an instructor in the Hollywood Writers School, a Communist-dominated school run by the League of American Writers. He has been a follower of the Communist Party line for many years.

This was a mild understatement. Long past his blacklist and the revelations of Stalinist atrocities, Cole remained a Believer in the wonders of Bolshevism to the day he died.

A native New Yorker born on June 19, 1904, Cole was the son of Polish-Jewish parents who were making their way in America on widely divergent paths. Lester remembered his father giving radical soapbox speeches to small crowds, and later making an attempt to run for mayor on the socialist ticket. Unlike his old man, however, Cole's mother was an energetic, industrious woman who ran several small business enterprises. When the senior Cole refused to borrow money for a business his wife wanted him to start, the result was a bitter divorce. While Cole always insisted his father's politics made sense, his mother's "driving ambition for wealth did not." His reading of *The Communist Manifesto* further helped decide him on a radical course. Though he promised his capitalist mom that he would be a lawyer, doctor or dentist, instead, he spent much of his time reading Communist pamphlets and attending Communist meetings. One of these gatherings had as its main speaker a fiery young radical named John Howard Lawson.

Cole joined left-wing theater companies in Manhattan and appeared in two plays on Broadway in the late 1920s. According to Cole, one of the shows he worked on had the unusual title of *The Polish Jew*, a description which actually fit Cole's father. (Like many leftists, however, Cole would ignore his own Jewish background and stress his aversion to what he perceived as decadent religious dogma.)

Cole later took on the responsibilities of assistant director, stage manager and crew person for various theatrical companies, finally joining a traveling repertory outfit headed for Los Angeles. He was assistant-directing a rehearsal of a West Coast production of *The Miracle* (directed by the great Max Reinhardt) when he was spotted by Cecil B. DeMille. According to his biography *Hollywood Red*, Cole claimed that all the big studio heads were in attendance: Jack Warner, Louis B. Mayer and Harry Cohn, as well as DeMille. Apparently impressed by Cole, DeMille fought past the other moguls and offered the fledgling A.D. a job as *first* assistant director for his studio, a very responsible position for a 22-year-old neophyte. After announcing his resignation to the company, Cole went to DeMille's studio to start work on the appointed day only to be told that DeMille was off on location and wouldn't return for a month.

Here was an interesting situation. Cole would have us believe that the great DeMille (whom Cole portrays as both "arrogant" and "anti-Semitic," which, in fact, he *was*) would hire a young *assistant* director out of a West Coast repertory company; and that all the studio heads ignored their own usually busy schedules and attended an L.A. theater company *rehearsal*, apparently, all on the same day.

Whether the great DeMille actually screwed over Cole or not (as he had John Howard

Lawson around the same time), apparently, the young radical reluctantly joined the proletariat by digging ditches on, of all places, the Warner Brothers lot.

After months of trying, Cole got his first screen credit when he contributed to a screenplay filmed by Paramount in 1931, the same year the company released *An American Tragedy*. It was the multi-directed, multi-written *If I Had a Million*, a powerful little Depression-era melodrama about a dying millionaire who sends anonymous checks to different people who don't know each other. (In the 1950s, this premise would be used for *The Millionaire*, a TV series with Marvin Miller.) Cole's sequence had a convict on Death Row receiving a million dollar check. Packed with radical speeches that made sense to Cole, but did not thrill Paramount (who already had their hands full with a troublesome Theodore Dreiser), the sequence was rewritten *sans* speeches, but still retained the story's irony.

As the years passed, Cole traveled the studio writers' circuit, cranking out scenarios for low-budget productions, including two Charlie Chan films, and helped write the treatment for *Dante's Inferno* (1935). He tried to insinuate leftist politics where he could and, like many a radical scenarist, loved injecting passionate speeches into his screenplays, regardless of whether they slowed the film's pace or not. However, to his credit, he sincerely tried to bring up problems concerning society's have-nots that the studios usually ignored, like the unemployed, racial minorities, exploited workers, and those who were wrongly accused of crimes.

But in the meantime, the problems of the masses were to be buried in South Sea island schlock.

In what may be considered an oddball, low-budget harbinger of Arthur Hailey's *Airport*, *Sinners in Paradise* begins by introducing various characters in an airport. Anne Wesson (Madge Evans) is a young woman who is flying to China to get away from a loveless relationship; Mrs. Sidney (Nana Bryant) is an old woman looking for her son whom she knows is in China; Thelma Chase (Charlotte Wynters) is a wealthy heiress looking to distance herself from labor troubles in her family's factories; Senator John Corey (Gene Lockhart) is a pompous ass of a politician; Bob Malone (Bruce Cabot) is a gangster taking it on the lam with mob dough; Iris Compton (Marion Martin) is a gun moll who hooks up with Malone; two rival agents for munitions manufacturers, T.L. Honeyman (Milburn Stone) and Harrison Brand (Morgan Conway), are looking to profit off the war situation in the Orient; and last but not least, Jessup, the plane's steward (played by future cowboy star Don "Red" Barry).

Whale starts the film with an in-joke: The man escorting an incognito Thelma past reporters is *Frankenstein* veteran Dwight Frye. After the takeoff, the characters are given just enough time to be established before a storm threatens their plane. After they crash-land into the ocean, the life-jacketed passengers swim to a supposedly uninhabited island. Cole's injections of leftist politics into the screenplay are obvious. The Senator starts ordering everyone around and assumes leadership, but the castaways treat him like a joke; Thelma is a rich snob, and Jessup, a working stiff, delights in deflating her; Malone and Iris, society's outcasts because they're criminals, are devoted to each other and come through the desperate situation with dignity; and, of course, the two capitalist arms dealers are seen as murderous thugs.

Soon the castaways find a hut occupied by a mysterious man named Jim Taylor (John Boles) and his Chinese servant, Ping (Willie Fung). Though he has a boat, Taylor refuses to return them to civilization. When Honeyman and Brand physically attack Taylor, he is saved by a gun-toting Malone, who comments on how funny it would be if he were the island's cop. Here, this "honest" gangster has far more integrity than two cutthroat capitalists. Predictably, the Senator is seen as a useless windbag, a wry attack on American politicians.

After the two arms dealers kidnap Ping and force him to take them off the island on Taylor's boat, Honeyman fires at those on shore and hits Mrs. Sidney, who dies soon afterward. It is revealed that her son (whose picture is in her locket; the picture is that of actor Jackson Gillis) is the man killed by Taylor for driving his sister to suicide. In fact, when a newspaper is found with a picture of Mrs. Sidney's son, he is in the exact same pose and wears the exact same suit that he's wearing in the locket picture!

Meanwhile, as Taylor bonds with Anne and the castaways go through moronic comedy bits, a storm rages out on sea (Whale got good use out of the studio's wind and rain machines). When Honeyman mortally wounds Ping, the Asian pushes Brand into the sea and then stabs Honeyman to death. After returning the boat to the island, Ping dies and the castaways finally leave. Jessup and Thelma decide to marry; when she offers the former steward a job, he replies with a typical Cole line: "What as, a *strikebreaker?*" However, it is implied that Thelma has become more compassionate about her employees, as well as Jessup. Malone and Iris will get married and Taylor and Anne will also wed. In fact, in this simple B flick, the gay helmsman comes up with a record *three* heterosexual couplings. However, some things will never change: The Senator will remain a pompous ass.

Cole not only tried to inject a Utopian theme onto this desert island flick, but also to comment on the growing fascist menace in Europe and Asia. The two arms dealers are seeking to sell weapons in China and, if one looked at any newspaper of the time, it becomes obvious that their buyers are the Japanese.

When Taylor's radio is turned on (he claims that the island is "thousands of miles" away from any shipping, yet he gets radio broadcasts clearly), the newsman mentions the "tense" situation in Europe and "No one will know where the *dictator* will move next." It was obvious just who this anonymous dictator was, since, when the film was released on May 19, he was already in the Sudetenland and had just annexed Austria. Still, Cole couldn't have been pleased at what Whale added to this sequence. As the radio announcer is mentioning the situation in Europe and "the dictator," Whale has Ping cackle mindlessly, almost obscuring the announcer's words. The helmsman had always loved grotesque comedy; his films, from *Show Boat* to his horror output, are full of characters shrieking, cackling, whining, and even mooing loudly; in comedy scenes, his actors make funny faces, do physical distortions and wave their arms constantly. It was obvious that he injected an otherwise pointless cackle over Cole's controversial lines.

The screenplay went through several changes. In Harold Buckley's original treatment, titled *Halfway to Shanghai*, the group crashes on a desert island and, facing the task of finding food and shelter, all react differently to their dilemma. Thelma Chase was originally called Doris Dodd, and she is described as the "richest girl in the world"; there is no mention of her escaping labor troubles. Corey was still written as a U.S. Senator, though he was less of a pompous ass in Buckley's original treatment.[18] In Cole's version, the Senator even boasts of using government influence in making private deals in the Far East ("It's easy for the government to wink an eye," he says at one point). Buckley's script also has two representatives of large oil companies competing for business in the Orient; Cole changed them to munitions salesmen. (There was also a line that these men will be responsible for "approximately 100,000 lives."[19]) Still, it was not a Lester Cole film, but a James Whale film, though minor Whale at that. The depressed helmsman, whose career never recovered after the

Laemmle family was forced out of Universal, left the business altogether by 1942; he committed suicide fifteen years later by drowning himself in his swimming pool.

His Communist scenarist, however, would continue his rise within the B units of both Universal and later Paramount, giving audiences escapist adventures and his co-writers plenty of headaches as they fought to reduce the persistently radical elements in his plots.

Meanwhile, as the world was sinking into chaos, Hollywood's most socially conscious studio was launching their newest star.

On August 9, 1938, Warner Brothers released what was in effect just another silly family-oriented comedy that would have little impact on the world at large, nor set any new trends for other studios to follow. Yet for all intents and purposes, as the Production Code Administration of Joseph Breen entered into its greatest years of power and influence with its insistence on portraying America as a problem-free society, Warners' new comedy augmented the film debut of a man whose life and film persona went totally against everything the PCA stood for.

Though the film starred Claude Rains, Jeffrey Lynn and the Lane Sisters, it was one supporting player who caught the attention of both audiences and critics. Set in small-town rural America, *Four Daughters*, based on Fanny Hurst's soap opera *Sister Act*, had its genteel trappings promptly swept aside by an intense young Jewish actor from the Bronx named John Garfield. Originally scripted as a minor character, the part of Mickey Borden was wisely built up by contract director Michael Curtiz. Garfield would always credit his stardom to the helmsman.

Here, amidst the longings and dreams of a Midwest musical family, Mickey Borden literally appears on their doorstep in a baggy suit and battered hat. Although Mickey is not outwardly portrayed as Jewish, his obviously big-city background, dark, brooding looks and New York accent strike a sharp contrast to the blonde gentiles of this eternally optimistic small-town family. As the various sisters pine for handsome Jeffrey Lynn, it is Garfield's Mickey Borden who stands as a stark reminder of the Depression and the working poor outside the Lemp family's self-involved world of musical radio contests and silly adolescent crushes. Garfield bites off his lines with relish as he comments on "they ... the fates" who have kept him in a low position in life. "They've been at me for nearly a quarter of a century [Garfield *was* 25 at the time], no let-up," he says. "What some people won't do for time and a half." This was a line that must have thrilled the working poor in the audience. Predictably, critics noted Garfield's appeal to the disenfranchised. In his *New York Times* review of August 19, 1938, B.R. Crisler wrote:

> As the most startling innovation in the way of a screen character in years — a fascinating fatalist, reckless and poor and unhappy, who smokes too much, who is insufferably rude to everybody, and who assumes as a matter of course, that all cards are stacked against him. Mr. Garfield is such a sweet relief from conventional screen types, in this one character anyway, so eloquent of a certain dispossessed class of people, that we can't thank Warner Brothers, Michael Curtiz, the director, Mr. [Julius] Epstein and Miss [Lenore] Coffee, the screen playwrights; and even Miss Fannie Hurst, the original author, enough for him.

It would soon be obvious to all that the actor playing Mickey Borden had more in common with the character than even Mr. Crisler might have suspected.

Born Julius Garfinkel on March 4, 1913, on New York's Lower East Side, he lost his mother when he was seven. His father remarried, moving some of the family to the Bronx. Growing up in a poor Jewish neighborhood, Julius eventually ran with Bronx street gangs and was involved in petty thievery. Expelled from several schools, the angry young man was saved from a life of crime by the groundbreaking educator Dr. Angelo Patri, who enrolled Julius in a drama class. Starting a pattern that would stay with him the rest of his life, whether the interest was acting, politics or the state of the world, Julius Garfinkel never did anything halfway. By the early 1930s, acting would be his salvation.

He would eventually come in contact with another angry young Bronx Jew named Clifford Odets. By the early '30s, this budding socially conscious playwright would introduce young Julius to the Group Theater.

Changing his last name from Garfinkel to Garfield, Jules made his Broadway debut in a forgotten work called *Lost Boy* in January 1932. He appeared in a supporting role in Elmer Rice's play about anti–Semitism among the Park Avenue crowd, *Counsellor at Law*, starring Otto Kruger. (Repeating the ethnic miscasting, when Hollywood filmed the play, they ludicrously cast John Barrymore as the assimilated Jewish lawyer.) After Odets wrote *Awake and Sing!* in 1935, the Group Theater wasted little time in casting their fastest-rising young member. In this domestic drama, Jules portrayed Ralph, the angry, frustrated son of the struggling Berger family. Set in the Bronx during the Depression, the play ran for a year. After losing out on the lead in *Golden Boy*, Garfield signed a contract with Warners, where the mostly Jewish executives changed his first name to the more gentile-sounding John.

The studio's 1939 production *Juarez* featured Garfield as Porfirio Diaz opposite Paul Muni in the title role. Both liberal actors found something in the film that was relevant to 1930s audiences: the theme of revolutionary action in the cause of democracy, comments on racism (Juarez is an Indian in racist Mexico), civil rights for the poor and the fight against foreign invaders. In reviews of the film at the time of release and in film histories many years later, much would be made about Garfield's Bronx-accented words coming out of the mouth of a Mexican general. However, if one doesn't dwell on the accent as much as his words and his physical presence, one would find it to be a sincere performance. When Brian Aherne's Maximillian visits a jailed Juarez and offers him a pardon, Garfield, gnawing on a chicken leg, looks up at him with a quiet defiance and skepticism which conveys a contempt for his offer of amnesty. It is the Bronx street kid staring daggers at his jailer; a man of principle who casts scorn on anyone who would make him sell out "the movement." Later on, impressed with Maximillian's integrity, Diaz will speak up for him when Juarez orders his execution. In this scene, Garfield also defines what democracy is and the principles behind it. The actor's transformation from cynical rebel to man of compassion is convincing. Certainly his performance in this film is not the camp laugh-fest that reviewers in later times seemed to think it is.

In 1939, Garfield not only appeared in his most powerful social protest film up to that time, it would inaugurate a lasting collaboration between the screen's most socially conscious actor and one of its most socially conscious screenwriters. In John Garfield, scenarist Robert Rossen, another denizen of the Lower East Side, found his Muse. The result was a film that attacked America's idea of itself as a successful, compassionate society where have-nots just didn't exist.

On September 16, 1939, 16 days after Nazi tanks and planes attacked western Poland and two days after Soviet tanks rolled into its eastern half, Warner Brothers released *Dust Be My Destiny*, with a screenplay by Robert Rossen and an uncredited rewrite by Seton I. Miller. Based on the powerful social protest novel by Jerome Odlum, the project was originally called *I Was Framed*. As one can tell from its title, if not by Rossen's involvement in the project, this was not going to be the fluff of *Four Daughters* or the prison clichés of

Blackwell's Island (despite its pertinent reform-the-prisons plot). In this film, Rossen and Garfield addressed issues that were close to their socially conscious hearts. Giving a voice to the poor and disenfranchised, Rossen used the actor to symbolize the other America, the one you emphatically did *not* see in films depicting the privileged classes, whether they were screwball comedies or not.

In an interoffice memo to Hal B. Wallis, dated May 13, 1938, writer-producer Walter MacEwen asks the head of production the question: "Do you want a happy ending to the new story *Dust Be My Destiny* which Jerome Odlum is writing?"[20] MacEwen describes the central character of Joe Bell as being "behind the eight ball," and continues:

> As Odlum sees the story at the present time, he is aiming towards killing off Joe, the principal character, at the end. He feels he can do this in a tear-jerking manner. On the other hand, if you do not want the principal character killed off, and want to end the story with everybody happy, he feels that he can do something about it at this stage. Personally, my hunch would be to let Odlum work out the story the way he sees it, because he is a good writer and that way we will get plenty of guts.[21]

This memo is revealing for several reasons, not least of which is that the novel's original author, Odlum, unlike other authors who refuse to change their works, apparently had no problem adjusting his vision to what the studio believed would result in a successful film.

Regardless of happy endings, *Dust Be My Destiny* is one of Garfield's most memorable works — even if the actor had shown us this character before.

Like Mickey Borden, Joe Bell (Garfield) has a chip on his shoulder. However, like Mickey's cursing "the fates," Bell has a damn good reason to be bitter. Having already been sent up to "the big house" for a crime he didn't commit, the unemployed ex-con–loser–Depression-era nobody hops freight trains around the country. (During one ride, he gets into a fight with bully [and future blacklister] Ward Bond.) Bell is sentenced to work on a prison farm run by Charley Alden (Stanley Ridges), the typical drunken prison farm commandant who loves to abuse a trouble-magnet like Joe Bell. Charley's step-daughter Mabel (Garfield's usual leading lady at the time, Priscilla Lane) at first badgers the downtrodden but proud convict and Bell heaps scorn on her. Needless to say, they are both in each other's arms when Charley catches them. In a brief scuffle, Charley falls to the ground and has a fatal heart attack.

BACKS TO THE WALL. One of the Depression era's most iconic figures of social protest, the great John Garfield, shares an anxious moment with Priscilla Lane in *Dust Be My Destiny* (1939). Robert Rossen's screenplay accentuated Garfield's character as just one of the nation's many social outcasts.

Fearing that he'll be blamed (for good reason, since Joe has been blamed for everything but the Japanese attack on Manchuria), Joe escapes with Mabel to parts unknown. In love with each other, but lacking money for a real wedding, the two get married for free on a stage in front of a rowdy, low-class audience. Here, we see Joe's pride and dignity as he detests the catcalls of the crowd; however, pictures are taken of the couple and this further fuels their fear of pursuit.

ON THE DODGE. John Garfield and Priscilla Lane hide from policeman Lee Shumway in a publicity shot for *Dust Be My Destiny* (1939). Warners had screenwriter Seton Miller rewrite Robert Rossen's unhappy ending to allow Garfield to end up with Lane.

Throughout the film, the couple are on the verge of separating as they have problems paying for an apartment, as well as food and bills. Both Garfield and Rossen throw the Depression and its brutal realities right in the audience's collective faces. We are instantly reminded of Garfield and Lane's making ends meet in *Four Daughters*. However, aside from the couples' status as "fugitives," Rossen is clearly giving us two basically decent people who symbolized thousands of other unemployed Joes and Mabels having trouble surviving in an economically disenfranchised America.

In a later scene, Joe takes a loaded gun (one wonders how he got it) and decides to rob a grocery in order for the starving couple to eat. Again, it is an act of desperation many other poor citizens had probably taken during the 1930s. In *Body and Soul* (1947), Anne Revere, playing Garfield's mother, rips her son over his decision to get involved in the crooked world of boxing. Hysterically, she screams at him, "Why don't you buy a gun and kill yourself?!" To which Garfield's protagonist replies, "You need money to buy a gun." The situations in both films, showing the desperate acts Americans will commit in order to keep from starving, are written by the same man: Robert Rossen.

Seeing Joe attempt to leave the house with the pistol, Mabel threatens to leave him. However, the robbery doesn't take place. Apparently, out of sheer coincidence, Joe happens to meet the most compassionate grocer on the planet. Ignoring Joe's surly demeanor, the storekeeper gives him kind words, as well as free food. The upshot of the grocer's generosity is that Joe is so humbled and ashamed by his robbery idea that he never once pulls out his gun. Seeing that Joe has changed his mind about committing a crime, the tearful Mabel immediately takes him back.

Bell happens to be present when a bank robbery takes place. With his camera, he takes pictures of the getaway and not only gets the robbers' faces, but also the license plate of their car. Wisely, Joe uses the photos to inveigle a photographer's job with kindly Mike Leonard (Alan Hale), the editor of the local newspaper. When the same robbers try to kidnap Mike, Joe is there to prevent it, and the police arrest the gangsters. Hailed as a hero, Joe tries to flee the publicity his good deed will bring him, until Mabel, tired of running, turns him in to the law.

Now put on trial, Joe tears into the jury by declaring that he will be indicted, not for any crimes he's committed, but for who he is. Here, Rossen and Garfield are revealing the prejudices that can lie at the heart of many decisions in American courts of law: that it isn't necessarily the committing of a crime that gets someone sent away to jail, but sometimes their economic status or even the color of their skin.

After his testimony, Joe is followed on the stand by Mabel, whose tearful pleading finally sways the jury to vote for acquittal. At the fadeout, a well-dressed Joe and Mabel are on a train where the ex-nobody now has "a place to hang his hat." (Ironically, instead of a scene depicting the couple in a stable home life, the two are again shown in transit.)

Though Priscilla Lane is impressive delivering her tear-streaked monologue in the courtroom scene, apparently her histrionics were the result of a little production interference from Hal Wallis. In a May 10, 1939, memo to director Lewis Seiler and studio scenarist Lou Edelman, Wallis noted:

> [After all] the girl sums up the boy's case, and unless she convinces the audience, it is going to be pretty hard to swallow the fact that she also convinces the jury in spite of all the evidence against the boy, he should be acquitted. It is an adequate performance, and does not rise to the height that it should. We will retake this and try again, and you'll just have to try to get the scene up to a pitch of where she is really pleading and selling the thing, and have a tear in

her eye, and really get some dramatics and some histrionics out of her. As it is, it is just the performance of an ingénue.

Apparently, besides the denouement, the screenplay itself was also altered radically. Early story treatments mention Joe and Mabel joining a mob of gun-toting gangsters and committing a slew of robberies with much gunfire and other scenes of violence. It was obvious these early scripts were influenced by the crime spree of Bonnie Parker and Clyde Barrow, who, in the historically inaccurate Warren Beatty film of thirty years later, would also be depicted as the economically disenfranchised; or, like Joe and Mabel, "jus' folks." Fortunately, producer-scenarist Mark Hellinger influenced Wallis' decision to tone down the violence and play up the couple's social victimization. In a letter dated July 15, 1938, Hellinger pointed out:

> It is my humble opinion that the screenplay of *Dust Be My Destiny* should be predicated on the bewilderment of Mabel and Joe. The bullets and murders are highly important, of course, but they should not be paramount. It is the love story of these two kids — their helpless gropings for happiness — that should key the picture at all times.
>
> You've got to feel sorry for Mabel and Joe from the very moment you meet them — and you must never lose your grip on the tenderness of their love. You must never lose the feeling that life is just too much for them.... Make them more childlike — because, in real life, that's exactly the way they should be.
>
> In other words, *Dust Be My Destiny* should be treated as a love story — not as a gangster film....

Indeed, looking at the finished film, it's hard to believe Joe and Mabel were written as another Bonnie and Clyde. However, according to Hellinger's letter, the original treatment had other contrived plot points which he insisted on changing. These include removing a scene where a pregnant Mabel collapses during one of the gang's robberies, her subsequent death during childbirth, and Joe witnessing the shooting of "two of his gangster-companions." At one point, Joe also foolishly insists on driving to a drugstore to help a sick Mabel while the gang is fleeing the police after a bank holdup.

Despite the above contrivances, it is also hard to believe that Garfield was not the studio's first choice for the role of Joe Bell. According to a Warner casting sheet from March 13, 1939, the studio wanted James Cagney (though a large X is penciled in near Garfield's name). Cagney's near-casting was probably done to emphasize the gangster angle; after changes to the script, the role was brought more in line with Garfield's screen persona. Warner starlet Jane Bryan was set to play Mabel, with Olivia de Havilland as second choice. However, considering Priscilla Lane's success opposite Garfield, she was cast instead. (The actor liked Lane personally, but behind her back, he reportedly belittled her acting abilities.)

In another version of the story treatment, Joe and Mabel are shot to death. However, Warners honchos had kept an eye on the box office of Walter Wanger's *You Only Live Once*, directed by Fritz Lang and starring Henry Fonda and Sylvia Sidney as the doomed couple framed for crimes they never committed. The film's tragic ending, where the couple are shot to death by the police, practically guaranteed its box office failure. Rossen refused to change *Dust Be My Destiny*'s original tragic ending, so Wallis brought in studio scenarist Seton I. Miller to write a new scene. Rejecting the ending of the Lang film, Joe and Mabel are finally allowed to live happily ever.

Frank Nugent, in his *New York Times* review of October 7, 1939, was hardly impressed by the film. After calling Garfield "the official gall-and-wormwood taster for Warners," the critic wrote that he is sipping another bitter brew at the Strand in *Dust Be My Destiny*, latest of the Brothers' apparently interminable line of melodramas about the fate-dogged boys from the wrong side of the railroad tracks.... It's not even fun anymore outguessing the script. The moment we met Joe Bell riding a freight car, looking for work, we know he was going to be sent to a prison camp.

Echoing Nugent's criticism of the film, while at the same time acknowledging the working class audience's identification with Garfield, Archer Winsten of the *New York Post* wrote, "He is fate's whipping boy, a personification of the bloody but unbowed head, and the embittered voice of the dispossessed."[22]

Soon, however, the Depression was going to be but a bitter memory. And as a new decade dawned on the horizon, England and France declared war on Germany, the Soviet Union attacked Finland, and in the coming months, the Nazis literally swallowed up most of Europe.

Pessimistic characters like Mickey Borden and Joe Bell were considered passé overnight. Continuing the typecasting, Warners attempted to put Garfield in B films which expanded his paychecks but wasted his talents. Garfield's films were usually hard-edged social commentaries which attacked America's ignorance of the poor; however, the studio realized it had to change with the times. FDR was a friend of Jack Warner's; and it soon became obvious that the Roosevelt administration preferred that Hollywood's premier social-criticism studio start criticizing something else. The success of 1939's *Confessions of a Nazi Spy* signaled the direction the studio had to go. It was time for Hollywood to attack those nations without, not those sacred institutions within. Therefore, Garfield would be squandered in non-controversial B dreck like *Flowing Gold*, *East of the River* and *Castle on the Hudson*.

In the meantime, as Warner Brothers was wasting Garfield's potential in the B-movie valley, the career of another socially conscious artist was on the rise.

"... a rousing salute to melodrama, suspenseful as a slow-burning fuse, exciting as a pinwheel, spectacularly explosive as an aerial bomb."[23]

The panting prose quoted above did not come from, believe it or not, some studio flack's ad copy, but actually the typewriter of one of the nation's most esteemed critics. In his unusually over-the-top comments, Frank Nugent of the *New York Times* praised the new B adventure flick that came out of RKO on June 23, 1939. And so, as Joachim von Ribbontrop and Vyachelev Molotov were still hammering out the details of the soon-to-be-signed Nazi-Soviet Peace Pact and German troops were consolidating their positions in Austria and Czechoslovakia, *Five Came Back* excited audiences all over the country.

Having produced the film for an estimated budget of $225,000, RKO would make back a profit of $265,000 in the U.S. alone. Though the cast would be headed by old reliable actors (Chester Morris permanently descending into Bs) and one gifted actress-comedienne on the rise (Lucille Ball), the suspenseful tone of the film could be attributed to artists behind the camera: director John Farrow and his screenwriters Jerome Cady, Nathanael West and a fast-rising young writer from Colorado named Dalton Trumbo.

Two of the above screenwriters would die tragically, their lives cut short while still relatively young. In 1948, Cady took a fatal overdose of sleeping pills on his yacht as it was docked off Catalina Island and died at the age of 40; West, the author of *The Day of the Locust* and other novels, perished in a car accident less than a year after the RKO film was released. Dalton Trumbo, however, would have a long — and sometimes controversial — life ahead of him. It began in the most humble of surroundings.

Born James Dalton Trumbo in Montrose, Colorado, on December 8, 1905, young

CAST OF CASTAWAYS. Chester Morris, Lucille Ball, Casey Johnson and Kent Taylor as stranded passengers of a downed plane in *Five Came Back* (1939). Dalton Trumbo's screenplay emphasized the need to destroy class divisions.

James was two and a half when his parents moved to the larger city of Grand Junction. Still, Grand Junction was not New York City or Chicago, and the child who would refer to himself as "Dalton" was immersed in the small-town sensibilities of the times. A look at one of Trumbo's screenplays will reveal the influence of rural America in his work: His characters are usually either from small towns or the settings are in small towns; everyone is a neighbor, people go to church, and Christmas is celebrated often and well as these simple folks go about their varied lives. However, Trumbo probably had more in common with small-town chroniclers like Sinclair Lewis rather than James Thurber. Not that Trumbo was anywhere near as brilliant a writer as Lewis; however, both men made it their specialty to give us a look behind the scenes of the bucolic small towns of their childhoods, to bring out the darkness behind the simple homey façade, the hidden meaning behind "hi, neighbor," the turmoil undercutting all that mistletoe and holly on December 25.

In his later novel *Eclipse*, chronicling the life of a small town rife with political corruption, Trumbo would refer to the make-believe hamlet as "Shale City, Colorado"; it was a veiled reference to the town he grew up in, Grand Junction. Trumbo would eventually use Shale City as the setting for many of his writings and screenplays.

In merry old Grand Junction, Dalton's parents were hard-working folks; his dad was employed in a shoe store and also ran a produce garden. Young Dalton sold vegetables from his father's garden and also had a paper route. While still in high school, he worked on *The Daily Sentinel* as a cub reporter. All these activities were typical of a small-town upbringing one can find in any Andy Hardy flick. However, in later years, Trumbo honestly admitted to another desire that destroyed the innocence of this small-town idyll: After World War I, he wanted five dollars from his father so he could join the Ku Klux Klan.

The five dollars for a Klan initiation fee was soon going to be hard to come by. During the 1920s, his father lost his job at the shoe store and, due to mounting financial hardships, moved the family to Los Angeles. Again, we have another instance of a famous American Communist who just happened to have a parent who failed in business and afterwards had trouble making ends meet. Meanwhile, Trumbo had gone to college and, in his spare time, worked as a cub reporter on newspapers in Boulder. But after his family moved west, Trumbo followed them, transferring to the University of Southern California.

When his father, now a broken man, died of anemia in 1926, Trumbo had to work to support his mom and two younger sisters. He had the usual array of odd jobs, including repossessing motorcycles and even bootlegging. Inevitably, he took a job in the Davis Perfection Bakery in downtown Los Angeles where he literally toiled the night shift. He lasted at the bakery for nearly ten years. It was miserable work for a young intellectual who, though aspiring to help the working class, had no desire to really be *among* them.

But Trumbo never let go of his writing aspirations. He sold stories to *Vogue* and *Vanity Fair*, wrote two novels (*Eclipse* and *Washington Jitters*), and eventually was able to procure a position on the *Hollywood Spectator*. Unfortunately, the paper, like other businesses during the Depression, was losing money, and Trumbo wasn't being paid. However, the job allowed him to meet some Hollywood people and soon he was hired as a script reader at Warner Brothers, recommending mostly left-leaning scripts to the liberally oriented studio. Eventually, the aspiring reader was offered a contract as a screenwriter for their B unit. In this hectic time, Trumbo met and married Cleo Fincher, and in the years ahead became the father of three children: son Christopher and daughters Nikola and Mitzi. Trumbo was a proud father: He had Phyllis Thaxter mentioning Nikola as a possible name for her baby in *Thirty Seconds Over Tokyo*; Ginger Rogers' baby boy is named Chris in *Tender Comrade*.

Trumbo then went to RKO where he ended up with the *Five Came Back* assignment. It was based on a story by Communist writer Richard Carroll, Nathanael West made a treatment out of it which only proved his lack of talent as a screenwriter. After converting the treatment into a screenplay, he had his stranded characters wax enthusiastic on the wonders of being close to the soil and using nature to make the land grow to feed everyone. How such an attitude was going to work in an Amazon jungle populated with headhunters and man-eating cannibals who had their own ideas about what to eat was a mystery.

Next on the list to shape the screenplay was Jerry Cady, who built up the character of Vasquez, the wise and witty anarchist, and brought the characters more in line to what appears on film. When Trumbo got the assignment, the characters were sharply realigned along socio-political lines. Figures of success and authority were going to be portrayed as either weak or evil once the stricken plane lands in Amazon country; those on the bottom rung of society's ladder were to be shown as brave and honorable.

In the finished film, a chartered plane called the Silver Queen is piloted by All-American Bill Brooks (Chester Morris) and co-pilot Joe (Kent Taylor). Headed south from Mexico, the plane has a passenger list that could have been made up by Arthur Hailey. First, we have the lovely Alice Melbourne (played by the lovely Wendy Barrie) eloping with Judson Ellis (Patric Knowles), an "obviously worthless young man" (according to Frank Nugent); next is the swarthy but cultured Vasquez (Joseph Calleia), an anarchist, though just what he's an anarchist *against* is anyone's guess; and a gangster named Pete (played by WB contract player Allen Jenkins). Since Vasquez is going to be hanged for his various (and never stated) crimes, he has to have an executioner traveling with him; of course, a hangman traveling on a chartered plane with the man he's to hang makes perfect sense, doesn't it? Anyway, this slimy creep is appropriately named Crimp (at times, Trumbo was not very subtle with his character names) and is played convincingly by John Carradine. Also on this flying Ship of Fools is Professor Spengler (C. Aubrey Smith) and his wife Martha (Elisabeth Risdon), as well as young Tommy Mulcahy (Casey Johnson). Tommy is the son of gangster Mike Mulcahy (Pat O'Malley), who is a target of the mob; it is he who sends Pete to be a reluctant baby-sitter for Tommy and fly the boy safely out of the country. Last, but certainly the most famous, is fallen woman Peggy Nolan, played by someone rapidly rising in the Hollywood firmament, a young, pre-comic Lucille Ball.

As the plane goes down, John Farrow's close-ups incisively capture everyone's reaction. Though everyone is naturally scared, Crimp, the officer of the law escorting Vasquez, *really* flips out, pulling a gun on the pilots until Joe decks him. Vasquez, condemned to die anyway, takes the plane's rapid descent stoically, but still has the presence of mind to grab Crimp's dropped revolver off the floor and deep-six it into his coat.

After the plane lands in the Amazon, the passengers discuss their new dilemma; a typical Trumbo line even has Vasquez comment on the fact that now that they have a classless society, everyone wants to escape it! However, this Marxist paradise has its own dangers; instead of the brutalities of the NKVD, we are alerted to the threat of cannibalistic headhunters lurking behind every bush. Here, Trumbo (or possibly West or Cady) inject a theme of native peoples fighting back against the "invasion" of their land by white interlopers. However, these poor, helpless victims of "imperialism" eat their oppressors buffet-style.

Farrow excels in these scenes, building the suspense as he cunningly refuses to show the headhunters; instead, we hear their drums beat incessantly in the distance. Somewhat of an expert on the Amazon, Vazquez explains that the passengers should be afraid when the drums *stop*, because then the tribesmen will attack. The best part of this mishegas is the relationship between Vasquez and the Spenglers; it is the most moving in the entire film. An odd chemistry is immediately established between the cultured revolutionary and the old professor and his spouse which lays the groundwork for the final, tragic scene between them at the climax.

Meanwhile, as usual in these pictures, the couplings begin as soon as the plane hits the Amazonian plateau. Bill and Peggy are attracted to each other, and Alice rejects the self-centered Judson (who, according to all Communist screenwriters, carries with him the ultimate curse that condemns him to a life of evil: he's got money) and finds herself pining for Joe.

Late in the film, there is a scene that must have warmed Trumbo's heart, as well as those of other Communists. When there is only one bottle of booze left, Crimp and Judson fight over it like animals (or what constitutes fighting like animals under the Production Code). Here, the symbolic respected figures of American society, the cop and the rich man, needlessly fight to the death over a liquor bottle.

Finally the plane is repaired and all are ready to take off except for one hitch: The damaged aircraft will not carry much weight and so only five passengers will return, or four passengers and one little boy anyway. Possessing the gun, Vasquez, the man who is condemned to death by society, must be judge, jury and executioner. When he finally decides who will live and who will die, of course, his decision is made along class lines. Judson stays with him (Crimp and Pete have already been killed off-screen by headhunters), while the "working class" are allowed to go off with their respective babes; whore will become Madonna and it is implied that Peggy (after marrying Bill) will become Tommy's new mom. The Spenglers, because they are old (and to Vasquez's sincere regret), must stay.

After the plane takes off, the drums stop beating. After killing Judson when he tries for the gun, Vasquez is forced to gun down the sympathetic Spenglers. With no bullets left, Vasquez stoically awaits his death at the hands of people whose struggle he ordinarily would have identified with; in this instance, the anarchist is literally eaten by the masses.

In his review of July 5, Frank Nugent wrote:

> Although Dalton Trumbo and his fellow-scriptists probably would be the last to insist their plot is virgin territory, they have landscaped it very well, writing punchy dialogue to fit the occasion and relying on John Farrow's direction and a well-ordered cast to make the melodrama grow. If it's excitement you're after, with a finale which omits the arrival of the Marines, then *Five Came Back* is a thriller to be seen.[24]

One must note Nugent's comment on whether the scenarists (including Trumbo) would be the last to admit that the plot was "virgin territory." For there are good reasons that the plot of *Five Came Back* sounds vaguely familiar. Certainly Trumbo himself wasn't going to admit it, but the entire situation and even some of the characters, closely resemble Universal's *Sinners In Paradise*. Released a little over a year *before* Trumbo's plane-goes-down-in-uncharted-territory flick, the earlier film boasts a screenplay by Harold Buckley, Louis Stevens and Trumbo's future cohort in the Hollywood Ten, Lester Cole. No one can prove that Trumbo, West or Cady had actually seen the Universal B and were "inspired" by it, but there are too many similarities between the two films to dismiss as coincidence.

Both films have women escaping romantic entanglements with wealthy but shallow men; both films have likable gangsters who become "good guys" once their respective planes crash-land; both films have likable older passengers; both films portray "respectable" figures of society as rotten heels (the two munitions manufacturers in the Whale film, Judson and Crimp in the Farrow film); both films have wise, strong "rebels" as the positive characters (Taylor in the Whale film, Vasquez in the Farrow film); both films have these outcasts judge who will return to civilization; and, of course, both films compare their respective settings (an island in the South Seas and an Amazon plateau) to a classless, Utopian society where the castaways can forget society's "prejudices" and everyone is equal.

Certainly, the rewards for writing these respective uncharted-territory/Utopian society adventures would be radically different for the two most famous Communist screenwriters associated with them. Cole would continue to write B movies for the next few years until his MGM contract in 1946, sneaking in his radical speeches and having them cut to pieces by others, all at a B scenarist's salary. After writing several more films of varying quality, however, Trumbo would land in Oscar territory with a screenplay nomination for RKO's *Kitty Foyle*. During this hectic time, he not only became Hollywood's highest-paid screenwriter, but he also joined the Communist Party.

Marxism and moolah; only in Hollywood...

Dalton Trumbo had always been a pacifist, and he was enraged by the body count in World War I, predictably seeing the conflict along Marxist lines as a war started for the sake of profit and land-grabbing. Certainly, there was much truth in this, with various munitions manufacturers being the war's real winners. However, Trumbo rarely noted (publicly anyway) that the war also benefited revolutionary movements as well as the capitalists. Kings and czars were overthrown, borders were realigned, new nations sprung up from old empires, and Marxism would be reborn as an actual form of government instead just of a dubious political theory. Like other Communists, Trumbo was well aware of the fact that the first Soviet leader, Vladimir Lenin, was in reality a bald-faced traitor who sold out his nation to German aggressors during wartime; his pulling Russia out of the war actually *prolonged* the conflict for the Allies until America's entry. The system of government he violently installed was unworkable until he allowed some capitalism into the Soviet economy. But Marxist dogma would reveal none of this; the villains of the First World War were the capitalists, period.

Then, in August 1939, came the alliance that shocked the world. In the shadow of the Nazi-Soviet Pact, with the Party portraying Germany as a peace partner and the democracies as warmongers, Trumbo wrote his most famous novel. It would replay the canard of the early Depression years which depicted the capitalist nations as the bloody villains of World War I while it ignored Bolshevik double-dealing.

The title, *Johnny Got His Gun*, is a parody of a flag-waving World War I song, as well as a wry comment on just what happens to a young soldier when he actually listens to the call to go to war and obediently gets his gun. A furious attack on all wars and the patriotic movements which promote them, *Johnny Got His Gun* tells the story of a young man who went to war and returned without arms, legs, ears, eyes or, for that matter, a face. He answered America's call to fight in this "patriotic war," and the conflict has literally turned him into a stump. Trumbo emphasizes the tragedy by reminding us of his youth through flashbacks: his first love, his first sexual encounter, his first job, his family, etc. Like his numerous screenplays, Trumbo is not subtle. He repeatedly shows us that the boy had so much to live for, but an unnecessary war has cut his active life short. He just exists to think and to remember.

Though *Johnny Got His Gun* was no Pulitzer Prize winner, it did win the National Book Award (though we can only assume it was a slow year for good literature). The background of Trumbo's protagonist is fascinating, that is, if you know the background of Dalton Trumbo. Joe Bonham is a youth from the author's typical small town in Colorado, the mythical Shale City (which stood in for Trumbo's hometown). In fact, the book is very much based on events in Trumbo's own life so much that the accusation can easily be made that the author left his creative imagination, something sorely needed when writing a novel, somewhere else. Bonham has a mom, dad and two sisters, just like the author, and leads a simple small-town life. Like Trumbo's father, Bonham's dad sells vegetable produce in his own garden and also works in a shoe store. He also takes young Joe on fishing excursions where, during one trip, the youth loses his father's precious fishing rod in a lake, breaking the old man's heart. (The implications of the fishing rod being a phallic symbol are not far from the surface.) Before his induction, Bonham works the night shift in a bakery, just as (surprise!) Trumbo would in the late 1920s and early '30s. Joe is also a bit of a racist (remember Trumbo wanting to join the Klan), and obnoxiously keeps calling his sweet Irish girlfriend his "little Mick."

Added to this mean-spiritedness, Trumbo does not have Bonham let up on his father (a barely concealed dig at the author's own dad), as we see in this paragraph:

> [All these things they had] and yet his father was a failure. His father couldn't make any money. Sometimes his father and mother talked together in the evenings about it. So-and-so had gone to California and had made a lot of money in real estate. So-and-so had gone and made a lot of money just by working in a chain shoe store until he got to be manager. Everybody who went to California made money and was a success. But his father was a failure.

Coincidentally, the Trumbo family had *also* gone to California after his father's ignominious firing from a shoe store. But for old man Trumbo, it was too late; he died, and young Dalton had to work the night shift in the Los Angeles bakery to support the family. The novel goes into Bonham's memory of his father's death. However, in a truly grisly insistence on linking himself for all time to Joe Bonham, when Trumbo later directed the film version of *Johnny Got His Gun*, he purposely filmed the scenes with Bonham as a living stump in the same hospital room where Trumbo's father had died (a decision that angered the formerly blacklisted Marsha Hunt).

However, the similarities between Trumbo and Bonham grind to a screeching halt when one realizes that Trumbo did not fight in World War I (nor would he have, had he been old enough). Added to the fact that *Johnny Got His Gun* is written by a man who is sick of war without actually having fought in one, the novel itself is clumsily written. The author impulsively threw in anything, and that means *anything* that he felt like throwing into the text, even if it slows the book's pace to a crawl. Echoing another overrated writer who just threw in anything he felt like, Louis L'Amour, Trumbo's work could have used a little thing called *editing*. Imitating what we assume is the boy's stream-of-consciousness thoughts, the author ridiculously dispenses with little things like periods, commas and semi-colons, making already awkwardly written sentences truly a chore to decipher.

However, Trumbo does succeed in getting us into the mind of his protagonist. There are excruciatingly boring passages when the dismembered youth is calculating little things like how many steps the day nurse takes when she enters the room and how far between are the intervals in which she arrives to change his sheets and wash him. Here, Trumbo is making *us* go through the same maddeningly innocuous details we would be forced to go into if we were also living stumps.

Indeed, when 40-year-old James Cagney played the teenaged Joe Bonham in a radio dramatization in 1940, the actor's performance actually brought much-needed energy and likability to the character. Also, despite his being middle-aged and only using his voice in his performance, Cagney actually out-acted Timothy Bottoms, who gave a dreadful performance as Bonham in the equally dreadful 1971 film version. In the FBI's file on Cagney, the Bureau duly noted the actor's appearance on the radio show, and also reported his widely diverse portrayals in war-themed projects. For instance, Cagney did the anti-war *Johnny Got His Gun* on radio while that same year he filmed the *pro*-war *The Fighting 69th* for Warners. The film depicted World War I (and, by inference, the coming war) as flag-waving, patriotic endeavors. One wonders if Trumbo had ever seen it.

Being a Communist, the author certainly couldn't resist letting anti-capitalist rage enter Bonham's thoughts, despite the fact that the youth had started out as a patriot, had not exhibited any interest in world politics before, and had no previous background which even implies Communist sentiments. This is another example of the author blatantly ignoring realistic character development in favor of Marxist speeches. Though Bonham hasn't even turned 20, he sounds just like John Howard Lawson and Lester Cole.

In this particular paragraph, the punctuations suddenly return:

> This was no war for you. This thing wasn't any of your business. What do you care about making the world safe for democracy? All you wanted to do, Joe, was live. You were born and raised in the good healthy country of Colorado and you had no more to do with Germany or England or France or even Washington D.C. than you had to do with the man in the moon. Yet here you are and it was none of your affair.

Trumbo's, or rather Bonham's, rhetoric becomes more passionate as the book progresses. The author constantly lets loose with bitter attacks on patriotic slogans and institutions, and he deals a particularly low-blow assault on brave men who die for their country (and who would yet again die for it shortly after the book's publication):

> No sir anybody who went out and got into the front line trenches to fight for liberty was a goddamn fool and the guy who got him there was a liar.... If there could be a next time and somebody said let's fight for liberty he would say mister my life is important. I'm not a fool when I swap my life for liberty I've got to know in advance what liberty and whose idea of liberty we're going to have.

The above quotes are just a small portion of Bonham's going on and on and (sigh) *on* for many pages, *ad nauseam*, on this kick. On page 114 of the 1970 Bantam edition, Trumbo even has Bonham say (in his mind), "When armies begin to move and flags wave and slogans pop up watch out little guy because it's somebody else's chestnuts in the fire, not yours." This is an interesting statement coming from the post–World War I Bonham since it parrots Stalin's late 1930s comment about the Soviet Union not willing to risk pulling other countries' chestnuts out of the fire (meaning saving England and France from Nazi aggression). There are even more attacks on patriotic rhetoric which, ironically, bring to mind the Soviet Union's call to arms in the *next* war. On page 113, Bonham declares, "Motherland fatherland homeland native land. It's all the same. What the hell good is your native land to you after you're dead?" When the Nazis attacked the Soviet Union in 1941, Stalin ordered that all propaganda for the war effort omit any reference to the nation fighting for Marxism or Communism; from then on, the Russian people were told that they'd be fighting for *Mother Russia*. After Hitler's double-cross, Stalin's patriotic slogans were now going to sound suspiciously close to those of Joe Bonham's warmongering boogey-men.

Finally, at the end of the novel, Trumbo bluntly calls for armed revolution if nations (meaning democracies) force young men to do their patriotic duty. These sentences are so shrill and angry that Trumbo again dispenses with punctuation. Certainly, if there had ever been any sympathy for Joe Bonham's plight, the novel's last paragraphs effectively destroyed it:

> Remember this you patriots you fierce ones you spawners of hate you inventors of slogans.... If you tell us to make the world safe for democracy we will take you seriously and by God and by Christ we will make it so. We will use the guns you force upon us we will use them to defend our very lives and the menace to our lives does not lie on the other side of a nomansland that was set apart without our consent it lies within our own boundaries here and now....

> Put the guns into our hands and we will use them. Give us the slogans and we will turn them into realities. Sing the battle hymns and we will take them up where you left off.... Make no mistake of it we will live. We will be alive and we will walk and talk and eat and sing and laugh and feel and love and bear our children in tranquility in security and decency and peace. You plan the wars you masters of men plan the wars and point the way and we will point the gun.

Of course, here is the paradox. To Trumbo, wars are all wrong, but revolutions are perfectly okay. Within the novel, Bonham continually raves that involvement in foreign wars calling for a preservation of democracy is not worth getting killed for, yet in the end he states unequivocally ("Make no mistake," Bonham repeats) that it is everyone's *duty* to die a violent death when the fight is an armed insurrection; or, in the youth's words, preserving "security and decency and peace."

In other words, Johnny *can* get his gun as long as it's to preserve Dalton Trumbo's version of democracy.

> It would be difficult to find a more malignant gang of petty robber barons than Miss Hellman's chief characters. Two brothers and a sister in a small southern town are consumed with a passion to exploit the earth.... It is an inhuman tale. Miss Hellman takes a dexterous playwright's advantage of a social occasion she suggests with the admirable restraint of her conspirators.

So wrote the brilliant Brooks Atkinson in the February 16, 1939, issue of the *New York Times*. What started him on this lavish praise was Lillian Hellman's newest play *The Little Foxes*, which had debuted at the National Theater the night before. Set in a nameless small town in Alabama in the spring of 1900, the play depicts the underhanded machinations of the dysfunctional Giddens family. Though banker Horace Giddens (Frank Conroy) is its nominal head, the *real* ruler of the roost is the malignantly deceitful Regina (flamboyantly played by Tallulah Bankhead). Collaborating with her brothers Ben (Charles Dingle) and Oscar (Carl Benton Reid), and to a lesser degree Oscar's son Leo (Dan Duryea), Regina hopes to open a cotton mill in the town that will exploit labor and give them maximum profit. The honest Horace blocks the deal; Regina allows her lame and sick husband to die after he discovers her scheme. Gradually, the Giddens' naïve young daughter Alexandra (Florence Williams) becomes more alert, not only to her mother's evil, but to the kind of greedy folks she had once cherished as her loved ones. There are those who "ate the earth," the black servant Addie (Addie Mitchell) had said; now Alexandra resolves to fight those who would infest the nation and eventually the world with greed and hunger for power, including her own mother, if need be.

The play was a hit, running some 410 performances. Hellman had "officially" been a Communist Party member, and supposedly left the organization in 1937 or '38. (Despite boasting of her defiance before HUAC years later, her waffling testimony before the Congressmen, including her uncertainty as to when she left the Party, betrayed the fact that she was scared of going to jail.) However, there were many who harbored strong doubts that she had *ever* left. A hard-line Stalinist who excused the show trials and supported the Soviets' genocidal purges, she would remain for decades a supporter and apologist for Communist tyranny. Her live-in lover was another Communist, an artist whose works stand the test of time far better than her own: Dashiell Hammett. The creator of Sam Spade, Nick and Nora Charles and the Continental Op was a talented writer who had met Hellman in the early 1930s. When her writing faltered or became too didactic (for instance, too many left-leaning speeches), Hammett went over her work, rewriting, red-penciling, and cutting. It is still said that his input helped make *The Children's Hour* and *The Little Foxes* the Broadway hits they became. Unfortunately, outside of doctoring Hellman's plays, Hammett's writing input virtually ceased not long after he hooked up with the playwright; he did not write another novel or story after finishing *The Thin Man* in 1934. By another coincidence, though one to be expected from a frustrated artist, Hammett's consumption of alcohol increased. Thus, by 1941, instead of using his creativity to help correct his lover's work, she would end up editing *him* when he delivered his haphazard screenplay of Hellman's play *Watch on the Rhine*.

Still, much of Hellman's work did reflect her new lover's politics (they had both allegedly joined the Communist Party at the same time). However, *The Children's Hour* was not political, unless one sees it (as many later did) as a harbinger of McCarthyism, with its basic melodrama about vicious rumors ruining innocent people. *The Little Foxes* was another story. The slam at exploitative capitalism and, not far beneath the surface, the racism that sometimes goes with the package, would become a growing theme in Hellman's work.

Though the play was written by the outspoken Hellman and directed by fellow Stalinist Herman Shumlin, most of the production's thunder was stolen by its tempestuous, over-the-top star. As Atkinson wrote:

> In a perfectly cast performance none of them fumbles his part. Sometimes our Tallulah walks buoyantly through a part without much feeling for the whole design. But as the malevolent lady of *The Little Foxes*, she plays with superb command of the entire character-sparing of the showy side, constantly aware of the poisonous spirit within.[25]

Hellman was never happy about the fact that the flamboyant Bankhead stole much of the attention of the production from her, but she apparently acknowledged that the actress also brought her didactic play much-needed fanfare. As usual with preachy works, it would only be a matter of time before audiences grew tired of such polemics. Shumlin's actors, especially Bankhead, kept the play popular for nearly a year. After its Broadway run, the star would continue to play Regina in the road company when it went on tour in 1941. In fact, in her autobiography Bankhead expressed gratitude to *The Little Foxes* for paying off all her debts; the actress collected ten percent of the box office receipts every week.

Anti-capitalism was still fashionable as a remnant of the 1930s, before global war would make the nation look outside its borders for suitable subjects to attack. Hellman's play would be her only work to fully attack capitalist exploiters before she would shift her focus to the world's growing fascist menace in her next Broadway hit.

However, Hellman the Communist still had blinders on in that hectic year of 1939. On August 14, she, Hammett, Shumlin and 400 other leftist "intellectuals" put out a newspaper advertisement denouncing the recently formed Committee for Cultural Freedom for its "fantastic falsehood" that the Soviet Union was no different than any other totalitarian nation (like, for instance, the one that flew the Swastika flag and whose army goose-stepped their way around Europe).[26] On August 25, the Soviet Union signed their pact with Nazi Germany, making the leftists' claims of Soviet enmity toward Nazism look absurd. In later years, the Left would disingenuously claim that the Soviets' signing of the Pact was a clever time-buying ploy.

After the Pact was signed, the U.S.S.R. lost little time in fulfilling its part of the conquerors' bargain. In November, the Soviet goliath attacked little Finland. Amazingly, the physically tiny nation showed themselves much tougher than their Bolshevik opponents by winning their first battles. Caught up in the high emotions of this naked aggression, Tallulah later wrote, "I thought the Russian invasion the brutal act of a bully. The people of the theater, their emotions inflamed by this wanton assault on a small and peaceful neighbor, were quick to volunteer aid for the victim."[27] In fact, with decent-minded people rushing to help, American Communists never quite explained just how the conquest of Finland had anything to do with putting off German aggression.

Incensed by the Russian attack, Bankhead and the other cast members announced to the press that they were giving a special performance of *The Little Foxes* that would benefit the Finnish war effort. Angrily, Hellman and Shumlin denied them permission. With the Soviet Union belatedly seen as a world bully, and her own cast seemingly turning against her, Hellman solved this public relations problem by slandering the victim. "I don't believe in that fine, lovable little Republic of Finland that everybody gets so weepy about. I've been there and it looks like a pro–Nazi little republic to me."[28]

"[Herman] Shumlin concurred," Bankhead wrote later.[29]

Besides the obvious dig at Bankhead supposedly getting "weepy" over the Finns' plight, Hellman was blatantly parroting the Party's new take on the Soviets' imperialism.

The controversy refused to die down, with Hellman now forced to deliver some pretty lame excuses as to why she spitefully refused to grant her own company a chance to give a show that would benefit the Finns. With Bankhead and the cast still angry over Hellman's behavior, the playwright spilled a little gasoline on the fire, claiming that they refused to give a benefit for Spanish Loyalists who had fled into France. If this was indeed true, then Hellman and Shumlin, like spiteful children, merely retaliated by turning thumbs down on their plan to help the Finns. Bankhead responded bluntly, "The charge that I had refused to play a benefit for Loyalist Spain was a brazen invention. Neither Shumlin or Hellman ever asked me to do any such thing. Nor did anyone else."[30]

The controversy clearly favored Bankhead and the *Foxes* cast. In the first place, Hellman never mentioned the request to perform for Spanish Loyalists when she publicly attacked the cast's idea of a Finnish benefit performance. Topping these evasions and fabrications, shortly after Bankhead's death, the playwright made certain dubious claims in her "memoirs," *An Unfinished Woman*. Continuing her theme of portraying Finland as "a pro–Nazi little republic," Hellman claimed that she was in Finland in 1937 where she had to turn her head from "the giant posters of Hitler pasted to the side walls of my hotel," and that a Finnish friend had taken her to a pro–Hitler rally.[31]

Much of this blather is blown out of the water by William Wright, the author of the definitive Hellman biography *Lillian Hellman: The Image, the Woman*. He noted that Hellman spent much of 1937 in Paris, Moscow, Prague and Spain, becoming deeply involved with the making of the documentary on the Spanish Civil War, *The Spanish Earth* (a film totally backed by the Communist Party), and then coming down with a case of pneumonia. It is hard to believe that Hellman would go for a leisurely two-week side-trip to Finland. Or, for that matter, why Finland in 1937 would have Hitler's image, of all things, plastered all over the outer walls of Finnish buildings when the dictator's cult of personality was still in its early stages in Germany. As Wright accurately deduces:

> It would seem, then, to be another example of the way in which Hellman, when convinced she was on the side of right and her enemies were on the side of wrong, felt no compunction about using whatever weapons were at hand, including her creative imagination.

On August 21, 1941, Samuel Goldwyn released the film version of *The Little Foxes* featuring much of the Broadway cast in their original roles, though with the notable absence of the original Regina, Tallulah Bankhead. At the end of the film, Alexandra, as played by

Oscar-nominated Teresa Wright, indicts her mother (a great performance from an Oscar-nominated Bette Davis as Regina) for being one of those avaricious folks who "eat the earth."

The Nazis had attacked the Soviet Union two months before the film's release, causing President Roosevelt to hastily welcome the Russians on the allied side. And few would remember the controversy behind the scenes in 1939 (and repeated in Eastern Europe in the postwar years) when the *Soviets* would be the ones accused of eating the earth.

South of Pago Pago was released by Edward Small Productions through United Artists in 1940 and starred Frances Farmer and Jon Hall. At first, the production looked like a rip-off of *The Hurricane*, but in reality it was one of the best slams at colonialism put on film up to that time.

Released on July 19, 1940, *South of Pago Pago* misled many critics into believing that it was just another South Sea island B adventure (Bosley Crowther of the *New York Times* called it a "token payment on the public demand for 'escapist' entertainment"[32]).

Crowther wasn't kidding; the film was still a "B" drowning in the racist casting conventions of the day. The natives on the idyllic island of Manoa are played by white actors and they speak halting pidgin English; the characterizations are along clichéd lines or, in other words, a Caucasian's version of indigenous peoples; and director Alfred Green's pacing could be a little faster. Still, it's a Frances Farmer film, and even if the actress does not have top billing, the socio-political themes are always fascinating.

In some dive in Singapore (set in "a time not long ago"), Ruby Taylor (Farmer) is sitting at dirty tables and drinking with slimy, randy sailors; in other words, she's a South Sea taxi dancer. Entering said dive is the evil Captain Bucko Larson (former Oscar winner Victor McLaglen, clearly in decline) and his stooges Williams (Douglass Dumbrille) and Foster (former silent star [and John Ford's brother] Francis Ford). Larson gets Ruby to convince two-bit sailor Ferro (former Group actor Abner Biberman) to take Larson's crew on a hunt for a treasure of fabulous pearls off the coast of Manoa. In almost a foreshadowing of John Steinbeck's *The Pearl*, the natives are exploited by Larson and his gang so they can go pearl-diving in dangerous waters.

Ruby meets the chief's handsome son Kehane (the usually wooden Jon Hall), and it is clear that the young man has a case of Caucasian-envy as he develops a crush on the former Singapore trollop. This does not thrill Kehane's native babe Malla (Olympe Bradna), who wants to carve up the gorgeous *shiksa*. Though Larson has fooled Kehane and the others as to his intentions, he doesn't fool the one white man on the island who truly loves the natives, drunken expatriate Lindsay (Gene Lockhart). Though Larson refers condescendingly to the natives as "a lot of kids," Lindsay has contempt for white men and what they have done around the world to "paradises" like Manoa. "I haven't seen a white man for nine years," he says, "thank Heaven."

With this biting comment, colonialism and racism are attacked as something white (meaning European) nations naturally engaged in. The film is clearly commenting on imperialism long before the Nazis were seen as a global threat; and it is obvious that Larson's "pirate" is a thuggish capitalist from the western democracies rather than the cradles of totalitarianism. (He is obviously American, not German.)

The film's politics are pretty much out in the open. Capitalist greed and the hunger for possessions are seen as poisonous compared to the simple lives of the natives. In order to ingratiate themselves, Larson's crew members distribute off-the-rack schmattas and cuckoo clocks to the natives, effectively "contaminating" them and their paradise with materialism. Or as the bitter Lindsay says to Larson, "[The natives] were happy *before* you came here!" Towards the end, when Larson boasts to Ruby that men like him enjoy grasping more and more cookies out of the jar, the comparison could easily be made to other "pirates" then exploiting native peoples around the globe.

In reality, of course, things were not quite that simple. Unlike the racial stereotypes in even a leftist film project, native peoples around the globe were not always "happy" or living in "paradises," and the lust for power was something that was not alien to them. Still, leftist films ridiculously maintained that these people were peace-loving lambs until white Europeans poisoned their minds with greed and hatred.

Larson tries to have Ruby play up to Kehane to keep him distracted from the natives' pearl-diving expeditions. This "distraction," however, unexpectedly includes Kehane falling in love with the former wanton woman. Though Ruby is feeling guilty about the scheme, she ultimately marries Kehane, and the two lovebirds go off to another island for a honeymoon while Larson and his gang make the natives dive for more pearls. After one diver drowns, the natives revolt, causing Larson and Williams to shoot down the chief, Lindsay and several other natives. On his return, the incredibly dense Kehane finally tumbles to Larson's scheme and he and Ruby have a trial separation.

Ruby has now totally turned against Larson. But that night, as she and the others are back on the ship, the natives swim out to it and, in a rousing battle to the death, kill Larson's crew and take it over. When Larson is about to shoot Kehane, Ruby throws her body in the way and takes the bullet. Kehane then drowns the fat captain. Now officially the chief, he orders Ruby to be buried on the island because "she was one of us." Then the new widower returns to Malla, the girl he so recently jilted who now gladly takes him back. Malla also happens to be Kehane's skin color, thus circumventing any problems with the Breen Office's rules on miscegenation.

By 1940, Frances had already started to drink, and her looks, though still lovely, are not as fresh and scrubbed as they were just three years before in films like *Exclusive*. The year before, her alcoholism and tardiness got her booted from the Group Theater's stage version of Ernest Hemingway's *The Fifth Column*, causing Broadway producers to stay away from her like the plague.

Still, we see the actress cavort in a sarong, go swimming in the man-made lake on the sound stage, and show convincing pangs of guilt when she considers her role in screwing over Kehane and his people. However, this film was no Paramount B escapism with a sarong-clad Dorothy Lamour. Its anti-colonialist message was probably the main reason (if not the only reason) for Frances' participation.

After calling Frances' Ruby Taylor a "caricature," Bosley Crowther said in his *Times* review of August 2, "The white men stand around in villainous poses; the natives are charming. Maybe it was just a couple of other pictures, but haven't we seen it all before?"

In the meantime, off screen, Farmer's bad reputation was spreading. Her drinking, her temper tantrums and her refusal to toe the line among sexist studio employees was not gaining her any friends in Hollywood. Another stigma was her leftist politics. Her home studio, Paramount, couldn't wait to get rid of her. After her loan-out on the Edward Small project (loan-outs which richly profited the studio, not the artist), Paramount next loaned her out to that liberal studio in Burbank.

John Garfield had known Frances at the Group Theater (they both appeared in the long-running *Golden Boy*). When Ann Sheridan and Olivia de Havilland turned down the

ROAD TO NOWHERE. John Garfield and Frances Farmer in Warners' *Flowing Gold* (1940). Garfield pulled strings to get Farmer cast as his leading lady. Both actors would eventually be destroyed by Hollywood's ignorance.

female lead in Garfield's next Warner vehicle *Flowing Gold*, the actor pulled strings to cast Frances instead. The actress was signed to the film on June 10 for a salary of $2,500 a week.³³ Opposite an old friend like Garfield, Frances literally comes alive and, in her scenes with the actor, never looked lovelier. Still, this B film was a severe setback for both of them, action-packed though it was. Garfield would survive this dreck and inevitably rise from it; Frances, never.

Back at Paramount in 1941, Frances appeared in *World Premiere*, a comedy with plot elements that included Hollywood, John Barrymore (in his second-to-last film) and Nazis. In a loan-out to Universal, she portrayed a gorgeous Calamity Jane in *Badlands of Dakota*. Typically, she got on the studio's nerves by demanding that her Calamity Jane be portrayed more along historical lines, with the actress insisting on making the character homelier and grittier; a gutsy move considering her already controversial reputation.³⁴

Then, on December 19, 1941, Paramount released their last film featuring Frances, the underrated B horror opus *Among the Living*, with a story and screenplay co-written by Lester Cole. As he did with the previous year's *The Invisible Man Returns*, amidst all the horror elements Cole injects a subplot concerning the town's working class.

Cole is credited along with Brian Marlow on the original screen story; however, looking at the plot elements we can accurately guess whose ideas and politics dominated. The treatment relates the story of twin brothers who grew up separately shortly after birth. One is good Paul, an industrialist who is seeking to destroy a town's disease-ridden slums and do right by the workers and their families, which include African Americans. However, bad Paul is a psychopath who had seen his German-born Nazi father abuse his mother; he remembered her covering her ears to escape his madness. Now grown-up, bad Paul murders a young woman and positions her with her hands covering her ears in death. A doctor falsifies bad Paul's death certificate so that he (the doctor) can open a clinic to serve poor minorities.

Producer Colbert Clark was having none of it. "The explanation here can be edited," he wrote. "The phony fascism can be dropped."[35] When Garrett Fort, who worked on the classic Universal horror films in the early 1930s, was assigned to the screenplay along with Cole, the fantasy-film veteran brought the script more in line with the traditional horror film. However, Stuart Heisler's nourish approach would take it into a more stylish direction than the creaky Universal films Fort had earlier worked on.

In the released film, good Paul is now called John Raden (liberal actor Albert Dekker), and he is a businessman who wants to reopen the mills and put people to work. However, in the finished film, the people may still be poor, but they're also Caucasians.

Farmer plays Elaine, John's loving wife, but her footage is negligible; it was obvious that a concerted effort was made to cut down her screen time. Ironically, the film was a good starting point for another Paramount starlet whose career was on the rise as Farmer's fell: Susan Hayward. Here, the actress from Flatbush makes the most of her opportunity as greedy bitch Millie Pickens. (Like other Communist scenarists, Cole was never very subtle with character names.) At one point, Millie boasts that for money she would even face death; a line written by Cole meant to show how sick the hunger for money was.

John's unknown twin brother Paul (also Dekker) is a child-like man who, when hearing screams, goes crazy and murders people, mostly women (like tart Jean Phillips). At the climax, though Paul is shot by Millie's loutish boyfriend Bill Oakley (Gordon Jones), he escapes an angry mob seeking to lynch him. However, *John* is mistaken for his killer brother and is attacked by the people who were chasing Paul. Again, as in far too many films featuring Frances Farmer, the action climaxes in scenes of rioting mobs. Before they can kill John, however, Paul's now-dead body is discovered in a graveyard. Still, the end result of the film was to be expected. Though Frances got the guy, Susan Hayward got all the good reviews.

After this opus, Frances appeared in a supporting role in Fox's *Son of Fury*, and was then unceremoniously fired from a Monogram film for allegedly slugging her hairdresser. Soon Frances was arrested for drunk driving on the Pacific Coast Highway (as well as having her headlights on during a wartime blackout) by the not-very-gentle LAPD. After even more public skirmishes and more arrests, Frances was taken by her horrific mother back to Washington, where she was eventually committed to the state's insane asylums. Unlike the asylum experiences of bad Paul, it is said that the former beauty was drugged, raped and lobotomized, though the accuracy of all this is still up in the air.

Talented, beautiful and passionate in her beliefs, Frances Farmer suffered tortures of the damned that no Hollywood Communist ever had to face. Though Party members from John Howard Lawson to Lillian Hellman had compared America to a fascistic state that imprisoned dissidents ("This is the beginning of the American concentration camp!" Dalton Trumbo would later scream at HUAC investigators[36]), none of them had ever received shock treatments, were dunked into tubs of freezing water or physically abused by any American law enforcement officer.

A ROLL IN THE HAY-WARD. Albert Dekker's psycho is amused by the attentions of the up-and-coming Susan Hayward in *Among the Living* (1941). Paramount doctored Lester Cole's screenplay, removing the presence of black workers, as well as the killer's Nazi father.

II. The Old Left Hook (1937–1941)

Though Farmer returned to the limelight in the late 1950s, it was as a shell of her former self, a dead woman who didn't know she was dead; a performer whose dreams of stardom had been shut away in a tiny room with bars on the windows and her meds in a paper cup.

Hooray for Hollywood...

In order for socially conscious artists like John Garfield and Robert Rossen to continue to have any kind of impact, they had to change their tune if they were to survive the war years. In 1941, both actor and screenwriter would get their chance to make subtly powerful attacks on fascism in two films they made that year. However, since the country wasn't yet at war with the Nazis, and Jack Warner feared any more controversy since *Confessions of a Nazi Spy*, these films would employ euphemisms instead of blunt attacks. One film was based on a literary classic written in the early part of the century, the other was a hit Broadway play that was set in a poor Brooklyn neighborhood near the waterfront.

In a year which would end with the Japanese sneak attack on Pearl Harbor, Garfield and Rossen used these films to remind us of the penchant of fascist nations to double-cross the rest of the world.

> For me to okay a story based on a book whose screenplay will be so remote from the original that it may not even be recognizable is rather a precarious position. Certainly it has an enticing element, but how can I, at this time, definitely decide to okay it?[37]

So wrote the great Paul Muni from New York to agent Mike C. Levee in Hollywood on November 1, 1937. The "story based on a book" that Muni was rejecting had been filmed several times before and ultimately ended up with David O. Selznick. In September of that year, Warner Brothers bought the property from Selznick with the vague idea of starring Muni in it. However, just like the story's psychopathic protagonist, Wolf Larsen, the property called *The Sea Wolf* remained an unmanageable force that refused to play by the rules.

With a screenplay by Norman Reilly Raine and leftist scenarist Abem Finkel, the film was to be directed by Mervyn LeRoy, whom Muni liked. Indeed, the star wanted the same three men to be involved with the project, but he knew the way things worked at Warners, where even more screenwriters would be involved in the mix, as well as a different director.

Predictably, Muni's fears would soon come true: LeRoy left Warners for MGM and Hal Wallis shelved the project, though the studio did have the vague idea of casting Edward G. Robinson as Captain Wolf Larsen. Eventually, the actor accepted the offer; however, in the next two years or so, Robinson got involved in *The Amazing Dr. Clitterhouse*, *I Am the Law* (on loan to Columbia) and *Confessions of a Nazi Spy*, leaving the *Ghost* (Wolf Larsen's ship) literally without a captain at the helm.

Then, late in 1939, with the war well underway, Robert Rossen was appointed sole screenwriter for the production. Yet as late as the spring of 1940, some at the studio still had reservations about working on the project.

Communist screenwriter John Wexley, for instance. (Wexley had co-written the anti-Nazi *Confessions of a Nazi Spy before* the signing of the Nazi-Soviet Pact.) Wexley added his two cents in a letter to Walter MacEwen, dated March 22, 1940. While expressing fond memories of reading the Jack London novel as a young boy, Wexley insisted, "I can't find it within me to work up any enthusiasm to any considerable degree — especially when I try to see it in any modern form such as the treatment attempts."[38] A good Communist who went into lockstep with Party doctrine at the time and openly supported the infamous Pact, Wexley had other reasons for casting doubts on a proposed film. Quickly seeing (perhaps with the help of Party functionaries) the implications of anti-totalitarianism in the novel, Wexley wrote:

> Returning to the book itself, with its Nietzschean philosophy of the Super-man — Might Makes Right, and the survival of the fittest, which is symbolized by the chief character [of] Wolf Larsen, it not only strikes me as terribly antiquated at this date, but also quite confused. And for the life of me, I can't see any way of resolving it on such short notice as overnight. Perhaps if I had more time to think about it, I might feel differently: I don't know.

Topping off this observation, the film's proposed star, Edward G. Robinson, saw the exact same subtext in London's novel; unlike Wexley, however, the actor hoped to retain it for the film. In his autobiography *All My Yesterdays*, the actor referred to Wolf Larsen as "a Nazi in everything but name." A dedicated liberal and *not* a Party member (despite his blacklisting in the early 1950s), Robinson was not subject to any kind of Party discipline. However, Wexley, still obeying Party dictates that the Nazis were *not* to be attacked during the duration of the Pact, claimed in his letter to MacEwen that the time element would make his involvement in the film prohibitive. In reality, in that spring of 1940, it was the desire of the Party not to involve their members in projects that cast scorn, even euphemistically, on their new allies, the National Socialists.

In an interoffice memo, Hal Wallis warned producer Henry Blanke to "be sure to watch Rossen carefully on the *Sea Wolf* script and confer with him frequently." The producer wasn't worried about Rossen's politics as much as the studio's desire that the picture not become too expensive.

Rossen hated the Nazis and, to his credit, felt no need to adhere with Party dictates that insisted that it was the "warmongering" capitalists who wanted to take over the world. To the scenarist, Wolf Larsen was a fascist whose ship was a Nazi slave state. "Better to reign

"A NAZI IN EVERYTHING BUT NAME" was how Edward G. Robinson (pictured) described Captain Wolf Larsen in the 1941 film version of Jack London's *The Sea Wolf*. Robert Rossen's screenplay compared Larson's cruelty to the methods of the Third Reich.

II. The Old Left Hook (1937–1941)

in Hell than serve in Heaven," says Larsen, quoting from Milton's *Paradise Lost*; a line that in 1941 implied that he'd rather be an all-powerful fuehrer than a "weak-willed" servant of democracy.

With Robinson's enthusiastic participation ensured, casting continued for the other roles, though the studio did reach a kind of impasse. For instance, who was going to play George Leach, the ex-con roustabout who represented the only person willing to openly stand up to Larsen's dictatorship?

A Warner casting sheet from September 26 lists an X next to Edward G. Robinson's name for the role of Larsen, with George Raft and Humphrey Bogart as second and third, respectively (with Wallace Beery, Victor McLaglen, Edward Arnold and Raymond Massey after them). For the role of George Leach, however, an X is next to George Raft's name, with Bogart, Garfield and Anthony Quinn below him. However, Raft had his own stubborn version of his self-image to consider. His dictates to Warner producers about his screen image were as follows: He was not to die at the end of a film, he was to get the girl, and he was to be a manly tough guy, but basically a *decent* manly tough guy. George Leach had all of these things, as well as a chance for some social commentary (which, however, never interested Raft).

After Wallis offered the part of Leach to the self-proclaimed "tough guy" actor, the producer received a quick reply on October 23, 1940. If anything, the letter revealed that Raft (a real-life confidante of gangsters Bugsy Siegel and Owey Madden) was not the brightest bulb in the marquee: "My dear Mr. Wallis, just read *Sea Wolf* [the script]. You told me in your office that [the role of Leach] would be a fifty-fifty part. I am sorry to say that it is just the opposite."[39]

After Raft continued to describe the role as "little better than a bit," the man who would turn down *The Maltese Falcon*, *Casablanca* and *Double Indemnity* predictably did the same for *The Sea Wolf*. Not only did rejections like this pave the way for the rise of future superstar Humphrey Bogart, but in this case, the rejection prompted a reply from Wallis the same day:

> It is the kind of part you have been wanting to play., namely the romantic lead in a good gutty picture. You are not a heavy and you get the girl. Possibly in actual number of lines it isn't the biggest part, but I assure you it will come through equally important as [Edward G.] Robinson.[40]

Perhaps the producer was deluding himself on the perceived size and importance of the roles discussed. With very little effort, Robinson couldn't help but blow anyone else off the screen no matter what part he played; Wolf Larsen was no exception. Whether it was played by Raft, Garfield or Quinn (or Cornel Wilde or Lloyd Nolan further down the list), the former Little Caesar would have wiped them off the screen. (How Warners could have had Raft as number two man after Eddie G. for the part of Larsen is shocking in itself.)

Next up for the part of Leach was Bogart, the one actor who might have given Robinson some competition for screen attention. But the actor was instead unceremoniously thrown into the Cagney starrer *City for Conquest* (and then, after filming on *The Sea Wolf* had already started, Bogart would be replaced in his role by Elia Kazan!).

An admirer of Jack London, Garfield expressed enthusiasm for the role and was finally cast. Unlike Bogart, and certainly unlike Raft, the actor put a social commentary spin on the part. Tough, embittered, an outcast even in the slimy waterfront dives of turn-of-the-century San Francisco, his George Leach is not a criminal as much as he is one of society's angry have-nots. Indeed, as played by Garfield, the character's righteous rage makes him a much more dangerous opponent to Larsen than some ordinary cutthroat (whom Larsen's crew would have welcomed with open arms).

Hunted by the law, Leach wanders into a waterfront dive where innocent men have been knocked out and shanghaied onto the *Ghost*, Wolf Larsen's own version of a Voyage of the Damned. When he is about to be slipped the proverbial mickey by one of Larsen's men, Leach knocks the man down but, fearing capture by the law, promises to join him on the *Ghost* anyway.

Rossen's screenplay works overtime in showing Larsen as an intelligent, articulate and highly dangerous man who makes his slimy, criminal crew dance to his own mad music. It is the typical Communist canard portraying the man in charge as a dangerous maniac (of course, making no obvious comparisons to Josef Stalin, who wasn't even half as well-read as Wolf Larsen). Rossen's comparisons with the behavior of the Third Reich are not coincidental. Like Hitler and his fanatical followers, Larsen can't say an honest word or do a decent thing for another person without betraying them two seconds later. He sets up Cooky (Barry Fitzgerald) as a stoolie, only to turn him over to the crew and have them toss him to the sharks (where he gets a leg chewed off). When ex-con Ruth Webster (Ida Lupino, beating out Geraldine Fitzgerald and Brenda Marshall for the part) arrives on the ship and puts on airs, the captain plays along until he announces, to the crew's derisive laughter, that he'll give her a cabin "with bars on the windows!" When drunken ship doctor Louie (Gene Lockhart) insists on Larsen treating him with respect, the captain cruelly trips him and throws him to the crew, who strip him of some of his clothes. The doc commits suicide by diving off the ship's mast.

Also taken on board is Dutch writer Van Weyden (a star-making role for Alexander Knox, who was not even originally on the Warner casting sheet). Van Weyden is clearly a political moderate, someone with whom Larsen can carry on conversations since the angry Leach hates his guts. Indeed, Rossen rejects the intellectual approach to life as personified by Van Weyden and clearly throws all hope for mankind to Leach, the angry young man. It is he who bonds with the felon Ruth and longs for a place where both outcasts can live in dignity; almost a parallel to Joe Bell's longing for a place for him and Mabel to "hang their hats." When Leach volunteers to give some of his blood to a wounded Ruth, Larsen sarcastically tells Louie to work fast or else the blood will cool off. Leach's reply, however, could be a coda for any character played by John Garfield: "Don't worry, Captain. *This* blood never cools off."

The scene also emphasizes the healing properties of "working class" blood. It is the blood of one of society's outcasts which is used to save another. In Stalin's Soviet Union, Communist propaganda would emphasize the blood and toil of the Soviet Man, a creation every bit as ludicrous as Germany's Aryan Supermen. Coming in line with this ridiculous theory, the blood of the proletariat is used to bring life to a dying person. In *The Invisible Man Returns*, as written by Party member Lester Cole, it is the blood of the English province's working class which brings visibility back to Vincent Price's falsely accused protagonist. In *The Sea Wolf*, George is a Leach who *gives* blood, rather than saps it away.

After Larsen's brother's ship fires its guns at the *Ghost* and makes it one for real, the crew escapes, but a gun-toting Larsen forces Van Weyden to stay with him. Mortally wounded, the writer smuggles a key to Ruth, enabling her to release Leach from a locked room. At the end, both fascist and moderate go down with the ship, while the film's anarchist characters, George and Ruth, escape to a life of happiness.

In a letter from November 7 (three days after the start of filming), Joseph Breen insisted that there not be any implications that Ruth was a prostitute. He also insisted that the screenplay "keep away from the idea of suicide" for any of the film's characters, completely forgetting that Louie clearly takes a suicidal dive off the ship's mast. However, Larsen covers it up by saying that Louie slipped and fell, a remark meant not only to hide his own complicity in driving the man to his death, but obviously to appease the Production Code Office.

Under Garfield's favorite director, Michael Curtiz, and screenwriter Rossen, *The Sea Wolf* added to the actor's screen persona as the movies' Last Angry Man. Had Raft or Bogart played Leach, their reputations as screen gangsters would have affected their portrayals. With Garfield as Leach, the film clearly became a not-so-subtle *mano-a-mano* between the forces of oppression (as symbolized by Larsen) and the forces of liberation (as symbolized by the angry Leach). Larsen may make his crew his unwilling slaves, and even gets an intellectual writer to talk to him as an equal and not an enemy, but Leach is the only man in the film who openly refuses to buckle under the captain's tyranny. The role fit the old street kid from the Lower East Side to a T.

Garfield's next role would put him back into a poor New York neighborhood; only this time, instead of playing the rebel, the liberal actor would be playing the fascist.

Bury the Dead, a satirical anti-war play, debuted at the Ethel Barrymore Theater on April 18, 1936, a time when both Hitler and Stalin were consolidating their power and the Imperial Japanese army was overrunning China. Millions of Americans were still broke and unemployed, despite FDR's radical efforts to fix the problem with the WPA, CC camps and the Social Security Act. And though Irwin Shaw's play was a warning for the future, the piece was mired in the past.

In the play, after dead soldiers on the battlefield rise from their makeshift graves as a hideous reminder of the horrors of war (with one arrogant general attempting to machine-gun the zombies), one immediately notes that the reasons these men died were not the same reasons other men were going to die in the next conflict. In other words, Shaw was attacking the capitalist powers who presided over the debacle of the First World War, not the genocidal maniacs in Europe and Asia who were just then formulating their plans.

Produced by the Group Theater, *Bury the Dead* ran for 97 performances, not exactly a long run, though it did entertain audiences for two and a half months.[41] Needless to say, Hollywood stayed far away from the piece; though one actor in the production would gain fame in Tinseltown years later: Communist actor Will Geer, who played the small role of a reporter.

However, less than two months after the Nazi pogrom known as Krystallnacht occurred in November 1938, the Group staged Irwin Shaw's *The Gentle People,* an ironic title for a play that was a call to arms. Debuting at the Belasco Theater on January 5, 1939, the play (which the author called "a Brooklyn fable"[42]) was a moderate hit, running some 141 performances. As directed by Harold Clurman, *The Gentle People* went in the opposite direction of Shaw's anti-war satire of three years before. In the farcical *Bury the Dead,* war is wrong and so are those who promote it, and it is heavily implied that those evil warmongers were the capitalist, industrialized nations who "profited" from the mass killing.

In *The Gentle People*, Goff (played by Franchot Tone), a small-time racketeer, terrorizes two old fishermen on Brooklyn's Sheepshead Bay waterfront. Afraid of his brutality, the two old men are forced to pay Goff protection money or else something will happen to their fishing boat, their only means of a livelihood. When the law is unable to protect them and the courts are biased against them, the two old men are forced to take matters into their own hands and destroy the strutting gangster themselves.

Unlike *Bury the Dead,* the anti-war Communists who staged the play now suddenly found a reason to go to war. In Shaw's pacifist piece, those who rattle sabers and push their nation's youth to fight are ruthless, sadistic exploiters; in *The Gentle People*, those who fight are victims bullied by an aggressor, with exploitation and profiteering having very little to do with the reasons for fighting back.

Named Jonah Goodman (Sam Jaffe) and Philip Anagros (Roman Bohnen), these old men are ordinary folks; and, like most characters in plays produced by the Group Theater, are struggling to make ends meet. The casting is along Communist Party-Group Theater lines: Elia Kazan as neighbor Eli Lieber; future director Martin Ritt as the wonderfully named Polack; Sylvia Sidney as Jonah's daughter Stella; Lee J. Cobb (formerly Leo Jacob) as failed Jewish businessman Lammanawitz; and a new face who was not a Party member, a young Karl Malden as Irish cop Magruder.

Bullied and physically abused, and with Jonah's daughter dazzled by Goff's materialism, the two old men scheme to murder their tormentor by taking him out on their boat and drowning him in Sheepshead Bay. At the end of the play, the murder completed, the two are suspected of the crime by Magruder; but instead of arresting them, the cop turns the other way and walks off, leaving the two persecuted victims unpunished for their crime.

The message was clear: Those who fight the world's fascistic bullies should do so by any means necessary, especially if the law, international or otherwise, is unwilling to help. With the Communists backing the leftist government in Spain against Franco, Japan conquering parts of China, and Germany marching into Austria, Czechoslovakia and the Sudetenland, all while the western democracies refused to get involved, *The Gentle People* made an impact on Broadway audiences. Shaw himself promoted its theme: "It is a fairy tale with a moral. In it, justice triumphs and the meek prove victorious over arrogant and violent men."[43]

Reinforcing the Communist anti-business viewpoint of the piece, Shaw has an old Jewish businessman named Lammanawitz, played by Cobb (and Christianized to Russian businessman Propotkin and played by Warner comic relief George Tobias in the film version of the play), comment wryly on the pitfalls of capitalism. Lammanawitz is a now-bankrupt furniture dealer who used to have a store on Pitkin Avenue in the Brownsville section. In one incisive scene, we are introduced to this curmudgeon in the local Russian steambath the two fisherman use as a meeting place to plot Goff's murder. At one point, Lammanawitz confides to them that he is an anarchist, "but please do not repeat this," he begs. But the lion's share of his comments are what fuel the scene. So as two "businessmen" plan to save their "business" (their boat) by killing someone who's impeding their ambitious plans, one failed businessman cynically talks about the system that brought him down.

His remarks, said between snatches of the fishermen's dialogue, are bitter, caustic and not very subtle:

> What is government? It is an invention of Wall Street. Government is a knife at the throat of the ordinary man.... All men are created free and equal it says in the book. Am I equal to Henry Ford? Am I equal to John D. Rockefeller? Throw out the books! ... I overheard the word God. God is in the service of the large banking establishments. There is no God for a small businessman.

To the playwright, a character like Lammanawitz is as natural a denizen of the American urban jungle as a greedy, exploitative thug like Goff. With failed businesses to look forward to, social and racial inequality influencing the law, and ruthless gangsters on our streets waiting to rob and murder us, the playwright presents a capitalist society on the verge of a massive breakdown (as had almost happened during the Depression).

Needless to say, Shaw benefited from the play's doom-laden, anti-capitalist viewpoint with profits from the Broadway production as well as the property's sale to Warner Brothers.

The play had more Jewish characters than Hollywood cared to deal with; Warners dictated that names had to be changed for the movie version. (Even the character of gangster Harold Goff, despite the Nazi analogy, implied a kinship with Brooklyn's Murder Incorporated, a group of not-so-nice Jewish boys whose headquarters were in the borough's Brownsville section. With little room for Jewish guilt, these killers made an art of the protection racket and practically created the concept of murder-for-hire.)

The screenplay was written by Robert Rossen, Jerry Wald and the studio's usual scenarist for their proletarian screenplays, Richard McCauley. Without missing a beat, Macauley would soon become a member of the anti–Communist Motion Picture Association for the Preservation of American Ideals.

The casting for the plum role of fascistic gangster Goff soon became intense. Though Cagney was discussed for the role, director Anatole Litvak favored George Raft. After both men turned down the role, it soon became apparent that two more appropriate candidates were moving up the list far ahead of anyone else at the studio: Humphrey Bogart and John Garfield. Bogart wrote a telegram to Jack Warner expressing his desire for the part. Longing to get away from B gangster parts, the actor was shrewd enough to realize that if a gangster part was well-written, he could still make an impact in it; and if one notices (as Bogart apparently did), the actor's best gangster roles all came from hit plays and best-selling novels, not the trite screenplays written by the studio's B unit. Adding to this, the actor's liberal leanings helped fuel his desire to make an anti-fascist film. Jack Warner himself wanted Bogie for the role of Goff, yet producer Henry Blanke, who usually oversaw productions of the studio's more literary properties (like *The Treasure of the Sierra Madre* starring Bogart many years later), wanted a man who was already familiar with the work of the Group Theater. So while Warner wanted Bogie as Goff and Garfield as the romantic lead George Watkins, Blanke wanted Garfield as the hood and contract player Eddie Albert as George. The impasse was finally broken by Ida Lupino. In later years, the actress refused to say just why she hated working with Bogart, but others had already noted Bogart's penchant for criticizing his co-stars' acting ability, or perhaps (especially in the case of George Raft) the lack of it. Having worked with Bogie on *They Drive By Night* and *High Sierra*, she had no intention of repeating the experience. Garfield was cast as Goff.

And so, just a few years after he abandoned the Group Theater for Hollywood, here was the former Jules Garfield playing a role that originated in a play that he had previously turned down. The actor couldn't have missed the irony. But it didn't matter; compared to the dreck Warners was then putting him into, Garfield now had a role he could sink his teeth into. To the *Boston Daily Record*, he enthused, "The film has something important to say. It shows how men such as I portray are kicked around until they eventually turn against society, adopting the fascist idea of seizing what they want."[44]

This take is interesting in more ways than one. Here, Garfield is still in Depression-era, blame-capitalism mode, equating this slimy thug with being a victim of an oppressive society. Did the actor think of the treacherous Goff as another Joe Bell or Mickey Borden?

Axis envy. Ida Lupino and John Garfield in *Out of the Fog*, the 1941 film version of Irwin Shaw's play *The Gentle People*. Both play and film compare Garfield's gangster to the rise of fascism in Europe and Asia.

Did he consider this petty racketeer the darker side of his freight-hopping, constantly-stepped-on 1930s Everyman? Certainly Communist director Anatole Litvak and his leftist screenwriters didn't see the role that way. Though they obviously imply a fallible legal system under capitalism that would allow Goff to escape justice, the system itself is not impugned.

Shooting began on Valentine's Day and continued till the middle of April 1941. The story and its themes (if not the Jewish names) are basically the same as in the play. However, Jonah Goodman is now played by Irishman Thomas Mitchell; instead of Philip Anangnos, his friend is now named Olaf Johnson (we presume, one of Sheepshead Bay's few Swedish fisherman) and he is played by John Qualen; instead of Jewish actress Sylvia Sidney, we have upper-crust British shiksa Ida Lupino as Jonah's daughter, Stella; the whiny Florence Goodman is played by the wonderful Aline MacMahon, a long way past her 1930s heyday as Warners' number one character actress; and future Marine hero Eddie Albert is Stella's lightweight goyishe boyfriend George Watkins (a role that was not in the play).

When there is a fire on the Sheepshead Bay pier, the only one not surprised by the arson is Harold Goff (Garfield), since he obviously started it. He begins his little protection racket by threatening to burn Goodman and Johnson's boat if they don't come across with five dollars a week. In time, his demands will increase.

As soon as he enters the first scene in the cafe, Garfield steals the film without even trying. His Goff is both casual and menacing; he's a man who's quite comfortable being a thug, yet his relaxed, easy manner hides a dangerous tension beneath his expensive tailor-made suit and topcoat. Garfield plays him with charm and guile; his is an attractive fascist. Though a loner, he goes to the best clubs, wears his clothes as well as any member of the upper classes, and is able to bend the law as he likes. Yet Garfield also shows us the brute beneath the charming smile and glib patter, the monster behind the wisecracking imp. When Goodman idly calls Goff a chiseler, the gangster's smile disappears, he shatters Goodman's cane into little pieces and knocks Johnson to the ground. Garfield is frightening in these moments, and the actor imbues the thug with chilling mood swings.

As time goes on and the two old men are forced to pay Goff, the gangster also makes them sign a paper saying that they *owe* him the weekly $5 they're paying him! Fed up with Goff's violence, Goodman sics Officer Magruder on him. Hauled into court, Goff is able to show the court the signed contract "proving" that he is owed money by the two men. The case is thrown out. This scene clearly demonstrates how a legal loophole utilizing capitalist means, in this case, a binding contract, is used to protect fascists (like the Munich Agreement?). Though he is now free, Goff has no intention of forgetting this act of defiance. After Goodman hits the street, Goff is waiting for him with a rubber truncheon, the usual tool of the Gestapo. Earlier, in another scene comparing Goff to a fascist, the charming gangster hails Goodman and Johnson's boat with a Nazi salute.

Meanwhile, Goff is dazzling Stella with his ill-gotten wealth. (One wonders what kind of "wealth" could be attained by squeezing five-dollar bills from every old fisherman along the pier when guys like Meyer Lansky and Lucky Luciano were making millions from their various enterprises.) After introducing Stella to several ritzy clubs, Goff conspires to take her to Havana's more decadent hot spots (shades of Clifford Odets' aborted anti–Batista play!).

After Goff demands the money Goodman and Johnson had been saving for a new boat, and with Stella in danger of falling for the gangster and his flashy lifestyle, the two old men finally decide to take Goff out on their boat and murder him in the middle of Sheepshead Bay. But once out on the water, the two find they cannot commit the deed. Finally tumbling to the murder attempt, Goff pulls out his .45 automatic, but the rocking boat causes him to fall into the bay and sink to the bottom. ("I got rocks in me," the gangster boasted earlier when asked if he had any feelings.) Goodman delivers lines that bypass the Production Code office dictum on justifiable murder that were emphatically *not* in the play: "'And God shall rise up and smite thine enemies.' That's in the Bible, Olaf. (*Shouting skyward to God.*) Thanks, God, for stepping in." Thanks to Joseph Breen and the PCA, Shaw's message of defending oneself against fascists is muted considerably since God Himself has decided to "step in."

Out of the Fog premiered at Warners' usual New York picture palace, the Strand, on June 14 and was reviewed by the *New York Times*' Bosley Crowther one week later. Apparently, the critic had little patience for works of "meaning": "[It] is a heavy and dreary recital of largely synthetic woes, laced with moderate suspense and spotted here and there with humor.... It is mostly plot — conventional plot — with very little theme." However, Crowther saw nothing "conventional" in the acting of the film's star: "As told by the Warners in their familiar hard-boiled style, it has moments of sinister impact, especially when John Garfield as the gangster is turning up the heat. Mr. Garfield is a sleek and vicious character, a most convincing small-time racketeer."

However, very few readers would remember the esteemed critic's review due to the overwhelming world events that would dominate the news the following day, June 22. In a move that even shocked dictator Josef Stalin into three whole days of indecision, Hitler broke the Nazi-Soviet Pact by ordering German armies to attack the Soviet Union. For Hollywood's Communists, the German dictator had provided for them a kind of moral reprieve. It was now all right for them to hate Nazis again. The resulting propaganda from Hollywood's Communist screenwriters would whitewash the Soviet Union and portray it as the great humanitarian ally against the world's aggressors. Virtually overnight, Communists who called Roosevelt and Churchill "warmongers" and "imperialists" were now agitating for war against Nazi Germany, the same nation they had so recently praised as a nation of peace.

Years later, when referring to the need to protect the secret of the Normandy invasion, Winston Churchill would say that the truth is so precious it must be protected by a bodyguard of lies. In the next four years, Hollywood's Communists, aided and abetted by the Roosevelt administration, wartime censorship boards, and, to some degree, the Breen Office, conspired to hide the truth about the Soviets, and used deceptive means to present them in a positive light before the general public.

There wasn't a better time for the Party faithful to make the world forget that annoying little piece of paper the Soviets gleefully signed with Germany back in August 1939...

III

Bodyguard of Lies (1942–1945)

> If Hitler invaded Hell, I would make at least a favorable reference to the Devil in the House of Commons.
> — Winston Churchill

> No man is justified in doing evil on the ground of expediency.
> — Theodore Roosevelt

After the Japanese sneak attack on Pearl Harbor, America declared war on Japan, which predictably resulted in Nazi Germany declaring war on the United States. Suddenly, the fascists who were attacking the Soviet Union were now wartime allies with the fascists who had attacked the United States on December 7, 1941. This disaster would metaphorically put the United States and the Soviet Union in the same bed, though it wouldn't be revealed until shortly after the war just how weak those bedsprings really were.

In the meantime, it was business as usual for Hollywood and its sizable Marxist community.

On March 5, 1942, Paramount released *The Remarkable Andrew*, a film that attacked capitalist bankers and corrupt politicians. Based on the short story by Dalton Trumbo, which he later expanded into a novel, it tells how small-town clerk Andrew Long (William Holden, just before he enlisted in the army) discovers embezzlement in his bank. Framed by the crooked fat cat bankers and town elders, he is locked up and is in the depths of despair until he is visited by the ghosts of *real* Americans. Though the Seminoles, Creeks and other southern tribes might have a problem seeing General Andrew Jackson (Brian Donlevy) as a hero, one must wonder why Trumbo also included Jesse James (an up-and-coming Rod Cameron) for "hero" status as well. Also visiting the young man is George Washington (Montagu Love), and Thomas Jefferson (Gilbert Emery), apparently taking a time-out from Sally Hemmings.

Trumbo made sure that the film was full of controversial lines. For instance, at one point Jackson admonishes Andrew for thinking he could actually get a square deal in America: "You've been dealing with politicians. You've been standing up for your rights, haven't you? Naturally, you landed in jail."

This controversy in the material wasn't missed by Paramount executives or the Breen Office's Charles R. Metzger. In a report filed on June 17, 1941, Metzger wrote this telling paragraph:

"[Paramount executive] Mr. Luraschi particularly was aware of the dangerous angles connected with this story, more especially as to the possible communistic angles and the showing of democracy in an unfavorable light."[1]

Because the novel was written during the Nazi-Soviet Pact, Trumbo, still following the isolationism that the Party demanded of its members, also has Jackson make a case for letting foreign nations under attack simply *get conquered!* When Andrew tells the general about the then-current world war, Jackson chortles that the "British and the Hessians [Germans]" should "blast each other from the face of the earth!" At another point, in a thinly veiled attack on lend-lease efforts to aid the British, Trumbo has Jackson say, "There's no point in cooking up an alliance with a country that's already licked." Though this remark is meant to refer to Nazi conquests, particularly their attacks on England, it can also be seen as a defense of Soviet aggression in Poland and Finland.

However, by 1942, months after the Nazis attacked the Soviet Union, Communist screenwriter Ring Lardner wryly noted that Trumbo "no longer found his pacifism tenable."[2]

Still, Trumbo survived the war years and prospered. Hired by mighty MGM, the screenwriter would be in the flower of his screenwriting phase, with wartime classics like *A Guy Named Joe* and *Thirty Seconds Over Tokyo* in the offing.

And few would read between the pro-totalitarian lines of *The Remarkable Andrew*, a film where a "common man" like Andrew Long argues for democracy in an American court of law, while agreeing with his ghostly visitors that it should die everywhere else.

Meanwhile, as Trumbo was having his characters talk to Colonial Era ghosts, Paramount released a film exactly one week after *The Remarkable Andrew* that seemed far more relevant to the international situation.

"Lover without a heart ... killer without a conscience!" screamed the tagline for the studio's newest thriller, a skillfully blended hodgepodge of gangster film and wartime melodrama. Based on the novel by Graham Greene, *This Gun for Hire* made a fortune for Paramount; boosted Alan Ladd to stardom; helped augment the stereotype of the "good gangster" who murders, yet still fights for his country; and brought Communist screenwriter Albert Maltz back to the forefront of Hollywood screenwriters with a bang.

However, the screenplay was based on a novel by an icon of British literature.

Graham Greene had written his novel *A Gun for Sale* in 1936. During the late 1930s, he became an entertainment critic for the *Spectator*. His critiques were distinguished not only by a certain snobbery toward Hollywood's output, but by a withering scorn toward any American film that promoted patriotism. Even his criticism of the anti–Nazi *Confessions of a Nazi Spy*, while supposedly praising the film's ability to take a stand, was laced with nitpicking sarcasm:

> Our children must be allowed to hate, and we can really feel, when the British Board of Film Censors abandons the policy of appeasement, that it is really dead at last. So — repressing a slight shudder — let us give as whole-hearted a welcome as we can to this magnificently constructed engine-of-war.[3]

The review is also noteworthy for the fact that Greene praised the performances of Paul Lukas and Francis Lederer while Edward G. Robinson, the star of the film, was not mentioned once.

Coincidentally, Robinson also happened to be a Jew.

From Greene's own pen (and later, mouth), he would gradually be revealed as the perfect example of the British author stuck in a cherished past where everyone was white, Christian and had a sense of entitlement. This is unusual, since the author's left-wing sympathies always appeared to be for the downtrodden. However, when dealing with subject matter concerning Jews, his film reviews were sometimes distinguished by what Greene *didn't* mention as well as what he did; indeed, what he omitted in his reviews said a lot about the man who wrote them.

In his review of *The Life of Emile Zola*, Greene called it "[m]ore pompous than [*The Story of Louis*] *Pasteur* and far more false, this picture's theme is supposed to be the truth — but truth to the film's mind is the word you see on news posters."[4] In other words, Warners' Jewish producers used the film as a euphemism to attack global anti–Semitism, and Germany in particular. After mentioning a scene where Zola proclaims he would never live to see France groveling under "the German heel," Greene brings up the Dreyfus Case, never once mentioning that anti–Semitism was at its core.

Perhaps this attitude would have been considered (especially in those days) nothing more than an unpleasant character trait, but Greene, taking up where Theodore Dreiser left off, was consistent in his hate. And never did his stereotypes seem more vicious than in *A Gun for Sale*.

In the book, James Raven is a mutilated, hare-lipped specimen of sleazy British hit man, hired by unknown powers-that-be to murder a popular antiwar cabinet minister. Using a letter of introduction from his employers, the scar-faced man is able to obtain an audience with the minister. Gazing around the room, Raven notes a framed photograph of "a young Jew, with a small scar on his chin as if he had been struck there with a club...." This young Jew will turn out to be the novel's evil capitalist villain.

After murdering the minister and his elderly female servant, Raven leaves their flat and later notices the Christmas decorations in a shop window. Here, Greene's leftist contempt for the trappings of religion makes itself known, as he uses the gunman as a kind of vicious

ON THE DODGE II. Alan Ladd in a publicity shot for his star-making role in *This Gun for Hire* (1942). The Paramount film removed the social commentary, as well as the anti–Semitism, from Graham Greene's novel *A Gun for Sale*.

commentator. However, the venom will ultimately cross the line from mere atheism into outright bigotry:

> The shop windows were full of tinsel and hard red Christmas berries. It maddened him, the sentiment of it.... A Jewish girl with a neat curved figure bent over a dummy. He fed his eyes contemptuously on her legs and hips; so much flesh, he thought, on sale in the Christmas window.

Needless to say, Greene not only has this Jewish girl hypocritically advertising Christmas in her shop window (in order to make a buck apparently), but he gives her a lisp. And so, to the horror of the reader, Greene sadistically turns the girl's dialogue into a painful stereotype of someone with a speech impediment ("It's been vewwy much admired," she says of a certain dress). In the same scene, the leftist author even mentions that the girl was "catching the eye of a Dago in a purple suit...."

Apparently, when the author wanted to slam a certain people, whether they be Italians, blacks or Jews, he made them the most repugnant physical specimens in the universe. Years after he wrote *A Gun for Sale*, Greene's review in the *Spectator* of the Yiddish-language film *Yiddle with a Fiddle* (starring a young Molly Picon) leaves no doubt as to his racial preferences. After calling the story "in which even the music seems to have the dignity and patina of age and race," Greene goes on to refer to the film as "full of ugly people in bowler hats ... people of incredible accomplishment happy for a while among themselves on a hill-top while the world dies."[5]

It would be this portrayal of the Jew as an accomplished, selfish and physically ugly specimen of barely acknowledged humanity that would influence the social and international politics of *A Gun for Sale*. (Greene's physically ugly Jewish villains permeate the intrigues of *Brighton Rock* and *Confidential Agent*, as well as other novels.) Though Raven is portrayed as a bigot, Greene never once condemns the killer's hatred; in fact, since the gunman is portrayed as the novel's *real* hero (the heroine's policeman boyfriend is clearly an ineffective second fiddle), his anti–Semitism is portrayed as honest and clean, the brutally frank words of a man of integrity sounding off against "Jewish influence." When Raven finally discovers that the young Jew in the photograph is the multi-millionaire capitalist who is angling for war (so his steel manufacturing firm can reap a windfall from defense contracts), the reader cannot miss the inference: The Jew wants war, and is willing to kill millions of Christians so he can make a profit.

Hitler couldn't have said it any better.

Then again, *A Gun for Sale* is full of British neurotics and socially repugnant people to begin with. In this endlessly talky book, those with religious preoccupations are depicted as slatternly, eccentric and dimwitted losers. Even those women who show up at church are there for a flea market sale, with these God-fearing, pious ladies ready to bowl over *anyone* who gets in their way of a good bargain. (Even the vicar is portrayed as cynical and disillusioned with his job.) Later in the book, a medical student playing a prank on another student realizes that he has nothing to look forward to but a life of middle-class mediocrity full of boring parties and brainless, chattering dullards; in other words, a slow bourgeoisie death. It is set in the fictional Nottwich; the hamlet is actually Greene's mean-spirited attack on the real city of Nottingham. Even the cop hero and dancer heroine are dysfunctional people clinging out of need, not genuine love. Besides them, the hare-lipped gunman is portrayed as Jesus in a trenchcoat.

Eventually, Raven and the heroine agree that the minister whom he murdered was just like them, an ordinary Joe who fought for the little guy. Hence, warmongers killing an antiwar activist are also against "the people." It was probably this element that appealed to leftist screenwriters Albert Maltz and W.R. Burnett. For their screenplay, they switched the setting from rainy Nottingham (Nottwich) to sunny Los Angeles (after brief scenes in San Francisco).

After using his gangster novels *Little Caesar* and *High Sierra* as social commentaries in the 1930s, Burnett later evolved into a reactionary. His later Western novel *Adobe Walls* (written around the time of the Cold War, in 1949), slammed the Apaches (and by extension, other minorities). Using the novel's 19th century setting as a euphemism to attack twentieth century liberals, Burnett likens the efforts of Washington politicians for a peace plan with the Indians as the misguided effort of "bleeding hearts" who seek to maintain a socialist welfare state. However, in 1942, Burnett was hired as a scenarist who knew his gangsters and used them as the cogs in a much larger landscape of capitalist manipulation and chicanery. Raven fit in perfectly with this theme; a gangster used by a "big boss" is portrayed as an anti-hero much more honest and righteous than the society in which he moves.

However, Maltz, being a Communist, was going to use Raven's story as a vehicle to attack super-capitalists who had always been supporting Europe's and Asia's fascists. The film had finished shooting as the Japanese bombed Pearl Harbor. Consequently, Greene's fantasy about a World War in 1936 had become true three years later (though he does not mention Germany or Japan as the other countries). However, unlike the novel (which took a page from World War I), it was not triggered by an assassination — and this time America, a nation the author had always held in contempt, would be involved.

One wonders what the Jewish Maltz must have thought of Greene's anti–Semitic stereotype of the book's villain. Nevertheless, the dedicated Party member had no problem with Greene's slam at capitalist warmongering, and turned the book's Jewish Sir Marcus into the power-hungry, and very gentile, Alvin Brewster (Tully Marshall). Sardonically, Maltz, with Burnett's approval, turned the aging, decrepit Brewster into a twisted version of the anti–Semitic, union-busting, and pro–Nazi industrialist Henry Ford.

Portraying Philip (not James) Raven, Alan Ladd literally shot to stardom in the film, now called *This Gun for Hire* (subsequent copies of the novel would now use this title). Many critics have unjustly called Ladd "a wooden actor," yet there are very few performers who would have been able to pull off the portrayal of a taciturn, monosybillic loner and gunman and turn him into a sex symbol. Maltz and Burnett remove Raven's anti–Semitism, his harelip, his all-around nastiness, his anti–Christmas spirit, and his overall disgust with humanity. Raven's angst is personal, not social or political. (An evil aunt broke his wrist with a hot iron; he kills her, is sent up to reform school, yada, yada.) Similarly, since the capitalist villain can't start a war that had already been going on for three years, the newly christened Brewster is now selling secrets and weaponry to the Japanese, or as Veronica Lake's heroine says, "Japanese birdseed for American soldiers."

As directed by Communist Frank Tuttle, *This Gun for Hire* skillfully enacted a delicate balance between wartime patriotism and an attack on capitalists who betrayed their country by collaboration with fascists. The film marked Maltz's return to major Hollywood screenwriting success after spending the late 1930s as a teacher at New York City's New School for Social Research.

At the climax, Raven is now able to sneak into the villain's Nitro Chemical plant as the company's officers enact a wartime drill by shooting harmless smog throughout the building. The gas drill enacted in the novel becomes, for the film, a more pertinent precaution since America was now really at war. In the book, Greene uses the World War I symbol of a gas mask as the tool in which Raven disguises himself in order to infiltrate Sir Marcus' firm. However, when looking at the film years later, the billowing fog spreading through the company's hallways would remind one of World War II's own particular use of gas — and how it was utilized to destroy a race of people.

In the novel, as Raven holds Sir Marcus at gunpoint, he expresses his contempt in a way Graham Greene was far too comfortable with: "Don't you want to pray? You're a Jew, aren't you? Better people than you believe in a God."

Years later, complaining about Hollywood (and its Jewish producers) in an issue of *International Film Annual*, Greene couldn't help taking another shot:

> The film producer can alter anything. He can turn your tragedy of East End Jewry into a musical comedy at Palm Springs if he wishes.... One gets used to these things and it is a waste of time to resent them. You rake the money, you go on writing for another year or two, you have no just ground for complaint. And the smile in the long run will be on your face. For the book has the longer life.[6]

In the case of *This Gun for Hire*, Greene was sadly mistaken. His novel was populated by nasty, dysfunctional and bigoted characters, who more accurately reflected the author's personality than real human beings. As of this writing, the novel has not been reprinted for twenty-first century readers.

However, Ladd, Tuttle, Maltz and Burnett had collaborated on a screen classic that will last much longer than the hateful words of that overrated "master of suspense," Graham Greene.

In September 1939, with German troops invading the western half of Poland and Soviet forces invading the eastern half, the nation's Jews, already existing under the yolk of Polish anti–Semitism, now had to deal with two more oppressors. However, for the time being anyway, the Red Army had other fish to fry.

In the next few months, the Red Army and NKVD rounded up thousands of Polish army officers, soldiers, intellectuals and other members of the bourgeoisie. They would take these men and march them back into the Soviet Union, after which they would be transferred to some 138 prisons around the country.

However, in the spring of 1940, in the prison camp in the Katyn forest several miles outside the small town of Smolensk in Soviet-occupied Byelorussia, the NKVD took what was first assumed to be 4,430 of these men out into the woods. Later it would be revealed that more than 9,000 men were in this group, with thousands more soldiers and civilians unaccounted for. What would happen to these men had already been duly reported to the Soviet government from the field.

According to a memo marked STRICTLY CONFIDENTIAL and addressed to the Communist Party Central Committee, dated March 5, 1940, NKVD Chief Lavrenti Beria wrote:

> I. To instruct the NKVD of the USSR that:
> 1/ the cases of 14,700 people — members of various counter-revolutionary spy and sabotage organizations, former landowners, factory owners, former Polish army officers, government officials and fugitives arrested and remaining in prisons in the western districts of Ukraine and Byelorussia — be considered in a special manner with the obligatory sentence of capital punishment — execution by firing squad.[7]

However, the term "firing squad" implied a group of men punishing the condemned while actually facing them. The Polish officers herded into the depths of the Katyn forest were denied even this show of respect. With almost frightening dispatch, NKVD troops shot thousands of men in the base of the skull and pitched their bodies into mass graves, never once having looked into the eyes of their victims as they killed them.

Three years later, after Nazi forces attacked the Soviet Union and overran the town of Smolensk, a lone wolf, hungry for food, started sniffing among the hundreds of mounds in the topsoil around the Katyn forest. The animal was soon joined by other wolves and, doing what wolves did best in their search for food, started digging up the ground. By the time German troops arrived to check out the prison campgrounds, they easily discovered the now-exposed corpses. Besides making this blunder, the NKVD had goofed royally on another detail: The dead men still had their identification papers and pictures of their families in their uniforms. Obviously these men were captured Polish soldiers and civilians.

The news made its way to the highest levels of the Nazi government and Joseph Goebbels personally ordered German forensic scientists to spare no expense in discovering how these men died. With typical German efficiency, the scientists soon came to the inescapable conclusion, inevitably broadcast to the world on April 13, 1943, that the Polish officers and civilian personnel were shot in the back of the head by agents of the NKVD.

Even the method of death was typical NKVD, though a bullet in either the nape of the neck or the base of the skull had also been used by the Gestapo, who called the method "the Nackenschuss." Ironically, the NKVD had killed the Poles with bullets later found to have been made in Germany. These bullets were probably shipped to the Soviet Union during the Nazi-Soviet Pact.

Stalin would deny the charge that his men murdered the Poles, and the Soviets referred to the accusations as "Nazi propaganda." However, Goebbels had invited (or more likely *ordered*) scientists from Nazi-occupied countries, with not one German among them, to ascertain the findings for themselves. They even brought, under guard, captured Allied soldiers to witness the findings. American P.O.W. Lt. Colonel H. Van Viet Jr. told army investigators in 1950:

> I believe the Russians did it. I hated the Germans. I didn't want to believe them. I believed the Germans would do their best to convince me that Russia was guilty.... It was only with great reluctance that I decided finally that it must be true.[8]

Stalin's allies, the same ones who did nothing about the Holocaust, also did nothing about the Katyn Forest Massacre. They wanted to keep the Soviets as allies against Germany. After the Nazis were driven out of Smolensk and the Red Army took control of the area (as well as the ubiquitous NKVD returning to the scene of their crime), the Soviets ordered a *new* study of the Katyn murders. And if anyone had any doubts as to who would *really* be deemed responsible for the massacre, the title of this less-than-impartial agency gave us a clue: The Special Commission for Ascertaining and Investigating the Circumstances in the Shooting of Polish Officer Prisoners by the German Fascist Invaders in the Katyn Forest.

Though the Soviets had murdered these men in the winter of 1940, the "impartial" commission, parroting the Soviet government, found that the Nazis had murdered them when they conquered the area in the summer of 1941. Other observers were invited to corroborate the Soviets' "findings," including Catherine Harriman, the 25-year-old daughter of the U.S. ambassador to the Soviet Union, Averill Harriman. But then Ms. Harriman asked the Soviets an embarrassing question: If the Poles were murdered in the summer of 1941, why were they all wearing heavy winter coats? At first, Soviet officials got flustered;

then they claimed that the day the men were murdered was unusually cold for that time of year.

Meanwhile, as the bones of dead Polish officers continued to rot in the grounds of Katyn, Warner Brothers decided to film a love letter to their murderers.

"He gives the impression which is composed and wise. His brown eye is exceedingly kind and gentle. A child would like to sit in his lap. And a dog would sidle up to him."[9] This was written by former ambassador to the Soviet Union, Joseph P. Davies, in the memoir of his years in the U.S.S.R., *Mission to Moscow*. The person he was waxing enthusiastic about was Soviet dictator Josef Stalin.

In the summer of 1942, at FDR's insistence, Jack L. Warner had green-lighted the filming of Davies' book, which seemed especially timely in view of the new Soviet-American alliance — an unholy union that we now know was based on evasions, deceit, expediency and bottomless ignorance of the facts.

Or as producer Robert Buckley stated in a letter of August 24 to "Colonel" Jack Warner*:

> We are all convinced that we can make a truly great and important picture from *Mission to Moscow*, but we also agree that the vital facts should be faced squarely and honestly, without pulling any punches or compromising for any squeamish reason whatsoever.[11]

The making of the film was not a road paved with good intentions, but a road paved with substandard asphalt.

In a letter dated February 3, 1943, Herman Lissauer, head of Warners' Research Department, apprised the film's technical advisor, Jay Leyda, of a little problem: "Mr. Buckner feels we ought to go to the Russian Consulate for the Russian text of the NON-AGGRESSION PACT between Germany and Russia but that we ought to try to work out something here that would save us the trouble." Ah yes, that nasty, inconvenient "non-aggression pact." Indeed, if one wanted to clean up the image of the Soviet Union being a peace-loving nation, how the hell was the studio going to ignore *that*?

Now we go into some of the personalities who were *really* responsible for the film's pro-Soviet point of view. Though the film was directed by Michael Curtiz and starred liberal actor Walter Huston, the screenplay (based on Davies' book) was by Howard Koch. Blacklisted in the early 1950s, the screenwriter was always mistakenly referred to as a "liberal" in later years; a harmless, politically moderate kind of guy unfairly condemned by the Right. Actually, by his screenplay for this picture, as well as his fanatical statements about Stalin's Russia, Koch demonstrated that he was about as moderate as John Howard Lawson, whom, Koch outrageously claimed, might have "made sainthood."[12]

In fact, it was quite possible that Koch was a secret Party member. As a co-author of the screenplay of *Casablanca*, Koch made a case for a united fight against fascism, an attitude he noticeably didn't have when he backed the Nazi-Soviet Pact. In *Mission to Moscow*, he wrote a scene early in the film in which Ethiopia's Haile Selassie condemns Mussolini's aggression in Africa while the ambassadors of the world's democracies ignore him. The only one to condemn the fascists is Soviet Foreign Minister Maxim Litvinov. Koch doesn't bother to mention that at the time of the infamous Pact, Stalin replaced the Jewish Litvinov with the gentile Vyachalev Molotov so as not to turn off his new Nazi allies.

---

*The studio head leaned on Washington to give him a military commission, which was amazing since Warner had never fought in any military battles, led any soldiers, or ever once made an appearance in a war zone.

III. Bodyguard of Lies (1942–1945) 121

But the scene was a withering condemnation of capitalist appeasement, as the supposedly neutral Koch gloated decades later in his 1979 autobiography *As Time Goes By*: "Let the Soviet-haters scream!"[13]

And scream they did — justifiably. Aiding Koch in his whitewash was the film's supposedly impartial technical advisor, the infamous Jay Leyda. A hardline Stalinist, skilled archivist, former assistant to Eisenstein, and somewhat of an expert on Herman Melville, Leyda had a direct pipeline to the Kremlin (that is, through the Comintern) and had the distinction of receiving their personal input into just how Stalin and the U.S.S.R. were going to be portrayed. Tragically, a former American ambassador enthusiastically added to Koch and Leyda's lies.

In *Red Star Over Hollywood: The Film Colony's Long Romance with the Left*, Ronald and Allan Radosh wrote:

> One of the changes that the former ambassador [Davies] demanded was that the film include the claim that Finland was not invaded by the Soviet Union in 1939. Producer Bob Buckner bridled, not realizing that both Koch and Jay Leyda welcomed this falsehood as a propaganda coup and enjoyed being able to attribute its assertion to Davies.

In the film itself, businessman Joseph P. Davies (Walter Huston) is appointed by FDR to be the ambassador to the Soviet Union. Accompanied by his wife (Ann Harding), he travels to Moscow, but first must pass through Germany. It is the late 1930s, and Davies

THE SHOW TRIAL MUST GO ON. Several unidentified extras populate the jury in Warners' *Mission to Moscow* (1943), the film version of Joseph Davies' book. Like the book, the film excuses the Soviet Union's show trials. Manart Kippen (first row, right end) plays a kindly Josef Stalin; John Abbott is the juror in the second row in the light suit.

accurately guesses that German officials are being rather sneaky about something; this is ridiculously obvious when one notices how the Germans comically shush themselves before revealing their plans for world conquest by some badly timed slips of the tongue. Davies also notices the rather horrifying spectacle of German youths doing military marches.

However, when they arrive in Moscow, they meet a smiling citizenry that has apparently forgotten their own problems with midnight callers and concentration camps. Soviet officials are portrayed as wiser than Methuselah and they can predict the future far more accurately than Nostradamus. All of them, in fact, *know* that the Germans are up to something very, very bad. This belies the fact that Stalin, in order not to insult his German allies at the time of the Pact, had anyone who warned him of Nazi military moves on the Russian border (the Soviets, remember, annexed half of Poland) arrested and quickly shot — including members of his own military and intelligence apparatus.

Then came the Moscow Show Trials, the pride and joy of the world's leftist "intellectuals." In the film, just as in real life, Davies actually believed that the poor bastards in the dock were all agents of Trotsky, who, Koch and Leyda inform us, was a Nazi collaborator.

Totally forgotten was the fact that Trotsky and his wife, after escaping Stalin's Russia, were chased out of every European country in which they thought they had found sanctuary, chased out under pressure by Stalin's government as well as Hitler's. In 1940, an NKVD assassin finally murdered Trotsky in Mexico by imbedding an ax (some say an ice pick) in his skull. After the murderer served his time in Mexico, he returned to the Soviet Union and was promptly hailed as a hero by the government.

Letters found in Warner studio files show a busy correspondence between Robert Buckner, Jack Warner, Chicago attorney Albert Goldman and studio legal counsel Roy Obringer concerning the feasibility of libeling the now-dead Leon Trotsky as a Nazi collaborator. Goldman had been looking after the interests of the still-living *Mrs.* Trotsky. In a letter to the Warner legal department dated October 14, 1942, Goldman was brutally frank in his assertions:

> It is a fact that *all* allegations made in the course of those frame-up trials, either by the prosecution or by any of the defendants or witnesses intimating that Trotsky had any connection with Hitler have been *proved* complete falsehoods.[14]

In fact, Koch's original script even had a scene between an outrageously sinister Trotsky and Nazi Foreign Minister Joachim von Ribbentrop in which the former Bolshevik icon gloats over taking over the Soviet Union. Goldman's implied threat of litigation forced Wallis and Curtiz to cut the offending sequence from the script.

Another problem for the filmmakers were the accusations that Warners played fast and loose with the actual transcripts of the show trials. In a letter to studio official Charles Einfield, dated September 28, 1943, Buckner wrote:

> The trial of the conspirators in *Mission to Moscow* is almost a verbatim transcription from the actual report of the trial as published by the Soviet Government.... Naturally, we had to condense the enormous mass of testimony for picture purposes, but at least 90% of the dialogue was taken directly from the published report. We were especially careful about this matter because we didn't want to be open to the charge of rewriting history.[15]

In reality, it shouldn't surprise anyone that Buckner and company actually did use the transcripts the Soviets gave the media since they weren't about to publish the *real* transcripts. Soviet Prosecutor Andrei Vishinsky, without a doubt one of the most evil, vindictive men ever to hold such a powerful post, was known, as was the manner of the Stalinists, to fire his questions and deliver his summations in true Bolshevik/schoolyard fashion. Those poor souls who had the misfortune to appear before him on the witness stand were routinely called "mad dogs," "wreckers" and "filthy curs," language unbecoming to barristers in most other parts of the world. All this infantile name-calling had been shouted at the top of the allegedly impartial prosecutor's lungs (witnesses even noticed Vishinsky frothing at the mouth several times) — and this was subtle in comparison to his frequent descent into language that would have made an NKVD torturer blush.

Of course, Koch and Leyda knew the truth, and it seems they effectively suckered the sincere Buckner into swallowing the bilge that the transcripts they used were authentic.

In the film, the Russian people are portrayed as happy and prosperous. Ayn Rand may have been a right-wing activist, but she was correct in her assessment that the portrayal of the Russian citizenry in *Mission to Moscow* was totally false. Writers and historians, many of them interested in whitewashing the Soviet regime, slammed Rand for her testimony before HUAC — particularly her assertion that no one in Russia smiled. Many of these leftists obviously had never lived in a nation where people routinely informed on their neighbors and police took them away, never to be seen again; where merely putting one's coffee cup on a newspaper picture of Stalin was a sure death sentence; or where those factory workers who screwed up the manufacture of a product were accused of being "wreckers" and "saboteurs" and quietly shot — with entire families that had nothing to do with the alleged "crime" also taken away and shot with them — or worked to death in concentration camps (or the kinder word, *gulags*).

Try smiling in a country like that and it would be a good bet you're on laughing gas...

Though not laughing, the film brought big smiles from "the usual suspects." In a letter to "Colonel" Jack Warner shortly after the film's New York and Washington premieres, Alvah Bessie wrote:

> I trust you will pardon my presumption in offering you my personal gratitude for *Mission to Moscow*.... You cannot help but be aware how mighty a weapon *Mission to Moscow* offers for our inevitable victory over fascism. It has the power of divisions of well-equipped troops; there can be no doubt of it.... The existence of the Union of Soviet Socialist Republics is, in my opinion, one of the greatest *facts* of our time. For many years now, those of us who have urged a closer understanding and an alliance with the Soviet Union have felt that this great fact would yet emerge — and that when people understand it, they too would see that such an alliance was the strongest guarantee of peace and freedom from aggression.

"Peace" and "freedom from aggression," two phrases that emphatically do *not* bring the Soviet Union to mind. However, shortly after Bessie's letter, another Communist screenwriter aired his two cents to "Colonel" Warner. Printed with the letterhead of his new (and lower budgeted) home studio, Republic Pictures, former Warner alumnus John Bright's letter was practically a carbon copy of Bessie's:

> All my trifling criticisms and differences were forgotten at the theater last night, engulfed by the admiration for the courage and patriotism of our organization, I actually experienced a glow of old school pride.
> This morning I read Dorothy Thompson's petty and irritable attack upon the picture. To state that I disagree with her and in indignation, is unimportant; I am saddened that liberals cannot stand together in defense of a film which does so much for democracy and for ultimate world peace.

Leftist playwright and scenarist Edward Chodorov even got into the act, writing Warner on July 20. In a letter slamming the "Writers' War Board," Chodorov takes issue with the group's audacity in challenging the accuracy of the film:

> [The Board] did not criticize [the film] on artistic grounds, but if you please, historic ones. *They* decided it falsified history. They blandly ignored the fact that a controversy rages and just passed judgment. And this is from a quasi-official board. A group of us in New York got together to tell these gentlemen, or whoever speaks for them, what we thought of such idiotic tactics.

After offering to give Warner "a list of native fascists," that is, those who "might want to beat Hitler, but save fascism for the world," Chodorov continued,

> [T]ake your bitterest critics of *Mission to Moscow* and you will find them there. I am not acquainted with the liberal fight in America and the old enemies we always had are the same dubious gang in high and low places who are screaming the loudest about *Mission*. But the louder they scream, the more you know you have done the right job.

The vultures were cawing their usual noise. Those who attacked the film's accuracy *must* be fascists. Echoing his first letter, Alvah Bessie again praised Jack Warner for trying to "create a better understanding between nations." How so much would change in two short years. By the spring of 1945, with the Nazis beaten and the Soviets not needing American help any more, the Party attacked their former allies with a vengeance. So much for a "better understanding between nations." On a more personal level, Bessie had no kind words for Jack Warner when the mogul kicked him out of the studio in 1945 for backing the striking Conference of Studio Unions.

However, in 1943, Jack Warner swallowed this Communist praise hook, line and sinker. In a letter to Robert Buckner, dated May 22, the studio head even called the film's critics "facists" [*sic*].

But the final word may have come from a man whose own questionable politics and controversial persona vastly influenced the times in which he lived. In a personal telegram to Warner, dated May 20, William Randolph Hearst had his own take on the film—and it wasn't pretty. After the opener "I certainly do not wish anything to impair our friendship," and that any criticism of Warner films "will not be considered an unfriendly act," the publisher praised Professor John Dewey and Suzanne LaFollette for slamming the accuracy of *Mission to Moscow*. Then the model for Orson Welles' *Citizen Kane* let J.L. have it right between the eyes:

> You say our papers "should state the other side of the case in reply to such attacks as Dewey and LaFollette."
> Your film, Mr. Warner, gives "the other side of the case"—the Communist side—quite completely.
> I think it is quite as much the duty of the American press to defend democracy against Bolshevism as against fascism or Nazism or any other form of totalitarian tyranny.
> I am sorry that we disagree on the proper function of the press—and of the moving picture. But I am sure you will realize that our attitude toward your screen product (an attitude so frequently favorable, but in this case, frankly critical) is guided by no personal unfriendliness, but merely by a sense of public duty.

Hearst himself had certainly done much to bestow a kind of legitimacy to fascism during the 1930s, so portraying totalitarians in a positive way was something he definitely knew about.

Yet even in 1943, upon the film's general release, the public was clearly appalled by the ridiculous spectacle of a kindly, wise Stalin doling out advice to an American ambassador, as well as the bizarre sight of an affluent Soviet Union full of happy, prosperous citizens. The film tanked, and tanked *big*. Warner and company, always accused of leaning to the left, this time had gone too far. A film praising the working class was all right; a film slamming our Nazi enemies was fantastic; a film that was a cinematic love letter to a nation of arrogant bullies hiding behind a flag of "peace and freedom" and run by a psychopathic madman on a par with Hitler was a different matter altogether.

More to the point, the film would come back to haunt Jack Warner years later when he was called before HUAC. After previously slamming the film's critics as "facists," the studio head now had to eat his own misspelled words.

That's show biz...

> Am very enthusiastic about the script. Cast and the possibilities the picture affords together with thought that we can do as much for Merchant Marines as we did for the Navy *Submarine D-1, Here Comes the Navy* and *Devil Dogs of the Air*. I will do all in my power to make it one of the best.[16]

So wrote director Lloyd Bacon to his boss, Jack Warner, in a telegram dated September 3, 1942. Unfortunately, Bacon's professed "enthusiasm" didn't last beyond a few months into the project, titled *Action in the North Atlantic*. Midway through filming, Bacon's contract with the studio ran out. Warner told him, "Finish the picture and we'll talk about it," but Bacon wasn't going to talk about anything with the brothers Warner until he put his John Hancock on a studio contract. Predictably, Warner fired him and brought in their special

CHARTING A COURSE. **Humphrey Bogart and Raymond Massey as officers of a Marine Merchant ship in *Action in the North Atlantic* (1943). John Howard Lawson's screenplay emphasized the wartime contribution of the Communist-dominated Maritime Union.**

effects man, Byron Haskin, to direct. Haskin, who would be responsible for filming the later Cold War paranoid sci-fi *The War of the Worlds*, was the right man to handle the various explosions and fires scattered throughout the picture. Yet even this expertise wasn't enough for Warner, who also threw Raoul Walsh into the project to punch up the already over-the-top action footage.[17]

The movie was based on a screen story by Guy Gilpatric; the screenplay credit went to that old hand at Marxist dogma, John Howard Lawson, though with "added dialogue" credit going to A.I. Bezzerides (who would do the screenplay for the classic *Kiss Me Deadly* in 1955) and W.R. Burnett. These added screenwriter credits obviously meant that the words coming out of the mouths of Lawson's characters were altered in order to tone down any leftist speeches.

This little fact was underlined by Lawson's biographer, Gerald Horne, in *The Final Victim of the Blacklist, John Howard Lawson, Dean of the Hollywood Ten*: "As often happened with Lawson's ambitious screenplays, this one was whittled down by studio executives, film censors, and the presumed dictates of the box office."

Then Horne criticizes the film's production values as "chintzy." This critique actually parroted a comment by Lawson: "The fleet of ships that made up the convoy consisted of miniature vessels manipulated on a small bay in Santa Barbara."[18]

Both comments were rather unfair. Considering the times the film was made in, with the then-primitive special effects of the day, Haskin and the Warners special effects department do a commendable job with the various scenes of smoke, carnage, sea collisions and torpedo explosions. Indeed, only the Lydecker brothers at Republic could match the good work done here.

The film was a tribute to the Communist-dominated National Maritime Union, though, of course, Lawson didn't mention the union's pro–Soviet political stance (which the studio wouldn't have allowed anyway). Joe Rossi (Humphrey Bogart) is the first mate of the *Liberty*, a Merchant Marine ship delivering supplies to Murmansk, U.S.S.R.; his friend, Steve Jarvis (Raymond Massey) is the ship's captain. Joe is a womanizer from way back, and apparently, as the saying goes, has a girl in every port. Though it might be hard for some to accept the then 44-year-old Bogart as a womanizer, remember that the actor *did* eventually seduce and marry a 21-year-old Lauren Bacall. However, adding to the off-screen realities behind the movie image, Bogie was perfectly at ease playing a seaman. As a veteran of the U.S. Navy during World War I, Bogart was on a battleship when, during an attack by German vessels, an explosion scarred his lip, forever giving audiences the famous lisp that would add to his tough guy image. In his off-screen hours, besides boozing, the sea was his great love, and with his own boat, the *Santana* (which would later be the name for his production company), he became an even better seaman than he was during the war.

Since the *Liberty* was a supply ship, it has no weapons to protect itself when a Nazi U-boat sinks it. Most of the crewmen escape, with the possible exception of Glenn Strange in one his rare non-western, non-horror roles. The crew is played by Warner contract players Dane Clark (as the emotional, not-too-bright Pulaski), Alan Hale (as O'Hara), a Jewish sailor named Chips Abrams (Jewish Broadway veteran Sam Levene) and Peter Whitney (as the kitten-loving Whitey).

After the torpedoing, the Nazis not only ram the sailors' lifeboat for good measure, but then sail away into the night, laughing uproariously. At this point, Captain Jarvis waves his fist and promises revenge on the Aryan U-boaters. Here, we see Massey give the old

John Brown fire and intensity as he convincingly delivers his threat. When Rossi reminds him that the Nazis can no longer hear him, Jarvis replies, "No, but God can."

In her politically biased *Running Time: Films of the Cold War*, Nora Sayre commented: "[S]ome of the Communist screenwriters weren't at all shy of God.... *Action in the North Atlantic* proves that almost no one wrote more passionately patriotic movies than American Communists did in wartime."

However, Sayre's rather dubious claim misses the point of Communist objectives vis-à-vis the American media. No Communist artist was going to openly say damn God and damn religion, not if he wanted to stay employed in a God-fearing nation like America; you can't use the medium of film to influence anyone if you're on the unemployment line. According to Stephen Koch in his excellent *Double Lives: Spies and Writers in the Secret Soviet War of Ideas in the West*, the Comintern, which was supported by Hollywood's Red screenwriters, was never going to openly seek the overthrow of the American democratic system or attack its Constitutional guarantee of religious freedom. If Communist screenwriters had to use God's name in vain in order to stay in the industry and manipulate it, so be it. If they had to look and sound more American than Americans themselves, so be it. This explains why Lawson's script, as well as those of other Marxist scenarists, contain so many references to God and Jesus Christ, even more so than the works of so-called "conservative" screenwriters, who certainly had nothing to prove by constantly mentioning God and patriotism all the time.

In fact, one of Lawson's major pro-religious lines is said by Abrams: "I got faith in God, President Roosevelt and the Brooklyn Dodgers, in that order of importance." Karl Marx must have been spinning in his grave.

After Rossi hits dry-dock, he goes to a club and picks up a singer named Pearl (Warner contract actress Julie Bishop, whose singing is dubbed in this sequence). Then, in true Production Code fashion, after barely knowing her, chronic womanizer Rossi marries the singer. Predictably, the Production Code office had trouble with the "suggestiveness" of her song lyrics. This "offensive" song is replaced by Cole Porter's *Night and Day* (which Warners would use as the title of their Porter biopic three years later).

Back on their new vessel, the old crew is now part of a military convoy, and sets out to deliver those damn supplies to Murmansk. However, during one rather violent attack by a U-boat wolf-pack, our heroes' ship is all alone during a night fog when that exact same U-boat that sank them before just happens to be trailing them. Now it is a game of cat-and-mouse, or, more likely, shark and barracuda.

In Lawson's original version of the script, to emphasize the crew's ethnic mix, a black sailor worked in the ship's pantry. During one scene, he asks everyone why *he* should fight. Though Lawson is trying to bring out black anger about racism, his plausibility, as usual, is non-existent; for why would this black sailor ask why he should fight if he's *already* on a ship doing its part in the war? The time to ask that question would have been before he joined up!

Also, Lawson (or possibly screenwriter Gilpatric) created a Latino character. In a letter dated August 11, 1942, Joseph Breen cautioned Jack Warner, "We assume that the Portuguese Tony Gonzales will be handled throughout so as not to give any offense to the Latin-Americans." Breen had no reason to worry about this at all. Backed by Warners, Burnett and Bezzerides cut out both Tony and his fellow black crewman.

All through Breen's letter of August 11, the censor warns the studio against scenes of "sexual suggestiveness" between Rossi and Pearl (hence, they get married after just one quick scene); as well as "unacceptable gruesomeness" in scenes showing sailors getting mutilated during U-boat attacks. This included the classic suggestion: "The killing of the little kitten should be suggested rather than shown." He also wanted the deletion of a scene showing a sailor "chopped up by the propeller," and a bit "where the shark is wounded and eaten by his fellows."

Perhaps more controversial, though apparently a common practice in anti–Catholic England: "In Scene 113, the business of Johnny and O'Hara 'crossing themselves' will be deleted by the British Board of Film censors." Breen even complains about a sailor thumbing his nose at the laughing U-boat crewmen, considering it "a derisive gesture." (Wasn't that the point?) Instead, we see the American sailors ridiculously giving the Germans the thumbs-up sign, giving audiences the inescapable conclusion that these victims of Nazi aggression were wishing their enemies luck! Even O'Hara giving Hitler a "razzberry" over the radio was considered offensive since "this is on the list of prohibited sounds which may come from the screen." In the film, the radio announcer cuts off O'Hara before he can make the forbidden noise.

After Rossi takes command (Jarvis was wounded in the leg), he reads the last rites at the sea burial of dead crewmen. Unfortunately, Bogart, with his thick New York accent and tough-guy manner, is less than convincing during this solemn scene.

Then the final attack comes. By fooling the Nazis into thinking their ship was on fire, the U-boat takes Rossi's bait and comes to the surface. Blinded by smoke, the U-boat crew does not see the ship coming out of the fog and is too late to avoid the destructive crash. As Jarvis had promised, the Americans slice through the U-boat like a piece of cheese. The audience is encouraged to applaud as the screaming Nazis go to their watery graves.

Finally, the crew docks at Murmansk. We see gorgeous, babuska-wearing Russian babes (played by gorgeous, babuska-wearing Southern California babes) help bring the ship in, as they are backed by cheering crowds of happy Russian citizens. As written by Lawson, this scene is, quite plainly, absolute nonsense. At no time during the duration of the war were Russian citizens encouraged to applaud their American allies, and certainly not while they were on a pier where the Red Army was receiving much-needed American supplies. Any support shown to Americans or any other allies would have sent the offender to a Soviet concentration camp. Also, the American crew that unloaded and delivered the supplies were not even allowed to go on shore, and were blocked from leaving the piers by armed NKVD men.

Lawson omitted another crucial fact about the Soviet-American alliance: The Soviets accepted American aid while hating our guts for having to ask us for it. While damning capitalism, the Bolsheviks freely accepted the products of capitalism in their fight against the German invader. As historian Brian Moynihan revealed in his *The Russian Century: The History of the Last Hundred Years*:

> Two-thirds of Red Army trucks were American. Aid had started even before the U.S. entered the war.... Arctic convoys ran a gauntlet of U-boats and bombers in ice floes, drifting fog and heavy seas. The Russians provided no naval or air support. The crew of the City of Joliet was bombed eight times by torpedo and eight times by bombers in a day. The crews were not welcome; the dock laborers were prisoners under NKVD guard. The effort was immense. The Americans largely clothed, shod, fed and transported the Red Army. Enough cloth was sent for 54 million uniforms, together with 1.5 million dollars worth of buttons to do them up. Red soldiers marched on 14.5 million pairs of U.S. boots. They ate a quarter million tons of Tushonka canned pork produced to a Russian formula by Midwestern packers. Red Army cooks used corn oil from Cedar Rapids and Pillsbury flour from Minneapolis. As well as the trucks—

409,526 of them — the Russians were supplied with tens of thousands of Willys Jeeps.... Freighters supplied enough railroad equipment for a new trans–Siberian. Russian mobility, which so terrified increasingly horse-bound German units, was American-engineered.[19]

After an American ambassador named Standley accused the Soviets of having little gratitude, Foreign Minister Vyacheslav Molotov arrogantly claimed, "Every man in the street knows that we are getting lend-lease supplies." "That may be so," replied Standley, "but we have no contact with the man in the street. The man in the street does not dare talk to us."[20]

When *Action in the North Atlantic* was released nationally on June 12, 1943, the American man in the street made it a box office winner; the film made more money than even *Yankee Doodle Dandy*. Though Lawson, as usual, was unsatisfied with the finished film, where he *again* complained about outside tampering with his prized words, the end result is still, to this day, an entertaining World War II action film.

Just try to remember that the cheering Russians on the docks at the end of the film probably had bayonets in their backs.

Meanwhile, as Hollywood's romance with the Soviet Union reached its apex, the Red Army proved their resolve by retaking the city of Kharkov from the Germans in the spring of 1943. While in Kharkov, the Nazis had murdered some 35,000 Jews and shipped 120,000 members of the populace to concentration camps in Germany, especially the infamous Sachensausen camp in Orenienberg, which "specialized" in political prisoners of a Communist stripe.

At the beginning of the Nazi invasion, Stalin had ordered that all propaganda should encourage citizens to fight the German invader, not for the sake of Marxism, but for "Mother Russia." However, shortly after the retaking of Kharkov, as historian Brian Moynihan wrote, "Now the Party and its ideological baggage came out of the closet." After the Germans retreated, the miserable citizens of Kharkov could hardly celebrate their "liberation." As in other newly liberated Russian cities, the NKVD was back in force as soon as the last German left. With little hesitation, they continued the killing of the populace that the Germans started. As many Red Army prisoners of war would find out, to their horror, Josef Stalin had no tolerance with those Russians who were "contaminated" by outsiders. Though the NKVD was also liquidating those whom they perceived as having helped the Germans, it was obvious that the agency never really bothered to sort out the "traitors" from the loyal citizenry.

With the loss of Kharkov, the Germans held the city of Orel to the north; with the Red Army massed in a salient west of Kharkov, a battle royal was in the offing. In fact, as the Germans continued to hold the area north of Kharkov, Soviet commander Marshal Zhukov convinced Stalin to launch an attack on the Germans in the summer when Soviet tanks would have time to ring the area. (During the early years of the war, Stalin had impatiently ordered attack after attack, not on the advice of his military advisors, but to augment the anniversary of a Bolshevik victory during the civil war. This rash policy led to many of the Red Army's worst defeats. Needless to say, Stalin blamed his senior officers.)

The salient the Russians held was about one hundred miles wide and eighty miles long, but this barely noticeable area of rolling plain interspersed with streams and valleys would be the locale of one of the most horrific battles of the war. The Germans, seeking to dislodge the Soviets from the area, referred to their own planned offensive as "Citadel," but few Russians of the day would ever forget the battleground that was always known as Kursk.

A Nazi deserter had informed the Russians of the date of the German offensive; it was not known what happened to this man, but we can conclude that, looking at previous examples of Soviet gratitude, he didn't survive the experience.

As Hollywood continued to produce films showing battles between our Russian allies and Nazi armies, none would dare come close to the horrors of Kursk, the bloodiest tank battle in modern warfare. Not as famous as the battle for Stalingrad, Kursk was, in its own way, a more powerful symbol of the Nazi defeat in Russia. For if the Germans couldn't keep a worthless piece of land in the middle of nowhere, how were they going to keep entire cities in their grasp?

On July 3, 1943, two days before Marshal Zhukov ordered his men to strike the German lines at Kursk, Warner Brothers continued their love affair with our Soviet allies by releasing a film that was originally the work of a master of espionage fiction.

"Love in the midst of intrigue!" screamed the publicity blurb, a tagline far more appropriate for *Casablanca*. *Background to Danger* was certainly no *Casablanca*, but unlike the Bogart-Bergman classic, the film was based on a novel by Eric Ambler.

The Bantam editions of Ambler's novel bear the copyright dates of 1937, 1938, 1939, 1940 and then a date of 1943 for the edition published by Alfred A. Knopf, probably a final version of the story to coincide with the release of the Warner film. But the above dates also reveal that the author kept updating his work as the events of the coming world war unfolded. Certainly, the novel itself is set in an unspecified, obviously pre-war time period, taking into account the burning fuse of international intrigue long before the final explosion of global conflict.

Our story begins with a board meeting of the Pan-Eurasian Petroleum Company. The chairman announces that, with nations like fascist Italy purchasing more of the company's oil in Romania, their agreement with the Romanian government be revised, thereby increasing the company's profits. When the nation's Communists react adversely to foreign oil companies extending their claim on Romanian lands, a plot is hatched by secret forces to discredit the Soviet Union.

Meanwhile, at Nuremberg, a down-at-his-heels British newspaper correspondent named Kenton, heading to Austria on the Frankfort-Linz train, meets a shady little man who begs him for help. Explaining that he is a Jewish metallurgist escaping Nazi brutality, the little man begs Kenton to conceal an envelope of currency (all the profits left from his confiscated business) to smuggle past German guards at the Austrian border, since they won't search a foreigner. The little man is also terrified by a hulking stranger in the usual dark topcoat and felt hat peeking in on the compartment he shares with Kenton. With a payment of hard cash, Kenton gets to Austria and not only discovers the little man's corpse in his hotel room, but that the envelope was filled with photos and maps that reveal phony Soviet war plans to attack Romania. As it turns out, the man is not a Jewish refugee, but a turncoat Soviet in the employee of the pro–Nazi villain.

If that isn't enough, the Austrian police are now after Kenton for the murder and his picture is on every newspaper in the country. (You'd think the coming Anschloss would be on their minds instead.) Our hapless Hitchcockian hero is also being trailed by two spies, a brother and sister team of Bolshevik humanity named Andreas and Tamara Zaleshoff. Kenton (like Cary Grant and Joel McCrea in Hitchcock films) is kidnapped by the *real* villain, a sophisticated international spy with the obviously phony name of Colonel Robinson. Robinson had sold his services to foreign powers, including the Soviets, as far back as the

First World War, and now seeks to incite a Romanian war with the U.S.S.R. and increase petroleum profits at the same time.

Because Kenton will not reveal the location of the phony war plans, he is left to the tender mercies of Robinson's sadistic British henchman, Mailler. But before Mailler can repeat a strike at Kenton's head with a blackjack, Kenton is rescued by Andreas Zaleshoff.

As the three bond, it is inferred that the beautiful Tamara is fond of the British newshound, though this affection doesn't get past the fondness stage throughout the book. Indeed, through the book's 245 pages of contrived adventure and death-dealing peril, it is *Andreas* who will be the hero's constant companion. This was done to portray the wily Soviet agent (who is far more colorful than his sister) as a hero worthy of our respect.

While Kenton is locked in a room in Robinson's castle hideout awaiting another beating by Mailler, our international journalist hero (created by an ex-international journalist) ruminates on the men who *really* start all the conflicts in the world:

> It was difficult ... to spend any time in the arena of foreign politics without perceiving that political ideologies had very little to do with the ebb and flow of international relations. It was the power of Business, not the deliberations of statesmen, that shaped the destinies of nations. The Foreign Ministers of the great powers might make the actual declarations of their Governments' policies; but it was the Big Business men, the bankers and their dependents, the arms manufacturers, the oil companies, the big industrialists, who determined what those policies should be. Big Business asked the questions that it wanted to ask when and how it suited it. Big Business also provided the answers.... The Big Business man was only one player in the game of international politics, but he was the player that made all the rules.

Brecht, Hellman and John Howard Lawson couldn't have put it better than that if they tried. The amazing thing about the above paragraphs is that they were written, not by a hard-line member of the Comintern, but a British capitalist espionage writer.

Nevertheless, this anti-capitalism is combined with an admirable portrait of a Soviet agent. Throughout Russian history, their intelligence community, from the early Cheka to the NKVD to the post–Stalin MGB and KGB, and especially those agents who worked under Vladimir Putin, were not exactly the lovable Teddy bears depicted by Eric Ambler. However, his novel claims otherwise. Instead of being agents of repression and sadistic torturers, we have a brother and sister team who are only trying to save their nation from a planned war and, in the process, right wrongs and clear Kenton of murder. Instead of being agents of Soviet tyranny, Andreas is portrayed as a resourceful and cherished ally to our innocent hero, and Tamara is a gorgeous Russian beauty any red-blooded American capitalist boy would want to sleep with.

Though Ambler implicated the Nazis for their treachery (with Colonel Robinson revealed to be an agent in their service), the author also ignored Soviet machinations. Throughout the book, we hear nothing of the Nazi-Soviet Pact or the Soviets' attack on Finland or eastern Poland; nor do we get the impression, even in a pre–Anschluss Austria, that the country was a fascist power long before Hitler invaded. In fact, the novel is an amazing document full of convenient historic omissions from a man who was reportedly an international correspondent in real life.

Though the book is fascinating in its behind-the-scenes boardroom manipulations and political backstabbings which lead to acts of war, with oil being the prime catalyst (the book is ahead of its time in this respect), Ambler's ignorance of Soviet duplicity and a less-than-accurate look at the international political scene do not do the reader justice. Rejecting global realities, the author is forced to rely on old Republic serial standbys for suspense, like locking the hero and his companion in a hot, airless metal container in some old factory.

The NKVD would really laugh at that one...

In a letter to Jack Warner, dated November 6, 1942, Joseph Breen gives his own review of the material submitted for *Background to Danger.* Dated September 26, 1942, the three-page letter is a detailed attempt by the Breen Office to apprise Warners of the international situation *vis-à-vis* Turkey.

But why Turkey? The book is set in Austria, and then ends up in Romania, which is the country that is supposed to be provoked into a war with the Soviets. At this point, even without Ambler's inaccuracies, the location of the plot *had* to be changed by late 1942. When the film was released on July 3 of the following year, the global situation had altered radically: Romania was now a German ally under the leadership of the fascist Iron Guard; and provoking a war with the Soviets, who were already at war with Germany, might be considered a bit redundant. Therefore, scripter W.R. Burnett and the studio conceived the bright idea of Turkey, a nation in a state of neutrality with its European neighbors (with the possible exception of *Greece*, for whom it had always harbored contempt).

After referring to Turkey as "Europe's uneasiest neutral," Breen outlines his objections, a few of which are worth quoting:

> Unintentionally the script creates the impression that should anything happen to disturb Turkey's neutrality, it is likely that she would be easy pickings for Germany. It is also suggested

DON'T BOTHER TO KNOCK. **Peter Lorre as a Soviet agent and George Raft as an American one in** *Background to Danger* **(1943). The actors were antagonists off-screen as well.**

> that it would be fairly easy—although not as easy as the Nazis imagine—to turn Turkey against Russia. Isn't this treading on pretty delicate ground?[21]

With the above paragraph, the censor not only pointed out something to alert the studio to Turkish sensitivities, but he brought up a big reason why Ambler's plot has more holes in it than cheese from that supposedly neutral nation, Switzerland.

Breen also mentions that Turkey had been playing "very wily politics to have stayed out of the conflict for such a long time," a comment that ignored the country's still-festering anger at being "dragged" into a war with Germany as an ally in 1914. Turkey, which still has its own crimes to answer for concerning the Armenians, was well taught by dictator Gamel Ataturk about keeping out of the wars of other nations. Ataturk may have died in 1938 (of cirrhosis of the liver, aka too much booze), but his philosophy of "isolationism" lived on all through the war years. Earlier in Breen's report, he noted that the film's foreword "does a good deal to explain Turkey's precarious position and why she has so jealously guarded her neutrality." Or, in other words, "very wily politics."

Then Breen makes some interesting points about the portrayal of the Russians in Burnett's script:

> While it is, of course, obvious that much of the suspense of the story depends on uncertainty whether the Russians shown are friends or enemies, still is it entirely necessary to build up this suspense by showing one of the band (Zaleshoff) as querulous, ill-tempered, somewhat duplicitous, and sometimes indecisive? Despite the fact that the Russians are given a verbal whitewash in two speeches, one is left with the impression that these speeches have been grudgingly inserted, and that the Russians are not perhaps entirely trustworthy allies. At this time, we can ill afford to create such feeling.

One wonders what Breen's reaction was to finding out that our Soviet allies spied on us all through the war, culminating in their theft of the A-bomb secret.

However, in this instance, Breen's political naïveté pales in comparison to that of Nelson Poynter of the Bureau of Motion Pictures, a wartime censorship department within the Office of War Information. In a letter to producer Jerry Wald, Poynter rambles on at length about the dangers of pointing accusing fingers at "allies" like Russia and neutrals like Turkey:

> Don't paint Turkey as a democracy as we know it—the Near East, like Russia, has been growing towards "Political Democracy" by giving more and more people a stake in the economic system. Thus it's not "neutrality" the Nazis are trying to upset. They have no illusions about that—it's merely their "Divide and Conquer" technique.

Besides the fantastic claim that Turkey and Russia have been giving their people "a stake in the economic system," Poynter, the man responsible for gauging the international scene for American audiences, has another zinger for us:

> [A]s long as the German military dominates, peace is jeopardized, and Russia needed peace to develop internally (like Turkey). When this peace was jeopardized, then all nations are unsafe, especially those bordering Russia—hence the Finland episode.

Here, our crack government representative in the censorship office somehow links German's belligerency with "the Finland episode." Of course, the only way German belligerency helped create Finland's subjugation was by specifying, in the Nazi-Soviet Pact, that Russia could attack Finland without any interference from Germany. However, continuing with the whitewash of Russia, Poynter ends the letter with: "The advantage of all this is that it definitely makes only *one heavy*—the German military. Pan-German, Deutschland Uber Alles idea."

Eventually, the script was revised by Daniel Fuchs and another writer whose best work lay elsewhere: William Faulkner.

Our story begins with all–American oil company salesman Joe Barton (George Raft) as he boards a Turkish train. Somehow, trying to picture the limited Raft doing a British accent and pretending to be a journalist would be almost as implausible as friendly Soviet agents. In his compartment, he meets a young woman named Ana Remzi (Osa Massen) who, besides praising America after meeting Joe, asks him to smuggle her money across the border. After he does this, he later finds the woman's corpse in a sleazy hotel room. The Turkish police are alerted and Joe is soon a hunted man. After being kidnapped by henchman Mailler (the always excellent Kurt Katch) and taken to the hideout of Colonel Robinson (Sydney Greenstreet; wonderful casting), Joe is rescued by Nikolai (not Andreas) Zaleshoff (eccentrically played by Peter Lorre) and his sis, Tamara (Brenda Marshall).

Lorre was the *only* actor in the film who saw it for the nonsense it was and played it accordingly. Impetuous, full of temper tantrums, yet facing loaded guns with incredible fatalism, Lorre effectively steals the film from the usually annoying Raft and even his (Lorre's) good friend Greenstreet. (Though usually a team in Warner espionage pictures, the two share no actual dialogue in this film.) The heavyset Greenstreet is excellent as Robinson, a traitorous variation of his Caspar Gutman from *The Maltese Falcon*. At one point he tests Barton by giving him a gun to kill Zaleshoff. Director Raoul Walsh screwed up big-time here: Raft reaches into a desk drawer, where we plainly see him take out a revolver, but in the next shot he is pointing a Luger.

Apparently, Raft and Lorre were a handful for Walsh. In one scene, Raft claimed that while he was tied to a chair, Lorre purposely blew cigarette smoke in his face. After he asked Lorre to stop it, the actor refused and Raft slugged him. However, according to Lorre's stunt man, Raft was lying through his teeth. Apparently, Lorre, a master at scene-stealing, was demonstrably waving his cigarette around a little too much to suit Raft. The tough-guy actor was *not* tied to a chair (something that would be faked on screen anyway) and was *not* in danger of being burned by the cigarette. Angrily, he asked Lorre what he was doing. Being the irrepressible pixie that he was, Lorre frankly admitted that he was simply stealing the scene from Raft and Brenda Marshall. Unlike Lorre's friend Humphrey Bogart, Raft clearly couldn't take a joke, and so the former New York tough guy attacked him. Walsh broke up the fight, but Hal Wallis quickly heard about it. It came exactly one year after Raft had physically attacked Edward G. Robinson on the set of *Manpower*. Predictably, the actor's days at the studio were numbered.

As the film progresses, we see that Joe is really an American intelligence agent. He is even given a Turkish assistant (played by an actual Turkish actor, Turhan Bey). After being caught yet *again*, Joe escapes with Tamara, but Nikolai is killed. Pursuing our heroes, Mailler and other Nazis crash their car (after the driver is shot by Joe) and are killed.

Joe makes it to the newspaper office that will publish the phony plans and smashes the printing plates. In the book, the publisher is an out-and-out Nazi. Holding a gun on Kenton and Zaleshoff, he accuses them of aiding the cause of "Jewish Bolshevism," a line which, thankfully, doesn't appear in the finished film.

Now having failed in his mission, Colonel Robinson is sent back to Germany; he is even met at the airport by two top-coated men sent by "Himmler the hangman." Good-bye, Colonel Robinson. At the end of the novel, Kenton, holding a gun on an unarmed

Colonel Robinson (whose real name is Saridza) somewhere out in the woods of Romania, actually lets him go after ludicrously mentioning Britain's sense of humor (not mercy, *humor*):

> The Anglo-Saxon sense of humor, Saridza, is one of the most emasculating influences known to mankind. I am the unfortunate possesser of such a sense of humor. You can go. Go on. Clear out. But I warn you. If you show your face within the next 24 hours, I shall shoot you on sight.

Ian Fleming's James Bond would have waited for Saridza to turn and, instead of letting this enemy of humanity go free, justifiably shot him in the back.

The film's tagline about "Love in the midst of intrigue," is shown when Joe leaves on a plane with Tamara. His closing line: "We're going to cement Russian-American relations."

The Hollywood Communist Party must have loved that one.

Helmut Flieg was born in what was then known as Chemnitz in Germany in 1913. As a young man, he became a writer and, because he was a writer who lived in pre–Hitler Germany, he soon became a member of the Communist Party. As his fame as an author grew, he changed his name to Stefan Heym. Since he was not only a writer and Communist Party member, but also a *Jew* (something that was a part of him long before his other activities) in a Germany where the Nazis now ruled, he fled the country and emigrated to the United States.

He learned English, worked at the University of Chicago, and eventually moved to New York where he edited a Communist newspaper. After the U.S. entered World War II, Stefan (unlike most American Communists, especially the Hollywood variety), joined the American army and fought the hated Nazis on the battlefield. Since he was an intellectual who knew German, he was enlisted to translate leaflets and pamphlets to distribute to Axis soldiers urging them to surrender.

After he returned to the U.S., the postwar anti–Communist mood caused the FBI to increase their surveillance of perceived Communist spies and potential threats to the nation's security. Heym claimed he was targeted by the Bureau. After being denied an entry visa into Communist Czechoslovakia, like Bertold Brecht, he settled in East Germany. Discovering that the U.S. government had used Nazi war criminals in their intelligence community, the compassionate author angrily sent his Bronze Star back to President Eisenhower.

Heym continued to write pro–Communist themed novels (with the permission of the East German regime) until he finally wrote one that backed the 1953 workers' revolt against the Communist government. Receiving the usual reward from Communists after so many years of supporting them, Heym's novels were banned in all Communist states for twenty years. However, Stefan bucked the system by having his manuscripts smuggled into West Germany, where he had more freedom to express his themes, and had his western royalties secretly deposited in a Swiss bank account. (Apparently, the Swiss bankers never tumbled to the fact that their new depositor was a prominent *Jewish* author.)

However, despite this obvious "disloyalty" towards the Communist government, when asked why he didn't live in *West* Germany, Heym replied acidly that he didn't want to live in an American colony. Yet the Germans, whether in the eastern half or the western half, apparently still had one thing in common. Though elected to a seat in the first all-German Bundestag after the fall of the Berlin Wall, his pride in being a Jew elicited hostility from the nation's dominating Christian Democratic Party, who refused to applaud him after his speech and refused to have the text of it printed in the Bundestag's press releases.

His books were acclaimed all over the world. He had been a soldier in the United States Army who fought against fascism. He had files on him compiled by the Nazis, the Stazi, and, to a much lesser degree, the FBI; however, unlike the totalitarian powers who kept files on him, he was able to obtain the Bureau files through the Freedom of Information Act.

Helmut Flieg aka Stefan Heym died in Israel at the ripe old age of 88. He never repudiated his Marxism, or at least his kinder, gentler version of it, and died a Jew among a free nation of Jews in 2001. Dying just before the shadow of 9/11 rose into the foreground of world events, Heym did not live to see a new fascistic enemy on the horizon, one whose dictates echoed his old enemies, the National Socialists, in their bigotry and insane hatred. Indeed, one wonders what the feisty Heym would have said about *them*.

But in the meantime, in that turbulent year of 1943, while Heym was fighting in the American army, Hollywood made the only film version of his work. Paramount Pictures bought the rights to his wartime novel *Hostages*, and one of the screenwriters was an old Communist hand at anti-fascist melodrama, Lester Cole.

The film is set in occupied Czechoslovakia. When a drunken Nazi officer named Glassnap (funnyman Hans Conried in a rare dramatic role) commits suicide, the local villagers are arrested for his murder. Also arrested is Nazi collaborator Lev Pressinger (Oscar Homolka). Though a German coroner finds that Glassnap killed himself, Gestapo chief Richard Reinhardt (Paul Lukas) and Reich Protector Kurt Daluege (Reinhold Schunzel) conspire to change the findings to murder so they have an excuse to massacre the hostages and confiscate Pressinger's vast coal syndicate. Also caught in this conspiracy is Pressinger's daughter Milada (Luise Rainer, in her last film for decades); Paul Breda (the underwhelming Arturo de Cordova) and a Czech guerrilla leader with an unusual New York accent (William Bendix).

The film was, of course, a thinly veiled account of SS Reich Protector Reinhard Heydrich's brutal control over occupied Czechoslovakia, though this time, through the character of Pressinger, it is mixed with old-style capitalist greed and collaboration with Nazi conquerors.

Luise Rainer is clearly affected as the heroine, and de Cordova is terrible as hero Paul Breda (an in-joke referring to Comintern-NKVD man Otto Katz, who used the alias of Breda in Hollywood). Directed by Party member Frank Tuttle (who just recently had a huge hit with *This Gun for Hire* and whose name shows up quite a bit in the FBI's COMPIC files), the film is a good B adventure, but it did not augment a stampede by Hollywood producers to buy up the rights to Stefan Heym's books.

In the meantime, Cole claimed he was having some problems with his collaborators. In his autobiography *Hollywood Red*, Cole describes his screenwriting partner for *Hostages*:

> Assigned with me was one of the studio's most experienced writers of comedies and melodramas, Frank Butler, a very amiable, completely apolitical man. Butler's salary was at about two thousand a week, and a common practice then, a purely business matter, was to make certain no contract writer was unassigned. Put him on anything whether he was right for it or not, as long as his salary could be written off on the picture's budget and not be charged to studio overhead.

Though Cole admitted to liking Butler, the leftist scenarist already emphasized the qualifier: Butler was not assigned to *Hostages* because he was familiar with political material, or even the genre, but because he was ordered to. However, to his credit, Cole writes that

Butler "certainly contributed to what was a difficult problem of construction"; in other words, taking Heym's eight stories about the heroism of the Czech underground and squeezing the various elements into, as Cole put it, "a single, coherent dramatic narrative."

After ten weeks, the partners had a first draft. Then, at a meeting in the office of Paramount executive Buddy De Sylva, which also included B producer Sol Siegel and Frank Tuttle, the script was praised and De Sylva "congratulated us warmly." However, despite the good vibes, Cole sensed that something was wrong when he noticed Tuttle averting his eyes from him. Admitting that the script was "political," De Sylva gave them some good news: The studio was able to sign Luise Rainer, the Oscar winner, or "real box office," as Cole wrote. Unfortunately, this was a bit of an overstatement. Rainer had angered Louis B. Mayer by walking out on her MGM contract. After more than two years off the screen, whatever "box office" clout she had at this time was certainly questionable.

Still, Cole wanted Rainer's character, Milada, the pampered daughter of a rich capitalist-Nazi collaborator, to secretly meet with the underground and then fall for the (implied Communist) guerrilla chief, Paul Breda. However, De Sylva (Cole has him speaking in the vernacular of every stereotype of a Hollywood producer you've ever seen) had a quite different conception of the hero. To De Sylva, the hero is handsome, attractive, well-dressed, high-class and, though he is supposed to be as an evil Nazi collaborator, the heroine *wants* him.

Or as Cole has De Sylva crudely put it:

> She knows nothing from politics and couldn't care less. Nazi-Schmazi, a man is a man to her, and here is this gorgeous hunk of meat who looks at her and she melts. Like hypnotized. Before she knows it, she's in bed with him, and he is *something*. She's hooked and I mean hooked! Completely. And it is then and only *then*, that we learn he was *posing* as a collaborator and is really a part of the underground.

After mentioning what "a great lay" the heroine has experienced with this man, De Sylva allegedly said, "It's just that sex hooks her into the underground, not that intellectual political crap."

Cole, the author of that intellectual political crap, was appalled. Instead of a scenario slamming a capitalist collaborator (that would have gotten Cole praise from his Party comrades), the studio had the heroine join the leftist underground not because of any sense of political commitment, but because the fighter for freedom and liberty was "a good lay." Though De Sylva's version, if true, carried with it the stigma of sexism, ironically, it would have brought a little much-needed color to the usual virtuous hero-heroine combination. Still, Cole did not bother to mention that the Production Code office would have censored any mention of the heroine getting "laid," something De Sylva, Siegel and Tuttle would have been well aware of.

In Cole's version, Butler readily agreed to this "radical" script change, but he also had Tuttle, the Communist helmsman, meekly acquiescing as well. Cole claimed that he fought for his version of the script, and was willing to risk getting fired to protect it. Then, according to Cole, after De Sylva suddenly came around and agreed to let the screenplay remain as it was, the producer had Butler rewrite the script behind his back.

However, what is amazing here is that very little of De Sylva's alleged version made it into the finished film either. Though Paul Breda *is* posing as a collaborator, Milada does not jump into bed with him and is, in fact, supposed to be engaged to another character. If anything, by having the hero pretending to be a fascist collaborator, the script also makes the underground look better by showing them as having the foresight to plant an important spy among high-ranking Nazi personnel (as we would see rescuer Oscar Schindler

GUESTS OF THE SS. Arturo de Cordova and Luise Rainer in the domain of Nazi officer Paul Lukas (right) in *Hostages* (1943). Stefan Heym's stories of underground resistance in Czechoslovakia closely resembled the assassination of SS Commander Reinhard Heydrich.

palling around with Nazi officials in the early parts of *Schindler's List* before he begins to save Jews).

Yet Cole saw none of this. To the leftist screenwriter, everyone on the production had turned against him and had rewritten his script to lessen its "politics." Of course, Cole never explained how a film that still contained fascist and anti-fascist characters was somehow *not* political.

Claiming to be fighting the good fight, Cole wrote, "There was a stop line for some of us, as time would show, and no dismal depth to which others would sink." (And how many of us can claim to have sunk to "dismal depths," or for that matter, have the nerve to express it just that way?) Cornering the supposedly milquetoast Tuttle (Cole has him stuttering some pathetic explanation by way of defending himself), the scenarist said to him, "You're a stooge, comrade, or a mouse. Or could it be a louse?" The above phrase "as time would show" was Cole's way of foreshadowing Tuttle's alleged treachery years later when he appeared before HUAC.

Most autobiographies contain a certain amount of self-love from the author that usually makes their version of events border on the fantastic, and it's extremely rare when the subject of said autobiography tells us the *whole* story. Predictably, they portray themselves as the honest and true hero and fighter for justice that they probably were *not* in reality. Cole adds

III. Bodyguard of Lies (1942–1945)

a variation to the fantasy by having himself tell off those Party members who later (as he puts it) "squealed" to HUAC. At a later point in *Hollywood Red*, he also claimed to have called in to a radio program that Budd Schulberg was guesting on and called him several choice names. He wrote that Schulberg responded by stammering out a lame explanation, something Cole also has Tuttle doing when *he* was confronted. Or as Cole rather cruelly put it, after "giving an audible gasp, Schulberg was once again stuttering, as he had done in his youth."

Despite the fact that the above remark will not endear Cole to those with speech impediments, his version of his collaborators might not have been, as one might have guessed by now, totally sincere. According to Bernard F. Dick's *Radical Innocence, a Critical Study of the Hollywood Ten*, Frank Butler was having his own problems with the Communist screenwriter. To his credit, he was taking no guff from a scenarist who typically distorted the facts to fit his politics:

> Frank Butler, who eventually received co-screenplay credit, had to curb Cole's anti–Nazism, which had exceeded even the sky-high 1940s limit. Butler reminded Cole, who had a German lieutenant commit suicide when his wife is sent to a breeding camp, that married women were *not* sent to breeding camps. When Cole had the heroine blanch at a German's touch, Butler politely informed him that the Czechs "are living with these people and this isn't their first encounter." When Cole had the heroine speak like La Passionaria, Butler reprimanded him for making her sound "like a heroine in a cheap melodrama."

With Butler's last phrase "cheap melodrama," the acerbic scenarist slyly put Cole on the same level that the leftist writer had previously put Buddy De Sylva. Adding to the authenticity of the above comments is that Dick took his information from the actual Paramount studio files.

"Cheap melodrama," a genre Hollywood could make in its sleep, permeated the war years on American movie screens. For the foreseeable future, the movie industry's Communists were going to continue to make cliché-ridden anti–Nazi films in which heroes and heroines give passionate speeches for liberty as Nazi characters unrealistically stood by like mannequins and waited until they were finished.

However, on Broadway, audiences would be galvanized by a slightly different take on the anti–Nazi subgenre, with a plot that brought fascism to the manicured lawns and comfortable surroundings of the nation's capital. This famous work was also written by a woman whose own Stalinism was legendary.

Opening on April 1, 1941, at Broadway's famed Martin Beck Theater, *Watch on the Rhine* turned out to be quite an April Fools' prank on the Communist Party. Lillian Hellman had finished the first draft of her play on August 15, 1939, a mere week before the signing of the infamous Nazi-Soviet Pact. (She would lie to President Roosevelt and claim she had finished the play in 1938.)

In this powerful (but long-winded) work, Hellman attacks fascism and all those who support it at the same time that Stalinists were ordering the Party faithful to lay off the Nazis. The reluctance to change the material according to Party lines was probably done less from a sense of commitment than the playwright's quite sizable ego.

In her excellent dual biography *Hellman and Hammett: the Legendary Passion of Lillian Hellman and Dashiell Hammett*, Joan Mellen noted:

> Lillian would not put aside or revise this work, which called openly for the involvement in the struggle against Hitler, no matter that Stalin was soon to decree that Communists now concern themselves, not with the anti-fascist struggle, but with peace.

Reviewing the play, the *Daily Worker* slammed the playwright for failing to mention that a land run according to Communist standards was a land that "already established a permanent new life of peace and freedom."[22]

However, in the FBI's file on Hellman, agents noted that the *Daily Worker* review of April 4 was "extremely favorable." According to the Bureau, the Communist paper had written that Hellman and producer Herman Shumlin had given Broadway "the first real play based on 'the third alternative' for the revolutionary way out."

Still, the Party faithful weren't going to swoon over the play's controversial themes without some nitpicking. Alvah Bessie would argue that the play would be "misused by those who would like to whip us or cajole us into imperialist war under the banner of fighting fascism in Germany."[23] Bessie had apparently forgotten that he recently fought against fascists in Spain who were armed with German weaponry.

Sticking with the Communist playbook, Hellman had reportedly based the central character of Kurt Muller on the bizarre yet fascinating figure of European Communist Otto Katz. A Czech Jew born in the Sudetenland, Katz became the right-hand man of enterprising Communist functionary Willi Munzenberg. Under the older man's tutelage, Katz became one the Comintern's brightest stars. In Europe, he had worked the journalistic circuit, at first writing stories against fascism, then bribing newspapermen in France and England (with the wealthy Munzenberg's Moscow bankroll) to write pro–Soviet, anti–Nazi pieces. In the mid–1930s, Katz journeyed to Hollywood to spread the wisdom of the Popular Front among the wealthy but intellectually simple denizens of the film community. He was reportedly the secret husband of film superstar Marlene Dietrich and, if you believe Diana McLellen's *The Girls: Sapphoes in Hollywood*, he was used as a "beard" for the singer-actress as she embarked on her many lesbian affairs.[24] However, he was also later married to a German woman named Ilse, though it is uncertain when the marriage to Dietrich, if there was one, ended and the one to Ilse began.

Exploiting the fact that Hitler was frightening many of Hollywood's Jewish executives, Munzenberg and Katz saw a potential gold mine in bilking the film community and funneling its money to the Party's coffers. In 1935, Katz, an instant charmer with the in-crowd, organized the Hollywood Anti-Nazi League. Along with authors (and Communist Party members) Dorothy Parker and Donald Ogden Stewart, Katz worked behind the scenes to ensure the popularization of anti-fascism within the film industry. A worthy cause indeed, but the dictates of Katz's organization came with Comintern strings attached. In April 1936, a fundraiser was given at Hollywood's Victor Hugo Restaurant in which Katz (using his alias "Rudolph Breda") told stories of "the Nazi terror" he personally witnessed in Germany, and how he risked his life many times to bring to Americans his eyewitness accounts of fascist barbarity. In reality, Katz was not in Germany at the time he was describing, and it soon became obvious to some in the glittering crowd of movie people that he was not a genuine refugee. In fact, unlike real refugees from Nazism, Katz had ample traveling funds from his "handler" Munzenberg and from Moscow, with the activist able to move everywhere at will while the real victims of Nazism were thrown into recently built concentration camps. During this time, Katz actually boasted, "Columbus discovered America and I discovered Hollywood." Indeed, there is some evidence that Katz was with the NKVD. Nevertheless, John Cantwell, the archbishop of Los Angeles who attended Katz's fundraiser, smelled a rat and quickly left.

Katz met Lillian Hellman the following year and, at a lunch in Paris, suggested that she become involved in helping the Republican government in Spain then under attack by

Franco's armies. She soon helped to make the documentary *The Spanish Earth*, and her deep friendship with Katz also evolved into an affair. Erika Mann, wife of the author Thomas Mann, referred to Katz (under his European alias "Andre Simone") as "probably a Comintern agent" and referred to the Abraham Lincoln Brigade, the volunteer force that was then fighting Franco, and of whom Katz was promoting as a liberating army, as "definitely a Communist-inspired and dominated organization."[25]

When one goes into the background of *Watch on the Rhine*, one would have to read between the frequently lecturing lines on international politics to conclude that the person who is the noble anti-fascist hero (and the centerpiece of the play) is also a Communist. Hellman knew she had to water down the character's Marxism in order for him to be appealing to Broadway audiences. Yet there is no mistake that in Kurt Muller's speeches calling for a free world and a never-ending fight against fascism, he is also parroting the same words used by Hollywood Communists like Katz and Munzenberg; that is, if not their actions. In the play, Muller bribes fascists to release guerrillas in a way that Otto Katz never did. Instead, the Comintern used the Nazis' prisoners for propaganda purposes, with little regard given to actually freeing them. In the play, to make him more appealing, Muller is given a loving family, and we never hear about the real-life Katz's long-suffering wife (who had to endure his many torrid affairs with Hollywood's A-list starlets), or his reportedly being a "beard" for Marlene Dietrich. In fact, in giving Kurt a loving wife who joins him in his fight against fascism, Hellman may have merged the propaganda image of Otto Katz (who was certainly no one's idea of a family man) with real-life anti-fascist heroes Muriel and Joe Buttinger. (According to Hellman's memoirs, written decades later, her anti-fascist heroine Julia was reportedly based on the life of Muriel Gardiner Buttinger. However, it turned out that Hellman had never even *met* Buttinger, much less risked her life in any wartime mission.)

In the play, Kurt and his wonderful family are put through the wringer in a steadily growing fascist Europe; they are starving as he continues his anti-fascist work; he marches with the Republicans in Spain as his family is forced to wear clothes that are not much more than hand-me-downs; he has kidnapped Gestapo chiefs and suffered the tortures of the regime that have literally broken many bones in his aging body. Meanwhile, Otto Katz, one of Hellman's "inspirations" for Kurt, was enjoying the high life among the jet set in Hollywood and living a cushy existence all over Europe spreading the good word about Marxism and being supplied with ample funds from Moscow.

However, Broadway audiences knew none of this. It didn't matter to them just who Kurt was based on; the play was a hit, instantly appealing to New York audiences as it took a strong anti–Nazi stand before America's involvement in the war. The play lasted for 378 performances. It starred Paul Lukas as Kurt Muller; Communist Party member Mady Christian as his wife Sara; George Coulouris as the double-dealing former Romanian aristocrat Tech; Lucille Watson as Sara's mother Fanny Farrelly; and even had a young Ann (then spelled Anne) Blyth as their precocious daughter Babette.

The April 14 *Time* magazine review of the play (which, in those days of lazy reviewing, really just told you the *plot*) reported that "tall, brown-haired, courtly Paul Lukas" was the son of a Hungarian advertising man and had served in the Austro-Hungarian army during World War I (in the play and subsequent film, Kurt is also a World War I veteran).[26] "Often he uses his acting talent for practical jokes, such as ordering people out of his house for supposed insults to his wife." The magazine didn't explain why anyone would think this was funny.

Though Hellman had a certifiable hit on her hands, one voice of hopeful praise remained silent: that of her then live-in paramour Dashiell Hammett. Unlike Hellman, Hammett was not in love with the playwright's words enough to cross his bosses in the Party. So while Hellman waited in vain for her lover to show up at another Party, the one at Sardi's after the play, Hammett avoided anything to do with *Watch on the Rhine*. With the Party damning its anti–Nazi stance, the slavishly devoted Communist author stayed away from rehearsals, run-throughs and even withheld his usually bombastic opinions — that is, until May. He accused his lover of ruining "a great play with sentimentalism; anti-fascist sentimentalism."[27] In truth, the author of *The Maltese Falcon* and *Red Harvest* was right. Though fascism is rightly condemned throughout the play, it is done in the most pretentious and downright corny way possible. Indeed, one could easily have called it "Watch on the Whine." However, after June 22 and the Nazi invasion of the Soviet Union, both Hammett and the Party would radically (pardon the pun) change their opinion of the play.

In 1942, with the United States now at war with Germany, Warner Brothers quickly bought the rights to the play. According to author Joan Mellen, Hellman had discussed of possibility of Hammett doing the screenplay with producer (and Hellman's ex-husband) Arthur Kober and the film's director, Herman Shumlin, in December 1942. Yet studio files suggest that the idea of Hammett doing the screenplay was already approved as early as January.

With this project, not only do we have the irony of Hammett working on the script of a play that he once referred to as containing "anti-fascist sentimentalism," but the assignment was given to him at the insistence of his former pupil, Hellman. Hammett had not finished a novel, story, screenplay or play (except for rewriting Hellman's early works without credit) since 1934's publication of the excellent *The Thin Man*. Now, Hellman insisted that Hal Wallis use the unpredictable and alcoholic Hammett to do the screenplay of her work. Grudgingly, Wallis offered to pay Hammett $30,000 (capitalist money apparently spoke a lot to Marxists), but also made sure that Hellman was paid $11,500, obviously for final revision work.[28] As it turned out, Wallis was right to have misgivings.

In a memo to the producer from the studio's New York office, dated March 6, Warner executive Jacob Wilk wrote:

> I talked with Shumlin on the phone yesterday and told him I did not think that the script was coming through fast enough. It has been five weeks since we made a deal with Hammett, and so far I have twenty-two pages of script and a good deal of this twenty-two pages is descriptive material and camera direction.
>
> Shumlin told me that he had spoken to Hammett and that Hammett said he "will have the script out on time." ... I appreciate it if you call Hammett and give him a gentle goosing for, with the play to work from, I do think he should be making a great deal more progress than he is.

In a letter to Wallis, dated a week later, Wilk groused:

> After six weeks during which time I received twenty-two pages of script, I have just received, in the mail from Hammett this morning, the next batch of six pages.... I want you to have a talk with Hammett immediately and find out just what is going on because unless I see more concrete evidence that he is working, I want to put another writer on the job to write the script out here. Please get right into the matter as it is serious.

Meanwhile, director (and Party member) Shumlin, whose loyalties were more to Hellman and Hammett than to the studio, had his own take on the situation. In a March 26 letter to Wallis, he wrote, "Dash ... is firmly confident that he will finish on time," and claimed that the author had "hurt his back earlier in the week and assumes that set him back a couple days." Then the Broadway maven goes on for many paragraphs to complain about the "dangerously tight" production schedule that the studio insisted upon. Again defending Hammett, Shumlin also claimed that the author had "hardly gone away from the house where he is living and working." In reality, Hammett was known to frequently cheat on Hellman with much younger women, especially when she wasn't in town, with the novelist having a particular preference for Harlem prostitutes.

Meanwhile, the production was having cast problems. Though both Shumlin and Hellman were insisting on casting the actors in the Broadway production, the studio was dragging its feet, hoping to fill the cast of the film with more established stars.

In an interoffice memo dated April 21, Wallis wrote to Jack Warner:

ANTI-FASCISTS IN LOVE. Bette Davis and Paul Lukas in the 1943 film version of Lillian Hellman's play *Watch on the Rhine*. Hellman's play was supposedly based on real-life counterparts.

> [Paul] Lukas has apparently become very much annoyed because we haven't made up our minds about him. As a matter of fact, he told Phil in one of his letters not to do anything more about him here as he decided he didn't want to do the part. I know that if we make tests of anyone, Lukas will hear about it, and he may keep his word about not playing the part.

Wallis then suggested that if Lukas was cast, the studio should pay him $25,000. Two weeks later, in a letter from studio attorney Roy Obringer to casting chief Steve Trilling, the role was finally offered to Lukas, with the actor getting $2500 with a ten-week guarantee. (On the strength of the film's success and Lukas' Best Actor Oscar, the studio would eventually give him equal billing with Errol Flynn in the wartime opus *Uncertain Glory*, written by another alcoholic author, Max Brand.) On a studio casting sheet from March 6, Lukas' name is at the top of the list for his role (as are the other members of the Broadway cast for their roles), and the other casting choices for Kurt were the French-accented Charles Boyer; star of the successful *Casablanca*, Paul Henreid; and Philip Dorn (with George Sanders, Raymond Massey and Conrad Veidt as alternate choices).

As it turned out, most of the Broadway cast would make it to the film, with perhaps one glaring exception, the actress in the role of Sara. Mady Christians had already done films since the 1930s, including that left-leaning attack on materialism, *Come and Get It* with Frances Farmer. Unfortunately, Christians was not only a Party member, but she also had the misfortune of not being a box office name. Instead, the studio cast their number one female star; though typically, said star would not cooperate willingly.

"Bette Davis is insisting that she take second co-star position in the billing of *Watch on the Rhine*," wrote Roy Obringer to Jack Warner on May 14.

> I have been arguing with her attorney for three days and he claims he cannot change Davis' mind, as she takes the position that while she is willing to do the picture, Lukas has the choice part and she does not want to appear ridiculous by taking first position billing.
>
> Putting Davis in second position will have a detrimental effect on selling the picture as, naturally, Davis is the attraction as to picture publicity and sales, rather than Lukas.

Though known to throw temper tantrums at any perceived threat to her star status, this time Davis, one of the organizers (along with John Garfield) of the Hollywood Canteen, believed so much in the play's anti-fascist message that she was willing to give Lukas, a lesser player, top billing. Ultimately, in a compromise move, the studio maintained her top billing status, but it was on the same level as Lukas' name.

Instead, the studio would get an ego trip from a different actress. In a memo to Steve Trilling, dated June 5, Wallis complained:

> Geraldine Fitzgerald is kicking up her heels, doesn't like the part [of Marthe] wants it built up, and the usual routine.
>
> Shumlin is telling her that we will put back a few lines from the play for her last big scene in the picture, but that is all we can do.

The producer ends the memo by suggesting that if Fitzgerald rejects the part, "let's get Margaret Lindsay lined up."

As the film opens, the Muller family arrives on the Mexican border (Warners' western town set) and is ready to enter the United States. They are Kurt (Paul Lukas), his wife Sara (Bette Davis), older son Joshua (Donald Buka), daughter Babette (Janis Wilson), and younger son Bodo (Eric Roberts). Though the children are supposed to be cute and charming, unfortunately, according to the movies' conception of the foreign-born (as well as Hammett's and Hellman's conception, apparently), they all talk in pidgin English and say unintentionally stupid things. Particularly annoying is Bodo. At one point, he loudly announces, "I am surprised the United States of America is a sunlighted, dusty country with vegetation of no great height and…" before Joshua interrupts him. One does wonder why Hellman and Hammett insisted on making Bodo a strutting little pompous ass (Mrs. Farrelly refers to him as a "midget"). Given to mouthing loquacious platitudes about freedom and the need to fight fascism that sound no less pretentious than their old man's speeches, the Muller children are far less fascinating to watch and listen to than the vindictive young girls of *The Children's Hour*.

On the train, the Mullers run into a refugee Italian family; the husband is played by Warner contract player Anthony Caruso. Here, the Italian-American actor is forced, by Hellman and Hammett's screenplay, to sound like any other just-offa-the-boat Italian stereotype you've seen in the movies. At one point in Hammett's screenplay, the supposedly tolerant author has a character referring to Caruso's baby as "a little cutthroat." Hellman wisely removed the line.

The Mullers are going to live with Sara's family, the Farrellys, in the wealthy Georgetown section of Washington, D.C. Sara's mom Fanny (Lucile Watson) is the curmudgeonly matriarch of the household; Donald Woods is her son, David; George Coulouris is former Romanian diplomat Teck; and his dissatisfied wife, Marthe, is played by the dissatisfied Geraldine Fitzgerald. In the homecoming scenes, it is quickly established that David loves Marthe, though she is unhappily married to Teck. A product of the former European aristocracy, Teck sees in the Nazis a way to return to his former glory. Again, all through Hellman and Hammett's scenario, all monarchies are seen as decadent, shabby, disgusting and uncompromisingly pro-fascist.

Ultimately, Hellman cut out most, if not all, of Hammett's speeches about the disparity between America's rich and poor, comments on Marxism, and even shots of newspaper headlines announcing a candidate for the socialist ticket. Billed in the credits as writing "additional dialogue and scenes," Hellman didn't hesitate to cut every line written by Hammett that was not absolutely essential to the plot. Unfortunately, what Hellman left in was unabashedly cornball, with Max Steiner's all-too-lush music emphasizing the way we're supposed to feel about the characters.

Hammett's best contribution may be the scenes where he "opens up" the play (even though Hellman pared down most of his dialogue), especially the memorable scene in the German embassy. Though Hellman graciously credited the sequence to Hammett (and indeed, most of the lines are his), she reworked this scene too. Fortunately, however, the scene is blessed with two actors who give the film some bite, as well as a sorely needed respite from the constant platitudes on fighting evil. One of them is Henry Daniell, outstanding as sardonic Nazi officer Von Ramme, and the other is the underrated Kurt Katch, as "Butcher Boy" Blecher (who is possibly a Gestapo agent). Katch, a former star of the Yiddish theater, as well as a refugee from Europe, shines in the scene, as he verbally takes apart the various Nazis and their industrial backers seated at the poker table. It is Hammett at his hard-boiled private eye dialogue best:

> We Nazis are always funny. We have a funny leader with a funny mustache. His name used to be Schicklgruber and he was a paper hanger. That too is funny, yes. And we have divided the world into two parts. Those like you [Von Ramme] who want to work for us. And those who lie awake trembling and hating us because they are afraid of us.

A Warner contract player who usually graced the studio's adventures whenever they were set in foreign locales, Katch would later steal a scene from Marlon Brando (as a ridiculously compassionate Nazi officer) in Edward Dmytryk's film version of Irwin Shaw's *The Young Lions*.

Sara is reunited with her family and the corn and phony sentimentalism return with a vengeance not seen since the Hatfields and the McCoys. Max Steiner's music is raised in volume and tears are supposed to well up in our collective eyes. At this point, Bodo, sounding like a little Stalin, pompously announces, "There is never a need of boasting. If we are to fight for the good of all men, it is to be accepted that we are to be among the most advanced!"

Somebody smack him!

Teck suspects Kurt of being an underground leader. After Teck attempts to blackmail the Mullers, Kurt gets the jump on him and forces the decadent monarchist out into the Farrelly garden. With little hesitation, he shoots dead the blackmailer in the Farrelly tool shed. After this, Lukas has an excellent monologue expressing his guilt over the "necessary" killing. Kurt then makes the Farellys promise not to report Teck's death until he is on a plane to Europe (where he will attempt to rescue an underground leader).

After this killing, which is enacted amidst their estate's well-pruned hedges and sweet-smelling tulips, the Farrellys are now shaken out of their cushy existence and become committed anti-fascists; David ends up with the newly widowed Marthe; and Sara has no choice but to allow her now grown-up son Joshua to follow his father into Nazi-occupied Europe to search for him and fight for the Cause. (Too bad they couldn't send Bodo.)

However, things weren't going to be that simple. Right away, Hellman and the studio hit a buzzsaw named Joseph Breen. The stuffy censor, who had always been isolationist before the war, predictably had issues with the film. In a letter to Warner, dated June 5, 1942, he sniffed:

> You will recall our concern about this picture because of the suggestion that Kurt commits a deliberate murder and is permitted to go off scot-free. Such a suggestion would, of course, be completely in violation of the Production Code.

Breen suggested that there either be a line of dialogue that "unmistakably establishes" that Kurt realizes he will be assassinated if Teck reports him to the German embassy, or that it be "clearly and unmistakably established" that at the end of the film Kurt is killed by the Nazis. Interestingly, "Butcher Boy" Blecher had already explained that he and his men *couldn't* murder Kurt on American soil, and that their target would have to be in Europe in order for them to assassinate him.

Again, Shumlin circumvented the studio to give Hellman a copy of important correspondence; this time, it was Breen's objections. In a letter to Hal Wallis, dated June 22, the playwright wrote, "Herman sent me the Hays office objections.... The objections are not only unintelligent [*sic*] as they were in the old days, but they are growing downright immoral." Not getting a satisfactory response to her demands, in a letter to Wallis from July 13, a fed-up Hellman issued a not-so-veiled threat:

> I hope this letter is not too strong. I wanted to make it stronger. I wanted very much to say that if you continue with the insistence that Kurt be punished, I would like to gather some more material and do a piece about the Hays office censorship.

And then the playwright tartly ends the letter with, "How are you and my very warm regards."

Apparently, Hellman's threat somehow did the trick. There was concern that the Hays Office and the far-from-perfect Production Code system would come under too much scrutiny, especially by feisty playwright Hellman (and her passionate argument that since American soldiers were now killing Nazis in war, according to Breen, we couldn't kill them in films). Breen backed off. In the film, Kurt goes to Europe and it is left up in the air whether he's dead or alive.

Hellman and Shulman weren't through yet. Both of them complained about the delay in the picture's release, the marketing, and even the venue the studio wanted to open it in (Warners' traditional picture palace, New York's Strand Theater). The complaining didn't help either their careers at the studio, or for that matter, Hammett's. Though Warner congratulated Hellman on the film winning the New York Film Critics Award for Best Picture, after *Watch on the Rhine* his studio never used Hellman or Hammett again. As far as Shumlin was concerned, two years later his only other directing effort would be the studio's spy drama *Confidential Agent*, and then in 1952, he would produce a Ronald Reagan comedy called *She's Working Her Way Through College*, two films that weren't going to win Oscars or critics' awards.

Though Davis' performance is affected, she *tries*, and it's obvious her heart is more in the film's anti-fascist message than in her own dialogue delivery. However, she was right; it was Lukas' film, and the actor was rewarded for his excellent performance with a Best Actor Oscar for 1943. George Coulouris, the film's villain, was signed to a Warner contract.

However, if anyone thought that Lillian Hellman was through with the subject of Nazi chicanery, they were wrong. Unfortunately for her, her next foray on the subject would be one of the screen's funniest films...

On November 4, 1943, Samuel Goldwyn released *The North Star* to a war-weary nation. With an original story and screenplay by Lillian Hellman, the film told the story of the people of a Russian village happily going about their lives until Nazi armies invade their country. As directed by Lewis Milestone, who made the anti-war *All Quiet on the Western Front* thirteen years before, and scripted by the pro–Soviet Hellman, the film was hardly going to be a real-life portrait of the U.S.S.R. Instead, the end result was a mockery of the very real courage of Russia's citizens, many of whom were dying by the millions *before* the Nazis invaded.

After the German invasion, Stalin ordered the Red Army to form into partisan groups to attack Nazi troops wherever they were. Unfortunately, this quite natural desire to defend one's land from a ruthless invader was coupled with a callousness towards its citizenry not seen very often in world history. Books like Matthew Cooper's *The Nazi War Against Soviet Partisans, 1941–1944* graphically detail, not only Nazi atrocities against the Russian people, but equally cold-blooded treatment from Red Army partisans who were supposed to defend them. For instance, while blowing up strategic targets or attacking Nazi troop positions, government-sanctioned Soviet guerrillas were known to use ordinary Russians as human shields in the event of a firefight with the Germans. Whenever a sabotage mission was formed, these partisans grabbed unwilling passersby, or sometimes whole families, including children, to weather the blasts of explosives. All this could not have been done without full authorization from Josef Stalin himself. This is one of the main reasons why Hollywood's various films depicting ordinary Russian citizens as babuska-wearing guerrillas with rifles and home-made bombs were ridiculous. The Russian citizen-partisan was a myth. If anything, no one should ever underestimate the courage of Russian citizens during World War II; however, much of this bravery is based on their incredible endurance while being caught between two evils.

The film begins when old Karp (Walter Brennan) drives his buckboard through a nameless village in the Ukraine (which the Soviets had always treated as *their* territory) where we are introduced, sledgehammer style, to the film's various characters. There is Boris Simonov (Carl Benton Reid); his sons, Russian officer Kolya (Dana Andrews) and Damian (Farley Granger in his film debut); Damian's girl, Marina Pavlova (the up-and-coming Anne Baxter); Clavida Kurina (Jane Withers); Rodion Pavlov (Dean Jagger); Dr. Pavel Grigorich Kurin (Walter

PARTISAN POLITICS. Anne Baxter and Farley Granger as unlikely Soviet guerrillas in Lillian Hellman's *The North Star* (1943), one of the funniest films of *any* decade.

Huston); Professor Iakin (Paul Guilfoyle); and young Grisha Kurin (played by Eric Roberts, the obnoxious Bodo in *Watch on the Rhine*). As one can tell by these actors' names, not a one of them is Russian; nor do any of them even attempt to deliver their hopeless lines with a Russian accent.

It is June 1941. At the Siminov household, the family is shocked to find that German troops are gathering on the Polish border; Hellman's screenplay neglects to inform us that Red Army troops were then occupying the entire eastern half of Poland, therefore the Germans couldn't possibly be on the Polish border without the station also announcing an attack on the Red Army inside Poland. (Soviet radios, of which there were few for the Russian public, also continued to report that all was well in the country and never once mentioned the approach of Nazi troops.)

We see the citizenry of this collective singing and dancing to songs with music and lyrics by Ira Gershwin and the soon-to-be blacklisted Aaron Copland. The "young" characters jostle, playfully shove and lightly ridicule one another all through the first half-hour of this opus so much that one almost prays for a Nazi attack and put an end to this phony scene of clichéd camaraderie. When they journey to Moscow (or is it Kiev?), after interminably wishing each other "good journey," they are all picked up on the road by Karp (Walter Brennan at the buckboard again). They are interrupted by a mess of Messerschmidts overhead bombing the daylights out of the country. Looking over some dead victims of the bombers, Karp intones to the young people (in Brennan's typical cowboy drawl), "The face of war is ugly and it is not for the young." To which Marina replies, "We're not young any more."

Military man Kolya quickly takes charge and decides to return to the village. It is never stated if this fellow is with the dreaded NKVD or the Red Army; nevertheless, his black uniform actually reminds us of the Gestapo. Meanwhile Boris galvanizes the village to use firearms, home-made bombs, clubs, rocks, whatever, to fight the Nazi invaders; oh, and yes, they had to set fire to their homes to leave the Germans with nothing. This "scorched earth" policy, which worked so far as transferring important heavy industries to the rear as the Germans advanced, was also the height of hypocrisy as far as the Soviet government was concerned. Ordinary Russians were supposed to burn their own homes, while in reality, Communist Party members never set the torch to their own abodes. In his speech to the villagers, Boris promises arms to all so that they can fight "the fascist invaders." Unfortunately, Hellman avoids the painful reality of this situation as well.

A paranoid dictator like Stalin would never allow his men to distribute loaded weapons to the citizenry, knowing full well that after years of oppression, they would turn these guns on the NKVD who had murdered so many of their loved ones. The ugly truth, of course, was that many citizens, especially those in the Ukraine, welcomed the Germans (including the psychopaths in the Waffen SS) as liberators. It was only the twisted Nazi racial policies that deemed Slavs as inferiors that ultimately turned the citizenry against them.

Soon, after all the interminable waving of hammer-and-sickle, the two most interesting characters in the film (played by two actors whose accents actually fit their characters) enter the scene 54 minutes into the picture. Dr. von Harden (Erich von Stroheim) and Dr. Richter (Martin Kosleck) are both surgeons, as well as Nazi officers. The dignified von Hardin is a man of the old school, a dedicated Nazi who is not a brutal man, and deplores the violence involved in turning the world on to the New Order. Richter, on the other hand, is a thug, plain and simple; Kosleck was an actor who had already played Goebbels twice (and was a passionate *anti*-Nazi in real life). Richter is gladly willing to drain the blood of children

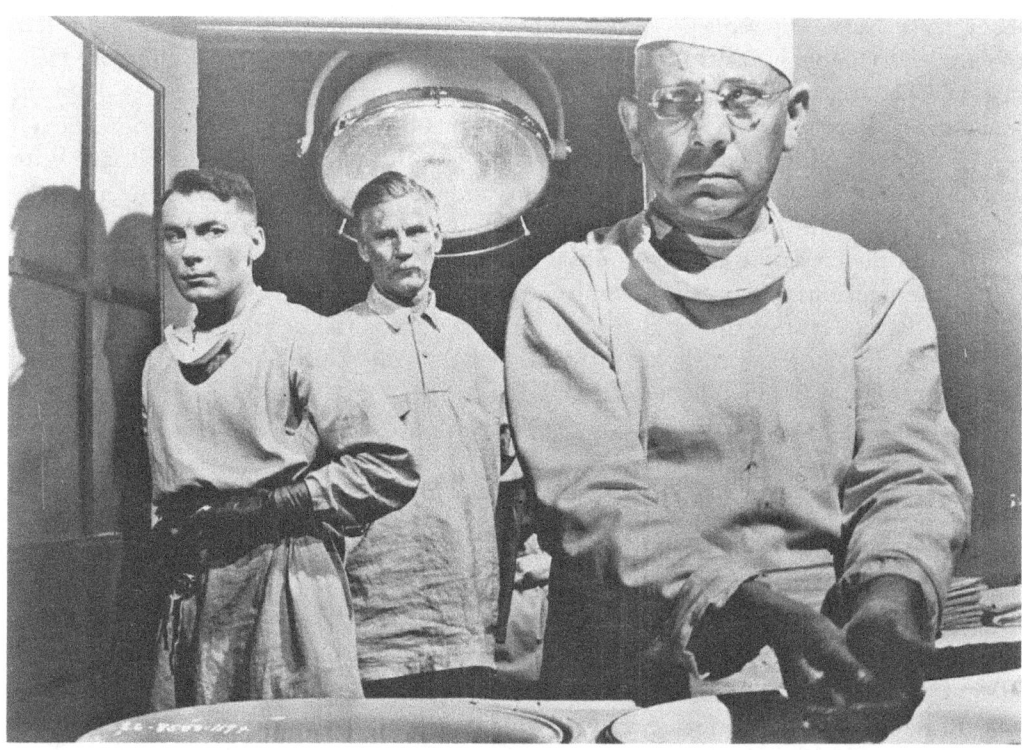

MALPRACTICE—NAZI STYLE. Martin Kosleck (left) and Erich von Stroheim (right) as Nazi surgeons about to be blown away by the miscast Walter Huston (center) in *The North Star* (1943). Ironically, Kosleck and von Stroheim, as the film's main villains, provide the best acting in the whole awful mess.

for wounded German soldiers. The scene between these two old pros is almost, though not quite, worth the effort to catch this poorly made film. The dialogue crackles between them, and here Hellman actually makes the script come alive, much helped by von Stroheim and Kosleck's acting. As the former director of classics like *Greed* and *The Merry Widow* heaps contempt on the younger man, Kosleck icily wonders why von Hardin's being taught surgery by a Jew didn't bother him. "I never thought about it *then*," the colonel replies. Had the playwright given us scenes like this, with two actors whose natural accents actually fit the characters they were playing and with the same sizzling dialogue, *The North Star* could have been a wartime classic. As it is, we were stuck with Walter Brennan's prairie *muznik* and Dana Andrews' kinder, gentler NKVD man and a village full of Hollywood extras who can't carry a tune.

"A strong people, a hard people to conquer," says an admiring von Hardin, a line that no Nazi officer would ever have uttered. When the German patrol arrives in the village, von Hardin apologizes for all the fuss (as the Nazis break the leg of a village woman who won't talk). Here, the colonel is brought up against his ideological opposite, another doctor of the old school, Dr. Pavel. The two surgeons respect each other, and when Richter insists that Pavel be arrested, the colonel replies that as a physician the man is harmless to the Reich.

Soon the doctors (with von Hardin apologizing for the waste of life *again*) start draining the blood of Russian children to give to wounded German soldiers, an act that made little, if any, sense. Nazis followed a perverted philosophy of racial superiority and the preservation of pure Aryan blood; why would wounded Nazis accept the blood of Slavic children? Hellman never addresses this discrepancy. To her, the Germans are evil because they drain the blood of children, regardless if it was contrary to their own precepts of racial superiority.

Finally, Dr. Kurin, pushed too far, leads a group that recaptures the village. With amazing luck, he walks through all the firefights and blood, waving a loaded gun, and finally enters the compound, confronting von Hardin and Richter.

Again, thanks to the characters of the two principal villains, the final scene is a good one. Walter Huston, who wisely underplays (except for an atrocious musical number scene), now has his gun trained on the two Nazi surgeons; one is full of regret, the other full of hate. Dr. Kurin's bitter words, like the scenes between von Hardin and Richter, is the kind of dialogue that shows Hellman at her best:

> [To von Hardin] I have heard about men like you — the civilized men who are sorry. This [Richter], his kind are nothing. He'll go when his bosses go. But men like you who have contempt for men like him. To me, you are the real filth — men who do the work of fascists and pretend to themselves they are better than those for the beasts for whom they work, men who do murder while they laugh at those for whom they do it.

Then he promptly guns down both of them.

At the end, the final lines are given to Anne Baxter. After proclaiming that this will be the last war, the future Eve Harrington passionately cries, "We'll make a free world for all men. The earth belongs to us — the People, if we fight for it. And we will fight for it!"

Regrettably, in just a few short years, the west would discover just what the Soviet Union's idea of "a free world" was. In fact, the film's curtain line, "The earth belongs to *us*," signaled the Kremlin's ideology in more ways than one.

Rarely in the history of motion pictures has a film been so consistent in its ignorance of political and historical realities. In fact, *The North Star* seems to exist in an alternate universe in which those who are noble and brave and true all sing off-key to background music pretending to be authentic tunes from the Russian provinces. Not only that, the "Russians" all seem to have American accents. Perhaps this was a move to present the Russians as really no different than us, as they are portrayed by such authentic Slavic performers as Walter Huston, Dana Andrews, Anne Baxter, Jane Withers, Farley Granger, Walter Brennan and Carl Benton Reid.

Milestone, who accepted the project because of his admiration for Hellman, was shocked to discover that she would be the fly in the ointment, standing in his way of making a good film. Though Hellman claimed to have painstakingly researched the subject matter, the helmsman later bitterly claimed, "As it turned out, Lillian knew *nothing* about Russia — especially the villages."[29] This was perhaps no surprise. Whenever she visited the USSR, Hellman hobnobbed with Soviet officials and dined in their dachas (villas). When she did see the country, it was usually at the behest of her NKVD escorts who didn't dare allow her to actually venture out among the citizenry. From her pro–Soviet statements through the years, Hellman, who probably would have ignored the plight of the citizenry anyway, had no problem fabricating a fantasy village that could have only existed in Oz.

Again, as in much of Hellman's wartime work, she ironically gives the best lines to the characters she claims to hate so much, the Nazis. Just as in *Watch on the Rhine*, where the German embassy's Nazi bureaucrats are seen as wry, witty and piercing in their assessments of those around them, *The North Star* is neatly stolen from all the noble, courageous and American-accented Russian characters by the screenplay's two principal German officers,

Dr. von Harden and Dr. Richter. As portrayed by von Stroheim and Kosleck (ironically, the only two Jewish actors in the starring cast), one is almost curious about *their* stories. Richter was a surgeon back in Germany, and is now an obedient Nazi; but von Harden, who was a surgeon before World War I and still has some respect for a man's principles before Nazi brutes stormed to power, roundly detests him. Indeed, instead of a phony project extolling the Soviets, Goldwyn could have made a film indicting Nazism by just focusing on these two characters (and played by these two fine actors) and how the Nazi system eroded the principles of two formerly decent men.

Meanwhile, Hellman's penchant for backstabbing treachery was as strong as ever. Milestone would later claim that Hellman told him that if he had any changes to make, to go directly to her, not Goldwyn. Taking her at her word, the helmsman provided the playwright-scenarist with a mind-boggling fifty pages of script changes. Hellman, who hated changing her golden words for anyone, promptly complained to Goldwyn, who promptly put Milestone on the carpet. Angry at this betrayal, the director was invited by Goldwyn to dinner and a script conference with Hellman at the producer's mansion. After a sumptuous meal, Hellman was infuriated to find that Goldwyn agreed with practically all of Milestone's script changes. Now feeling vindicated, the director cheerfully left the mogul and his strident scenarist to scream at each other. The bitter result of the row would be Hellman buying her way out of her lucrative contract for $30,000, a sad end for a collaboration that produced three classic films and one rotten (but financially successful) one over a period of eight years.

There is a story that during a screening of *The North Star* in Goldwyn's projection room, Hellman burst into tears, with the mogul shouting at her to shut up while the film was being run. In later years, Hellman would always maintain that the producer had changed her script into sentimental musical nonsense. However, back in 1943, Hellman was apparently proud enough of her corny script to have her original published in book form. According to Hellman biographer William Wright, her original is not much different than the script the playwright accused Goldwyn of changing.

Regardless of whether the script was altered or not, the film was a box office hit, with the general public keen on seeing Russian guerrillas as the noble heroes they were definitely *not* in real life.

In the *New York Times* review of November 4, the usually incisive Bosley Crowther called *The North Star* a "lyric and savage picture" which states "in passionate terms the outrage committed upon a peaceful people by the invading armies of Nazi Germany." However, after calling it "a heroic film," the critic noted a problem with its general structure:

> The first part of the film, in which the village and its inhabitants are idyllically introduced, is distinctly in the style of operetta. There is music (by Aaron Copland) and rollicking gaiety of the sort that is familiar to light-hearted peasants in musical comedies set in mythical foreign lands. When the people of the village gather for a sociable evening al fresco, it might even be a scene from *Oklahoma*.

But Crowther ended his review with the observation that the film is so "moving and triumphant that its sometime departures from reality may be greatly overlooked." "*Sometime departures*"??

As Joan Mellen noted, there were enough Communists in the industry to make sure that Hellman and the film were nominated for Oscars for Best Original Screenplay, Musical Scoring, Cinematography and Art Direction.[30]

Meanwhile, real Russian citizens would win no awards as they suffered the cruelties of their Nazi conquerors as well as their own government.

"Errol is very enthusiastic about the script and he worked until 6:48 last night. This looks like a record day."[31] So wrote director Raoul Walsh on April 21, 1943, when he apprised Warner executives of Errol Flynn's cooperation on the wartime adventure *To the Last Man*, soon to be changed to *Northern Pursuit*.

Though the screen story was by Leslie T. White, the actual screenplay was by two men who had done other work elsewhere: pulp western-mystery author Frank Gruber, and Communist scenarist Alvah Bessie. Bessie, a veteran of the Spanish Civil War, was now a contract writer at Warners, and would have the shortest screenwriting career of all the Hollywood Ten (1943 to 1948). He would be kicked out by Jack Warner for backing the CSU strike against the studios in 1945. But for now, the leftist writer was at the beginning of a career where he seemed to specialize in screenplays of wartime intrigue.

Gruber was a pulp writer of the old school whose usually absurd plots would be used again and again and yet *again* in the coming years. One of his favorite plots, a B movie cliché even then, was that of the hero (marshal, detective, cowboy, FBI agent, whatever) pretending to be a bad guy in order to get the goods on the outlaw gang. In this case, "the outlaw gang" is a group of Nazi saboteurs who have insane plans to take over Canada. However, the Aryans hit a brick wall when they come up against the Royal Canadian Mounted Police and one of their dashing Australian-accented Mounties.

Mountie Corporal Steve Wagner (Flynn), of German ancestry, has been badmouthing Canada, all to the chagrin of his girl, Laura McBain (Warner contract cutie Julie Bishop) and his best friend, fellow Mountie Jim Austin (longtime WB contract player John Ridgely). When his comments cross the line into disloyalty, he is chastised in public by Austin and his commanding officer Inspector Barnett (Tom Tully), both of whom he slugs. (At this point, we get to see Flynn's skills as a former roustabout back in Tasmania; his punches are the quickest on screen.) After this assault, he announces, "The devil with Canada!" A court of inquiry judge declaims that whoever says "The devil with Canada" might as well be saying "Heil Hitler!" In record time, Wagner is drummed out of the Mounties.

At this point, he is accosted by Nazi collaborator Ernst (Gene Lockhart) who hooks him up with Colonel Hugo von Keller (anti–Nazi activist and former inmate of one of Germany's early concentration camps, Helmut Dantine). The Nazi colonel needs Wagner to guide him to the frozen Canadian north to find a hidden German bomber and use it to blow up the country's defense installations. Unfortunately, Gruber and Bessie don't bother explaining just how this bomber got in the Canadian woods or who hid it there. Nevertheless, to make sure Wagner will cooperate, von Keller has kidnapped Laura. The group trekking deep into the north woods now includes Wagner, Laura, von Keller, his various Aryan henchmen, an Eskimo collaborationist named Tom Dagar (Communist Bernard Nedell), his wife Rose (Rose Higgins) and a very queasy Ernst.

The Dagar character is interesting for the fact that it is one of the few times we see an Eskimo in films outside of a comedy set in Alaska that resorted to stereotypical igloo jokes. In potent lines written by Bessie, Dagar is helping the Nazis because of British racism. Claiming that the Eskimos will be free "when the Germans come," we see the bitterness in this man whose people are considered second-class citizens in Canada.

The trek in the high mountain air takes its toll on Ernst. Not wanting to wait up for him any longer, von Keller orders Wagner and Laura out of the cave and then, with little ado, shoots the wheezing spy. Since Ernst is played by Gene Lockhart, of course he's given a scene where he pathetically begs for his life. He whimpers that he has always been loyal to the Reich; a bullet from the colonel's Luger puts a stop to his blathering.

When Austin shows up and tries to rescue Wagner and Laura, von Keller guns him down as well, giving our hero that "Now it's personal!" motivation to get back at the fiends. Bitterly, Wagner accosts Dagar and throws his own words back in his face (things getting better when the Germans come). Seeing the Nazis' madness, the Eskimo tries to escape on skis until von Keller's men shoot him down, giving him a just reward for collaborating with National Socialists.

Von Keller's plan is to fly the hidden bomber plane over Canada and drop a huge deadly payload; essentially the Nazi is doing a 9/11 in the middle of '43. Now that he and his men have reached the plane, the colonel orders one of his thugs to dispose of Wagner. But the hero ain't played by Errol Flynn for nothing! Turning the tables, Wagner kills his would-be assassin, takes his sidearm (which mysteriously changed from a Luger to a revolver) and dresses in the Nazi's heavy

COLD COMFORT. Errol Flynn and Julie Bishop huddle in the Canadian wilderness in *Northern Pursuit* (1943). Screenwriter Alvah Bessie also throws in a subplot dealing with bigotry against Eskimos.

parka. When it's time for von Keller and his men to board the plane and bomb Canada, Wagner boards as well. In short order, Wagner disposes of the remaining henchmen and he and von Keller shoot each other in a crossfire. Yet the Mountie still has the nards to put on a parachute, leap out of the falling plane and float to safety. Von Keller, however, gets a bird's-eye view of his impending death as the now derelict plane crashes far away from Canada's big cities.

At the fadeout, Wagner is hailed as a hero and he and Laura plan to wed. At this point, her deliriously happy Scottish father announces he'll pay for the wedding, then says, "What am I sayin'!" and faints. Though rejecting stereotypes of Eskimos in his screenplay, apparently Bessie had no problem stereotyping Scotsmen.

"A woman's lips set the frozen north aflame!" cried the film's tagline; though it looks like Julie Bishop's lips have little to do with the plot, or for that matter setting the frozen north aflame. However, the *New York Times* did say that she "models fur wraps very prettily."

Joseph Breen basically approved of the script, though he insisted that sequences that show von Keller hitting the sled dogs with whips and rifle butts be cut out. Also deleted should be von Keller's lashing Rose and his kicking a prone man in the head. Filmed in lovely Sun Valley, Idaho (substituting for northern Canada), *Northern Pursuit* continued Flynn's string of wartime box office hits for Warners.

Meanwhile, over at Columbia, a studio not known for pushing the envelope during the war years, Lester Cole wrote one of his best screenplays. Rejecting the typical antifascist propaganda, the film contained one of the most powerful scenes depicting Nazi persecution ever shot during the war.

> The story was called *None Shall Escape*, by two European refugees, one Alfred Neumann, an established German writer of short stories, and the other Joseph Than, about whom I knew nothing. But they had written a tale of the Nazi occupation of Poland and the extreme torture and human degradation to which the Jews were being put on their journey to the gas chambers. The story was projected into the future: following the Allied victory the Nazi Gauletier was on trial in a Polish court. His accusers were those victims and witnesses who had survived.

So wrote Lester Cole about the origins of his best screenplay filmed during the war. Burt Kelly, Cole's associate producer on some of his Universal and Paramount films, was now at Columbia, and it was obvious that Kelly used his influence to hire the leftist writer.

The film begins some time after the war, when a Colonel Wilhelm Grimm (Cole's unsubtle names again; and played by Alexander Knox) is charged with war crimes in occupied Poland. Then the film flashes back to just after the First World War.

The little village of Litzbark is celebrating the end of the war and the chance for Polish independence. When one villager (Western actor Ray Teal) expresses cynicism about the prospects for peace, another villager says that "German imperialism" (a phrase straight out of the Communist playbook) has been defeated. One of the town's elders expresses confidence in the Treaty of Versailles and yet another says that Poland's main worry is a rearmed Germany.

This is another example of Cole's usual penchant for historical inaccuracy. Poland's main enemy at the time was not a defeated Germany, but the recently established Soviet Union. After the Bolshevik revolution, Poland fought tooth and nail to take back land that the czar's armies had seized. Applying a little imperialism of their own, the Bolsheviks hoped to keep the land for themselves and the Red Army fought the Poles in a bloody border war that lasted from 1918 to 1921. Marshal Tukhachevsky's Red Army divisions became victims of the Miracle of the Vistula, where newly minted Polish troops, tasting independence at last, encircled the supposedly infallible Bolsheviks. Lenin's naked grab for Polish land was a disaster and the Communists were forced to relinquish the territory to a people they had always deemed inferior (Poland's strong Catholicism was anathema to the Bolsheviks). Over 100,000 Red Army troops were captured and 40,000 fled into, of all places, a defeated Germany. The Treaty of Riga ended the Russo-Polish War, but not the bitterness of the Communists over losing to the bourgeoisie Poles.

Twenty years later, after the Nazi-Soviet Pact was signed, one of the "Secret Protocols" within the deal was for the Soviets to conquer eastern Poland without German interference. In the winter of 1940, when the Red Army and the NKVD took back Smolensk from the Germans, many of these Soviet commanders (that is, those who survived Stalin's purges) remembered the humiliating defeat of their army by the "reactionary" Poles. The result of this festering hatred culminated in thousands of Poles being shot and thrown into mass graves in the Katyn forest.

Another gross inaccuracy in the film is when the village priest, Father Warecki (Henry Travers), says, "Let me talk to my friend, the rabbi." In Poland, the gentile clergy didn't exactly consider rabbis on the same level as they were — as legitimate clergy or, for that matter, as human beings. Rabbi Levin (Richard Hale) is also allowed to walk among the Christian villagers without getting stones thrown at him. And the Litzbark in this film amazingly has no Jewish ghetto, those Polish-created slums where Jews were ordered to stay and never leave; indeed, the town is as integrated as a big American city.

Grimm is the local German schoolmaster. He is bitter about Germany's defeat in the war and, as the years go by, this anger will grow into a pathological hatred of his country's enemies. By the time National Socialism arrives in the 1930s, Grimm goes to Deutschland and joins the army. Rising to the rank of colonel, he is front and center when Nazi armies overrun Poland. (Needless to say, Cole does not mention the Soviets overrunning the eastern half of the country.)

Soon, the ethnic cleansing begins and the nation's Jews are thrown into cattle cars. Though the action takes place in 1939–40, Cole's use of the cattle cars foreshadows the Holocaust which started in 1943. Taken to a train station by Grimm's men, the Jews are about to board the train on their last journey until Rabbi Levin addresses his people. Cole's words, well-delivered by actor Hale, are still powerful to this day:

> Let us prepare ourselves to face the supreme moment in our lives. This is our last journey. It doesn't matter if it's long or short. For centuries, we have only sought peace. We have tried to take our place honestly, decently alongside all mankind, to help make a better world, a world in which all people would live as free neighbors. We have hoped and prayed, but now we see hope was not enough. What good has it done us to submit? Submission brought us rare moments when we were tolerated — tolerated! Is there any greater degradation than to be tolerated? To be permitted to exist? We have submitted too long. If we want equality, we must take our place along with other oppressed peoples.... By our actions we will be remembered. It is our last free choice, our moment in history. I say to you, let us choose to fight, here, now.

The rabbi's answer is a bullet in the stomach fired by Grimm. When the other Jews turn to attack the Nazis, they are ruthlessly cut down by Lugers and submachine guns. A platform signpost casts a cross-like shadow on the ground suggesting the figure of another Jew murdered by brutes centuries before.

Bernard Dick wrote that the speech was obviously "phrased in the idiom of the class struggle," and he was right. Cole may have been a Jew, but unfortunately he was also a Communist; therefore, the special circumstances that found Jews persecuted down through the centuries is subverted by leftist dogma that encouraged Jews to forget their own concerns and instead "take their place along with other oppressed peoples." The flip side of this philosophy is the famous quote by the great Jewish author and Holocaust survivor Elie Weisel. He said that during the Holocaust, not all victims were Jews — but all Jews *were victims*.

This conscious attempt to reduce the tragedy of Jewish victimization during the Holocaust wasn't restricted to the film's Communist screenwriter, but also included the Breen Office. In an MPPDA memo marked CONFIDENTIAL, and dated February 8, Breen insisted on the deletion of Grimm's line "Anyway, those weren't people, they were Jews."[32]

According to Cole, Harry Cohn himself watched the rushes and then said, almost in awe, "Hey, this is *controversial!*" Whether Cole was immodestly putting his own opinion of his screenplay into Cohn's mouth is uncertain. However, the awe-struck compliment doesn't fit into the crude yet canny profile of the Columbia president. Cohn rarely praised anything, and he was certainly not the type of mogul given to complimenting screenwriters like Lester Cole to his face. If he had done that with all the people who worked for him, they might actually ask for more money. And Cohn, like other Hollywood moguls, was not a man who liked to waste a buck.

Certainly, a qualifier as to whether Cohn ever complimented Cole on his screenplay would be what happened afterwards — or rather *didn't* happen.

Cole did not work at Harry Cohn's Columbia ever again.

Meanwhile, the war continued, as did production of war movies and the Communist screenwriters' participation in them. Dalton Trumbo was in his most profitable period in the early 1940s as a contract scenarist for mighty MGM. But before he signed with the studio with the lion, he had to do propaganda penance for that *other* studio with the initials on the corporate stationery.

RKO premiered *Tender Comrade* in Los Angeles on December 29, 1943, and released a final version nationally on June 1 of the following year. Scripted by Trumbo, the film's other leftist distinction is its direction by another future member of the Hollywood Ten, Edward Dmytryk.

After an apprenticeship as a prop man and editor, the Canadian-born Dmytryk rose in the studio system to become a director of Bs in the early 1940s. A dedicated Party member, Dmytryk had a long and sometimes controversial career. His films contained elements of political and social themes which were so deeply rooted in the man himself that they were evident even in his post–Communist period; in fact, it's hard to distinguish between the leftist films he made while he was a Party member and the leftist films he made after he testified before HUAC. Unfortunately, mixed with his attempts at social comment, his films also tended to be sleazy and violent; and not just Production-Code-good-taste violence either. Though the Code restrained his more outrageous excesses, we are still left with crude scenes of violence and torment, like the bit in *Behind the Rising Sun* where a Chinese infant is tossed in the air by Japanese troops with raised bayonets. We are grateful that the scene cuts quickly before the child starts to fall, though one gets the impression that, if he had had his way, Dmytryk would have shown the bit uncut and with close-ups. Certainly, this opinion is proven when one gets the chance to see his much later, and much gorier, *Shalako*. In this violent Euro-Western, a scout captured by the Apaches is tied up with a pointed lance at his back (done in such a way that a slight movement will send the lance through him). Soon the poor man is impaled and, to make sure we don't miss any of this, Dmytryk's camera quickly zooms in for a close-up as it thrusts through his body.

However, this was still 1943 and *Tender Comrade* is set on the home front. A talented actress (and an Oscar winner with help from Trumbo's screenplay of *Kitty Foyle*), star Ginger Rogers was adept at both comedy and drama. However, in *Tender Comrade*, she is turned into a strident and sanctimonious pain in the butt courtesy of Trumbo's plea for democracy and freedom.

The plot deals with six women, most of whom are airplane factory workers, and another who is their housekeeper; they share a house while their men are fighting the war. The women are Jo (Rogers), Barbara (Ruth Hussey), Helen (Patricia Collinge), Doris (Kim Hunter), Mrs. Henderson (Jane Darwell), and their German housekeeper, Manya (the underrated Mady Christians). Jo's husband is Chris (played by Robert Ryan before his racist-psychopath phase), and we see flashbacks of their happy marriage — or what passes for it, since their many arguments portend a bitter divorce if not for Chris getting himself killed in the war. Here, Trumbo *again* uses the flashback device as if he had invented it. One expects flashbacks in *Johnny Got His Gun*. But what was his excuse for using them for

Kitty Foyle, Captain Ted Lawson (in *Thirty Seconds Over Tokyo*), Yacov Bok (in *The Fixer*) and several other films? This device, along with having his characters talk to the dead, are just lazy gimmicks which call into question the theory that he was the most talented member of the Hollywood Ten. In truth, Albert Maltz's work was far more interesting.

Rogers portrays a character who keeps making speeches about democracy, yet is presented as a bossy, dictatorial woman who essentially has made herself the House Fuehrer. Added to the scenarist's portrayal of the heroine as authoritarian, the dialogue from the other women is *not* Trumbo's best:

"Gee, aren't men fools?"
"Yes, but aren't they sweet?"

Meanwhile, as the sweet fools are getting themselves killed in Europe and Asia, the women attempt to run their household as a free nation; this is emphasized by Manya, the most interesting character in the film (played by the most interesting actress). Communist Party member Christians does well here as the anti–Nazi refugee from Deutschland. Unfortunately, the women can't seem to make a move or express a thought without one of them spouting a moral statement about the war effort. Manya actually says that she will no longer purchase meat from a butcher who gives her more to the pound because it takes meat away from someone else. Wartime audiences suffering from shortages of gas, sugar, rubber, and especially meat, must have roared with laughter at that one.

Nevertheless, shortly after her arrival, Manya says that Germany was a democracy until "we let it be murdered—like a child." Here we have the amazing example of a Communist writer actually admitting that the Weimar Republic, the same system that Bertold Brecht and hundreds of other Marxists had relentlessly attacked before 1933, was actually a democracy.

At the end, we find that Chris has been killed, which gives Trumbo a chance to have the dead soldier talk to his wife; much as dead pilot Joe talks to his girlfriend in *A Guy Named Joe*; dead soldiers (as well as Jesus Christ) talk to Joe Bonham in *Johnny Got His Gun*; General Andrew Jackson and other historical figures talk to Andrew Long in *The Remarkable Andrew*; and various conversations in other Trumbo-scripted films of startling unoriginality.

Notice how Trumbo and Dmytryk snuck "comrade" into the title. At the end, after she learns of Chris' death, Jo talks to her baby, also named Chris (Trumbo's affectionate tribute to his own son). She tells the poor kid that his dad died for democracy, or rather,

GINGER SNAPS. Ginger Rogers and Robert Ryan in one of their quieter moments from Edward Dmytryk's *Tender Comrade* (1943). The film portrayed the lives of five women who share a house during wartime.

BRAZEN HUSSEY. Kim Hunter, Patricia Collinge and Ginger Rogers watch as lunchtime Romeo Richard Gaines attempts to add Ruth Hussey (right) to the menu in *Tender Comrade* (1943). Dalton Trumbo's dialogue is still laughable to this day.

Dalton Trumbo's version of it, and if he didn't follow those principles, he might as well be dead too. Oy!

At one point during the film, when the women are discussing the money they'll have left after all the bills are paid, Doris proclaims, "Share and share alike, isn't that right?" To which refugee Manya answers wistfully, "Democracy." Unfortunately, and perhaps a little hysterically, many leftist writers have attacked Leila Rogers, Ginger's mother, for later telling HUAC that she saw the exchange as Communist. It was obvious that Leila Rogers was attacking a line about sharing written by the highest paid screenwriter in Hollywood who enjoyed his money yet slammed capitalism; she wasn't attacking the act of sharing or charity. Indeed, no political system on the planet actually promotes "share and share alike," which is why, knowing the human animal for what he or she is, the concept of Utopia is about as real as the land of Oz or Shangri-La.

Bosley Crowther in his *New York Times* review of June 2, 1944, didn't have Shangri-La on his mind when he wrote:

> Dalton Trumbo, who wrote the story, was apparently more intent on being cute and wistful than he was on cutting close to life. And the consequence is that his female is a thoroughly incredible lot. The scenes that she puts on with her husband just to dominate the poor man are of such ungenerous nature that they manifest spiteful selfishness. And her curious expressions

of affection appear just too coy and contrived. But worst of all, from the viewpoint of writing, it is the scene at the end of the film, when the lady reacts to the blunt news of her husband's death by giving a lecture to her infant child.

Calling Trumbo's screenplay a "poor script," Crowther also faulted Dmytryk's "stagy" direction, Rogers' "weak" performance and the rest of the cast as below average. Indeed, the critic was quite democratic about laying the blame for the film on everyone equally.

Talk about "share and share alike."

Soon, Trumbo left RKO for MGM. Assigned to contribute to the studio's war film output, the Dalton Trumbo of those years did his part for Hollywood's (and, in effect, the Party's) propaganda effort in a way the pacifist author of *Johnny Got His Gun* never would have. The sudden transformation from anti-war activist to Johnny Shoot Your Gun was noted by the observant Richard Corliss in *The Hollywood Screenwriters*:

> Within four years of writing a novel denouncing World War I and, by extension, all wars, Trumbo was churning out chauvinistic screenplays propagandizing World War II — the *good* war. His specialty was movies about American bomber units, and one of these films contains an irony that would have elicited pages of well-wrought cynicism from Trumbo the letter-writer [Corliss admired the screenwriter's correspondence.—BH]: the protagonist of *Johnny Got His Gun* was a guy named Joe Bonham whose legs, arms, and face were blown off on the last day of the Great War; in 1943, Trumbo wrote a bomber film for smiling Van Johnson called *A Guy Named Joe*.

In 1944, Trumbo wrote the screenplay for *Thirty Seconds Over Tokyo*, based on the book by Captain Ted Lawson. Unfortunately, except for Spencer Tracy's fleeting but memorable performance as Colonel James Dolittle, and the final third of the film set in war-torn China, *Thirty Seconds Over Tokyo* is one long bore. The soldiers, sailors and pilots are all a little *too* perfect, and a little *too* team-player to be real. In one bit, an army man insists on taking a bunk with a harder surface, obviously so Van Johnson's pilot can sleep on a softer mattress, as if the bunk he sleeps in will guarantee his not being shot down by Japanese Zeros.

Once Lawson's team is, in fact, shot down over China (after successfully doing their thirty seconds over Tokyo, that is), the screenplay rejects heroic derring-do and we see the downed flyers, now realistically wet and bedraggled after swimming to the beach in the midst of a driving rain. When Robert Walker's gunner pulls out his .45 and is about to pop a "Jap" in the distance, Lawson orders him to hold his fire; fortuitous, since the approaching group are Chinese guerrillas. Again, when one designates a friend or enemy merely by their racial appearance, disaster could result.

At this point, Trumbo's work is indeed memorable. The Chinese are portrayed as strong allies *and* distinct individuals, despite the language barrier of some of them; of course, Benson Fong's doctor speaks perfect English. Still, what is important is that the Chinese allies move Heaven and Earth to help the downed Americans, and it is this warmth and compassion from the villagers, not the first two-thirds of the film, that make it memorable.

Unfortunately, Lewis' mangled leg has to be amputated, a harrowing scene aided by Johnson's strong performance. (It is said that the real Ted Lawson was on the set that day.) After the surgery, two moving scenes occur, both dealing with the gratitude of the Chinese villagers to their American friends. One finds a chorus of beautiful Chinese children singing a Chinese translation of "The Battle Hymn of the Republic"; the other is when an old Chinese man gives Lawson a present of a pair of sandals. Director Mervyn LeRoy skillfully uses

BROTHERS AGAINST TYRANNY. Ching Wah Lee as the Chinese guerrilla leader and Robert Walker as an American bomber pilot come to an understanding, despite language barriers, in *Thirty Seconds Over Tokyo* (1944). The best part of Dalton Trumbo's screenplay emphasized brotherhood with our Chinese allies.

his camera to show the old man's point of view; we see the angle go from Lawson's crestfallen face down to the missing leg. Realizing his *faux pax*, the old man covers his face in anguish, but a quickly smiling Lawson takes his hands away and thanks him, accommodatingly putting one sandal on his good foot.

When Lawson returns home, he doesn't want his wonderful wife Ellen (the always wonderful Phyllis Thaxter) to know that he lost a leg; however, the tough but compassionate Colonel Dolittle thinks otherwise. And as we all know, what any character played by Spencer Tracy wants, any character played by Spencer Tracy gets!

When Ted and Ellen finally embrace on the cold hospital floor (he had fallen down), audiences the world over got a bird's eye view of Lawson's horrible facial scars — except that these scars were *not* makeup. Van Johnson nearly got his head torn off in a horrible motorcycle accident and was almost replaced on *A Guy Named Joe*, but Spencer Tracy threatened to walk off the set if Johnson was ousted. In *Thirty Seconds Over Tokyo*, LeRoy figured that Johnson's scars would add realism to Captain Lawson's injuries and no makeup was used. By 1954, we still see these same scars on Johnson's face in Edward Dmytryk's *The Caine Mutiny*.

"Heart-warming Romance ... Stark, Sensational Drama! Thrills! Action! Adventure! ... Ripped from the Heart!" cried the taglines, though the real war was hardly an MGM flack's idea of a B movie. Despite the silly advertising, *Thirty Seconds Over Tokyo* made an

III. Bodyguard of Lies (1942–1945)

estimated $4,471,000 in the U.S alone. Though it was a tribute to the men who risked their lives to give Imperial Japan a dose of its own medicine, its major contribution, thanks to Captain Lawson as well as Trumbo, was its positive portrayal of the Chinese people as friends and allies in the fight against tyranny.

Meanwhile, Japanese aggression in Burma was finally going to get some screen time.

In 1941 Burma, there was activity on a road that would connect the village of Lace to Kunming, China. This 700-mile road, which wound through the mountains and valleys of both nations, was supported by Britain, which retained Burma as a colony under its domination. However, the road wasn't constructed to aid the Burmese people as much as it was to give Britain an important supply route to aid Chiang-Kai Shek's army battling Japanese forces in China. The project also helped keep Burma in well-manicured British hands.

However, the Japanese had their own ideas of colonialism and they helped a growing independence movement in Burma, granting the nation limited home rule in 1943 to thwart British designs on the country—though, predictably, with Japanese strings attached.

After the Japanese sneak attack on Pearl Harbor, American troops under General Joseph Stillwell landed in Burma, but resistance was heavy and the troops were forced to fall back to India. In 1943, the British, under the command of General Ord Wingate, established a specially trained jungle fighting force called the Chindits which fought the Japanese in bitter attacks throughout the country. Eventually worn down by the Japanese, the unit was also in danger from the constant threat of contracting jungle diseases.

Besides the Chindits, the Japanese also had to face the battalion commanded by Brigadier General Frank A. Merrill, known as Merrill's Marauders, which aided the pro-British guerrillas after they landed in 1943. Worn down by the strain of the campaign, General Merrill suffered several heart attacks, but he persisted. Though a puppet government was set up in Rangoon in 1943, by early 1945, with British and American troops gradually taking back the country, the Burmese Quislings followed their Japanese masters back to Tokyo to escape being arrested by the Allies for war crimes.

However, the Japanese government's plan for Burma to shake off British rule would come true not long after their own defeat. The Burmese, especially the guerrillas who had fought the British under limited Japanese rule, were given a taste of independence they would never forget. Reluctantly, the British were forced yet again to abandon another of their "possessions" after the war.

Yet many a British soldier, as well as Americans, died heroically in the jungles of Burma to keep it free of Japanese domination. However, when Warner Brothers made a film about the battle for Burma, they neglected to mention the crucial participation of one of these countries...

Production commenced on *Objective, Burma!* on May 1, 1944, and continued into the hot California summer until it finally ended on August 26. As directed by Warners action specialist Raoul Walsh, the film is a sprawling work that keeps up a good level of tension for over two hours. Based on a screen treatment by Alvah Bessie, the screenplay was written by Lester Cole and former radio writer Ranald MacDougall (who would be signed to a Warner contract after this film).

It was obvious that Cole had already worn out his welcome at Harry Cohn's Columbia. As he demonstrated in his autobiography, his bitterness at studio interference in his work never left him, and the book portrays *every* studio head he worked for as a crude, empty-headed moron. But especially galling to him was their insistence on watering down the Communist rhetoric in his screenplays. Certainly, his next assignment for William Cagney Productions would bear out Cole's tendency to complain, and complain loudly, about his precious words being tampered with, long before the Blacklist came into being.

In the meantime, Cole was working for the brothers Warner on a screen story by a fellow Communist who had seen war against the fascists firsthand.

It is the early 1940s in Burma. A company of American soldiers parachutes into the country on a mission to locate and destroy a Japanese radar station. The men are led by Captain Nelson (Errol Flynn), an Australian-accented American officer; his second-in-command is Lieutenant Sid Jacobs (William Prince), this soft-spoken officer with the Jewish-sounding name was a former teacher in upstate New York. Next in line is Corporal Gabby Gordon (Warners' expert at ethnic characterizations, George Tobias). Though Gordon is the comic relief, he usually punctuates his killings of Japanese soldiers with "Mazal tov." Also along for the ride is American news correspondent Mark Williams (Henry Hull) and Private Nebraska Hooper (Richard Erdman): guess where he comes from. Bit part actor Erville Alderson makes a brief appearance as General Joseph Stillwell; unfortunately, we don't see Brigadier General Frank Merrill.

Having accomplished their mission, the men have to rendezvous with an American transport plane at an old air strip that apparently happens to be on the other side of Burma. The starving, exhausted men have to slog through miles and miles of jungle swamps while keeping alive despite mosquitoes as well as the Japanese. That Raoul Walsh was able to skillfully convince the audience that this was a Burmese jungle is an incredible feat since the movie was filmed in the Los Angeles County Botanic Garden in Arcadia. In his autobiography, Cole mistakenly refers to the location as a park in Pasadena, while Walsh in *his* autobiography *Each Man in His Time* writes, "We found some scrub areas in Orange County and shot the picture there." Anyone who's been to Southern California knows that Arcadia and Pasadena are nowhere near Orange County.

Midway through the film, the patrol is split, with Nelson taking one path through the jungle and Jacobs' company taking another. When Nelson later discovers the bodies of his men, including the dying Jacobs, in the ruins of a village hit by the Japanese (the film does not mention anti–British guerrillas supplied by the Japanese), the production exploded into some behind-the-scenes controversy.

The likable Jacobs had obviously been tortured to the point of Nelson barely recognizing him; here, Walsh cunningly focuses his camera on the horrified reaction of Nelson and Williams. The obviously mutilated officer weakly begs Nelson to kill him. At this point there is a painful pause as the captain agonizes over the decision; Jacobs suddenly dying of his own accord conveniently circumvents Nelson having to shoot his close friend. Though the captain quietly mourns Jacobs, Williams, the non-combatant, lets fly with the film's most controversial speech:

> I thought I've seen or read about everything one man can do to another, from the torture chambers of the Middle Ages to the gang wars and lynchings of today. But this — this is different. This was done in cold blood by people who claim to be civilized. Civilized! They're degenerate, moral idiots. Stinking little savages. Wipe them out, I say! Wipe them off the face of the Earth!

The original speech was rewritten by Ranald MacDougall, who assumed co-screenwriting credit. In Cole's version, Nelson calmly answers the hysterical journalist: "There's nothing

ON PATROL. Frank Tang, Errol Flynn and John Whitney find what's left of their men after Japanese troops got hold of them in *Objective, Burma!* (1945). Raoul Walsh's suspenseful direction made this one of the best films produced during the war.

Japanese about it [torture]. You'll find it wherever you find fascists. There are even people who call themselves Americans who'd do it too."[33] Needless to say, Cole and Bessie neglect to mention Soviet concentration camps, but why nitpick over a Communist screenwriter's version of man's inhumanity to man?

Nevertheless, in the finished film, after Williams' diatribe, Nelson is silent; no pearls of wisdom about fascists, nor any unsubtle comments about Americans torturing anyone, or anything else. Actually, in the real world far from the pampered one of the Hollywood screenwriter, politics mattered little, if at all, to the foot soldier. No matter who they were fighting, to those men in frontline combat the main objective was to *survive*, period. In far too many war films, you often see soldiers keeping their eyes peeled for enemy snipers while at the same time discussing political systems, a rather suicidal lack of concentration that could get them killed. In real life, soldiers were concerned with not getting their heads blown off, and when they were on point, the class struggle was the *last* thing on their minds!

Of course, Cole and Bessie ignored this logic, believing that combat soldiers should babble on like magpies about what they were fighting for. Unfortunately, Williams' speech, delivered passionately by Henry Hull, also sounded unmistakably racist. In this case, a mature, highly charged entertaining film, now had an uncharacteristic racist speech added to it that almost, though not quite, parroted the infamous "dirty little yellow monkey" epithets that were often heard in anti–Japanese wartime films of much inferior quality.

Certainly Spanish Civil War veteran Bessie wasn't going to let producer Jerry Wald or Warners get away with it. In an interoffice memo to Wald, dated December 2, 1944, Bessie aired his complaints:

> I'd like to put on the record what we were discussing yesterday on the phone. Namely — the scene in *Objective, Burma!* in which the newspaper correspondent says the Japanese should be "wiped off the face of the earth." I've discussed this with Lester Cole, and he feels precisely the way I do about it — that the statement, as used, can be a very dangerous one and, in a film that so sedulously avoids political statement of any kind, this one highly political statement sticks out like a sore thumb. It seems to me that if you are going to dramatize Japanese atrocities — and I think they *should* be dramatized — then you owe it to yourself to make it plain that such atrocities are not the private property of one nation or one race of people.

At this point, Bessie also reminds Wald of Nelson's reply that "you'll find it [inhuman behavior] wherever you find fascists," and it is here revealed that Bessie, not Cole, wrote this line in his original screen story.

Later in the missive, Bessie again implores Wald to reconsider leaving the line in without some response from Nelson, and warns him of the moral consequences of his decision:

> I am not asking you for a complete explanation of things. But I assure you that if you do not answer the racist statement: "They ought to be wiped off the face of the earth," you are falling into the enemy's trap. Wiping people off the face of the earth is the private idea — and policy — of fascists.

After quoting from Roosevelt's speech on bringing no charges against "the German race," Bessie argued that the line is "quite ambiguous, and could be interpreted to mean the Japanese people. And since that is obviously not the policy of our government or any other Allied governments, a very bad impression could indeed be created." Bessie's final P.S., however, takes a not-too-veiled swipe at an implacable foe of the Communists: "Also, I am sure neither [Jack] Warner, nor [Steve] Trilling would want our film to be misinterpreted, or to apparently carry the tone of a typical [William Randolph] Hearst editorial."

Despite Bessie's letter, Wald kept Williams' lines in, and kept Nelson's reply out. Though Cole wrote in his autobiography that he got along "famously" with MacDougall, as usual with Cole, the collaboration soured soon enough. In his book, Cole claimed that Bessie did about a dozen pages of screen story until Wald pulled him off the project, prompting the studio to bring in MacDougall. Still, Cole insisted that his fellow Communist share screen credit. According to Cole, MacDougall suspected that Bessie would be given top billing in the credits; the young writer also accused his leftist colleague of political favoritism for allying himself with Bessie over him, and was further incensed when Bessie was nominated for Best Screen Story. (According to Cole, Jack Warner stole the idea for the film from a book about Merrill's Marauders. If this was indeed the case, then Bessie should never have even been nominated for "original story.") However, if MacDougall feared being squeezed out of a script credit as Cole had claimed (it was MacDougall's first screenplay), the young writer was obviously backed by his producer. In an interoffice communication to Jack Warner, dated January 26, 1945, Jerry Wald enthusiastically raved about "MacDougall's excellent script." Notice that Lester Cole's name is not mentioned once.

Meanwhile, the British were infuriated by the film and, being the British, banned it for many years after protests from veterans' groups. To them, it was another example of Hollywood hoarding the glory for Americans and completely ignoring British participation in liberating Burma. Of course, during this controversy, the British neglected to mention their own colonialism and that Burma would *really* be liberated in 1947 when they finally left.

In 1951, Warners remade *Objective, Burma!* as a Gary Cooper Western called *Distant Drums*, again directed by Raoul Walsh. This time, instead of the Burmese theater, the screenplay is set in the jungle marshes of Florida in the 1840s. Also, the Seminoles were substituted for the Japanese.

Amazingly, this time the British had no complaints...

With the Nazis recently defeated, Columbia released *Counter-Attack* on April 26, 1945. Based on a Soviet play called *Pobyeda*, the screenplay was by Soviet-phile John Howard Lawson and directed by Zoltan Korda. Though shot on a low budget (90 percent of the film is set in the basement of a collapsed building), the film does have Paul Muni. Long past the years of his biographical roles, the great Muni spent his 1940s Hollywood years making anti–Nazi war films like Columbia's *Commandos Strike at Dawn*, where the former Louis Pasteur and Emile Zola could be seen throwing grenades at Nazi troops and drowning a Quisling member of his guerrilla group.

In *Counter-Attack*, Muni is once again a guerrilla, but a Soviet one. Predictably, Lawson's propaganda is blatant, if not downright idiotic. When the guerrillas capture a German

GUERRILLA MY DREAMS. The great Paul Muni gives the old koochy-koo to the beautiful Marguerite Chapman in an unusually light moment in *Counter-Attack* (1945). John Howard Lawson's screenplay ignored the cruelty that Soviet partisans inflicted on the populace and instead turned them into heroes.

soldier, the man is frightened, but guerrilla leader Kostyuk (Party member and Group Theater alumni Roman Bohnen) is a clever character who uses psychology to make the Nazi spill vital information. In reality, the soldier would have been lucky to escape with all his body parts, since the guerrillas and the NKVD would have gutted him for laughs.

During one battle, Muni's Alexei finds himself trapped with several Nazi soldiers in the basement of a crumbling building (one of the Nazis is played by perennial Three Stooges villain Philip Van Zandt). Holding his Kalishnikov on them, Alexei has to fight sleep until the good ol' Red Army arrives in the nick of time to save the day. However, things aren't all that bad; trapped along with our Bolshevik hero is sexy brunette guerrilla Lisa Elenko (the beautiful Marguerite Chapman, taking a hiatus from Columbia Westerns).

In one of the few times in a film scripted by a Communist, a Nazi is actually shown to be a good character. Stillman (played by anti–Nazi German actor Rudolph Anders) is grudgingly trusted by the two guerrillas for one reason: He had previously been a member of the working class — a great reason to trust a Nazi if there ever was one.

All through the war, Communist screenwriters seem to ignore something very important about their fascist enemies: Many of them were formerly poor and working class. However, to the leftist screenwriters, the Nazis were all wealthy capitalists in neatly pressed uniforms with swastika armbands and high leather boots who never worked a day in their collective lives. And how quickly Communists like Lawson, Maltz, Bessie and Cole forgot that the Nazis started out as a *leftist* group (they were, after all, National *Socialists*), with thousands of poor and working class Germans flocking to join them.

At the end, just as the chief Nazi officer shouts loudly of victory over the Soviets, Alexei riddles him, of course, just before the Red Army breaks into the house above and rescues them. At fadeout, Alexei gets a kiss from Lisa and some much needed sleep, while audience members puzzle as to why Rhode Island–born and –bred George Macready is cast as a Soviet general.

Also in the cast is Columbia contract player Larry Parks (as a Soviet guerrilla), who would break through to stardom in the studio's *The Jolson Story* (with some screenplay work done by an uncredited John Howard Lawson). *Counter-Attack* would be just one of the films noticed by a few Congressmen convening a subcommittee on un–American activities. They couldn't help but notice their pro–Soviet point of view, or some of the Communists involved in these productions.

The times, they were a-changin'...

"To know their secret is to court death!" No, the tagline is not talking about what the Party does with its money; it was the ad blurb for James Cagney's latest action film, only his second under the banner of William Cagney Productions. There are very few today who can recall *Johnny Come Lately*, the first Cagney brothers production. But *Blood on the Sun* is still remembered today, especially in the wake of 9/11 and the rise of Islamofascism, for its message of revenge at the end of the film.

Released nationally on April 26, 1945, shortly after the Allied conquest of Nazi Germany, *Blood on the Sun* kept up the attacks on the still active but dying Japanese enemy. Based on a screen story by Frank Melford and Garrett Fort, the screenplay was by Lester Cole.

One must give credit to Cole for *not* attacking the Japanese on the basis of race, as so many rather brainless wartime B flicks had. In *Blood on the Sun*, the nation's politics were the enemy, not its people.

It was a hectic time for the Party. With the Red Army's victory over Nazi Germany now a foregone conclusion, the Soviet Union didn't need American help any more (especially the thousands of tons of supplies and weaponry being shipped to the U.S.S.R. which the Russians never publicly acknowledged or thanked us for). In January 1945, with the Red Army headed for the gates of Berlin, Stalin ordered the sacking of American Communist Party chief Earl Browder. Accused of "social imperialism," something few people could claim as a major personality flaw, Browder was inevitably replaced with the more militant William Z. Foster.

It was time to hate America again.

The change would be noted by Norma Barzman (wife of Communist screenwriter Ben Barzman) in her book *The Red and the Blacklist*. At a party at the Barzmans' house after Browder was replaced, ex-journalist Norma was present when Cole raised his glass and proclaimed (supposedly "jokingly"), "Now we can toast the revolution again!"

However, in an interesting example of Cole's contempt for the work of others, Ms. Barzman relates a time when Ben and Cole were to start collaborating on a comedy about the "Hungarian Invasion"—that is, the invasion of Hungarian screenwriters to Hollywood (Cole wouldn't be caught dead slamming the Soviets over the *real* invasion of Hungary in 1956). Norma, who was writing a story of her own upstairs in her nightgown ("as many women writers do," she claimed), would hear the two men downstairs, and through her open window, she couldn't help hearing Cole's "loud rasping voice": "[Cole would] pounce on what Ben said, shred it, relinquish it. Another flow of quiet words from Ben. Lester leaped on them, chewed them, spit them out, winding up with 'D'ya know?'" This is certainly a revealing little anecdote about the man who usually fought like a demon when his own words were challenged.

His work on *Blood on the Sun*, however, was no comedy.

Set around 1928 (President Herbert Hoover's portrait hangs from the wall of an American newsman's house), the film deals with the search by the growing fascist government to retrieve the infamous Tanaka Plan, the secret document supposedly detailing Japanese plans for world conquest. However, like the Protocols of the Elders of Zion which alleged that Jews were also planning world conquest, the Plan was considered fake by many scholars, a myth created by racist hate groups. (Because of continued anti-Semitism, however, the Protocols would have a much longer shelf life, and to this day this fantasy document is frequently published in Arab-language periodicals, certain literary outlets in Europe, many global websites and, ironically, even Japan.)

In the late 1920s, the Japanese government and their secret police organs are literally up in arms by an article by American news correspondent Nick Condon (James Cagney, perfect for this role), mentioning Japanese plans for world conquest, as per the Tanaka Plan. The Japanese officials are a varied and badly made-up lot: Premier Tanaka (character villain and stage actor John Emery); Colonel Hideki Tojo (Robert Armstrong, wearing outsized buck teeth that threaten to leap out of his mouth and attack the audience); secret policeman Hijikata (Leonard Strong, later *Get Smart*'s Asian Kaos villain, the Claw); and secret police official Yamada (Marvin Miller, future star of the TV series *The Millionaire*). Since he is played by Cagney, Nick is still the Professional Againster, a tough guy who doesn't compromise his beliefs to save the Japanese government's face or anybody else's.

The newsman is also playing footsy with one of their top secret agents, Iris Hilliard (a totally miscast Sylvia Sidney). Wearing preposterous half-Asian makeup, Sidney is playing a woman who is half-Chinese ("She is *Chinese*!" is spat out like a racist epithet by Tanaka when he is asked about her). Apparently, Cole never explained just why the racist Japanese have employed a female Chinese secret agent to work for them. During a romantic clinch with Nick (who is half-Irish, half-Norwegian, like the actor playing him), the newsman shrugs off any qualms about the interracial coupling by asking her, tongue in cheek, "Hey, you runnin' down the Irish?" "Oh, thank you, Nick!" she replies happily, as if that solved all their problems. Certainly, it doesn't solve the problem of Japanese sexism. "Japanese women aren't allowed to think. It's against the law," Iris says. Again, Cole was wrong. Japanese sexism wasn't decreed by law. In many societies around the globe, sexism was maintained by centuries of tradition in male-dominated cultures and cut across all racial and political lines, even Communist ones.

However, Cole does brings out the racial angle again with the character of double-dealing newsman Cassell (Rhys Williams), who declares that he has nothing against the Chinese. "All my best friends are Chinese, eh?" Nick replies sardonically. Cassell had raised funds from anti-fascist Asians back in the States, then absconded with the money. Of course, the Japanese will double-cross him as they double-cross everyone else.

Frequently throughout the film, Cole mentions certain anti-militarist characters as "liberal," a ridiculous term which was never a part of Japanese feudal culture. Unfortunately, the scenarist tried to recast Japanese politics more along American lines with a term that would easily be recognized by the audience (and use the term "liberal" instead of the more damaging word "Communist"). Even in Communist director Edward Dmytryk's *Behind the Rising Sun*, an anti-militarist minister uses the term "liberal" to describe enemies of the regime.

Meanwhile, Nick is put through the wringer. Iris is really (big surprise here) an agent for the Chinese, and is intent on taking the Plan out of the country in order to expose (I have to say this) *the whole insidious scheme!* But the Imperial police are closing in. Nick rejects official protection by U.S. ambassador Johnny Clark (Beaver's dad, Hugh Beaumont), and races to a waterfront shack rendezvous with Iris and an aging "liberal" ex-government minister who vouches for the Plan's authenticity with his signature. However, the old man is shot dead as soon as he leaves (another big surprise) by Imperial police thug Captain Oshima (hulking John Halloran, another actor in need of dental hygiene due to the oversized buck teeth he's forced to wear).

In pure *Casablanca* farewell mode, Nick tells Iris to escape with her friends in a rowboat behind the shack while he (rather needlessly) faces down the man who murdered his newsman friend (Wallace Ford) and his wife (Warner contract player Rosemary DeCamp). (Younger than Cagney, DeCamp played his *mom* in *Yankee Doodle Dandy*.) In a knockdown drag-out karate-judo-boxing match that makes frequent use of stuntmen, Nick throws the hulking secret policeman into the drink behind the shack.

Hunted by the Imperial police, Nick finally hitches a ride on a truck and ends up in front of the U.S. embassy. Attempting to run a gauntlet of Yamada's men, he is shot and wounded. Not finding the incriminating document on Nick, Yamada is given a dressing down by Johnny Clark for shooting an American citizen.

However, when a humbled Yamada attempts to shake hands with Nick, begging him to "forgive one's enemies," Nick replies with the famous line: "Sure, Yamada, forgive your enemies ... but first, *get even*!" It is a controversial line that leaves no room for turning the other cheek, or in forgetting the crimes of your enemies any time soon. I can plainly say that, in the wake of 9/11, many New Yorkers were reminded of "the Jimmy Cagney movie" which promised revenge on this country's enemies; in this case it was replacing revenge against Imperial Japanese forces with revenge against the Islamofascists who murdered close to 3,000 New Yorkers on September 11, 2001.

Apparently without telling Lester Cole, the Cagney brothers hired scenarist Nathaniel Curtis to rewrite the film's final scenes; and it is Curtis whom we can credit with the classic line.

Cole's ending wouldn't have been half as memorable. In his version of the climax, Nick and Iris fly the Tanaka Plan to the League of Nations in Geneva to show that the Japanese were already planning to attack Manchuria. According to Bernard F. Dick, Cole was implying that "the League, catering to Chiang Kai-shek's anti–Communism, was indirectly responsible for leaving Japanese imperialism unchecked during the 1930s." However, to the endless frustration of Cole and other Hollywood Communists, Chiang, though an arrogant leader in his own right (Secretary of State George C. Marshall reportedly couldn't stand him), the Chinese leader was still considered an important ally. As Dick wrote:

> While not an icon on the order of General MacArthur, the Generalissimo and his wife always drew applause from World War II audiences when they appeared on the screen in a newsreel. To cast doubt on Chiang's integrity would verge on the sacrilegious.[34]

Cagney was a leftist himself during the 1930s, and in the film, he actually delivers Cole's coded line, "Let's toast to ten days that shook the world." Though it supposedly alluded to the time he'd known Iris, those "in the know" will interpret it as celebrating the Bolshevik Revolution.

However, with Curtis' changed ending, done on the direct orders of the Cagney brothers, Cole smelled a reactionary rat crawling around the Cagney production offices. Indeed, Cole must have felt the same way Ben Barzman did when he "chewed" and "spat out" his collaborator's words at the Barzmans' house. Since Cole was not one to let anyone mess with his Golden Marxist words without damning them to hell, the scenarist's response was predictable.

In a confidential FBI memo, dated July 11, 1946, the SAC (Special Agent in Charge) of the Los Angeles field office took note of a Cole article in the *Hollywood Quarterly* that criticized the Cagneys. Apparently proud of his attack, Cole devoted several pages to the controversy in his autobiography *Hollywood Red*. Having claimed in his article that the Cagneys were pressured by William Randolph Hearst to change the ending, Cole goes on to describe his reaction to the ending after the film's preview. Ironically sounding like the fictional Nick Condon, Cole wrote: "I was furious. After the preview I told Jimmy Cagney that it wasn't just me he sold out, but the American people, and he would hear more about it. Always a decent guy, he seemed embarrassed." Once again, Cole is portraying himself as the Noble Hero of our times who tells off the Powers That Be and gets no back-talk in return. However, he was right about one thing: Cagney *was* a decent man. During the 1930s, the actor had sincerely contributed to funds that would help the Loyalists defeat Franco, gave generously to help striking workers, and was one of the celebrities who lobbied FDR to stop doing business with Nazi Germany.

However, by the mid–1940s, the actor had gotten fed up with those on the left. Especially galling to him was the fact that they did nothing while liberals like him were being thrown into the same political bed as Communists. Indeed, liberal actors like Cagney wanted to preserve their careers, and the John Howard Lawsons and Lester Coles of Hollywood didn't lift a finger to help them by declaring that they were *not* members of the Party (as Clifford Odets would later do before HUAC on behalf of John Garfield). Already spooked by his HUAC appearance in 1940 (along with Bogart and Fredric March), Cagney knew he had to fend for himself, and if that meant rejecting Party dogma (despite the "ten days that shook the world" line), so be it. Obviously, Cole's attack on the Cagney brothers did *not* make Cagney feel "embarrassed" at all; it should have made him angry. The actor's quiet slide over to the conservative side of the aisle had already begun. Thanks to Communists like Lester Cole, he embraced the right wholeheartedly from then on.

Ironically, when the anti-racist Cole recited the film's final scene in *Hollywood Red*, he unwittingly fell into some racist stereotypes: "At that point, the embassy guards [there was only Hugh Beaumont] rescue him. The Japanese say, 'So sorry. Big mistake. Very sorry. Excuse please!'"

The pidgin English apologies, so common in wartime propaganda films using anti–Japanese stereotypes, are nowhere in the finished film.

Ultimately, *Blood on the Sun* made $3,400,000 in the U.S. alone.[35] It continued Cagney's bankability and, despite his churlish complaining about changes to his script, the bankability of Lester Cole's work as well. MGM official Jack Cummings (Louis Mayer's nephew) called Cole's agent and offered to have the Communist screenwriter work for the studio with the lion. Now having cut loose Dalton Trumbo, mighty Metro was going to hire another Communist screenwriter.

However, Cole's tenure at MGM, like his tenure at other studios, wasn't going to last for long...

"I look at the material as a combination of two elements; a love story, and an important, timely piece of material. In this respect the change of title from *Al Schmid—Marine* to *This Love of Ours* has been good. This *is* a love story of two American kids, not a war story."[36] This was Albert Maltz writing to producer Jerry Wald on June 26, 1944. The project in question would soon go through yet another title change, to *Pride of the Marines*. The love story about "two American kids" was apparently going to be put on the back burner.

As a Warner contract writer, Maltz had certainly contributed to the wartime propaganda effort. In 1943's *Destination Tokyo*, the Communist screenwriter gave us a fine, suspenseful submarine adventure, but at least one line blatantly reminded us of American corporate dealings with the Axis. When Cary Grant's captain brandishes a metal bolt that had been part of a Japanese bomb, he notes that the piece was stamped "Made in the U.S.A." Wryly, he remarks, "The appeaser's contribution to the war effort."

In *Destination Tokyo* and *Air Force*, John Garfield had been just part of the gang, clearly reduced to supporting player until the studio could find something worthy of him. Not that the star wasn't patriotic; he contributed greatly to the war effort, including starting the Hollywood Canteen with Bette Davis. However, his appearance in outside projects like *The Fallen Sparrow* for RKO made Jack Warner sit up and take notice.

Again, Garfield appeared in a war-themed film, but this time he was center stage. Al Schmid was a foundry worker who lived in a rented room in a poor section of Philadelphia. After enlisting in the Marines, he became a hero who was blinded by a Japanese grenade while fighting on Guadalcanal. Based on the *Life* magazine article (and later book) by Roger Butterfield, the film was adapted by Marvin Borowsky, with a screenplay by Maltz and an uncredited Delmer Daves, who also directed. In a letter to Daves, dated November 7, 1944, Jerry Wald wrote, "Garfield is literally floating on air" after having read the script. Considering his previous Warner outings, how could he not be?

Garfield is supported in the film by new contract starlet Eleanor Parker, less mannered than usual, as Schmid's girl Ruth Hartley, and Dane Clark as Lee Diamond, the unit's Jewish leader of the machine gun squad. Maltz and Daves have Schmid go from a happy-go-lucky Joe, sparring with a tempestuous Ruth, to an embittered man forced to deal with permanent blindness. To his credit, Maltz makes a forceful case for a blind man's still being productive in our society, but the scenarist *really* excels in a scene in the veterans' hospital rec room, as the wounded vets (whose wounds are so negligible, they could only have been approved of by the Production Code) worry about their futures in a postwar America.

Chief among the griping soldiers is the tactfully named Irish (new WB contract player Don McGuire) bitterly slamming companies that would "sell oil to Japan or do business with another Hitler." He also expresses the fear that he and other vets will not end up selling apples on street corners, as many of them did after the previous world war. Maltz's Communist social politics are front and center here, especially in the part of wounded veteran Ainslee (Mark Stevens, here called Stephen Richards). Ainslee is the rich kid of the group, so of course he is also shown to be a racist when he criticizes foreigners for not fighting in the war, saying this right in front of a Latino veteran in a wheelchair. The brainwashing is a bit sledgehammer here; not only is the rich kid a racist, and not only does he look fine for a recuperating veteran, but he also wants to run for Congress! If anything, one must praise Garfield's incredible lack of ego; the film's undisputed star, he quietly hangs back and allows the supporting players to dominate the scene.

Still, Maltz's creative talent and his compassion towards the returning vets help push the film into making an urgent, ahead-of-its-time statement. In a letter to Wald, dated June 26, the scenarist expressed his concerns:

> By the time this film will be released there will be not a few boys home from the battlefield, some with permanent disabilities. Everybody is going to be thinking of this question of the returning veterans. Our film will face it squarely — and we will come up with the answer that *there is* a future for the Al Schmids, as well as for all the returning soldiers.

However, other considerations also came up; including not making the hero spout the typical racist epithets of the type heard often in war films of lesser quality. In an October 20 letter to Wald, Herman Lissauer of the Warner research department warns the producer about allowing Schmid to make racist statements *before* he even gets on the battlefield. In Scene 40, Maltz has Schmid say such lines as "The only Japs I've ever seen are those slant-eyes at Atlantic City" and "Those Japs always did look slinky. Shootin' Japs oughtta be more fun." Lissauer convincingly argued:

> This indicates that Al was prejudiced against all Japanese long before the war. American policy towards American Japanese is to avoid lumping the good Japanese with the bad, and every effort is being made to make the American people feel that there are innumerable good, loyal Japanese citizens in this country. Many soldiers of Japanese descent have died in the defense of our country.

Unfortunately, copies of Lissauer's memo were not distributed to those policy-makers who ordered the Japanese into interment camps on the West Coast.

However, Maltz making Schmid sound anti–Japanese did not make the screenwriter a closet racist. In a long letter to Wald, dated December 2, Maltz gave the producer detailed script suggestions. One of them concerned Schmid's controversial lines:

> Al's talk about the Japanese he used to see in Atlantic City is right out of the Butterfield biography, I know.... This is an essentially backward and racist approach that Al manifests here to the Japanese people. What makes the Japanese our enemies has nothing to do with slant eyes.

BLIND MAN'S BLUFF. Eleanor Parker watches the bitter John Garfield as he projects phony cheerfulness to the innocent Ann Todd in *Pride of the Marines* (1945). Albert Maltz's excellent screenplay emphasized the need for veterans to get better employment opportunities in the postwar period.

> If it did, we'd be fighting the Chinese too. If we were doing a novel about Al, a statement like this would absolutely belong — but in a novel we would be able to show all sides of Al's character. We would then understand that this came out of the backwardness which a great many Americans suffer and as such we would make a point by stating it.

The film solves this problem by making Schmid's bigotry for the Japanese become murderous hatred, but these statements are made *after* he is blinded by the Japanese, while standing on a train platform getting a ride home. In fact, after he says these lines, Ruth and Diamond look at each other worriedly. This implies that Al's bitterness is natural, but still unsettling.

At another point in the letter, Maltz makes a good argument for building up Schmid's Jewish buddy, Diamond:

> [It] is essential for the health of America to take every opportunity to counteract the insidious Nazi propaganda in our country. One of the especially spread lies has been the statement that the Jews of America have not taken their part in the fighting forces.

Garfield's performance was his best in films so far, and Maltz's work was nominated for a Best Screenplay Oscar. In the next few years, both men would rise artistically to even greater rewards in the film industry; bigger pictures with higher budgets and even more Oscar nominations. With the war now over, it looked like a bright future for Garfield and Maltz.

But the Communist Party and HUAC were about to submit their own scripts...

IV

A Revolution from Above (1946–1951)

> Gratitude is a dog's disease.
> — Josef Stalin

World War II had been good to the Marxist screenwriters. Never in their careers would they be so busy, or would their bank accounts grow so much.

So as millions died in the gas chambers and crematoriums of Nazi-occupied Europe, in the prisons and concentration camps of the U.S.S.R., and on the battlefields of Europe and Asia, the scenarists of the Hollywood Communist Party were at the peaks of their careers. Living in a free country run by a president sympathetic to the Soviets and naïve about Stalin's madness, the Marxist screenwriters had no idea that things would change quickly in a few short years.

With the war over and the Soviet Union triumphant over Germany, the U.S.S.R. sought to flex its muscles outside its borders. Its wartime allies, led by the weak-willed and dying FDR, did literally nothing to curb the Soviets' many outrages, from the murder of Polish officers in the Katyn forest to their allowing the Nazi massacre of fighters in the Warsaw Uprising; instead, the democracies accepted its belligerent and harmful behavior in order to keep it as an ally. Reluctant to take on the Soviets in a new war, the democracies told themselves that Stalin and the Communists would change, and took as gospel truth Uncle Joe's unconvincing assurances that Eastern Europe would live under the banner of freedom. Rather predictably, the result was the Soviet annexation of Eastern Europe.

Appeasement had once again returned after a brief vacation in the late 1930s.

Certainly, if the democracies thought that exposure to democratic nations would turn Stalin and his followers into allowing freedom for the people within Russia's own borders, they were sadly mistaken. There was more paranoia, more state-sponsored liquidations, more persecution and more censorship. The number of those citizens murdered by the Soviet government grew to over twenty million. It is in the shadow of these world-shaking events in the U.S.S.R. that one must look at the new situation of the Hollywood Party screenwriters.

Earl Browder, who had steered the Party on a more cooperative footing with the U.S., had been unceremoniously kicked out as head of the American Communist Party (also known as the "Communist Political Association," or CPUSA in many FBI files). During the wartime alliance, Communist attacks on America were basically non-existent. The

United States was the main supplier to the Soviets of machinery and building materials for their shattered industries, as well as weapons for the Red Army. The Communists needed the U.S. more than the Americans needed the U.S.S.R. With orders straight from the top (meaning, of course, Stalin), the CPUSA was not to attack America for the duration of the struggle. In fact, while the lynchings of African Americans continued unabated, Japanese citizens on the West Coast were thrown into internment camps, and the employment of low-paying, non-union labor went on, the Party was remarkably silent. "Don't attack those who were helping the Russian war effort," was the Party's ironclad rule for four long years.

That rule was about to be broken.

In March, 1945, as both American and Soviet forces were speeding to crush remaining Nazi armies trapped in Berlin, the streets outside a certain Hollywood studio would be the scene of another kind of battle; in its own way, just as ideologically symbolic as the battle taking place outside the gates of Germany's capital.

Though it remains debatable whether Moscow actually dictated the policies of certain Communist-dominated Hollywood unions, one particularly violent labor action in early 1945 calls into question whether the timing was a coincidence.

The Conference of Studio Unions, consisting of a mostly Communist membership, fought to become the dominant union among the Hollywood studios. However, they were opposed by the left-leaning but anti–Communist International Alliance of Theatrical Stage Employees (IATSE). Though this was at first considered a jurisdictional dispute, the issues soon became much larger, with the very real fear of Communist domination of all Hollywood labor in the balance. The head of the Hollywood Communist Party, John Howard Lawson, instantly backed the CSU and demanded that the Screen Writers Guild do so as well. Typically, Lester Cole, Dalton Trumbo and other hard-line Communists went into lockstep with Lawson's demands, though the writers' union itself wanted to remain more or less neutral. Other Hollywood unions wanted to keep out of it as well (with the Screen Actors Guild alone voting 3,029 to 88 not to support the CSU strike[1]); but Herb Sorell, head of the CSU, as well as Lawson, Cole and their allies, had a certain talent for throwing gasoline on the fire.

The conflagration officially started at 7:00 A.M. on the morning of October 5, 1945, when 800 members of the CSU, led by Sorell, fought against the LAPD outside the gates of Warner Brothers. Armed with knives and baseball bats, CSU members not only injured cops trying to put down the riot, but any worker trying to enter the studio, with several unfortunates getting hot coffee purposely splashed in their faces. The "Battle of Burbank" became a legend in Hollywood. It forced actors and studios technicians to ride in studio-hired buses as CSU members threw stones and even pipes at the windows. As fists, missiles and tear gas dominated the air outside Warners, this horror show did not escape the attention of Jack Warner. Justifiably seeing a Red boogeyman behind much of the violence, the formally leftist studio head was rapidly swinging to the right. Other studios would also be struck by the CSU until late 1946. Though there are many who can justifiably condemn the Hollywood moguls for acquiescing to the blacklist years later, they might have had a little push in this direction after viewing (safely from a distance, that is) the violence outside the gates of their own studios.[2]

While the CSU strikes were still going on in 1946, future SAG president Ronald Reagan heard of a meeting at Ida Lupino's house where Communists were trying to sway guild members to side with the CSU. Lupino was no Communist, and the actress was appalled that the 75 or so people on her patio were *not* being constructive about the dispute. When

Reagan and his pal William Holden showed up, Lupino was grateful for their appearance; the Communists assembled around her pool and tennis court clearly *weren't*. Waiting for the right moment, Reagan took the floor and, in his own words, "confronted one of the most hostile audiences I ever hope to address."[3] He spoke for 40 minutes and somehow kept his own anger in check despite "interruptions and boos and the customary name-calling."

Despite his fury, however, Reagan was quite familiar with this type of audience by now. At a previous union gathering, the future SAG leader came face to face with the redoubtable John Howard Lawson. Putting his long index finger under Reagan's nose, the screenwriter allegedly shouted, "This organization will never adopt a statement which endorses free enterprise and repudiates Communism! And for your information, I may add that a two-party system is in no way necessary or even desirable for a democracy!"[4]

Now Reagan stood before the same type of audience and tried to sell a basically anti–Communist agenda to a group of Marxists. However, not everyone in the crowd was hostile to other points of view. At one point during the numerous boos, catcalls and personal insults heaped upon Reagan, John Garfield stood up and admonished them: "Why don't you listen to him? He does have information you don't have."[5]

This show of support shocked Reagan, who previously suspected that Garfield "seemed too close to the other camp to be on his feet defending me." Grateful, Reagan later said that he and Holden always regretted not inviting Garfield to join them afterwards for a few friendly beers.

After Garfield's noble act, Communist performer Howard DaSilva physically escorted Garfield to the back of the garden. Crowding Garfield against a tree and grabbing his shirt front, DaSilva then read him the riot act ("punctuated by a jabbing finger," Reagan claimed). It must also be emphasized that DaSilva was a rather tall, hulking actor perfect for playing villains (he menaced Alan Ladd through many a Paramount vehicle) while Garfield, though taller than Ladd, was still physically smaller than DaSilva. In his fine Garfield biography *He Ran All The Way*, Robert Nott commented: "It was later revealed that Reagan was an undercover agent for the FBI; he told about seeing Howard DaSilva ... silence Julie [Garfield] at a politically charged meeting in Hollywood in 1949."

Reagan may have been an undercover agent for the FBI (and it was hard *not* to be one after having John Howard Lawson's finger waved under your nose), but a few details are wrong here. For one, the CSU mess was considerably muted by 1949, with Herb Sorell eventually fired from the union and the CSU more or less put out of action. Another is that, in his autobiography, the future president never once mentioned the name of the thug-like actor who crowded Garfield against a tree and read him the riot act.

In fact, in *Where's the Rest of Me?*, Reagan merely calls Garfield's tormentor "a well-known character actor."[6] In 1965 when his autobiography came out, tell-all bios were still written with a certain amount of class and consideration to those still living. With the formerly blacklisted DaSilva starting to get hired again by the mid–1960s, Reagan gracefully backed off from labeling the future portrayer of Benjamin Franklin as a most un–American bully.

Two months after the release of *Pride of the Marines*, one of showbiz's greatest icons was doing his part for the cause of the American Way. On November 1, 1945, Frank Sinatra paid a visit to the Froebel School in Gary, Indiana, where white students and faculty led a strike against an effort to desegregate the school. At the time, the former poor kid from Hoboken, New Jersey, was a performer who publicly fought the good fight against racism and anti–Semitism. The ideology of brotherhood, however, didn't necessarily carry over into Sinatra's personal life, especially in his later years. He was known to angrily spit out racist epithets (sometimes about his close friend, Sammy Davis Jr.), as well as express feelings of anti–Semitism, despite having many Jewish friends (again, like Sammy Davis Jr.) and being a supporter of Israel.

Yet Sinatra, for all his penchant for bullying, his palling around with Mafia thugs, his crudeness, his blatant sexism, his outrageous vanity and his oversized ego, he could also rise to the level of greatness when he wanted to, as a later FBI summary of his activities on November 1, 1945, proved. Compiled in 1950 by the FBI field office in Indianapolis, this confidential memo shows us Sinatra the Man as he faced down Gary's bigots:

> Confronting a rowdy and antagonistic audience in the school auditorium, Sinatra stood center stage, his arms folded, staring down the crowd for two anxious minutes, until the catcalls and stomping gave way to absolute silence. Then he stepped up to the microphone, and announced, Hoboken-style, "I can lick any son of a bitch in this joint." Hostility gave way to cheers, but his impassioned plea for tolerance ended up insulting some locals and failed to end the strike. It also cemented the boyish singer's status as a hero to American liberals of every stripe, including Communists.[7]

Of course, since he was Frank Sinatra, he didn't mince words either. And in the shadow of the encroaching blacklist era, the singer openly named names, only this time they were bigots who were masquerading as Gary's most respected citizens. He named undertaker Joseph Lach, city custodian Julius Danch and student strike leader Leonard Levenda. The FBI summary even goes further:

> As a result of Sinatra's attack on Lach and Danch, Father Lawrence T. Grothaus, Pastor of the Saint Anthony's Church and Director of the Catholic Youth Organization in Gary, left the stage in disgust. Father Grothaus told Sinatra's manager, George Evans, that Sinatra should not have delved into personalities. Evans reportedly replied that Sinatra's information was in part, at least, received from the confidential files of the FBI. He later stated that he could not recall who had made the statement regarding FBI files; however, Evans' statements pertaining to FBI files was witnessed by Police Captain Peter Billick and Patrolman (name blacked out) of the Gary, Indiana Police Department.[8]

A police investigation of Sinatra's activities, from the time he arrived in Gary to the time he left that same night, showed that the singer had no time to contact the Indianapolis field office. Did Sinatra, the well-known friend to notorious mob figures, have a secret contact with the FBI? And did said FBI contact reveal to the singer the identities of the bigots behind the school's racial strife? It was a given that the Bureau had information on the town's leading movers and shakers, but Sinatra's controversial activities obviously didn't end in Gary in 1945. Though there would be even bigger questions to ask concerning an FBI/mob/Sinatra/Kennedy/Monroe/CIA and God-knows-who-else connection in the turbulent 1960s, during the '40s the singer was already being referred to in FBI files as both a "Communist sympathizer" and a "fellow traveler."

Fully realizing this (or was he *told* this by friendly FBI agents?), in the early 1950s, at the height of the blacklist, Sinatra had his people contact the Bureau and offer the singer's services as an FBI informant — not against the Mob, but against the Communists (Sinatra was anything but suicidal). There were ample reasons for this sudden concern with the Communist menace; one major reason was that the singer's career was in serious trouble.

Whether producers were fed up with his social causes (which were usually backed by Communist front organizations) or, more likely, they took note of his string of box office flops for MGM, Hollywood backed away from the Voice. By 1952, Sinatra had to ask his lover, Ava Gardner, for plane fare to fly back to Hollywood to audition for *From Here to Eternity*. Columbia president Harry Cohn had Eli Wallach in mind for the role of the hell-raising Private Maggio. However, things were about to change.

It is not known if J. Edgar Hoover, the FBI director who ideologically sided with Gary's racists, found Sinatra's offer to inform on the Communists amusing. However, the results of the offer were revealing. Though Hoover ultimately turned it down, the offer itself had miraculously beneficial effects on Sinatra's career. Eli Wallach was out as Maggio and Sinatra was now *in*. The singer won an Oscar for his performance and the decade of the 1950s became, to put it in the singer's native Hobokenese, like a broad that didn't stop for nuttin'.

But in 1945, after one war ended and with a Cold one on the horizon, the singer was still working professionally with people who were featured regularly in the FBI's COMPIC files.

By the fall of 1945, formerly blasé American audiences who had weathered a non-stop glut of war movies were about to get a shock when they were allowed to view newly released Nazi concentration camp footage. These documentaries, emphatically *not* written by Dalton Trumbo or John Howard Lawson (Communist artists who were every bit as responsible for the clichés of the Hollywood war film as John Wayne had been accused of), horrified those who already believed the Nazis were evil, but never thought that even they could sink to such insane depths.

Then, on November 9, exactly three months after the A-bomb was dropped on Nagasaki, Frank Ross Productions released an 11-minute short subject to the nation's theaters. Directed without credit by Mervyn LeRoy, the film starred Frank Sinatra and was written by Albert Maltz. Footage of concentration camps may have made audiences cry, but *The House I Live In* was made to make audiences cheer. Not only did the film take a stand against bigotry, but it also instilled pride in our nation. When a rowdy youth accuses Sinatra of being stupid, the singer answers, "Not me. I'm an American."

Our story begins in a recording studio where the Voice is singing "If You Are But a Dream." Since Sinatra is singing it, the rendition is, of course, nothing less than perfect. But the picture is not about Frankie making bobby-soxers swoon, but a subject of more importance. After the recording session is over, Frankie leaves the studio by way of the alley where he is just in time to stop a pogrom.

Apparently a gang of kids has chased another kid (with dark hair and apparently Semitic features) into the alley's corner. When the singer asks the gang's leader why the kid is being chased, the answer is that they don't like his religion. No one could fault Albert Maltz for attempting to show his people as the victims of bigotry and to bring the matter front and center to movie audiences. Though the boy's religion is not mentioned, we knew that this dark-haired white kid wasn't Hindu or Buddhist, so what else could he be but Jewish—especially with theaters down the block probably showing documentaries on Auschwitz?

Sinatra is convincingly outraged and compares the gang to those "Nazi werewolves" he'd heard about. To today's audiences, the term may be laughable, and the picture of SS men turning into lycanthropes probably comes to mind; yet immediately after the war, Allied occupation forces had to deal with groups of diehard Nazi saboteurs euphemistically called Werewolves. These post–Third Reich terrorists also make an appearance in Samuel

Touch this kid and I break your face! Frank Sinatra confronts a group of little Hitler Youth in the Oscar-winning 1945 short *The House I Live In*. The Albert Maltz screenplay exposed the dangers of American youth being instilled with Nazi-like bigotry. Around the same time, theaters were showing newly released concentration camp footage.

Fuller's powerful *Verboten!* in 1959 (where a young would-be Werewolf is shown concentration camp footage to dissuade him from his path).

"No one calls me a Nazi!" shouts the gang's leader, claiming his father was a sergeant in the army. Here, Maltz had just broken a forbidden taboo under both the Production Code and the Bureau of Motion Pictures which oversaw propaganda dealing with the war. Before this moment, we never really had an implication of U.S. soldiers expressing bigoted sentiments outside the usual anti–German and anti–Japanese epithets during the war. But in this case, Maltz is showing a boy taught to hate another American; his bigotry is aimed at a citizen on these shores, not a wartime enemy. It is certainly implied that the boy learned his religious hatred from his American soldier dad; one of the first times on an American screen that a soldier of the United States, previously seen as a hero, was portrayed as someone who could teach their children Nazi-like hatred.

Sinatra explains that if the kid's father was wounded, the blood plasma needed to save his life might come from a soldier of another religion, like the father of the boy chased into the alley. Again, Nazi racial dogma is attacked, this time their cherished belief in a race that is of "pure blood." Despite Maltz's lapse of judgment when showing us a Japanese destroyer getting bombed by our Air Force, a bit that doesn't mix with the message of peace and brotherhood, we're back on track when the Chairman of the Board belts out the powerful "The House I Live In," a number which leaves these Aryan punks literally speechless.

At the end, after Sinatra is called back into the studio to cut another song, the gang, now full of love for all peoples everywhere, welcome the little Jewish kid into their ranks as a patriotic tune is played in the background.

Now if only Sinatra had sung "The House I Live In" in Arab countries…

The picture won the Oscar for Best Short Subject, the only time a production written by Maltz was so honored (though at other times he *was* nominated). Despite its obvious clichés, the film is still moving in its intended goal of showing bigotry as a disease not restricted to National Socialists.

In the coming years, as both the Cold War and the blacklist solidified its hold on the nation, Sinatra's career rose as Maltz's fell. However, by the early 1960s, the attempt to break Maltz's blacklist would have a far different outcome than the successful collaboration that brought the world *The House I Live In*.

> One day [Adrian] Scott and I were walking across the [RKO] lot and I happened to mention that I was reading an interesting book.
> "Which book?" asked Adrian.
> "[Arthur] Koestler's *Darkness at Noon*," I replied.
> Adrian stopped in his tracks, turned to me, and spoke in a hushed voice. "Good God," he said, "don't ever mention that to anyone in the group."
> I was honestly puzzled. "Why not?" I asked.
> "It's on the list," replied Scott. "Koestler is an ex–Communist. Everything he writes is corrupt, and no member of the Party is allowed to read him."
> That was the end of the honeymoon for me, but by no means the end of the marriage. That would be brought about by further events related to *Cornered*.

The above story was related by Edward Dmytryk in his autobiography *A Hell of a Life, But Not a Bad Living*. *Darkness at Noon* was ex–Communist's Koestler's devastating portrait of Soviet tyranny by detailing one man's inner fight against the inhuman Bolshevik prison system. What is shocking in Dmytryk's anecdote is that a political group that has declared one of its aims to be freedom of expression actually has a list of forbidden books that were not to be read, making said political group sound like some fascist entity.

Mind you, this is Dmytryk obviously telling his side of the famous break with his former leftist comrades in the Party; the same Dmytryk who refused to name names to HUAC in 1947, and then, desperate to get back in the Hollywood whirl, decided to name names on April 25, 1951. On the other side of the fence, the Party faithful always treated Dmytryk as something on the moral level of measles, though perhaps without the need for an inoculation.

Despite the Party's contempt for Koestler's groundbreaking expose (which, because of good taste, couldn't graphically relate *all* the violent acts committed by the NKVD on its prisoners), Dmytryk goes on to mention a film that audiences thought was just an entertaining little revenge melodrama from RKO. Indeed, they never suspected that *Cornered* would be the touchstone for one man's own Red Revolution.

By 1945, Dmytryk was RKO's Golden Boy. With his seventh RKO film *Murder My Sweet*, the helmsman had finally come into his own, breaking forever from his sometimes sordid B movie past. Despite the liberties taken with Raymond Chandler's novel (such as removing Moose Manson's murder of an African American), the film elevated Dmytryk to the status of Hollywood big-shot and also served as a comeback for former 1930s crooner Dick Powell. In fact, the film unleashed a dormant talent in Powell for playing wisecracking tough guys, putting the former singer on the course of producer-director that would extend his career past the 1950s, until his untimely death from cancer on January 3, 1963.

Philip Marlowe was one thing; *Cornered*, however, was a far different animal. It originated as a 54-page screen story by no less an author than Ben Hecht, with collaboration by Herman Mankiewicz and Czenzi Ormonde (who completely rewrote Chandler's screenplay, without credit, for Hitchcock's *Stranger on a Train*). The plot dealt with an American seaman, a former prisoner of a Nazi P.O.W. camp, who tracks down the man responsible for murdering his brother in Vichy France. The trail takes him to the Caribbean, where he finds that someone else has murdered the man he'd been seeking.

According to Dmytryk, producer William Dozier had purchased a 20-page treatment of "a tough suspense mystery written by Ben Hecht." But then Dmytryk changes his tune (kind of like his HUAC testimony) about the merits of the property: "Or was it [a treatment by Hecht]? It was such poor stuff that we were inclined to guess that Hecht had simply put his name to someone else's material and shared in the payoff, which was a fat $50,000."

Then Dmytryk explained how Hecht and his partner, Charles MacArthur, did this kind of thing *a lot*; that is, putting their names on inferior scripts and sharing a big paycheck with the hack who really wrote it. "*Cornered* was more of the same," claimed the helmsman.

The script was rewritten by another scenarist whose identity Dmytryk seems to have had trouble remembering. After Adrian Scott replaced Dozier as producer (and presumably he and Dmytryk had that supposedly life-changing walk across the RKO lot discussing *Darkness at Noon*), the two men hired, to their eternal regret, John Wexley ("a man of extreme leftist leanings," said Dmytryk) to rework the screenplay. Wexley, you might remember, was the hard-nosed Party member who wrote Hal Wallis and expressed misgivings about writing the script for *The Sea Wolf* that might imply any anti–Nazi message at the time of the Nazi-Soviet Pact. Now Wexley, not having any restraints on attacking National Socialism, was writing a script about a man taking revenge against fascists.

By the time Wexley took the assignment, however, the premise had changed somewhat. Now the hero was a Canadian flyer held in a Vichy prison camp who was searching for an SS officer who had been responsible for the death of the pilot's young French wife, and subsequently tracking the fiend to Buenos Aires.

However, as Dmytryk claimed later on, "[L]ong before Wexley had finished his version of the script, even Scott realized we were in trouble." In *The Last Mile*, the Broadway hit of 1930, Wexley attacks the capitalist prison system and the society that literally created a protagonist like the play's Killer Mears (played by such future screen stars as Spencer Tracy and Clark Gable). Wexley's politics did not change very much in fifteen years. To Dmytryk, the problem was soon obvious:

> At every turn [Wexley] inserted long speeches loaded with Communist propaganda thinly disguised as anti-fascist rhetoric — manifestos by the dozen, but little real drama. Major surgery was in order. Wexley was allowed to finish the script, politely thanked, and dismissed. Good old reliable non-political John Paxton was called in. The script was rewritten quite extensively, retaining a strong anti-fascist bias.

In Paxton's new script, the SS officer now becomes a Vichy collaborator who ordered the murders of several innocent civilians, one of whom happened to be the wife of the flyer.

The film begins as Lawrence Gerard (a wonderful performance by Powell) returns to postwar France to seek his bride's murderer. His quest takes him to Switzerland, where he bribes an official for a visa to Latin America. (Noting the country's later revelations of crooked financial dealings with Nazi Germany, the bribe is not a surprise.) After he arrives in Argentina, it is soon obvious that pains were taken by the producers not to insult the Peron regime and to avoid controversy at all costs; in fact, Paxton's screenplay bends over so far backwards to avoid stepping on any toes, it might as well be playing Twister. The police officers that our hero runs into are about as pro-fascist as Bozo the Clown; and we are led to believe that somehow the police under the Peron dictatorship *didn't* protect Nazi war criminals.

On the plus side, however, the film is an excellent mystery where all the characters appear to be one thing and are really another (usually the best elements of a really good mystery). It is filled with actors who have played assorted notorious types

SHOOTING FROM THE HIP. Former crooner Dick Powell revealed a hidden talent for playing tough guys. One of his best performances was in Edward Dmytryk's *Cornered* (1945). The director, as well as producer Adrian Scott, would soon find themselves in trouble with the Party over this film.

before: Party member Morris Carnovsky, Walter Slezak, Edgar Barrier, Jack LaRue, Gregory Gaye and Steven Geray, all of whose characters seem to have agendas that turn out to be something completely different by the time of curtain. Powell is deserving of credit for carrying the whole show and deftly maneuvering his way through all the intrigue with his incisive wit still intact. ("When I see a man packing his suitcase, it makes me nervous," is Gerard's excuse for attempting to shoot someone.) By deliberately making the characters' motives ambivalent, Paxton fails to fall into the trap, if Dmytryk's assertions are true, that John Wexley falls into in his own script draft. According to Wexley's version, various characters loudly (and rather stupidly in Peronista Argentina) pronounce their political beliefs in endless speeches that would have tipped off the audience right away as to their motivations and agendas and ultimately destroyed any kind of mystery in the story.

But then Paxton and Dmytryk pull off a royal boner by having the hero finally come face to face with the evil Vichy collaborator at the end; unfortunately, we've never seen this guy before at any point in the film. There is no big revelation, no big unmasking scene; Jarnac just shows up because the script says he's supposed to.

Party member Luther Adler, who oddly gets special billing in the film, shows up in the last ten minutes and announces he is the evil collaborator whom Gerard has been seeking. However, that is not all he announces; to the dismay of the audience, he delivers the Wexley speeches that no one else was allowed to make (if we are to believe Dmytryk). Holding a gun on our hero in the usual dingy cellar that is the climactic setting for so many of these films at the time, Marcel Jarnac delivers his reasons for being. However, two things make this final monologue a plus: One is that it's delivered in Adler's rich voice; another is that the speech, though promoting the Evil in Man, is politically ambiguous. Though Jarnac is a fascist collaborator, the tenor of his words could also be seen as being from a Communist point of view. Especially pointed is his claim that "wherever you find the hungry, you'll find us," a remark that makes no distinction between the appeal of fascism and the appeal of any other totalitarian movement. If Dmytryk's claims are true, then he, Paxton and Scott are to be commended for making a far more biting commentary on the nature of totalitarianism than a Lester Cole or Dalton Trumbo would have (or would have dared to).

Released to a postwar audience on Christmas Day, 1945, *Cornered* sparked controversy in Communist Party circles, with the radicals apparently forgetting about Good Will Towards Men when they finally confronted Dmytryk and Scott shortly afterward.

According to Dmytryk, he received a call from John Howard Lawson at the request of John Wexley. The Party poobah just wanted to meet with Dmytryk and Scott and discuss the matter, he said. Expecting to meet with Lawson alone to discuss a script credit for Wexley, the two men were surprised to see fellow Party members Richard Collins and Paul Trivers at the supposedly private meeting (Lawson now made "the discussion" a battle of three against two). According to Dmytryk, however, there were more "discussions" after this one where he and Scott would be facing "a *committee* of the Party," a phrase which implies a whole roomful of Marxists rather than three men. As the helmsman wrote:

> [Wexley] claimed we had completely emasculated his work to the extent that, far from being the anti-fascist film that he had intended, it was now definitely slanted to the other side. He demanded that we recall the film and re-shoot his propaganda scenes which we had eliminated. The situation was unbelievable.

Certainly, to many, the above story would be unbelievable. In fact, to this day, leftist historians still have a problem with *Cornered*, and have their own version of why the script was changed from Hecht's original. According to *Blacklisted: The Film Lovers' Guide to the Hollywood Blacklist*, leftist authors Paul Buhle and Dave Wagner had no problem taking alleged HUAC "squealer" Dmytryk to task:

> What Dmytryk failed to mention, however, was the extraordinary pressure [Dmytryk and Scott] came under from representatives of Nelson Rockefeller, the U.S. government and RKO brass well before shooting started; they wanted to scrap any but the most elusive references to Argentina's anti-fascist resistance and to the fact that its Nazi problem ran a good deal deeper than a group of sympathizers in elite social circles. In spring 1945 ... Argentina broke off diplomatic relations with an all-but-defeated Germany, and the U.S. government wanted to save its new ally from embarrassment.... Dmytryk waited until Scott was dead to give his highly questionable account of this film.

Though obviously biased, the authors do make a good point about government interference in a film project that might attack a new anti–Communist Latin-American ally. Party members Ring Lardner and Lester Cole had wanted to depict South America as a new postwar haven for Nazis in the same year's *Cloak and Dagger*; but Warners, apparently bowing to outside pressure, removed all references to the continent's disturbingly friendly relations with wanted Nazis. The script had also depicted South America as a new base of operations from which escaped Nazis would launch a Fourth Reich.

Yet Buhle and Wagner could not deny (though authors of their political bent always do) the Party's dictatorial way of doing things. To Lawson and other Party members, whose history of ganging up on those who deviate from the Party line is well-documented, demanding that a film be totally re-shot might not have been an impossible demand, especially coming from such a stiff-necked source. In fact, what Lawson and others in the Party might have found so infuriating was the fact that a fascist collaborator was allowed to express his own point of view (and that Wexley's Communist characters weren't).

However, when the fascist talks about using the evil in men and fertilizing it to their advantage, it's hard for anyone to see this character as a positive figure; and it's rather odd that the highly intellectual Lawson failed to see that Dmytryk and Paxton portrayed Jarnac as a figure to hate, not one to follow. Despite Wexley's huge ego not accepting the fact that his golden Marxist words were changed, it was quite possible that Lawson actually feared that the character of Jarnac is so deliberately ambivalent about his politics that an audience unschooled in such matters will instantly mistake him for a Red.

Dmytryk claimed that he and Scott made a decision at a later meeting to leave the Party, which apparently didn't matter since they also claimed Lawson kicked them out. Hearing this version of events, Lawson later scoffed at Dmytryk's claims that "discussions with fellow craftsmen were an attempt to 'intimidate' him."[9]

Oh, is that what it was?

Despite Lawson's gentle use of the word "discussions," certainly no artist expects to stand in a roomful of fanatics and political pygmies and receive a verbal mugging as payment for all of his or her hard work. Unfortunately, when Dmytryk and Scott paid their Party dues, they got what they paid for.

The talented Albert Maltz, outraged by Lawson's and the Party's attempt at censorship, backed Dmytryk and Scott, if only temporarily. However, shortly after this controversy, when Maltz attempted to get the Party to expand its artistic horizons past the usual Marxist dogma and proletarian rhetoric, the scenarist would soon find a new meaning to the word *cornered*.

Now with Germany defeated, the mood of the Party would go back to attacking America with a vengeance. (This also gives the lie to the oft-repeated litany that a bunch of right-wing Congressmen somehow started the Cold War, while the Communists were peace-loving lambs.) Still, it was quite possible that many Party members were under the assumption that the Stalinists' exposure to America would eventually trickle down to its membership, and that a new era of glasnost might actually make its way into the CPUSA.

Albert Maltz certainly emerged from the war a changed man. He was still a dedicated Party member, but there was something in him that started to question the rigid dogma of its members, especially the dictates of John Howard Lawson, who settled all ideological arguments within the Party, and not with very much charm or tact. Maltz had bravely backed Dmytryk and Scott in their fight against Wexley and company, even though, predictably, he would again fail to take his fight past the strident Lawson's rulings. He also *privately* criticized Lawson for his brutal attacks on Budd Schulberg for writing *What Makes Sammy Run?* Though Lawson had treated Maltz no more condescendingly than anyone else in the Party, he might have reserved a special contempt for him nevertheless, going back to

Lawson's quibbling review of one of Maltz's early Broadway works. Certainly the two writers had sharp differences in their approach. For instance, unlike Lawson, whose screenplays couldn't help being sledgehammer-blunt about Marxism, Maltz usually blended his politics into his own work seamlessly, with few sudden pit stops for speeches. He had grown considerably from the didactic ideologue who authored such Broadway propaganda pieces as *Merry-Go-Round*. Besides this, he was also a successful author of novels and prize-winning short stories.

Though Lawson was the author of several (highly biased) books on film theory, his work never equaled Maltz's literary contributions; nor had he ever grown very much as a writer beyond the sketchily written characters and Party-speak of *Success Story*. Another difference between the two men was personality. Albert Maltz was a man who didn't like controversy and rarely made waves within the Party. Sensing this, Lawson, like the intellectual bully he was, enjoyed making mincemeat out of someone who craved the Party's love.

Now that fascism was defeated in Europe and Asia, Maltz wondered whether there was a need for any further stridency in the way the Party did things; particularly if being a good writer also meant slavish adherence to the Party dictates on subject matter. Soon, he was going to learn the hard way that the Party's bunker mentality had only gotten worse.

It all started with an article Maltz published in the Party periodical *New Masses* on February 12, 1946, less than two months after the release of the controversial *Cornered*. He was merely responding to Party member Isidore Schneider's request in the October *New Masses* to a question dealing with a writer's relationship between creativity and the prevailing political situation. Taking note of Schneider's "frank and earnest article about writers' problems" and calling it "very welcome," Maltz's response was the article "What Shall We Ask of Writers?" In this pertinent work, Maltz questioned, many times brilliantly, the phrase "Art as a weapon" strictly followed by Party members:

> First of all, under the domination of this vulgarized approach, creative works are judged primarily by their formal ideology. What else can happen if art is a weapon as a leaflet is a weapon? If a work, however thin or inept as a piece of literature fabric, expresses ideas that seem to fit the correct political tactics of the time, it is a foregone conclusion that it will be reviewed warmly, if not enthusiastically. But if the work, no matter how rich in human insight, character, portrayal, and imagination, seems to imply "wrong" political conclusions, then it will be indicted, severely mauled, or beheaded, as the case may be.[10]

In a "recent example of this unhappy pattern," Maltz revises the subject of the two *Watch on the Rhine* reviews published in *New Masses*. His logic is right on target: Maltz wrote that when it was produced in 1940 as a play, the *New Masses* critic attacked it. However, "[W]hen it appeared, unaltered, as a film ... the *New Masses* critic hailed it." In other words, Maltz deduced:

> The changed attitude came not from the fact that two different critics were involved, but from the fact that events had transpired (the breaking of the Pact by an attack on the U.S.S.R.) in the two years calling for a different political program.

In another example of deviating from the Party line, Maltz also suggested that the oppressed might not be the one-note victims that the Party had always portrayed them as, or that racists might have a little more dimension than the comic strip villains usually portrayed by Marxists. For a Communist writer, it was an amazing admission that racism could be practiced by anyone, not just someone of a higher social strata:

> We are all acquainted with Jews who understand the necessity of fighting fascism, but who do not see the relationship between fascism and their own discrimination towards Negroes. We

know Negroes fight discrimination themselves, but are anti–Semitic. I am acquainted with the curator of a museum who has made distinguished contributions in his scientific field, but who sees no contradiction between his veneration for science and his racist attitude towards Negroes. Out of these same human failings many artists are able to lead an intellectual life that often has a dual character.

Seeing the human experience as something that did not begin or end according to Party dictates, Maltz really lowers the ideological boom when he comments more directly on his Marxist brethren:

> Writers must be judged by their work and not by the committees they join. It is the job of the editorial section of a magazine to praise or attack citizens committees for what they stand for. It is the job of literary critics to praise the literary works only.

Throughout this groundbreaking piece, Maltz mentions the works of Steinbeck, Galsworthy, Balsac, Richard Wright and James T. Farrell (the author of *Studs Lonigan*), among others, providing detailed examples of their diversity in approach and subject matter, while they still maintained their dedication to leftist ideals. It was an article which certainly demanded far more fulsome and mature debate than the Party was capable of; unfortunately, since only Party members read it in a Party periodical, only Party members would have the chance to comment on it.

And comment they did.

Despite the fact that Maltz gave some good arguments to his theories, including some examples of literary approach from the above-named authors, Party commissars Mike Gold and John Howard Lawson saw only the perceived dig at "citizens committees" as an attack on the Party, which meant, of course, an attack on *them*. For if Party members were actually allowed more freedom to express themselves and not limit their creative choices as writers, who needed Mike Gold and John Howard Lawson to show them the way?

The result was a thunderclap heard all around Hollywood's leftist dens, and the first one to fire the shot was Gold. Dripping sarcasm and bile in the place of logical discussion, Gold went schoolyard. After accusing Maltz of "preparing to retreat into the stale, old ivory tower of the art-for-art-sakers,"[11] he slammed Maltz's defense of former Communist author James T. Farrell with some choice rhetoric that further demonstrated the sophistication and class that was so much a part of Party debate:

> Farrell is no mere committee server, but a vicious, voluble Trotskyite with many years of activity. Maltz knows that Farrell has long been a colleague of Max Eastman, Eugene Lyons and similar rats who have been campaigning with endless lies and slanders for war with the Soviet Union. It is a sign of Maltz's new personality that he hasn't the honesty to name Farrell's Trotskyism for what it is; but to pass it off as mere peccadillo. By such reasoning, Nazi rats like Ezra Pound and Knut Hansum, both superior writers to Farrell, must also be treated respectfully and even forgiven for their horrible politics because they are "artists." ... Meanwhile, let me express my sorrow that Albert Maltz seems to have let the luxury and phony atmosphere of Hollywood at last to poison him.[12]

Then, after accusing the capitalists of "plotting to establish an American fascism as a prelude to American conquest of the world," Gold magnanimously concluded, "[T]he ivory tower may produce a little piece of art now and then, but it can never serve the writer who means to fight and destroy the Hitlers of the world."

After comparing those who disagreed with the Party as "rats" and that their enemies were the "Hitlers of the world" (except, apparently, between 1939 and 1941), Gold then allowed Lawson and the Party to continue the attack. Alvah Bessie, the brave veteran who fought fascists in the Spanish Civil War, showed a definite lack of backbone by referring to Maltz as "actually anti–Marxist."[13] Party member Howard Fast, the future author of *Spartacus*, accused Maltz of promoting the "ideology of liquidation."[14]

Then, at a meeting at Morris Carnovsky's house crowded with Party members, the group let Maltz have it right between the eyes. Ex-Party member Leopold Atlas bluntly referred to them as an "intellectual goon squad." When Maltz tried to explain what his intentions were when he wrote the article, he was ruthlessly shouted down, as were Atlas and Conrad Bercovicci when they tried to defend him. As Atlas testified years later to HUAC investigators, Maltz was worked over with "every verbal fang and claw at their command; every ax and bludgeon."[15] In fact, he said that two of the Communists invited to the meeting of the "goon squad" flew in from New York especially for the occasion — like hit men imported from out of town.

Maltz, attacked by both friends and enemies, rivals and collaborators, was finally broken. He apologized profusely for the article and wrote another that appeared in the *Worker* on April 7 called "Moving Forward." Taking note of the Maltz episode in his excellent *Decline of American Communism: A History of the Communist Party in the United States Since 1945*, David Shannon put it quite accurately: "He recanted, utterly and abjectly. He crawled."

In later years, Maltz, a man who apparently liked being liked, would be an essential part of the propaganda that depicted the Hollywood Ten as persecuted victims maintaining a united front against their accusers. And the outside world would never know until years later of the other "witch hunt" that the Party faithful committed on their own.

For in the years ahead, HUAC would be the ones to deal with the question "What shall we ask of writers?" And the answers they were looking for had little to do with Balsac...

> [Lillian Hellman] found the Red Army "too well disciplined" for individual reprisals against Germany, but was impressed by the Russians' resolution for "complete and absolute punishment" of German war criminals.

The above reportage from the March 2, 1945, *New York Times* article on Lillian Hellman's recent trip to the Soviet Union was found in the playwright's FBI file. Her faith in the Red Army's "discipline," however, would be a bit misplaced less than two months later when Soviet troops stormed Berlin. With Stalin's direct encouragement, Russian soldiers raped German women and young girls and murdered unarmed civilians at will. When Churchill complained about this barbarity, Stalin reportedly laughed and said, "Let the boys have their fun!"

In the same article, Hellman also claimed: "Artists are treated like kings in Russia in their respect and remuneration accorded them."

Unfortunately, as Hellman said these words in Moscow, the Lubyanka was loaded with people of allegedly royal blood being deprived of sleep by NKVD men with burning cigarettes.

Certainly, Hellman's penchant for selective historical condemnation was probably never more evident than in the new play she had started writing in 1942 just before the filming of the also historically biased *Watch on the Rhine*. On April 12, 1944, the new work finally opened at Broadway's Fulton Theater. Another parable on the growth of fascism and the decent people of the world who ignore it, *The Searching Wind* ran over 300 performances; this, despite less than enthusiastic reviews from critics, and even Hellman herself, who later referred to it as "a bad play." However, this comment was nothing compared to Dashiell Hammett's remark that the play had the makings of "a good comedy."

More strident and demanding then ever, Hellman's unrestrained arrogance during the rehearsal process also alienated her frequent director, fellow Stalinist Herman Shumlin. He was not only angered by Hellman's insistence on taking over as director, but also by the playwright's cramming so many set changes into the play and having so many background extras on stage, that they needlessly increased the production's budget. More responsible for Hellman's great success than anyone else (with the possible exception of Hammett who rewrote her work), the infuriated Shumlin never worked with her again.

Hellman biographer William Wright, in his well-researched and intelligent *Lillian Hellman: The Image, the Woman* calls *The Searching Wind* "a rambling, talky three acts that sets out to show the culpability of well-meaning people of privilege who do not use that privilege to stop an evil like fascism before it is too strong to stop." Wonderful writer that he is, Mr. Wright was a bit mistaken here. *The Searching Wind* is a rambling, talky *two* acts that sets out to show the culpability of well-meaning people of privilege who do not use that privilege ... yada yada.

The plot deals with easygoing U.S. diplomat Alexander Hazen; the mannered and haughty rich girl he married, Emily; and the socially committed woman he *should* have married (according to Hellman anyway), Catherine (or "Cassie") Bowman, as they live out their lives through catastrophic global conflicts. As a career diplomat, Hazen just happens to be at most of the world's hot spots during the rise of European fascism. He and Cassie are at Rome's Grand Hotel in 1922 as Mussolini takes control of Italy; they're at a Berlin restaurant around the time of Hitler's Munich putsch; and the two are at the Hotel Maurice in Paris as the Munich agreement is being signed. If anything, we assume that through the years the couple at least had some great food.

The play featured Dudley Digges (Smithers from *The Emperor Jones*), Cornelia Otis Skinner and, four years before his film debut in *The Search*, Montgomery Clift as the Hazens' disillusioned son who lost a leg in the war. At the end, it is he who condemns his parents' lack of values and expedient compromises that allowed the rise of fascism. Seeing the intense actor he would become in his Hollywood films, one can only imagine today the controlled emotion the young Montgomery Clift must have given to the powerful lines he delivers to his parents just before curtain:

> I am ashamed of both of you, and that's the truth. I don't want to be ashamed that way again. I don't like losing my leg, I don't like it at all. I'm scared — but everybody's welcome to it as long as it means a little something and helps to bring us out someplace.

In its review of April 24, *Time* magazine said:

> The play's great merit is its genuine bite; its worse weakness, that it bites off more than it can chew. It is more like two plays — and two very unequal ones. When it seizes its theme and blows across the blackened grass of the age, *The Searching Wind* is bracing and sharp — a drama of adult talk and challenging ideas. But the theme both hampers the plot and holds aloof from it. The love story lacks fullness. The women lack freedom. They live only in hurried, gasping moments of crisis — and in an atmosphere too often dominated by proclamations, rioting and the boom of guns.[16]

Booming guns were about to be heard again, this time on movie screens. Paramount and Hal Wallis filmed *The Searching Wind* in late 1945 and finally released it on a weary postwar audience in August 9, 1946. Robert Young played Alex Hazen; Ann Richards was his wealthy wife, Emily; Sylvia Sidney, recently (and unconvincingly) having played a half–Chinese spy in *Blood on the Sun*, was cast as the liberal Cassie; Dudley Digges repeated his stage role as disillusioned ex-newspaper man Moses; but unfortunately, Clift, still doing plays on Broadway, was replaced as Samuel Hazen by Douglas Dick. Hellman did the screenplay, which allowed her to show fascists literally taking to the streets of besieged European capitals (all filmed on the Paramount back lot).

The plot is the same. Alex loves Cassie, but ends up with Emily, a woman who doesn't care about dining with Nazis as long as the silverware is polished. Unfortunately, Cassie has her own neurotic tendencies. When nervous, she has an awful habit of dropping things; kind of like comediennes Joan Davis or Judy Canova in their usual slapstick set-pieces. However, Hellman and director William Dieterle also deliver scenes of unusual power; as when a policeman of the Weimar Republic arrests a Hitler Youth member in front of the restaurant Alex and Cassie are dining in. As the couple look on in horror through the restaurant's large window, another Nazi thug pulls out a Luger and shoots the cop in the back. It is a scene obviously not in the play that perfectly shows fascist contempt for democratic law and order, and their use of violence to overthrow it.

Hellman also includes another scene not in the play, that of Madrid being bombed by Franco's forces, of course while Alex and Cassie just happen to be there. Perhaps the spread of fascism wouldn't have happened if these two lovers just weren't around, especially since Nazis seem to show up *every* time they meet!

Another change in the film is the happy ending. *This* time, after Samuel delivers his speech indicting his parents (Douglas Dick was no Montgomery Clift), Alex and Emily decide to end their marriage, and the diplomat meets Cassie far from his home (and far from his kvetching kid) and they decide to marry and build a better world. One can see the results of their efforts in a few short years when Soviet troops stationed themselves in Eastern Europe and war criminals escaped to South America.

In its review of July 1, *Time* noted:

> Robert [Young] struggles desperately and particularly against his love for Sylvia [Sidney], fighting his own Leftist Conscience. Over a couple of decades, Robert and Sylvia keep running into each other all over seething Europe. They make love, part, meet again and swap Miss Hellman's acid-etched lines while Jews are being slugged in Berlin (1928), while fascist bombs are crashing into Madrid (1936), and Paris diplomats are hatching the Munich deal.[17]

Of course, the critique in the July 14 issue of the *Daily Worker* by the usually hysterical David Platt had another take on the film's unevenness: "One wonders why Miss Hellman did not state frankly in her picture that behind [Alex's] neutrality and appeasement was fear of the Soviet Union, fear of the Working Classes." What fear of the Soviet Union or the working classes had to do with *The Searching Wind* remains a mystery; though one must remember that Platt was never, at any point in his career, the Richard Schickel of his time.

Hellman had her greatest popularity during the 1930s and the war years. However, with the rise of anti–Communism paralleling the rise of Soviet belligerence in Eastern Europe (not to mention Communism in China), the playwright soon found herself in an uncomfortable position. The postwar years on Broadway would still accept a play that attacked the excesses of capitalism, but never again in the blatant, sometimes forced and decidedly "acid-etched" manner of writing that Hellman had mastered. Postwar audiences were tired of polemical speeches from cardboard characters whose social standing automatically broadcast either their virtues or their vices.

From now on, capitalism was going to be attacked by a new left-wing artist, one who had the talent and the skill to attack America's hunger for money and yet make its audiences love him just the same. The rise of Arthur Miller's career would occur around the same time that Hellman's started to decline. (The two would feud many years later.) She would still have an occasional hit like *Toys in the Attic*, but her heyday as the theater's socially conscious spokesperson for a generation was clearly over. Broadway audiences were sick of the Popular Front brand of political theater as practiced by Communist playwrights like Hellman and Clifford Odets. (Odets, long past *his* prime, would survive on Broadway and Hollywood only by abandoning the Left.)

With her every move noted by FBI agents and her long affair with the cheating Hammett a relationship in name only, the struggling but still arrogant Hellman started to retreat into a world of fabrication and perhaps self-delusion. In the decades ahead, as her many "memoirs" have proven, instead of using her imagination in her plays, Hellman now used contrivance and outright lies to recast herself as a virtuous heroine and fighter for justice, as if she were giving herself the role of the dedicated Cassie Bowman or the courageous Sara Muller.

Continuing to call the enemies of Stalinism blatant liars and fascists well into her final years, her writings would prove that she picked up some valuable knowledge on making the lie look like the truth from her Marxist colleagues. In fact, when Hellman boasted during the Blacklist Years that she refused to cut her "conscience to fit this year's fashion," she forgot all about cutting her conscience to fit Soviet policy.

The postwar years became an odd time for artists of the left. Perhaps they thought that with the war over they could merely continue to make films that criticized materialism and success; and that they could unmask the scourges of racism and exploitation and expose the underbelly of American society. Just as naïve liberals thought the Soviet Union would loosen up with Stalin's exposure to the democracies, the Communist Party, for all their anti–American rhetoric, naively thought that the powers-that-be in America would continue to accept Communist critiques with a shrug and a mild grumble.

They were dead wrong.

In the meantime, Hollywood Communists were going to conduct business as usual.

"Love-wrecked!" screamed the tagline for Walter Wanger's new production *Smash-Up: The Story of a Woman*, released by Universal-International in March 1947. Party member and talented wit Dorothy Parker worked on a screen treatment for the studio (along with Frank Cavett) chronicling one woman's battle with alcoholism. Though John Howard Lawson did the screenplay (with additional dialogue by Lionel Wiggam), it was obvious that Parker's influence over the story, and especially the character of Angie, was immense. A tormented alcoholic who had tried to commit suicide several times, Parker knew all too well the inner workings of the pathetic Angela Evans Conway, the talented nightclub singer who marries, has a child, and gradually sees her ambitions crumble into dust as her husband's career rises. Almost a reverse of *A Star Is Born* (the 1937 original was co-written by Parker), the film is still remembered for its ahead-of-its-time feminism and the impressive, star-making performance of Susan Hayward.

However, Lawson was not a screenwriter who was known to write good female characters (not that, admittedly, there were all that many in *Sahara* and *Action in the North Atlantic*); and he was infamous for being unusually harsh and insensitive towards the actresses who appeared in his films. Because of this, it was soon obvious that he took far too much credit for a screenplay whose feminism is more due to the influence of the tragic Parker. In fact, at the time Parker wrote the story, she was going through a painful divorce from her husband of many years, screenwriter Alan Parker (who also co-wrote *A Star Is Born*). For weeks at a time, Dorothy would stay in bed and rarely venture outside her home. Depressed and feeling unloved, she would have crying fits, and pathetically wait for a letter or phone call from Parker, a liquor bottle frequently within reach.

Hollywood gossips would claim that Parker based Angie Evans Conway on Bing Crosby's alcoholic, long-suffering spouse, Dixie, an impression Parker herself did little to discourage.

However, the Algonquin Hotel wit knew better. When not agonizing over her divorce from Alan, she had been seeing a much younger man named Ross Lynn Evans (he was 31, she was 53), who happened to be a radio announcer. (Evans is Angie's last name; her husband Ken becomes a radio performer.) Hence, just as in *A Star Is Born*, an older artist has her self-esteem reinforced by a younger and financially successful lover (Parker was getting few offers of work after the war). Former husband Alan Parker, nine years her junior, was also her collaborator on *A Star Is Born*. All this would obviously make Dorothy Parker, the alcoholic artist constantly craving attention from her lovers, the *real* model for Angie Conway. Surrounded by wealth (which she didn't keep for long), but ignored emotionally (Ross Evans exploited her celebrity to enhance his own standing in the entertainment industry[18]), Parker had no trouble creating the pathetically needy Angie Conway. This also calls into question why leftist authors still insist that Lawson, who had never lived Parker's tormented life, could have possibly had such influence on the supposedly feminist *Smash-Up*.

Even Universal-International was aware of Parker's sizable influence on the film. On January 24, 1947, studio executive J.J. Kaufman wrote to the New York office:

> Walter Wanger is most anxious that the New York office tie-in Dorothy Parker in any and every way possible in connection with the motion picture, *Smash-Up: The Story of a Woman*.
> As you know, Miss Parker wrote the original story and of course she is excellent copy.
> If you can conceive methods and means of utilizing her personally or her name in connection with our picture, it will of course enhance our campaign.[19]

One of the supporting cast members didn't care for the film's take on women's problems. In a 1997 interview with Patrick McGilligan and Paul Buhle for their *Tender Comrades: A Backstory of the Hollywood Blacklist*, outspoken liberal actress Marsha Hunt had her own strong opinions about the film. However, it was obvious that during her tirade, the actress thought she was just criticizing Lawson, and probably didn't realize she was also criticizing

Do I look plastered to you? Charles D. Brown is uncomfortable with Susan Hayward's drunkenness in *Smash-Up: The Story of a Woman* (1947). John Howard Lawson took credit for the film's feminism, when in reality, Dorothy Parker had put her own personal stamp on the story.

Dorothy Parker: "It's a story of a weak, self-pitying woman who acquires a serious drinking problem because her husband isn't paying attention to her.... I don't understand why it is so popular."[20] Predictably, in his biography of Lawson, Gerald Horne snidely wrote: "[H]er opinion was not widely shared."[21]

However, one person's opinion *did* matter, the one man who controlled what audiences saw. On the heels of the success of Billy Wilder's *The Lost Weekend,* Joseph Breen despaired over the making of pictures showing "excessive drinking" which the censor felt was "not good for the industry."[22] He felt that "showing a drunken woman moving about" was "both distasteful and repulsive" and that the film's moral will be forgotten in "the reaction of disgust."[23] Unfortunately, the above quotes not only revealed a shocking ignorance of the problem of alcohol abuse, but a barely concealed sexism; as if somehow showing a drunken *man* moving about was going to look much better on screen.

At rise, we see that Angie Evans Conway is a nightclub singer. (Parker's original treatment was called *Angelica*. At other times, the project was called *Smashed-Up* and *One Woman's Story*.) To give herself a little "courage" before the crowds, Angie takes a drink backstage, treating it as if it were some kind of life-giving elixir. Hayward would carve out a reputation for playing tormented women, particularly alcoholics; unfortunately, the actress was also known for being able to put it away off-screen, though her "social drinking" apparently didn't stop her from getting nominated for Best Actress for the first time in this film (or finally picking up the Oscar years later).

Angie is married to Ken Conway (Lee Bowman), a pleasant enough fellow whose career as a radio singer-songwriter is on the rise. His songwriting partner is Steve Nelson (Eddie Albert). Lawson's use of the name might have been an in-joke; off-screen, according to FBI files, there *was* a Soviet spy whose American alias was Steve Nelson. (In Warners' *I Was A Communist for the FBI*, the murderous commie boss is based on real-life spy Steve Nelson.[24]) However, in this film, Nelson is the hero's best friend and the film's conscience. He sees Angie spiraling into alcoholic torment and slams Ken for his ignorance of the problem. In fact, it appears that Steve has no life of his own at all; we never see him with a woman or even a home life. His only reason for existing is merely to support his two best friends.

As the film continues, Lawson, a man who lived in a mansion near Hollywood and was well-paid for his services, slams the wealth and affluence the Conways attain as Ken's fame grows. Supposedly because of this opulence, a frustrated Angie not only takes to the bottle, but Lawson contrives situations where the poor woman can't help but run into booze. If anything, one must praise Hayward's ability to go from disoriented to blotto in mere seconds. No Crazy Guggenheim she, Hayward gives an excellent portrayal of a woman who is literally crashing while still (barely) on her feet. Even a cheerful new father whose wife just had a baby (an excellent Robert Shayne, pre-Inspector Henderson on *Superman*) can't help but indirectly turn Angie towards the sauce. Eventually, Ken, fed up with seeing Angie doing Claire Trevor in *Key Largo*, divorces her.

Also on the cusp of this triangle is not Steve (who, of course, lives merely for the Conways and nothing else), but the secretary of Ken's sponsor, Martha (Marsha Hunt). In one memorable bit at a nightclub, a drunken Angie, believing that Ken and Martha are doing the nasty ("Careful, Angie," says the secretary doing her best Joseph Breen imitation), attacks her rival in the ladies' room. Meanwhile, the understanding Dr. Lorenz (Carl Esmond) chastises Ken for not taking Angie on a long vacation far away from that horrible mansion with its loyal servants and beautiful surroundings.

Eventually, the drunken Angie's smoking causes a fire that burns down her mansion.

She is able to rescue her baby, but her face is disfigured in the process. After a while, with her face almost better (director Stuart Heisler wisely does not show us Angie's face, letting our imagination fill in the picture), Ken realizes what a self-centered ass he's been and the two reconcile, a highly ridiculous ending as there ever was in a social problem film. It would be far more realistic to discover that Angie is scarred for life (after all, alcohol *slows* the healing process), and that, despite her injuries, she still has the thirst. In fact, just before the happy ending, Heisler shows us a scene where Angie, her face still swathed in bandages, still craves a drink.

Certainly, the film's final scene had been changed somewhat from the original. According to a studio Synopsis (#1510), dated July 31, 1946, the film ends this way:

> After reawakening in [the] hospital, she is reunited with Ken and they move from city penthouse back to country place. There, Angie and Ken celebrate their wedding anniversary with Steve and Dr. Lorenz as guests. Angie proposes a toast, but doesn't fill her own glass. It is clear that she is off the stuff, and will never take another drink as long as she lives.

An ironic postscript to Lee Bowman's appearance in this film was his role in Warners' *My Dream Is Yours* (1949). In that film, Doris Day is the up-and-coming radio singer and Bowman plays the has-been, drunken singing star. It's an excellent performance, skillfully capturing the ego, the vanity, and the violent temper of the man he was playing; in fact, Bowman might have been watching Hayward's performance closely during his off-camera breaks. (In his Lawson biography, Gerald Horne couldn't help commenting that Bowman would go on to become "a TV advisor to Republican politicians," as if this made him some kind of war criminal.)

Newsweek's review of April 28 was reminiscent of Joseph Breen's earlier warning about how unattractive a drunken woman would look on screen (though Breen never took into account how beautiful Susan Hayward looked no matter what role she played): "Miss Hayward's bouts with demon rum are more to be censored than pitied, considering that she is attractive drunk or sober and is apparently immune to hangovers."[25] After predictably comparing the film to another picture about "success and drunkenness, *A Star Is Born*," Bosley Crowther, in his *New York Times* review of April 11, wrote:

> [I]n the writing, this complex tension has been so weakly and unconvincingly drawn that the reason for the lady's dipsomania seems completely arbitrary and contrived. Furthermore, the writer, John Howard Lawson, has so muddled the lady with mother-love that the story becomes a wallow less in liquor than in mawkish sentiment.... Artificial and hackneyed in construction, the story tends further to assume the qualities of a daytime serial with the injection of several soapy songs. One of them, "Life Can Be Beautiful," is moaned and groaned so many times that a less than complete juke-box fanatic may be tempted towards the end to scream in disgust.

Premiering at New York's Capitol Theater, the film made money in the Big Apple if only for one reason: The rising comedy team of Dean Martin and Jerry Lewis were the accompanying stage show (along with Xavier Cugat and his band).

Meanwhile, as HUAC started to open investigations in Hollywood, Party "commissar" John Howard Lawson had no idea that *Smash-Up: The Story of a Woman* would be his last credited screenplay ever. The man who was the "last word" in all Party matters was about to become a non-person, his name forever missing on screen from what few scripts he would work on in subsequent years. As the Red Scare progressed, the wealth and materialism he had always cherished for himself yet attacked in others, were about to be taken away from him.

Dorothy Parker would also be blacklisted, though her contributions to literature would make her far better remembered in the years ahead than the limited Lawson. Three years after the release of *Smash-Up*, she would remarry the declining Alan Parker, and they would stay married until his suicide in 1963. Still an alcoholic, and now a lonely one as well, Dorothy spent her remaining years in near poverty until she died of a heart attack in New York City on June 7, 1967. She had been borrowing money from Lillian Hellman just to survive, a fact the stingy playwright never let her forget. However, in her will, Dorothy stipulated that whatever money she had left was to go to Martin Luther King Jr. and the NAACP.

She bequeathed her ashes to Lillian Hellman…

> A soldier fed up to the breaking point with being left behind a desk job, hears a rumor that his wife has been unfaithful to him. He goes completely to pieces and on a wild binge in Washington becomes involved in murder. Through the efforts of a loyal friend he is finally extricated from all difficulties.[26]

The above summary, written by an RKO story analyst on May 11, 1945, is of a novel written by a recently returning soldier named Richard Brooks. The title of the novel was *The Brick Foxhole*. Pointedly left out of the RKO summary, however, was the fact that the murder victim in the novel was a homosexual.

On February 19, 1947, another RKO analyst summarized screenwriter John Paxton's (of *Cornered*) 102-page adaptation of the novel, now called *Crossfire*. Now the story's theme became "A drunken soldier murders a Jewish civilian for no apparent reason unless it be his hatred of Jews."[27]

Jews, the Nazis' prime victims, were now to be portrayed as the victims of American bigotry in a major Hollywood film in the postwar era. During the war years, filmmakers studiously avoided depicting Nazi persecution of the Jews and making it a central topic of their films. Anti-Nazi films depicted tyranny as the enemy, not the persecution of one particular religious group; though even Hollywood filmmakers once in a while *had* to face the reality of German anti–Semitism, occasionally showing us a European Jew getting bopped on the head by a Nazi's truncheon. For with the possible exception of scenes like the one at the railroad depot in Lester Cole's *None Shall Escape*, Hollywood and the Breen Office stubbornly avoided showing the Holocaust.

That same year, Fox made *Gentleman's Agreement*, directed by former Communist Elia Kazan, which won the Oscar for Best Picture. It also co-starred John Garfield as a returning Jewish combat veteran. At a time when actors rarely played Jews, and when Hollywood never wrote any roles where Jews had pride, Garfield gladly accepted the part of a Jew who took crap from no one. Because of the passion Garfield brought to his role, the Jewish performer neatly stole the film from the Goyish Gregory Peck (ludicrously pretending to be a Jew for a newspaper exposing anti–Semitism) and Dorothy McGuire as his confused, upper-crust fiancée. Yet Darryl F. Zanuck's "courageous" film always seemed like too little too late. As we see Peck get barred from staying in a ritzy hotel and suffering the indignity of having his "Jewish" name misspelled, just two years before, the *real* Chosen were getting beaten, gassed, and thrown into crematoriums.

Produced by Adrian Scott and directed by Edward Dmytryk, *Crossfire* dealt with a Jew's murder, a microcosm of the genocide that had so recently taken place in Europe. Dmytryk's direction is a film noirish delight, full of shadows, harsh lighting and low-angle camera setups. The helmsman does some of his best work in the scenes that show the actual murder (a startling way to begin the film), and in the way his camera catches the frightening performance of Robert Ryan as the psychotic Sergeant Montgomery. An ex-policeman, Montgomery is the right-wing bogeyman of every leftist's nightmares; in the film, he is the anti–Semite who is responsible for two murders. In later years, film historians would write that Hollywood would ignorantly replace the book's murder of a homosexual with that of a Jew, thus avoiding the issue of homophobia and, in the shadow of the Holocaust, making a more timely statement about anti–Semitism.

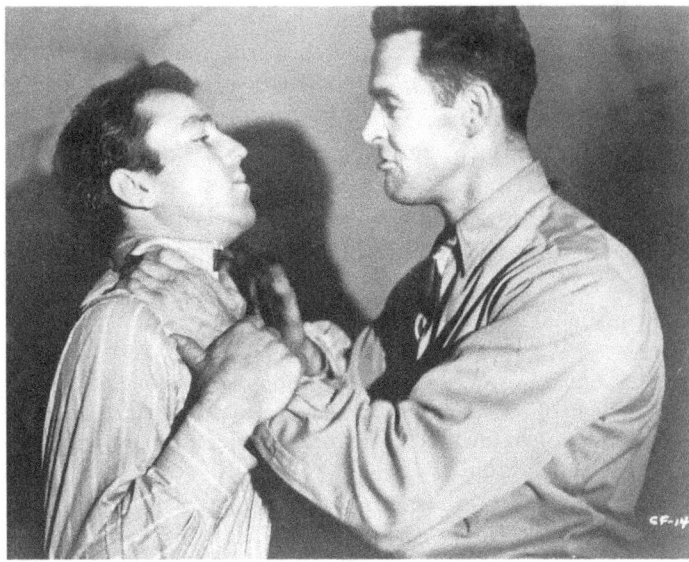

NO ROOM FOR SQUEALERS. Steve Brodie is being silenced by psychotic Jew-hater Robert Ryan in Edward Dmytryk's *Crossfire* (1947).

In other words, to Hollywood, one bigotry was replaced with another, a cynical ploy that neatly avoided discussing the deeper issues at stake behind these prejudices.

However, Brooks' novel clearly emphasizes the victim's Jewishness more than his homosexuality, a subject publishers in those days rarely accepted as the main theme of a novel (Brooks treats the character's homosexuality with restraint). Also, in the book, Sgt. Montgomery's bigotry is far uglier:

> I hope the little sheeny gets murdered. That'll teach him a lesson. Him and his kike father. You know, his father owns all those big stores. Twice he's been married. Both times to Christian girls. The sheeny sonofa bitch. If he don't lay down, soon he's hit, it'll be a pleasure.

Montgomery's epithets are indeed repugnant; however, Brooks makes the victim's father, Manny Brock, a Jewish self-hater. The thoughts he expresses to his confused ex-boxer son Maxie, are, in their own way, on a par with Montgomery's:

> [O]ne thing I know without any argument. There isn't any anti–Semitism. There are Jews and Jews. It's only natural that people should hate some Jews. But that doesn't mean there is anti–Semitism. That's only a boogie-man dreamed up by a lot of rabbis and extra-sensitive people.... Of course, I didn't think I'd be a better Jew by giving money to Father Coughlin. I just wanted to show him there are good Jews. That we're not all Zionists or something.

Throughout the chapter, the old man raves on and on to his soon-to-be-murdered son about his own skewered version of what a Jew's place should be in America and that the Chosen should stay in the limited roles the world wants them in. At the end of the chapter, he is clearly baffled by his son's questioning the experience of assimilation:

> It's a funny thing, mused Max's father. Here all the time am I, Manny Brock, with citizen papers and everything and I'm a first-class American. And here all the time is my boy, a real American, born and bred in the U.S.A., and he's a Jew.

Throughout the novel, there is an atmosphere of dread, of tension, of people going nowhere who might explode at any second. Brooks takes a dark look at America, and his various soldier characters refer to the nation's can-do business ethics as "dog eat dog" and "kill or be killed"—terms which would have been far more appropriate to the battlefield. Even an army chaplain who had been against killing before the war, was forced to call the Japanese "wicked people" and find a reason to approve of killing them to save Christian civilization. Full of tormented people who express themselves in only the crudest terms, *The Brick Foxhole* was a portrait of postwar America as a melting pot ready to boil over.

Besides "Monty," his soldier buddy Floyd has his own take on another minority, as well as a former First Lady. At one point, the disgusted soldier spits out:

> Dirty nigger.... Yes, and that woman in the White House. It's all her fault. Don't get me wrong, Eddie. I'm a good Democrat but that woman drives me crazy. She got them niggers in the service. Never was in before. Always a white man's service. Now she's got them niggers in. And the next thing you know there's niggers kissin' and makin' love to white gals out in front of everybody. That shows you, now don't it?

Unlike the film version, Brooks implies that bigots like Montgomery and Floyd are far more common in America. In the film, after Jewish war veteran Samuels (Jewish actor Sam Levene) is murdered, an army major (Kenneth MacDonald) claims that anti–Semitism is not tolerated in the American military. This line must have gotten howls of bitter laughter from many a returning Jewish combat veteran who had to fight Christian bullies in their companies to be accepted as equals. It wasn't until a decade later that Dmytryk, no longer restrained by the anti–Semitic Joseph Breen, was able to dispute *Crossfire*'s nonsensical claim about the army's intolerance to bigotry when he filmed Irwin Shaw's *The Young Lions*. As a Jewish soldier, Montgomery Clift has to fight four anti–Semitic soldiers to get back the book they stole from his bunk, as well as gain their respect. Obviously, such scenes were far more common in the army than the Powers That Be in Hollywood or the censor's office cared to show.

Not that Dmytryk was all that tolerant in real-life either. In his autobiography, while discussing the filming of *The Juggler* on location in Israel, his unflattering portrayal of Israelis, especially religious Jews, bordered on the anti–Semitic.[28] Both Stanley Kramer and Kirk Douglas, in *their* respective autobiographies, also detected a barely concealed bigotry toward Jews during the filming of *The Juggler*.

Crossfire made an estimated $1,300,000 at the box office, and compared with the Oscar-winning *Gentleman's Agreement*, it is better remembered today. Adrian Scott and John Paxton were praised for exposing a real problem in America, and Dmytryk's directorial approach is remembered for using the techniques of film noir and expertly applying them to the social problem film.

Two other artists who used the bleak point of view associated with film noir would make a classic comment on American excess in 1947. One was a liberal actor and the other a Communist writer-director. Both formed a vision that depicted America as a place where becoming a success and being guilty of exploitation go hand in hand. Needless to say, the project would get both men in big trouble...

There are those who see *Body and Soul* as the definitive John Garfield film. As a poor young man from an (implied Jewish) urban ghetto, he works his way up to become a champion boxer and get the gorgeous (shiksa) girl in the end. The plot is like one of Garfield's cliché-ridden 1930s Bs for Warners. However, in *Body and Soul*, in one of the first times seen on an American screen, it is hammered into us that one cannot be a success in America without losing one's soul in the process. Money and morality do not go hand in hand; in Garfield's and Rossen's version, *Boy Meets Girl and Becomes Success* needs the postscript *And Turns Into Heel*. Reportedly based on the life and career of Jewish boxer Al "Bummy" Davis (who was a hero to the Jewish residents of Brooklyn's Brownsville section), and his defiance of Murder Inc., *Body and Soul* pulls no punches.

Garfield's Charlie Davis is a decent young man, but bitter about the squalid life he and his family lead (gangsters murder his father, and his mother is forced to apply for welfare). Knowing that a local gangster will promote him as a fighter, Charlie grabs the brass ring, not realizing that in capitalist America it has strings attached. When his mom (Communist actress Anne Revere) tells him that he might as well get a gun and shoot himself, Charlie retorts (in Garfield's wonderfully biting delivery), "You need *money* to buy a gun." Here, the Depression-era lost soul of *Dust Be My Destiny* becomes another kind of lost soul; however, *this* time, he's getting lost with his eyes wide open.

Played by soon-to-be-blacklisted Lloyd Gough, Roberts is a ruthless gangster who exploits everybody. However, this vicious, amoral man in an expensive suit could easily have been written (with a few slight changes on the soundtrack) as an ordinary businessman. Setting up a fight with Ben Chaplin (an excellent Canada Lee), Roberts neglects to inform Charlie that Ben is sick and over the hill, and the younger boxer unwittingly throttles him. Belatedly finding out, a guilty Charlie hires Ben as his ring man.

Unlike many Hollywood stars, Garfield had made speeches to African-American groups on the need for racial brotherhood and equality. When he could, he tried to inject issues of race into his films by the casting of black actors. One certainly remembers Juano Hernandez (a Latino actor) as Garfield's black shipmate in 1950's *The Breaking Point*, a role that easily could have been played by a white actor. In *Body and Soul*, Canada Lee's role is incidental as well; we see he is the white hero's friend, but no one in the film comments on his skin color. Roberts is already characterized as a gangster and an exploiter; however, thanks to the casting of Canada Lee as Ben, we also see him as a racist. Rossen and Garfield's message is as plain as day: Racism is the natural outcome of capitalist exploitation.

One can easily see the camaraderie between Garfield and Lee on screen (they were also friends off-screen), and one will always remember the scene in which Roberts baits Chaplin to get him excited, aggravating a blood clot in his skull that will

BROTHERS. Off-screen friends Canada Lee and John Garfield in Robert Rossen's *Body and Soul* (1947). The film slammed the compromises made in capitalist society, while at the same time, emphasizing the friendship between two fighters of different races.

kill him. A talented performer (after a boxing career and acting on Broadway), Lee refused to play the stereotyped servant or "hanky-head," though others certainly attempted to make him do so. In Hitchcock's *Lifeboat*, Lee refused to deliver his lines in a stereotyped manner (and got little understanding from an ignorant Hitchcock). He was also furious when he discovered that Walter Slezak was apparently living his Nazi character *off*-screen as well.[29]

Lee was a decent man who passionately fought for equal rights and justice for his people. Tragically, racists and anti–Semites wielded far too much power in the American government at the time. Lee's name turns up several times in the FBI's COMPIC files, despite the fact that he was *not* a Communist. This "information" came out during the accidental release of the FBI's file on pro-Soviet spy Judith Coplin (though no Hollywood actor had anything to do with her or her Soviet contacts). In an article he wrote in 1949, Lee angrily referred to the implied tie-in with Coplin as "the drivel that has come from the so-called secret files of the FBI."[30] This was not a statement that was going to endear him to FBI director J. Edgar Hoover, a man whose own racism would cause him to block FBI involvement in investigating Klan lynchings down south (until the Kennedys forced him to become involved in the 1960s).

In *Body and Soul*, Roberts baits Ben into making him angry, triggering the blood clot that will kill him. However, unlike the usual stereotyped blacks in films of the time who would bow and scrape, Lee's Ben Chaplin gets *angry* and Charlie has to physically restrain him from attacking Roberts. Ben's tragic death brings Charlie to the realization that he has sold out to an exploiter, that his refusal to buck a crooked system has resulted in the deaths of his best friends (Joseph Pevney's Shorty gets run down by a car after being beaten by one of Roberts' men).

As written by Communist Abraham Polonsky, the fight game and the celebrity that comes in its wake is nothing more than a microcosm of the American success story (money, women, fame) at its worst (Charlie becomes "a money machine," a product owned and operated by murderers and thieves). Garfield was Oscar-nominated for the only time in his career for Best Actor, but lost. It took courage for him, Rossen and Polonsky to make a film that attacked capitalist exploitation with HUAC already in Hollywood.

To the left (both liberals and Communists), America had won its war against the fascists, and now it was time to turn its attention inward to solve its pressing social problems. However, not all of these social protesters were Hollywood veterans with years of film experience. Months before the release of *Body and Soul*, a brand new voice began to set America's moral compass, and it was first heard from the stage of Broadway's Coronet Theater on January 29, 1947.

"Everything that happened seems to be coming back." This line is delivered by the character of Kate Keller, the passionate, slightly dotty and clearly in-denial mother of Arthur Miller's new Broadway play *All My Sons*. Less blatant than the works of Lillian Hellman, and written with amazing skill by the 31-year-old Miller, *All My Sons* was cheered by theater audiences and praised by critics. Though set in 1946, immediately after the world war, *All My Sons* still carries with it an impact that is felt to this day; for the issues of corporate greed and manufacturer abuse are, unfortunately, just as timely as ever. Miller had been aware of such abuse during the war years, and had tackled the subject of the play on and off as he made his living as a struggling radio writer and occasional script doctor. (He worked in the Ernie Pyle movie *The Story of G.I. Joe*, but his contributions do not appear in the film.)

Born in Brooklyn in 1915, Miller was a playwright and author (he had written *Focus*; like *The Brick Foxhole*, it dealt with anti–Semitism) who had labored for FDR's Federal Theater Project during the 1930s. He had also flirted with membership in the Communist Party, and though he supposedly never became a member, it was quite possible that the Party made him an "unofficial" member; that is (as would be suspected of Lillian Hellman), an important artist who was a secret member, but still presented an anti-capitalist view in their works, or at least one that was critical of American society. Richard Schickel points out in his excellent biography of Elia Kazan that the director, who was a Party member in his youth (and had met Miller while the future playwright "flirted" with joining the Party), might have made a "deal" with Miller about the playwright's alleged membership: Miller would keep his silence about Kazan's testimony before HUAC in exchange for Kazan's silence about Miller's Communist Party membership.

Whether Miller was a Party member or not, his plays presented a definite leftist point of view that Party members clearly approved. For with very few exceptions, Miller used his plays to attack capitalist excess (*All My Sons*, *Death of a Salesman*) or American ignorance (*The Crucible*, *A View from the Bridge*). Even when he concentrates on the deteriorating relationships of his characters, it's a good bet that capitalism had something to do with it (*The Price* has two brothers whose father was wiped out by the Depression). *The Crucible*, obviously, attacked McCathyism, and it is implied that *A View from the Bridge* attacked those "friendly witnesses" who testified before HUAC (like Kazan). Even *After the Fall*, a pretty unfair portrait of ex-wife Marilyn Monroe (and the excesses of Hollywood, which rarely hired Miller), there is a subplot about one former friend ruining another with his HUAC testimony. A further irony is that the play was directed by, of all people, Elia Kazan.

But Miller's prolific output was in the future. For now, the playwright had *All My Sons'* mother speak of events "coming back," a comment that implied the phrase "chickens coming home to roost." This theme, so prized by leftist writers, consisted of rewarding exploitative capitalists with much suffering, despair, and even death, by the time of curtain. Therefore, within the play's subtext, dark secrets are revealed, it is discovered that the characters' success and happiness are based on outright lies, and good and righteous folks are unmasked as hypocrites and villains. Specifically, using the "chickens come home to roost" coda, amiable but ruthless manufacturer Joe Keller is about to be paid back for his own cutthroat business methods with the destruction of the status quo he had always known and loved. Again, the inference is unmistakable: A financially successful and happy America is a façade that is built on lies, and has some immoral skeletons in its closet that must be revealed.

Joe Keller (played on Broadway by Ed Begley) is a parts manufacturer who, during the war, had shipped out defective aircraft cylinders to the Army Air Corps. Though indicted for the crime (several pilots perished thanks to the malfunctioning parts), Joe feigned illness (he was therefore not at the factory when the decision was made to ship out the cylinders), and his innocent business partner goes to jail for it. Chris Keller (Miller's muse, Arthur Kennedy) admires his father, and though expressing little enthusiasm for inheriting Joe's business ("the rat race" is how he refers to the drive to make money), he is expected to carry on and be a good little businessman. Kate Keller (Beth Merrill), whom Miller refers to in the play's text as "Mother," though she is never called that, is in denial that her son Larry, a pilot in the war, is dead, and expects him to return from the battlefield at any minute. Ann Deever (Lois Wilson) is the daughter of Joe's jailed partner; formerly Larry's girlfriend, she is returning to her home to marry Chris, to the predictable chagrin of Kate. Ann's brother

George (rising star Karl Malden), after believing his father guilty of sending men to their deaths, pays an off-stage jailhouse visit to Pop, and now believes him to be innocent.

Of course, the upshot of all this sturm and drang is that Joe, a lively, charming and industrious man (if not a very bright one), is revealed to be guilty of the crime; he shipped out the defective cylinders in order to keep his business from collapsing. Claiming that the military would have ruined him, Joe's excuses to an angry Chris are an unsparing attack on the pressures capitalism puts American businessmen through:

> I'm in business, a man is in business; a hundred and twenty cracked [cylinders], you're out of business; you got a process, the process don't work you're out of business; you don't know how to operate, your stuff is no good; they close you up, they tear up your contracts, what the hell's it to them? You lay forty years into a business and they knock you out in five minutes. What could I do, let them take forty years, let them take my life away?

At the end, it is revealed that Ann had secretly been carrying a letter from Larry that revealed his shame at his father's crime, and that the tormented young man flew his plane on a mission that he was not expecting to return from; in other words, he purposely committed suicide by crashing his own plane, almost in a kind of morbid solidarity with the many pilots who were killed thanks to Joe's defective airplane cylinders. Upon reading the letter, Kate is now forced to acknowledge the inevitable; and Joe goes upstairs and shoots himself. But just before the suicide, when Kate asks Chris what they could do to make sure Larry did not die in vain, the young man says, "You can be better! Once and for all you can know there's a universe of people and you're responsible to it, and unless you know that you threw away your son because that's why he died."

All My Sons ran 328 performances and Arthur Miller won the Tony Award. This not only provided a much needed boost to Miller's burgeoning playwrighting career (if the play had failed, he was going to try to succeed in another medium as an author), but boosted the stock of former Group actor Elia Kazan. He had directed and stage-managed plays for years (he directed the successful *The Skin of Our Teeth* and *Jacobowsky and the Colonel*, among others), and was already getting a name as a director in Hollywood, but Kazan's work in this play started his golden period as *the* major director of actors on both Broadway and in Hollywood in the postwar era. Performers, whether of the Method school (like Brando and Dean) or more traditional veterans, thrived under Kazan's guidance. His distinctive style, which included being part father-confessor, part psychiatrist to his actors, caused them to expose raw memories within themselves to Broadway and film audiences. Unlike the usually escapist Hollywood product, Kazan's films brought psychic torment front and center in a way that was never presented before. Even in lesser vehicles, Kazan's sure hand never wavered. The scripts may have been trash, but the characters usually kept our interest.

While directing *All My Sons*, his former boss, Group Theater producer Harold Clurman, would backhandedly refer to Kazan as "my former stage manager," despite the fact that Kazan had stage-managed just *one* play for Clurman. However, with Miller's play, Kazan started to come into his own. As Karl Malden later explained, to the Group Theater, Kazan

> sensed he wasn't one of them, that he was an outsider, always an outsider until, goddamnit, he got to be a director and, buddy, he took over. No one was going to tell him what to do, and it sprang from being tied down so long.[31]

Malden, who had appeared in *Golden Boy* in the late 1930s, knew from experience what the Group was like. Though not a Communist, the actor must have witnessed Party discipline and how it affected Kazan, an artist yearning to escape its dictatorial control.

In the spring of 1948, Universal-International released the film version. Besides the usual "opening up" of the play when translating it to film, the picture made some other interesting changes. For instance, we actually get to see Joe's partner Herbert Deever (played by stage actor Frank Conroy) and he is given some of George Deever's stage lines when telling Chris how Joe bamboozled him into accepting blame for the cylinders' defects. We also see a hysterical woman berate Joe in a swank seaside restaurant as he's having dinner with his family. The scene is a harbinger of the hell to come, and already reveals that Joe, like some kind of Nazi war criminal, will not escape punishment.

Starring Burt Lancaster (as Chris), Edward G. Robinson (as Joe) and Mady Christians (excellent as Kate), *All My Sons* continued Universal-International's quest to be taken seriously as a major studio since its recent merger. That same year, it would release *The Naked City* (both films would feature new contract player Howard Duff). Shot on location on the streets of New York, the film was a groundbreaking work. Hinging the film's plot on the murder of a model, director Jules Dassin and screenwriters Albert Maltz and Malvin Wald didn't invent the police procedural (*The House on 92nd Street* did that), but they refine it in such a way as to make it their own. Henry Hathaway's film, being pro–FBI, was not going to be even a *bit* subversive; however, leftists like Dassin, Maltz and Wald had no such qualms. Skillfully, the three concoct a crime melodrama which subtly attacks American optimism and the comforts of capitalist society.

Duff is a rich gigolo, his well-dressed appearance revealing a jewel thief and con man (though he does partly redeem himself by helping to prevent a suicide). Another bad-guy is a wealthy professional in a beautiful office (of which he tries to jump from when caught by the police). The young would-be actress murdered at the beginning of the film, once had dreams of glamour and had escaped to the big city. After sampling café society's charms and joining a gang of thieves, she is strangled for her ambition. This later leads to the most powerful scene in the film, where detectives, led by Barry Fitzgerald, bring the murdered girl's small-town parents to claim her body. After bitterly declaring that she hates her daughter, the mother suddenly collapses in tears as she sees the body laid out on the morgue slab. "My baby, my baby!" she cries as she reaches out to her daughter's corpse. It is one of the best scenes Albert Maltz had ever written.

The mother had previously attacked the victim for her snotty ways and contempt of small town life, triggering her flight to the city for some excitement; typically, in the "chickens come home to roost" morality of Communist writers, Maltz and Wald have her killed for wanting to sample some of capitalism's excesses. At another point, the dead girl's father sneers about "this fine city," making the glitter of New York (coincidentally, the home of Wall Street) sound like a pestilence.

The moviemakers used concealed cameras in delivery trucks to catch the hustle and bustle of Manhattan's Lower East Side; we see an actual urban ghetto with Jews, Italians and Latinos going about their business as the actors do their lines. These scenes were a kind of time capsule, forever capturing the real-life activities of poor and lower middle class New Yorkers of the day: and with little effort, they made a mockery of Warner Brothers' idea of a poor neighborhood.

If one ignores Mark Hellinger's corny voiceover narration, *The Naked City* is a classic work, a stylistic *tour de force* that makes good use of its location shooting and eccentric characters to comment on a society that murders innocent young girls from the country and allows rich capitalists to con the public. As a police procedural, *The Naked City* not only inspired a later TV show of the same name, but obviously inspired hit 1990s TV shows like

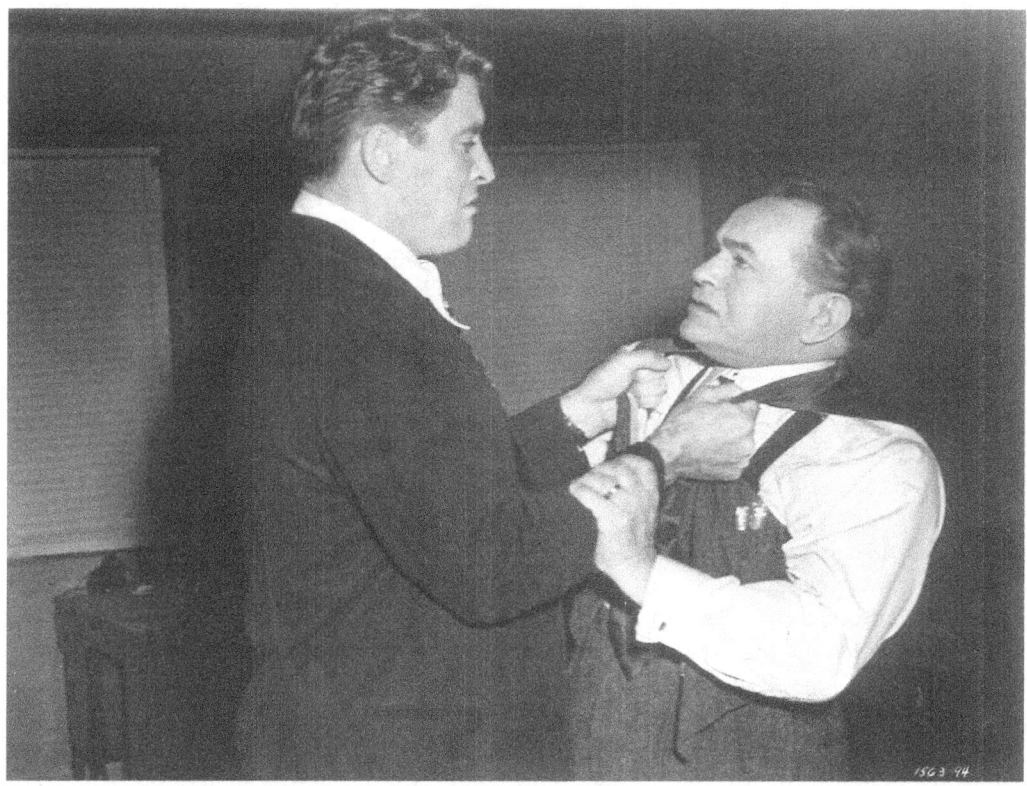

ONE OF MY SONS IS PISSED. **Burt Lancaster roughs up father Edward G. Robinson in *All My Sons* (1948). Like Miller's *Death of a Salesman*, the project portrayed big businessmen as callous and greedy.**

Law and Order. That much of this innovation was the work of Communist screenwriters and a liberal director is besides the point; unfortunately, *The Naked City* would be the last gasp of screenwriting fame for the brilliant Maltz. His name would not be seen on movie screens for 22 years, and even then, sporadically.

Indeed, another artist of the left was soon going to find out that the late 1940s weren't going to be as friendly or as profitable as the war years...

In 1942, Paul Robeson had performed in *Othello*, one of the first times a black actor had played the part. Opposite a rising Jose Ferrer as Iago, Robeson entranced Broadway audiences in a way that Hollywood movies would never allow. Disgusted by his part of a "po' sharecropper" in Fox's *Tales of Manhattan* from the same year, Robeson vowed never to return to Hollywood while racist stereotypes continued in their products. His affairs, many with white actresses (like Peggy Ashcroft), would continue unabated in both New York and London, all while the long-suffering Eslanda kept her silence, at least publicly. During the war, Robeson had promoted the Soviet-American alliance as the savior of the world against fascist duplicity. Predictably, he would continue to ignore Soviet tyranny and praise their supposedly courageous fight for human rights.

With the war now over, Robeson quickly forgot about the sacrifices of thousands of American servicemen and instead turned his criticism inward; it was now time to fight racism at home, he declared. However, with the Soviets quickly suppressing all human rights in Eastern Europe and the revelation that Communist spies had stolen America's nuclear secrets, Paul was about to discover that America wasn't going to listen to *anyone* about the supposedly good intentions of the Soviets, especially a well-paid performer who had swallowed Moscow's lies.

It wasn't as if Paul wasn't aware of Soviet bigotry either. According to Martin Duberman in his definitive biography of Paul Robeson:

> [T]hrough the years, he did come to know many of the Soviets' most prominent ambassadors ... and, in regard to one, Panyushkin, he bluntly told Paul, Jr., "that the SOB talked like a Nazi about the Jews.... He sounded like Goebbels at times." But Robeson was careful never to express such views in public, and only rarely in private. He did not transfer his dislike of particular leaders into a condemnation of the cause they represented, however poorly, or the political entities they headed.

Unfortunately, this hateful behavior from one of Stalin's officials turned out to be the rule, not the exception. Though constantly (and to many, ridiculously) parroting the litany that the Soviet Union had no racism against people of color, Robeson was blind to the fact that the Soviets had been persecuting Islamic peoples all over the U.S.S.R. for decades. For instance, it was well known that the Bolsheviks had been trying in vain to pressure Russia's huge Moslem population to turn away from Allah and embrace Marxism, all to no avail. The results were predictable: persecution, mass arrests, and one-way trips to Siberian concentration camps for thousands of Islamic families.

When Paul appeared at a concert in the Soviet Union in the late 1940s, he insisted that he be allowed to see his old friend, the Jewish poet Itzak Feffer, now a prisoner in the Lubyanka. Not wanting to blow off their most famous supporter, the Soviets released Feffer, had him cleaned up, awkwardly bandaged his wounds, put him in a shabby suit and had him meet the singer at his room in Moscow's Metropole Hotel. According to Paul Robeson Jr., the two men already knew that the room would be bugged by NKVD agents. In a frenzied combination of mime and quick scribblings on a notepad, Feffer indicated that that Jewish actor Solomon Michoels and many other Jewish activists had been murdered. At several points in the meeting, this great literary figure drew his finger across his throat, indicating the act of execution. Finally, as the meeting drew to a close, the two men, one a black artist and other a Jewish artist, embraced each other with tears in their eyes. Robeson knew he would never see his friend alive again.

In a blast at Robeson in his 1979 memoirs *Testimony*, Jewish activist Dmitri Sostakovich attacked the singer for maintaining his silence about the persecution of Jews in the Soviet Union: "Why don't these famous humanists give a damn about *us*, *our* lives, honour and dignity?" But Paul ignored these obvious examples of racist persecution and continued to praise his Russian friends, apparently too preoccupied to worry about this obvious double-standard.

On February 1, 1947, Paul marched with thirty other picketers to protest segregated seating at St. Louis' prominent American Theater. During the protest, Robeson claimed that he was through with concert performing so that he could "talk up and down the nation about race hatred and prejudice." This was an interesting remark to make since he was scheduled to do a concert at the Philharmonic Auditorium in Los Angeles a mere six weeks later.

Meanwhile, one of the film community's most vocal personalities had her own take on the ongoing drama that was the life of Paul Robeson. Hedda Hopper, in her "Looking at

IV. A Revolution from Above (1946–1951)

Hollywood" column in the *Los Angeles Times*, reported on Robeson's March 17 concert in L.A. Three days later, she wrote:

> When Paul Robeson sang the Communist "People's Battle Song" here and dedicated it to Gerhard Eisler, some members of his audience walked out. Why one remained is beyond me. To sit idly listening to a man abusing the precious heritage of freedom given us by our Constitution and flaunting the preachings of the most dangerous enemy is inviting disaster.[32]

Of course, considering "the precious heritage of freedom" Hopper mentioned, it never occurred to her that at the time Paul made his speech that no African American could ride on a Southern bus except in the back; that they couldn't get any job they wanted, but a low-paying, menial one; that they couldn't live anywhere they wanted except some disease-ridden slum; or that they were usually targeted for attack by men wearing bedsheets and soiled linens.

On April 17, Paul was scheduled to perform at the Shriners Hall in Peoria, Illinois. Then something odd happened: As it got close to concert time, the Shriners pulled the offer to use the hall. Though some of the city's union leaders and civil liberties groups wanted the concert to take place, Peoria's newspapers backed the Shriners and *also* protested Paul's appearance. As far as Peoria's top elected official was concerned, Mayor Treibel was going back and forth like a tennis ball; at first backing the Shriners and calling Robeson's appearance a safety issue, then calling for the concert to take place, then changing his mind *again*. But Paul had made other enemies among the country's political establishment. With little hesitation, he had spoken out against Mississippi's segregationist senator, Theodore Bilbo (a man who had contacts with HUAC), a daring act in the Cold War years.

There is some evidence, however, that not all Peoria officials were against Robeson's appearance, with some voices of support coming from unexpected directions. In a letter found in the FBI's file on Paul and Eslanda Robeson, an unknown officer of the American Legion (the Bureau blacked out his name) wrote to Senator Everett Dirkson on April 24. After relating that he had "no knowledge of any subversive activities on the part of Mr. Robeson," the man wrote:

> On Monday, April 14, Mr. Gomer Bath began a campaign in the *Peoria Star* to arouse public sentiment against Mr. Robeson. Here he cited some of the supposed incidents that occurred to prove his statements.
> 1. Robeson sang national anthem and dedicated it to [Gerhard] Eisler.
> 2. Robeson is supposed to be affiliated with 34 Communist organizations.
> 3. The fact that Robeson's son attended Russian schools.
>
> Withstanding these three items mentioned, true or false, I sincerely doubt the legality of Mayor Carl O. Triebel and his 20 Aldermen of branding one Paul Robeson of being a Communist and closing all public buildings to his appearance. I contend that it is an abuse of the civil liberties law together with the destruction of the Constitution of the United States.

Though the letter's author did request FBI and HUAC reports on Robeson to ascertain his ties, if any, to the Communist Party, it was obviously an attempt by the Legion's officer at fact-finding from totally unbiased sources — or rather what this fellow innocently considered totally unbiased sources in 1947. After this request, the Legionnaire wrote:

> Ev [Dirkson], these questions are very important in this community because of the fact that I've taken a stand in Robeson's behalf, based on the civil liberties law, which I deem my duty.
> I am enclosing a copy of my statement to the press [blacked out name] but withstanding this fact, they attempt to bring pressure that I denounce Robeson as a Communist, which I believe [is] an un-American act.

In the many biographies of Paul Robeson and other blacklisted artists, the American Legion is always portrayed as being in the vanguard of suppressing freedom of speech. Yet letters like this one reveal that some Legionnaires during the Cold War did *not* necessarily rush to judgment.

In the spring of 1948, Robeson campaigned for the candidate for the Progressive Party for president, Henry Wallace, a former official in the Roosevelt administration. Robeson's support for Wallace was based on his belief that the Truman administration was too slow in enacting anti-lynching laws and equal rights legislation. The results of this support could be seen in newsreels over the next four years showing Harry S Truman still in the Oval office playing the piano.

Certainly it was the many controversies he found himself in which prompted Robeson to explain his stand many, *many* times with reporters who were not necessarily the brightest bulbs in the world of journalism. Though he would occasionally lose his temper with them, Paul could also be quite loquacious when discussing his general political philosophy:

> On many occasions I have expressed my belief in scientific socialism, my deep conviction for all mankind that a socialist society represents an advance to a higher stage of life — that it is a form of society which is economically, socially, culturally and ethically superior to a system based on production for private profit.[33]

Noble words. Though it's highly doubtful this theory was any comfort to those poor souls languishing in the basements of Moscow's Lubyanka Prison as they were living their "higher stage of life."

Though few would accuse Hedda Hopper of being one of Hollywood's great political thinkers (did Hollywood ever have such a person?), another paragraph from her March 20 column is illuminating:

> When such people as Robeson are attacked, they scream "persecution" and "fascism" — the obvious dodge that our Red brethren attempt when cornered by people who they've goaded out of lethargy. Yet they believe it perfectly right that they be allowed to attack the very foundations of our country — simply because one of the principles provides freedom of speech.[34]

And this was the uncomfortable paradox, debatable as it may be. Robeson had courageously spoken out on behalf of his own people. He attacked the discrimination, the oppression, the lynchings that were openly allowed and *never* punished. (In 1946, for instance, black servicemen who had heroically fought for this country were summarily lynched once they returned to their homes down south.) Unfortunately, Robeson linked this fight against injustice with fulsome praise for the foulest, most barbaric political system on the planet. Hopper was right in this regard. It was hard to take Robeson seriously when he wore these blinders.

One wonders what would have happened had Paul been a little more honest, with himself as well as with others, about his Soviet "friends." Would his career have turned out differently in the 1950s had he portrayed himself as a fighter against racism in the United States *and* oppression in the Soviet Union? No one will ever know.

Still, there was no excuse for what came after. In the short-sighted America of the late 1940s, there was always the possibility that Robeson's controversial remarks might trigger violence. The Soviets certainly didn't help matters. In issues of *Pravda*, the *People's World*, the *Daily Worker*, and other Communist-run publications (all to be found in the FBI's files on the singer), the Party proclaimed Robeson a great friend of the U.S.S.R., doing everything they could to inflame the situation, not diffuse it. From what we can gather from this approach, it was pretty obvious that the Communists working for these tabloids cared little, if anything, for Paul's safety, or the safety of anyone else at one of his concerts who suddenly found themselves in the middle of a riot.

The nightmare that Paul's fans feared would happen exploded with devastating impact in the summer of 1949. The prelude to said explosion occurred in April, when Paul attended the so-called World Peace Congress in Paris. There was no doubt that the group was promoted, influenced and financed by the Communist Party. Everyone knew that, including the FBI, whose agents were sitting in on their meetings and quietly taking notes. Besides the usual America-bashing which permeated the conference, Paul said something that remains a controversy to this day. He announced that "Negroes" would never fight in a war against the Soviet Union, and especially in the armies of a nation which had enslaved them for generations.

If Paul wanted to shake up those in power in America, he succeeded beyond, as the cliché went, his wildest dreams. Meanwhile, the Soviets, seeking opportunities to divide and conquer, loved every minute of it.

Black religious leaders denounced him from the pulpits and whites who hadn't cared about Robeson one way or the other were now enraged, particularly war veterans. In fact, the singer's logic made little sense. He had supported the recent world war as a "people's war," and insisted on the nation making an all-out effort to defeat fascism. Why was it all right for America's black soldiers to fight and give their lives against Nazis and Japanese fascists, especially in a then-segregated army, yet *now* it was wrong to fight the Russians? Neither Paul, nor his wife Eslanda, ever answered this question to anyone's satisfaction.

Then, on August 27 of that year, controversy was followed by violence. Paul was scheduled to perform in Peekskill, New York, to benefit the Harlem chapter of the Civil Rights Congress. He had performed in Peekskill in recent years to receptive audiences, but in 1949, things were much different. Hours before the concert, an angry mob of white thugs wielding baseball bats, clubs, knives and rocks stormed the concert site; they even burned a cross on a nearby hillside. Loudly, the mob threatened to kill Robeson, as well as any blacks and Jews they found in the audience. Concert staff and teenage ushers were injured in the melee. At a Harlem rally attended by Canada Lee and some 10,000 supporters, Robeson defiantly announced he would return to do the concert on September 4.

Surrounded by an interracial phalanx of unarmed volunteers, Paul did the concert before some 20,000 fans who bravely defied the mob. Unfortunately, as the concertgoers were leaving, the racists returned and launched their attack. In the hell that followed, Robeson's fans were stoned and beaten, with the mob dragging many of them from their cars and assaulting them with clubs and knives as police and state troopers reportedly stood by and watched. There were 140 people injured by the mob (some reports put the number as much higher).

Robeson, Lee and civil rights groups demanded an investigation. State officials and Peekskill authorities ignored their request and the perpetrators remained at large. Concert promoters took notice. Watching the aftermath of the Peekskill riot, they came to the conclusion that a Paul Robeson concert was going to be a dangerous night out for many music lovers. Offers to book him started to dwindle.

On top of this, the State Department took his passport away. Seeing his concerts as excuses to promote the Soviet Union and make un–American speeches, the government, with J. Edgar Hoover's approval, saw Robeson as a security risk just as the Korean War started.

Blocked from performing both inside and outside the United States, Robeson remained defiant, even in a testy appearance before HUAC. Despite the obvious racism attributed to his persecution, his embrace of the Soviets while his country was at war didn't help his situation either.

Certainly, the words used to describe one of his greatest roles could easily have fit his admiration for the Soviet imperialists: "He loved not wisely, but too well...."

After the success of *Body and Soul*, Abraham Polonsky, ex–B scenarist at Paramount, now found himself to be Hollywood's newest golden boy. Why, he was even invited to the chateau of right-wing superstar Ginger Rogers (daughter of Leila, she of the *Tender Comrade* controversy). Apparently, the gorgeous blonde Oscar winner wanted the Communist scenarist to write a project for her. However, like other stories from Polonsky, there were apparently no other witnesses to give corroboration to such a meeting. Nevertheless, the story was recited with due reverence by leftist apologists Paul Buhle and Dave Wagner in their Polonsky biography.[35]

Despite the "meeting" with Ginger having gone nowhere, the scenarist wasn't through yet. Polonsky was now hired to direct John Garfield in Enterprise's next project, a crime melodrama based on Ira Wolfert's novel *Tucker's People*. Scripted by Polonsky and Wolfert, the film, now called *Force of Evil*, was Hollywood's first all-out attack on Wall Street. In previous years, certainly during the Depression, the film industry had always made fun of the rich, but never with such vindictiveness. For one thing, Hollywood *couldn't* attack Wall Street businessmen since so much of the film industry's money came from there. The Mayers, Warners, Cohns and Zanucks may have run their respective studios, but the money men who were on boards of directors in New York were the *real* owners. Biting the hands that fed them was bad enough, but Polonsky, Garfield and the Enterprise staff now endeavored to chop them off.

Only in America...

Joe Morse (Garfield) is a numbers-running attorney for a "combine," that is, well-dressed corporate types like Mr. Tucker (Roy Roberts) and his underhanded gang of suits. But Tucker sees an annoying gnat in the numbers operation run by small-timer Leo Morse (Thomas Gomez), Joe's moralistic older brother. Leo had put Joe through business college, but didn't expect the younger man to use his newly acquired knowledge to twist the law to work for Tucker and the combine. Here, Polonsky and Wolfert concoct a new kind of gangster: one devoid of machine guns, Molotov cocktails, and brass knuckles, and instead, dressing and acting like American success stories. Kind of like studio moguls.

Leo rather ridiculously refuses to join Tucker's combine and refers to himself as a "little guy" against the corporate monopolies of crime. (Apparently, the fact that he's still a dishonest SOB ripping off poor people doesn't occur to Leo, as long as he's not a *big* criminal.) In a gangster version of a hostile corporate takeover, and despite entreaties from Joe to spare Leo, Tucker's men revert to Warner Brothers form and blow Leo away. After finding out about his brother's death, Joe accosts Tucker and his associate Bill Ficco (Paul Fix) in their penthouse realm. After the subsequent shootout, Joe is the sole survivor. Ultimately pressured by the Breen Office, Polonsky was forced to write in a voiceover where Joe decides to cooperate with the D.A.'s office.

In an ironic counterpoint to the film's plot, Enterprise was losing money. *Force of Evil*, a film that was, in its own way, an American classic that influenced the later crime films of Martin Scorsese, was eventually released by, of all studios, MGM. Harboring contempt for the material, the studio gave it sparse bookings and it quietly died at the box office.

Meanwhile, Garfield and Polonsky's former collaborator, Robert Rossen, was over at Columbia writing and directing the film version of Robert Penn Warren's Pulitzer Prize–winning novel *All the King's Men*, with the director-scenarist presenting his own special portrait of an American political system gone out of control.

However, a half century later, long after Rossen's testimony before HUAC, the vindictive Polonsky would have his own take on the man whose direction of *Body and Soul* helped bring him critical acclaim: "You wouldn't want to be on a desert island with Rossen, because if the two of you didn't have any food, he would want to have you for lunch tomorrow."[36] It also couldn't have escaped Polonsky that his own directing career was cut short at the exact same time that Rossen won the Oscar for Best Director for *All the King's Men*. Rossen would not be around to hear the bitter words of his former underling because he had died in Hollywood on February 19, 1966.

Even cannibals didn't wait 30 years before devouring their enemies.

On December 27, 1945, a new play called *Home of the Brave* opened at the Belasco Theater, written by a young New Yorker named Arthur Laurents. A Jewish combat veteran who had endured anti–Semitism in the military, Laurents put his own experiences into his work. In this story of a Jewish soldier battling race hatred as well as Japanese fascism on an island in the South Pacific, Laurents began a trend of social problem works which exposed American bigotry by using the country's experiences in the war as a starting point. Politically to the left, the play was blatant in its charges against who was responsible for bigotry in America. Predictably, its main villain is the soldier who was a rich kid as a civilian, thus linking capitalist affluence with bigotry; as if somehow a poor person couldn't possibly harbor any prejudice because of his financial status.

Played by future director (and *Body and Soul* co-star) Joseph Pevney, Coney is a Jewish soldier sent on a suicide mission with a young major (Kendall Clark), his pal Finch (Henry Bernard), tough poet Mingo (Alan Baxter), and the anti–Semitic T.J. (Russell Harde). The Japanese, whom the audience never sees, terrorize the men from afar. During a moment of tension as they stalk a Japanese patrol in the jungle, the usually understanding Finch mimics T.J.'s bigotry and suddenly calls Coney "a dirty yellow"—He stops short, then ends it with "—jerk!"

Soon, Finch is captured by the Japanese out in the jungle. Shocked by Finch's reversion to anti–Semitism, Coney's anger at his friend causes him to believe that he purposely allowed him to be captured. As the enemy tortures Finch so his pals can come to his rescue and reveal their positions, a frantic Coney has to resist the urge to try to save him. However, the anguished young Jew is calmed by the compassionate Mingo, who recites a poem "written by his ex-wife" that perfectly comments on the need for all peoples to stand together in times of crisis. Mingo's poem is a powerful one, and is still moving to this day:

> We are only two and yet our howling
> Can encircle the world's end.
> Frightened,
> (FINCH screams weakly.)
> You are my only friend.
> (Slower now.)
> And frightened we are everyone.
> Someone must take a stand.
> Coward, take my coward's hand.

When the men return to their base (without Finch who died on the island), a traumatized Coney finds that he cannot walk. It is soon revealed by the compassionate physician Captain Bitterger (Eduard Franz) that Coney is suffering a psychosomatic reaction concerning guilt over Finch's death. After the doctor berates Coney with "You lousy, yellow Jew bastard, get up and walk!" Coney rises off his cot and is ready to kill the doctor until her realizes that the illness was all in his mind. Just before going home, Coney punches out T.J. and decides to open up a bar with Mingo (who had lost an arm in combat).

Home of the Brave ran 69 performances and won the New York Drama Critic's Circle Award before closing on February 23, 1946. Though not exactly a hit, it impressed a young producer-director in the audience who hoped to begin a series of pictures that would comment on the nation's social problems. But social problems or no, Stanley Kramer was still a businessman.

> I had thought of it as a possible film project ever since I saw it on Broadway, just before its sudden and unfortunate closing. I was able to buy the film rights to *Home of the Brave* from its brilliant author, Arthur Laurents, for $35,000, a steal.[37]

Kramer and his minions (including former East Side Kids writer Carl Foreman) now promptly changed it. Realizing that Fox and RKO had already produced films attacking anti-Semitism, Kramer wanted to switch ethnic victims. In his autobiography, he claimed that Laurents had always wanted to make the soldier-victim a black man, but dared not attempt it at the time. This was an incredible statement to make since Laurents, a recent war veteran, knew good and well that army companies were not integrated during the conflict. Laurents had suffered the outrages of anti-Semitism; how could he write about racism against blacks when they were never part of his segregated company?

In the film version of *Home of the Brave*, despite fine performances from all the actors (especially groundbreaking black actor James Edwards), the black soldier's presence on a reconnaissance mission is plainly absurd. The later play and film *A Soldier's Story*, which addressed segregation in the armed forces, was far more realistic. It showed black soldiers, more often than not, being forced to remain on base and assigned menial chores like painting and carpentry rather than fighting. Only when white units were decimated in battle did white officers design to send in black replacements for important missions (though these men died every bit as bravely as their white brethren).

The low-budget film ($365,000) is more or less like the play, except that Foreman "opens it up" by having Moss (Edwards) feeling the sting of racism even before he gets into uniform. At a party thrown by college classmates, Moss prefers to hang out on the front porch with his one white friend, Finch (Party member Lloyd Bridges), rather than be ostracized by the white crowd inside. During that heated argument on the island, instead of starting to call his friend a "yellow Je—," Finch stops himself before he says the N word. We are moved by the expression of hurt and pain on Edwards' face (which was reconstructed after an accident in the army during the war).

Edwards was a war veteran who, after surgeons saved his face and damaged vocal cords, decided to celebrate his "rebirth" by becoming an actor. He took elocution lessons, read plays and later appeared on Broadway in *Deep Are the Roots*, a play which attacked southern racism. He made his film debut as a boxer in RKO's *The Set-Up* with Robert Ryan. After *Home of the Brave*, though he would continue to act in films with an occasional role of servant or African tribal leader thrown in, Edwards would portray the quintessential African-American soldier. In the next 22 years, no black actor in film wore an American uniform better. Certainly, Edwards' talent for portraying the black man as American warrior was a slap in the face to those backward whites who preferred seeing black performers in subservient roles.

Despite his memorable performance in *Home of the Brave*, the film was Edwards' first and *last* starring role. He had less presence than a Robeson or Canada Lee; and the studios were still reluctant to give starring roles to black actors, so the underrated Edwards would usually be cast in both films and TV as a supporting player. An added impediment to his career were his uncompromising remarks against racism and Hollywood's typecasting of African-American actors. (Sidney Poitier, not as militant then as he would later become in the safer atmosphere of subsequent decades, would be Hollywood's new black superstar.) Though *not* a Party member, Edwards was graylisted for the duration of the Blacklist years, where he was mostly restricted to serviceman roles. He was a wonderful performer and usually stood out in anything he appeared in. (One of my favorites is his defense attorney in 1958's *Night of the Quarter Moon*. In the moving final scene, after successfully defending the black heroine, he is left to wander off alone outside the courtroom, unheralded and unrewarded, his isolation captured in a beautiful long shot as the end titles come up.) According to Kramer,

> Edwards was a pioneer. Until 1949, the only roles for black actors were in the Stepin Fetchit category.... Edwards never fit into such a role, nor should he or anyone ever have been asked to do so. He was an intelligent, cultivated actor with an excellent voice, and I was lucky to get him.[38]

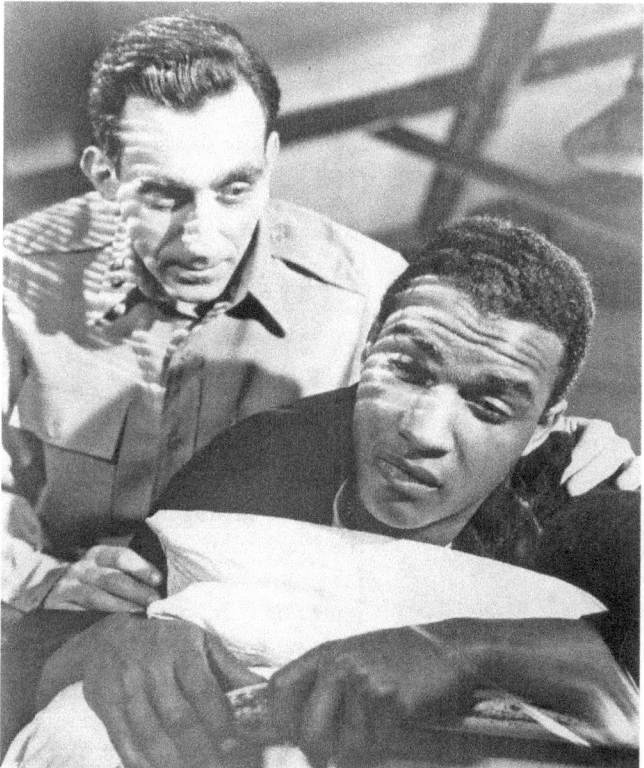

Filming the project in total secrecy (according to Kramer, he made the cast and crew take vows of silence, as if they were monks), he, Foreman and director Mark Robson referred to the project under the code name "High Noon," a title that would reappear to more powerful effect years later.

Despite protests from the usual quarters, *Home of the Brave* was a hit with both audiences and critics.[39] Bosley Crowther accurately wrote, "The only people who will scorn it are those who segregate the truth." Kramer said that after a preview in Westwood, California, audiences gave the film a standing ovation for several minutes.

HEROES IN TROUBLE. Jeff Corey and the underrated James Edwards in the film version of Arthur Laurents' play *Home of the Brave* (1949). The screenplay changed Laurents' Jewish soldier to a black man, but the film neglects to mention segregation in the armed forces during World War II.

Despite what many today see as the film's naiveté which implied that racism wasn't part of the system, but more of a matter of personalities, *Home of the Brave* laid the groundwork for films like *Lost Boundaries* (featuring Canada Lee) and the more direct attack on white racists (if not white racism) *No Way Out*, with new black star Sidney Poitier.

But in 1949, despite the rise of black actors like Poitier, Edwards and Lee, Hollywood had never produced a black *female* movie star (and, for the most part, continues to have that problem to this very day). When black actresses were on screen, they were usually stuck in small, worthless roles as either maids or café singers.

But what would happen in that turbulent year of 1949 if a script was to feature a black female character as the center of attention?

To practically no one's satisfaction, that question was going to be answered by Darryl F. Zanuck and Elia Kazan...

"The love story of a girl who passed for white!"

This was a movie tagline that, let's admit it, wasn't seen too often in 1949. Still, the same ridiculous plot points of light-skinned black people pretending to be white would actually continue with silly exploitation films produced well into the 1960s.

But this wasn't the cheesy filmmaking of Larry Buchanan or Joseph Brenner, this was the great Elia Kazan. How this giant got involved in such a film is a B film in itself, and it started with the involvement of another filmmaking giant.

Fox contract writer (and later director) Philip Dunne tries to answer the question in his memoirs *Take Two: A Life in Movies and Politics*:

> [W]ho was the auteur of *Pinky*? At film festivals you will see it billed as "a film by Elia Kazan," but Kazan had absolutely nothing to do with its preparation.
>
> Ironically enough, [John] Ford did. He was the director until, on the third day of shooting, he came down with a painful and crippling attack of shingles which forced him to withdraw. Kazan was hastily signed to replace him....[40]

Unfortunately, Dunne, who was one of the leaders of the anti–HUAC Committee for the First Amendment (which, thanks to the arrogance of the Communist writers they were defending, flopped big-time), was a bit disingenuous about the *Pinky* affair. Elia Kazan was far more open about his replacing Ford in a 1980s interview with Jeff Young:

> [Ford] pretended to have shingles. Some years later I said to Zanuck, "Jack Ford never had

COLOR SCHEME. Jeanne Crain as the African-American heroine in *Pinky* (1949), with William Lundigan as her boyfriend. Elia Kazan took over the direction from John Ford, who plainly couldn't handle the material.

shingles, did he?" And he said, "Oh hell, no. He just wanted to get out of it; he hated Ethel Waters and she sure as hell hated him." Jack scared her to death and she knew she didn't want to work with him. I also think he didn't like the whole project.[41]

Years later, Darryl Zanuck put it even more plainly:

> Ford's Negroes were like Aunt Jemima. Caricatures. I thought we're going to get into trouble. Jack said, "I think you better put someone else on it." I said, "Finish out the day," and I took Ford off the picture. Some directors are great in one field and totally helpless in another.[42]

"Helpless" was a nice way to put it. If anyone had seen any of Ford's 1930s film output when black characters were shown, it will come as no surprise that Stepin Fetchit had been the main African-American actor he would feature. Indeed, Ford's *Judge Priest*, set in the South, features Fetchit and other black performers in supporting roles playing the usual stereotypical singin' and dancin' "darkies" that white Southern audiences of the day loved seeing. In 1960, Ford would endeavor to show a proud black man (played by Woody Strode) in *Sergeant Rutledge*, but the film always seemed like too little and much, *much* too late.

Besides Ford's own problems with *Pinky*'s subject matter, he had to deal with cast player Ethel Waters, who apparently had her own racial prejudices concerning whites. At the *Pinky* wrap party, Kazan coaxed her into admitting that, though she loved him personally, she also hated him because of his skin color.[43]

Based on the novel *Quality* by Cid Ricketts Sumner, *Pinky* is the story of a black woman passing for white. Patricia "Pinky" Johnson is played by that famous portrayer of African-American roles, Jeanne Crain. She has a white fiancé, Dr. Adams (William Lundigan), who finally accepts her as black, but wants her to return up north with him and continue "passing" so it won't adversely affect *his* position at the hospital. Though this man lacks some moral fiber, at least he is still played by handsome white actor Lundigan. Unfortunately, it was the actor's good looks which clinched the studio's decision to reject another, obviously more qualified actress to play the lead role. Lena Horne, the beautiful singer-actress, already comfortable in front of a camera because of her appearances (mostly in musical numbers) in MGM films, campaigned long and hard for the role. However, as usual, it was felt that audiences would not accept an actual black woman in the role, especially opposite a good-looking white actor like Lundigan. In real life, Horne was married at the time (and for decades after) to a Jewish man, but due to the era's prejudices, they were forced to keep the marriage a secret.

In the meantime, Fox executives decided on the approach they would make concerning the screenplay; in fact, it was a foregone conclusion, the orders came from the top man himself. In a December 1, 1948, interoffice memo to Dudley Nichols, the film's first scriptwriter, Darryl Zanuck laid it on the line:

> I am writing in large letters on my script the following legend:
> "This is not a story about how to solve the Negro problem in the south or anywhere else. This is not a story particularly about race problems, segregation or discrimination. This is the story about one particular Negro girl who could easily pass as white and who did pass for a white. This is a story of how and why she, as an individual, finally decided to be herself—a Negress."[44]

A few days later, in a memo dated November 5, Zanuck admitted to Philip Dunne that "Kazan, confidentially, like everyone else, is insane about the first 75 pages [of the script], and while he likes many individual scenes in the last half he shares our opinion that it misses."[45] Still, Dunne backed the boss' dictum on how Pinky was to be portrayed, as he made clear in a May 1949 letter to studio manager Harry Brand:

> Jeanne Crain, as Pinky, portrays not a race but an individual. The story is Pinky's, not ours, and while the tragic dilemma of her life is induced by the facts of racial prejudice, the solutions she finds are her own and affect her.... Pinky is acted upon by many other characters in our screenplay. Some are kind, some brutal, some condescending, some just harsh. We have tried to present them fairly and objectively, as we have tried to avoid preaching and confine ourselves to the facts.

Just before Dunne ends his letter, his comments to Brand about America's race problems are revealing in that he segues into mentioning alleged Communist influence in American films. The remarks about Communist propaganda in a private letter to the studio hierarchy are not to be found in his self-serving memoirs *or* in his pronouncements as head of the Committee For the First Amendment:

> The future of our way of life, the survival of democracy itself as a world force, may depend on what we as a nation do about the Negroes among us. It is not a coincidence that Soviet propaganda has continually stressed the subject. It is chiefly from the motion picture that the foreigner gains his concept of American life. We have to try to consider what the impact of such a film might be, not only on domestic audiences, but on audiences overseas, on friend and antagonist alike.[46]

Besides his admirable and sincere comments about the need for improving the status of African Americans in the U.S., Dunne also admits that the motion picture was the only way for people, whether here or on foreign shores, to gain any portrayal of what America was like, and that the Soviets constantly brought up our racial problems for propaganda purposes. Ironically, by his support of the Communist screenwriters as head of the Committee for the First Amendment, Dunne would deny that HUAC Congressmen might also be concerned about what kind of image American films conveyed to the world through its films.

Pinky opened in New York and Los Angeles on September 29, 1949, just a few weeks after the infamous Peekskill riots. The next day, the *Hollywood Reporter*'s Irving Hoffman (in his column *Tales of Hoffman*) had this to say about the performance of the film's star: "Jeanne Crain's warm, sensitive and appealing performance of the title role adds such stature to her career that the worry is whether she will find the part to top it. The young actress is superb."[47] The film's director might have disagreed with Hoffman.

Kazan later referred to Crain as "a sweet girl, but she was like a Sunday school teacher ... she didn't have any fire."[48] However, he also admitted that "the only good thing about her face was that it went so far in the direction of no temperament that you felt Pinky was floating through her experiences without reacting to them, which is what 'passing' is."

Calling *Pinky* "a disappointment," Dunne claimed that Zanuck had wanted it to be the first film about "the race issue, but the delay resulting from the script problem ... allowed two low-budget pictures on the subject to beat us into theaters...." The pictures that Dunne apparently thought beneath him to mention were *Home of the Brave* and *Lost Boundaries*.

However, Zanuck sent a copy of Dunne's screenplay to previous scenarist Dudley Nichols, who was also a liberal. Afterwards, Nichols responded with a long, detailed critique, "the burden of which," claimed Dunne, "was that he couldn't conceive of a white man ever agreeing to marry a girl with even a drop of African blood in her veins."[49] After reading the letter aloud to Dunne and John Ford in his office, Zanuck "merely shook his head, dropped the letter on his desk, fixed me with a gleaming eye, and said, 'I could never understand the liberal mentality.'"

In the coming years, there would be very few in either Congress or the film industry who would.

On February 24, 1949, *The Big Knife* debuted on Broadway's National Theater. It was Odets' first play in seven years; in 1942, he had written *The Russian People*, a Communist-backed production extolling a Party-sanctioned version of what a Russian citizen was (i.e., loyal to Stalin, etc.). But 1949's *The Big Knife* was a far different animal. It starred John Garfield as Hollywood star Charlie Castle, former RKO B starlet Nancy Kelly as his estranged wife Marion, and J. Edward Bromberg as Louis Mayer clone Marcus Hoff. Directed by Method god Lee Strasberg, the play ran 109 performances, not exactly a big hit, but certainly not a failure either.

For Odets, it would be a year and a half after the closing of this show before he would put on another play; however, it would be the one that finally wiped out the stigma of left-wing theatrics in his works, the wildly successful, and emphatically *non*-political *The Country Girl*. The playwright's testimony as a "friendly witness" before HUAC didn't exactly hurt his career either; and when the committee pressed him to name names, despite his own disgust with the blacklist, he obligingly gave the name of the now-dead actor who had played the venomous Marcus Hoff: J. Edward Bromberg.

However, John Garfield wasn't going to have it that easy.

One must applaud the actor's wall-to-wall guts for filming material that, despite the rising Cold War, socked American institutions right in the teeth. Even when Garfield made a film that had nothing to do with America, he was attacked by the right. *We Were Strangers*, directed by John Huston (who co-headed the Committee for the First Amendment), dealt with the Cuban revolution of 1931 that put Batista in power (the same Batista whose police incarcerated Odets and his retinue on that pier in 1936). Though the film is a powerful indictment of Latin-American dictatorships, it took a slightly more benign stand concerning those who would foment violence to overthrow these despots. Here, Garfield and Huston both glorify and condemn the kind of armed insurrection that continued to be a Soviet specialty as the decades passed. Though Garfield's character, a New York–raised Cuban revolutionary, is sincere in his desire to free his people, he is also callous about the killing of innocents so that the overthrow can take place. To his credit, the actor plays it with his usual charisma, making the role of Tony Fenner (a revolutionary alias) both charming and obsessive, driven by his passion to help the people, yet using cutthroat methods in the way he goes about it; in other words, the usual Garfield screen character.

Still, the *Hollywood Reporter* called *We Were Strangers* "the heaviest dose of Red theory ever served to an audience outside the Soviet," which was ridiculous. Despite decent reviews, the film left behind it a taste of controversy merely by "promoting" the idea of how wonderful things would be if "the people" decided to knock off their leaders.

Already in hot water over the anti-capitalist *Force of Evil* (which, anti-capitalist or not, flopped at the box office) and the pro-revolution *We Were Strangers*, Garfield was now appearing in a Broadway play written by a known Communist playwright (who supposedly left the Party, not that the right-wing believed that anyway). Worse yet, it was going to rip apart Hollywood, the actor's bread and butter before HUAC came to town.

The play deals with film star Charlie Castle's rather screwed-up life in the land of Hollywood. Charlie was a former New York theater star (like Garfield); after a wild Hollywood party, a drunken Charlie runs over and kills a child, and his publicity man takes the rap. Studio head Marcus Hoff wants Charlie to sign an incredible 14-year contract to the studio or else Hoff will turn the key on Charlie. Meanwhile, Charlie's ex-wife Marion hates his hedonistic lifestyle and wants him to return to New York theater (and apparently ignore *its* hedonistic lifestyle).

Throughout the play is the usual Odetsian angst, sometimes ridiculously so, especially when the author attempts to give us his version of crackling, realistic dialogue. Still, there is the leftover resentment of what the need for money and a high-maintenance lifestyle does to a person, particularly a talented actor who is now a Hollywood "property." As his wife Marion makes clear:

> It's a fabulous deal. But it's for fourteen years, and I don't believe in the life that goes with it. Charlie, you're half-asleep right now! I haven't seen you sparkle since the day Billy was born! You used to take sides. Golly, the zest with which you fought. You used to grab your theater parts and eat 'em like a tiger. Now you act with droopy eyes. They have to call you away from a card game. Charlie, I don't want you to sign that contract — you've given the studio their pound of flesh — you don't owe them anything. We arrived here in a pumpkin coach and we can damn leave the same way!

If many of us can't find it within ourselves to excuse Odets for coming up with the sentence "Golly, the zest with which you fought," we can instead praise him for some insight into the actor playing the role. Certainly, the part of Charlie Castle (with the obvious exclusion of the act of child-murdering) comments rather accurately on the life and career of John Garfield. Though a basically decent chap off-screen, Garfield cheated on his wife Roberta with Charlie-like abandon; he did the Hollywood party scene with the best of them; and he actually didn't return to the theater for seven long years, until the town's political climate became unusually hot for socially conscious actors like himself (excluding the miserable Broadway bomb *The Heavenly Express* in 1940). And though the Marion in the play is not overtly political, as was Robbie, her desire to push Charlie back onto the New York stage accurately mirrors that of Garfield's off-stage wife.

In the Garfield biography *He Ran All the Way: The Life of John Garfield*, author Robert Nott commented on Robbie's dominance over her husband during this trying time. In fact, the following lines reveal a close kinship between her and Marion Castle: "Even if HUAC had struck a deal with Julie [Garfield] regarding his wife's activities, she was fair game to the media and the FBI. Robbie didn't care. She felt that Julie could set aside his film career and return to the theater."

All in all, it seems fairly certain that Odets, a close friend for many years, was fully aware of the actor's marital situation, as well as having intimate knowledge of the personality of Mrs. John Garfield.

However, besides the child's murder, there was another difference between Garfield and Castle. For instance, unlike Castle, Garfield *didn't* sell out. His films were not escapist pap (excepting the worst of the Warner years, that is). By the late 1940s, he was at the top of his game. He was an actor who was getting better and better as the years went on; he was a producer who believed in subject matter that brought attention to the poor and the disenfranchised; and he was a committed activist who fought against racism and worker exploitation.

He was also *not* a Communist.

Of course, this meant nothing to those who thought otherwise. In her *Los Angeles Times* column, Hedda Hopper attacked the play with her usual poison pen:

IV. A Revolution from Above (1946–1951)

> *The Big Knife*, Clifford Odets' play which pokes fun at Hollywood, with John Garfield starring, didn't get cheers when it opened out of town. Serves Garfield right. This town was very good to him, and since this is the way he shows his gratitude, perhaps he deserves a failure.[50]

By an amazing coincidence, the play opens with Charlie fending off an obnoxious woman named Patty Benedict, a powerful Hollywood columnist whose nasty demeanor and obvious lack of respect for others reminded many of a certain female columnist then working for the *L.A. Times*. As Odets described her, Benedict is "a famous movie columnist. She is authoritative, cynical and assured, insolently appraising, the world of Hollywood is certainly her intimidated oyster."

As far as "Hollywood being good to him," the vindictive Hopper may have forgotten Garfield being forced to make dreck like *Dangerously They Live* and *East of the River*, but apparently *he* didn't. Ignoring the controversy of a Hollywood actor starring in a play that ripped Hollywood, Garfield liked the challenge of an Odets play (even the silly dialogue); he felt he was an actor first, a Hollywood personality second.

In the play, when Charlie does defy Hollywood, it mirrors exactly Garfield's battles against film typecasting, as well as the town's political reactionaries. The following dialogue makes this comparison crystal clear: "I say the hell with bargaining, down with public opinion! Down with not being what we are! The hell with merchants and their tricks."

Despite the merchants and their tricks, *The Big Knife* did not become another *Death of a Salesman*, and this was not merely because Arthur Miller was a far more subtle playwright than Odets. For instance, latter-day critics accurately noted that studios, especially with TV on the horizon, didn't hand out 14-year contracts in 1949. A Hollywood veteran like Odets should have realized this. Just three years before, Olivia de Havilland's landmark suit against the studios proved that long-term contracts were illegal, so why was Odets using a process that no longer existed as a peg to hang his plot?

Nevertheless, the studios couldn't help noticing the depiction of studio head Marcus Hoff, a barely concealed and cruel portrait of Louis B. Mayer, the man whose studio had so recently released Garfield's *Force of Evil*. Hoff not only blackmails Charlie, but when a drunken starlet demands better parts from his studio, Hoff goes down on his knees and bursts into tears, a pathetic act Mayer himself would use to make recalcitrant actors come around to his viewpoint. The Hoff character also beats and kicks the actress when she laughs at his crying act. (Former working stiff Mayer had punched out Charlie Chaplin after an argument about his leftist beliefs in the late '40s, an episode that brought to light the mogul's latent penchant for violence.)

However, a more pernicious accusation about Mayer has now become accepted fact. At the end of the play, Charlie commits suicide by slitting his wrists in the bathtub, a Chekhovian ending favored by Odets (Remember the final guilt-ridden suicides at the end of *Golden Boy* and *Till the Day I Die*, as well as his screenplay of *Humoresque*, which had starred Garfield.). But Hoff's right-hand man (aptly named Smiley Coy), a vicious portrait of studio hatchet man Eddie Mannix, calls Hoff *before* he calls the police, to claim that Charlie died of a heart attack. This is as direct an accusation as could be made at the time of Mayer's duplicity in covering up the alleged 1934 suicide of Jean Harlow's husband, producer Paul Bern (which was later proven to be murder by an ex-girlfriend).

United Artists filmed *The Big Knife* in 1955 with Jack Palance in the role of Charlie Castle; however, a further irony in casting would be that of Shelley Winters as the play's drunken starlet. The actress was Garfield's final leading lady in his last film, *He Ran All the Way*.

In May 1949, Twentieth Century–Fox released *Under My Skin,* an above-average melodrama based on Ernest Hemingway's short story "My Old Man," which featured Garfield as a crooked jockey. Like Charlie Davis of *Body and Soul,* the Garfield character finds his integrity at the end of the film and actually *wins* (in this case, a horse race); but, unlike *Body and Soul,* he loses his life in the process. After this production, Garfield would star in his second-to-last film, the final one he would ever make for the studio where he gained his fame.

Meanwhile, on June 1, 1950, less than a year after the Peekskill riots, Paramount released a B film that refused to parrot the reactionaries' claims of America as a land of equality...

William Pine and William Thomas, sardonically known in the industry as "The Dollar Bills" for their low-budget but high-octane B adventures, had purchased the rights to the novel *The Voice of Stephen Wilder* by screenwriter Daniel Mainwaring, then still calling himself "Geoffrey Homes." As usual with their productions, the proposed film version was to be released by Paramount. The plot was an unusual one, even for 1950; it dealt with the bigotry inflicted upon a small California town's Latino minority by its white citizens, culminating in a race riot. Since Paramount wanted to get rid of contract players Macdonald Carey and Gail Russell, the studio cast them as the stars, figuring that a film which dwelled on racial issues wasn't going to be successful.

At first, the studio had planned to call the film *Outrage,* but that word had implications of something controversial, or possibly inflammatory. Then they called it *The Big Showdown,* a title which immediately implied a Western. Ultimately, Paramount decided on *The Lawless,* a title which brought to mind an old Western town besieged by outlaws. But as the film's foreword conveyed, the title referred to those Americans who had lost their sense of tolerance who *could* become the Lawless. It was a cynical title that was supposed to lure people into the theaters.

Mainwaring had written the script from his novel and, as was the usual procedure, it was sent to the Production Code office for their verdict. It wasn't exactly thumbs up. In a letter to Paramount executive Luigi Luraschi, dated October 5, 1949, Joseph Breen conceded that, even though the script (then known as *The Big Showdown*) was acceptable under the provisions of the Code, something else about the material clearly worried him:

> Certainly, it is that the story itself is a shocking indictment of America and its people and, indeed, is a sad commentary on "democracy at work," which the enemies of our system of government like to point to. The shocking manner in which the several gross injustices are heaped upon the head of the confused, but innocent, young American of Mexican extraction, and the willingness of so many of the people in your story to be a part of, and to endorse, these injustices, is, we think, a damning portrayal of our American social system.
>
> The overall effect of a story of this kind made into a motion picture would be, we think, a very definite disservice to this country of ours, and to its institutions and ideals.
>
> This whole undertaking seems to be fraught with very great danger, and, because of this, I wish again to urge that you study this matter with very great care....[51]

Despite the fact that Breen never once specified exactly where this "very great danger" was coming from, liberal director Joseph Losey was anxious to tackle the film. Two years before, he had made his directorial debut with RKO's antiwar Technicolor drama, *The Boy with Green Hair,* written by Party member Ben Barzman. Though the film's message stated quite clearly that war was wrong (big surprise here), there was more than a little hypocrisy attached to the project and its message. It seemed that after four years of Communist screenwriters exhorting us to go to war against Nazis, *now* war was wrong. Coincidentally, since our enemies at the time the film was made were Communists who had the A-bomb, *now* we were supposed to Give Peace a Chance.

Losey received (and deserved) praise for his sure hand behind the camera. However, it was certainly no surprise that RKO disliked the helmsman intensely. Vain, arrogant and cruel (his own wife and children reportedly couldn't stand him), Losey was rescued from studio-enforced idleness by MGM's Dore Schary, who generously bought up the director's contract. However, being Joseph Losey, the leftist helmsman promptly double-crossed Schary and signed with Pine-Thomas.

Predictably, relations between Losey and the Dollar Bills weren't all that rosy either. Thomas was known to hold staff meetings while sitting on a toilet with the door open; certainly a novel way to create entertainment for the masses. At one point, pressured by what he felt was interference, Losey reportedly threw his script at Thomas and told him to direct "his own f-----g picture!" Since Mainwaring was the only witness to this, Thomas admirably held his temper and allowed Losey to continue filming. In later years, the director also claimed that Pine and Thomas only gave him $150,000 to spend on the production; however, studio documents gave the lie to that one. The Dollar Bills had actually give him *$407,000* to spend, not the cheap figure Losey maliciously claimed they gave him.[52]

Predictably, the hostile director couldn't keep his temper in check for very long, ultimately getting into a fistfight with production manager Doc Merman. On the set, Losey's rages almost pushed the cast, half of whom were amateurs, to the breaking point. One scene between Carey and Russell went on for hours, much of it due to the alcoholic actress' need for a drink to steady her nerves. Paramount, who was quite familiar with Gail's affliction (and whose casting couch atmosphere didn't help her self-esteem), warned Losey *not* to give the actress a drink. Throughout the years, her managers at the studio also played a game of enabling with the sensitive woman, alternately prodding her with drink and, unfortunately, getting something else from her besides a performance in front of movie cameras.

Though cruel to a fault, Losey was surprisingly compassionate in his appraisal of her many years later, in an interview with Doug McClelland:

> Gail Russell died of alcoholism because she was deathly frightened of acting, but she had in her the makings of a great star. She had the most beautiful eyes I have ever seen, the most moving eyes. And she was immensely sensitive. Paramount had her under contract — like a horse. On *The Lawless*, I had absolute instructions from

SKIN DEEP. Macdonald Carey as the white editor of a small-town newspaper and Gail Russell as the Latina editor of a Spanish-language newspaper in a studio shot from *The Lawless* (1950). The film was based on a book by screenwriter Daniel Mainwaring (using the name Geoffrey Homes).

them not to let her have a drink. The first time I shot with her I had a long night-tracking shot. She couldn't remember a single line, and it was three or four pages of important dialogue.[53]

Grabbing her director with "icy cold" hands, Gail claimed that she really wasn't an actress and then begged him for a drink. Losey told her that she *was* an actress and then, whether out of pique with the studio or because he just wanted to shoot the scene and get it out of the way, he defied Paramount and gave her a drink. After she had her drink, the scene was quickly shot without a flub. Unfortunately, Losey's enabling little "pick-me-up" helped spell finish for the actress at Paramount. Her boozing forced the studio to drop her as the heroine of the western *Flaming Feather* with Sterling Hayden (her role would be played by Barbara Rush).

According to studio publicity for *The Lawless*, "Miss Russell ... turns in a smashing portrayal that proves her an actress of remarkable ability as well as beauty."[54]

Within a year, Paramount had no problem kicking the "actress of remarkable ability as well as beauty" off the lot.

Then, of course, the studio, Pine and Thomas and the Breen Office were also pressuring Mainwaring and Losey to water down the vindictiveness of the characters. A film slamming racism against a victimized minority now became a film slamming mob rule, something that Hollywood had *already* tackled in films from *Fury* to *The Ox-Bow Incident*; therefore, the material became less controversial.

Then there was the on-location shooting in Marysville, California, substituting for the film's fictional Santa Marta. Losey instructed the citizens of Marysville, whom he used as extras, to throw rocks during certain scenes, purposely *not* telling them what the scene was about. When the folks at Marysville discovered after the film's release that they were portraying a racist mob, they were justifiably angry, and probably wished they had saved a few rocks to hurl in Losey's direction.

Nevertheless, with *The Lawless*, the helmsman was going to show us more of his dark vision of America by depicting its worst nightmare (that is, besides Bolsheviks with their fingers on a nuclear trigger). Losey had studied news photos of the Peekskill riots, and used them as a framework when shooting the climactic race riot. It was this innovative approach which helped give the film its lasting power, and put it far above the usual Pine-Thomas schlock.

Our story begins in the little village of Santa Marta. In the town proper, the Caucasians hold sway as the movers and shakers while, in Sleepy Hollow, on the other side of the tracks, the Mexican citizens, working at unrewarding, low-paying jobs, have their own community. Latinos Paul Rodriguez and Lopo Chavez (newcomers Lalo Rios and Maurice Jara) are fruit pickers working for racist supervisor Jim Wilson (serial and B Western player Walter Reed). After knocking off for the day, the two Latinos get into a car accident with two rich kids, one of whom is Joe Ferguson (Johnny Sands). When Joe calls the Latinos a racist name, a fight starts. It is broken up by a white motorcycle cop who realistically would have sided with the rich boys. At home, Joe is chastised for not understanding his Latino brethren by his father (off-beat casting: character villain John Hoyt playing a nice-guy bourgeoisie).

Come Saturday night, there is the usual dance party at the old barn in Sleepy Hollow. Joe and his white pals (one of whom is played by future Warner Brothers star Tab Hunter) show up, if only to have their way with the Latino gals. Also attending, and looking for the fight he knows will "naturally" start, is newspaper editor Larry Wilder (Macdonald Carey). However, he runs into the compassionate Latina editor of the town's Spanish-language paper, Sunny Garcia (Gail Russell). Joe soon gets his randy hands on one of the Mexican gals and causes a fight. When the local police arrive, young Lopo, carried away with his punches, accidentally socks racist police sergeant Al Peters (B villain Ian McDonald). The officer throws the young Latino into the back of a police cruiser, but not before punching his face in. This brings a rebuke from his superior, Sergeant Boswell (Robert Williams): "Pick on someone your own size!" Another officer agrees with Boswell about Peters' surly disposition.

Here we have another rather unrealistic example of the studio attempting to water down the racism of the film's white characters. As we have seen, far too often, in many examples of police brutality down through the years, chances were that *all three* officers would have been belting Lopo, with not a word of compassion or restraint from any one of them.

Unfortunately, while Boswell chastises Peters, he fails to watch the road, and their car crashes. Boswell and the third officer are killed; Peters and Lopo stagger from the wreck, alive, but bruised. However, instead of shooting the unarmed Latino dead (which, this racist SOB realistically would have done), he fires warning shots in the air and allows him to escape. After fleeing in a stolen ice cream truck, a frightened Lopo tries to hide in a barn. When young teenager Mildred Jenson (Gloria Winters) discovers him, the frightened gal turns around and her head strikes a barn post, knocking her out. The local media discover the incident and concoct a story of Lopo sexually attacking the innocent farm girl.

Almost against his will, Larry is forced to take a stand. Aided by Sunny, he uses his newspaper to try to raise a fund for Lopo's defense. The white townsfolk have other ideas. Prodded by Wilson and the girl's father, mobs form in the streets and try to storm the jail (just like any lynch-mob Western), but the police (those fair-minded, anti-racist guys) hide the accused from their wrath. When Wilson angrily exhorts the mob to attack Wilder's newspaper office, some of the white men who had already attacked Rodriguez and his friends, now back off from joining him. Again, the studio is trying to show that not all white guys are bad, though the attack on Paul and his friends doesn't exactly absolve them.

When the mob does finally attack the newspaper office, they hit Rodriguez with a well-tossed rock. Sunny is in the building, but the members of the mob do not lay a hand on her. Afterwards, Wilder finds her unconscious (and unmolested) on an office couch.

Studio documents prove that the mob did much more to Sunny than we see in the finished film. According to a letter sent to Luigi Luraschi, dated October 4, Breen wrote, "[P]lease eliminate the action of the men slugging the girl, Sunny. In this sequence, no one should do more than push or shove the girl."

Despite Breen's chivalrous protection of Latina gals played by white actresses, the sequence of the newspaper office (the symbol of a free press) being overrun by a racist mob still retains a certain power. Losey films the mob having, literally, an orgy of destruction, breaking printing presses, throwing rocks through windows, tossing around newspapers and overturning desks.

However, according to a studio publicity sheet for the film (headlined *They Forgot They Were Americans*):

> The citizens of Marysville, California, are much too polite to suit motion picture director Joseph Losey…
> One scene in *The Lawless* which was filmed in Marysville with more than 2,000 townspeople as extras, called for a mob to charge through the door of a newspaper plant and wreck it. But Losey couldn't get the crowd to show enough violence until he told the group they were

through for the day and that the cashier would pay them inside the building.

The camera started turning and the resulting stampede was just what the director wanted.

This contrived copy certainly sounded more convenient to the studio as the reason the scene played so well, rather than Losey's assertion that he had modeled the violence on the racially fueled Peekskill riots.

After Wilder returns to his wrecked office, he gets a chance to punch out Wilson, then he addresses the mob outside the building. His speech unrealistically shames them, including Joe Ferguson, who suddenly feels guilt because the Breen Office apparently said he *had* to.

Throughout the film, every time Mainwaring and Losey depict a rotten white character, there seems to be a disclaimer further on in the picture. When sarcastic female journalist Jan Dawson (Lee Patrick, soon to play Mrs. Topper on TV) says, "They all look alike to me," right in front of Sunny, this newshound without a heart later tells her, apparently with sincerity, that she understands her pain. Ed Ferguson, the town's goody-goody capitalist, would have realistically been siding with the mob, but instead is willing to rebuild Wilder's newspaper and insists that the newsman stay and fight the good fight. Any racism on the part of the police is restricted to one officer with a bad attitude, Sgt. Peters. Indeed, only the film's depiction of a white-dominated media who portray Lopo as a Latino Jack the Ripper, seems to elude the (pardon the pun) whitewash; however, in 1950, moviemakers weren't about to have good words about the medium of television anyway.

The Breen Office apparently worked overtime to restrain the film's more sensationalistic elements. Concerning the alleged attack on Mildred Jenson, the censor insisted on deleting the word "rape" and the phrase "sex maniac." When the film's various characters get into racially fueled fights, apparently they were to be done according to Marquis of Queensbury Rules. Breen insisted on no "kicking or kneeing" of vital parts.

At the end of the film, Wilder is offered a chance to help Sunny print her Spanish-language paper. The last shot of the film is of the two journalists looking at each other lovingly over the printing press lever just before the Paramount mountain appears on screen to stirring music. The good fight will continue, though we assume it will be quite muted compared to what we've seen of the film's depiction of the white-dominated media.

In the coming years, actual race riots would not conclude with such pat endings, and it would take several more years before a preacher from Montgomery, Alabama, would set America straight on overcoming its numerous racial barriers.

Blacklisted soon after the film's release, Losey fled to England where there was no shortage of anti–American filmmakers willing to employ leftist artists. Mainwaring was also blacklisted, and he was forced to write under a pseudonym (which he was doing anyway). He later scripted the classic sci-fi of Cold War paranoia, *Invasion of the Body Snatchers*. Years later, *Invasion* bit player Sam Peckinpah tried to steal credit for Mainwaring's screenplay (that is, until Mainwaring's threat of legal action forced the macho big-mouth to make a retraction).[55]

In the meantime, another artist-activist was having his final day in the sun. In 1950, he returned to his home studio to make a film that skillfully merged rousing action with a biting commentary on the plight of Americans just trying to make ends meet.

> Look at me. I used to make $35 a day right through the season taking people out fishing. Now I get shot and lose an arm, and my boat, running a lousy load of liquor that's hardly worth as much as my boat. But let me tell you, my kids ain't going to have their bellies hurt and I ain't going to dig sewers for the government for less money than will feed them. I can't dig now anyway. I don't know who made the laws, but I know there ain't no law that you got to go hungry.

If the above bitter monologue was not delivered by a classic character of literature, at least it was written by one America's greatest authors. Like Harry Morgan, the two-fisted charter boat operator of *To Have and Have Not*, Ernest Hemingway also retained an anger against those in authority. Though he had lived an adventurous life, this vain author had an inflated image of himself as a two-fisted, plain-speaking Joe every bit as tough and fearless as Harry Morgan. Basking in a reputation as a no-nonsense he-man, Hemingway jealously guarded his past from those who might reveal certain embarrassing details. For instance, the allegedly manly author never mentioned how his own domineering mother used to make him dress like a girl and then insultingly call him Ernestine.[56] Other celebrities, perhaps prompted by jealousy, had already suspected the author of promoting a macho image to hide another side of him. Truman Capote famously referred to the author as a "bully."[57] Actress Louise Brooks thought he was "basically a homosexual putting on a fucking-and-fighting act to fool himself."[58]

Certainly, one can see how far the author got with his "tough-guy-with-a-heart" routine. Though supposedly maintaining a sympathy for the world's downtrodden in his novels, particularly the angry *To Have and Have Not*, Hemingway never quite explained how shooting down animals, getting into mindless barroom brawls, cheating on his wives and waving his *machismo* around like a pathetic flag actually helped the world's have-nots.

Warner Brothers certainly didn't care. During the war, they had bought *To Have and Have Not* and made it into a hit film with Humphrey Bogart and Lauren Bacall. However, director Howard Hawks' over-the-top celebrity kitsch, that is, promoting Bogart and Bacall's sex appeal over Hemingway's story, effectively killed the book's bitter social commentary. Set in Martinique, France, the film had our anti-hero protagonist abandoning his isolationism (something Bogart also did in *Casablanca*) to take a stand against the bad-guys of the Vichy regime. The novel, however, is set in Depression-era Key West, Florida. At one point in the book, Harry is forced to help four Cuban revolutionaries (who had just robbed a bank and killed two people) escape across the bay and back to Havana. In 1944, when the Bogart film was being prepared, the Office of Inter-American Affairs vetoed this plot on the grounds that it was dangerous to show Batista's Cuba as being so corrupt that revolutionaries were willing to overthrow the government. Therefore, the location of the story was now war-time France.

But Hemingway's novel isn't just about Harry Morgan and his efforts to break the law to provide for his family. Halfway through the book, the author introduces an obnoxious writer character (Hemingway speaking from a place he obviously knew well) who is cheating on his loving wife with the town's rich slut. In fact, the book is full of miserable people, especially poor folks who are constantly put down by the wealthy; who, in turn, are portrayed as neurotic, arrogant and pathetic. The poor are forced to work at horrible jobs, can't make ends meet and barely enjoy their lives. There are many, *many* long scenes set in Freddy's, the Key's popular watering hole. Here, the eccentric, arrogant rich rub elbows with the island's economically disenfranchised. At one point, Hemingway even goes into painfully boring detail on the wealthy inhabitants of the various yachts docked at a certain pier, damning every one of them as crooks, liars and social parasites. One wonders if the macho scribe ever considered saying the same things to his wealthy publishers.

Warners had always wanted to remake the Bogart film more in line with Hemingway's original story. By the spring of 1949, with the project officially green-lighted, the studio proceeded to start casting. In a letter to Steve Trilling, dated May 7, 1949, producer Jerry Wald wrote, "Spoke to John Garfield this morning. He is leaving *The Big Knife* May 28, and going away on a month vacation. If the studio wants, he could start *The Breaking Point* sometime in July."[59]

Garfield wanted Fred Zinnemann as the director; however, according to Wald, "if the studio twisted his arm" he would accept Michael Curtiz, then busy making *Young Man with A Horn* with Kirk Douglas. Further down in the letter, Wald even floated the film's screenwriter, Ranald MacDougal (the scripter of *Objective, Burma!*), as a possibility for director, noting that the studio also gave scenarists like John Huston, Delmer Daves and Norman Krasna a chance to direct.

Garfield wasn't the studio's only choice for the role of Harry Morgan. At other times, they threw around names like Kirk Douglas (too young), James Cagney (too old), Burt Lancaster, John Wayne and Errol Flynn (who had his own boat, and genuinely loved the sea). However, Garfield wanted the role, and Wald and Curtiz liked him personally and professionally. (Flynn, whom the studio was trying to get rid of, would play the heroic skipper of the studio's B adventure *Mara Maru* two years later; needless to say, it was not Hemingway.)

On June 8, Wald advised Trilling that Garfield would also accept Robert Siodmak as the director. In the same letter, Wald also mentions Garfield's possible participation in a film version of *The Glass Menagerie*.

Taking a definite hands-on approach, the actor wrote to Curtiz on January 16, 1950. His suggestions all seem to have made it into the film. Although Harry had been married to his wife for many years, Garfield suggested that the character show that he still "has a real kind of yen for her, which is usually very rarely shown in films." He also suggested that since the character of Eddie (changed to Wesley for the film) will be a black man, their regard for each other, "without being too sentimental, can be kicked up a bit more." Again, this is another example of the actor's commitment to civil rights, and his efforts to showcase African Americans in his films.

Garfield also thought one of the most interesting features of the book was the fact that Harry loses an arm, though the actor admitted, "It might seem a little grotesque." While also mentioning that Jack Warner might find it "a little too morbid," he suggested that "there is no reason why this couldn't be included." Towards the end of the letter, the actor neatly summed up the picture's social commentary: "The main theme which seems to me quite simple and direct is: the struggle of a man who tries to make a living for his family and to discharge his responsibilities and finds it tough."[60]

Having read and reread the book, Garfield understood Hemingway's novel better than most. After all, he had been performing in films and plays commenting on the problems of poor Americans making ends meet for close to twenty years.

However, the theme of economic disenfranchisement, as well as their star's activist credentials, weren't lost on the filmmakers either. In fact, in a letter to Ranald MacDougall, dated February 10, Wald ironically uses the name of his star to identify the character:

> Garfield's story is a violent and sometimes cruel one, but from it should come great pleasure in his eventually learning something ... that no man is an island to himself, and that he must assume responsibilities ... that there is a right way of living in the world. The aspirations of Garfield for peace and security for his family and for himself are the aspirations of all of us today.

In a Warner story analysis from March 8, critiquing MacDougall's early script draft, the producer continues with the theme: "The intention of *The Breaking Point*, I believe, is to show how difficult, if not actually impossible, it is for a returning war hero to adjust to the

BROTHERS II. Juano Hernandez and John Garfield in Warners' *The Breaking Point* (1950). According to studio correspondence, Garfield wanted to use the film to encourage racial brotherhood.

subtler conflicts of civilian life…." Then, in an almost chilling prophesy of Garfield's problems to come in less than two years, the following paragraph could easily have been commenting on the Hollywood of the Blacklist Years:

> In *The Breaking Point*, at present, there is no way out and no hint of one — because Garfield, and everyone around Garfield, has no faith, no hope, no decency — and in the last analysis, no courage. Examine the role carefully and you will see that Garfield, for all his physical bluster, has no real courage. He grabs at every quick device, he makes whatever shady or cheap compromise is offered him, essentially he thinks only in terms of himself, his own desires, and the gratification of those desires.

In reality, though he was a typical movie star hedonist, Garfield didn't only think of himself. However, the Hollywood of that time, ultimately bullied by vain Congressmen on the one hand, and militant Communists on the other, certainly made some "cheap compromises."

Hemingway's book, with its convoluted prose and over-long sentences, was an ugly indictment of capitalism in Depression-era America, and practically encourages breaking the law so that one's family can survive. In an indictment of the system's hatred of the poor, Hemingway has Morgan bitterly complain:

> [M]y my family is going to eat as long as anybody eats. What they're trying to do is starve you Conchs out of here so they can burn down the shacks and put up apartments and make this a tourist town…. I hear they're buying up lots, and then after the poor people are starved out and gone somewhere else to starve some more, they're going to come in and make it into a beauty spot for tourists.

CRUISING FOR A BRUISING. Guy Thomajan and William Campbell hassle John Garfield in *The Breaking Point* (1950). The climax, as filmed by Michael Curtiz, is one of the best shootouts put on screen.

After this speech, his doomed friend Albert calls him a radical. However, later in the novel, after Harry picks up the Cuban revolutionaries and hears a young idealist rant on about the "cause," Harry's brutal realism takes over:

> What the hell do I care about his revolution. F___ his revolution. To help the working man he robs a bank and kills a fellow works with him and then kills that poor damned Albert that never him did any harm. That's a working man he kills. He never thinks of that. With a family. It's the Cubans run Cuba. They all double-cross each other. They sell each other out. They got what they deserve. To hell with their revolution. All I got to do is make a living for my family and I can't do that. Then he tells me about his revolution. To hell with his revolution.

Lacking this objectivity, the Communist Party would have merely seen the revolutionaries as heroes and damned Harry as some kind of "fascist" for his realistic take on all insurgencies.

Still, Harry's refusal to see the world through socio-political blinders doesn't lessen the character's basic amorality. Certainly, every film version of the novel, including Garfield's, has made Harry far more likable (and far less sleazy) than he was in the book; he has few moral qualms about breaking the law, and at one point is even thinking about murdering his rummy pal, Eddie, to make sure he doesn't talk.

In fact, the dog-eat-dog tone MacDougall tried to convey in the first drafts of his script (the studio forced him to water them down) is very much in the novel. Ludicrously jumping back and forth between first-person narration and third-person, then focusing on altogether different characters who have nothing to do with Harry Morgan, Hemingway gives the novel a schizophrenic tone which calls into question whether the author had a bottle at his elbow while writing it. Besides the author's lack of focus, there is a mean-spiritedness throughout the book, with the character descriptions crossing over from the colorful into the inflammatory. Referring to Wesley, Harry's black friend (who is more like a fellow crook than a buddy), or any other black character, Hemingway's neurotically frequent use of the N word goes off the charts. This is when he doesn't refer to Asians as "Chinks" or call part of Key West's commercial strip "the five Jew Stores."

Meanwhile, having cast Harry, the studio now had to find the actress to play his wife. In the book, her name is Marie. She is a tall, hefty, bleached blonde example of trailer trash who used to make her living "swinging her hips." The writer character even refers to her as "big as a battleship," which seems a trifle unfair. If anything, she thinks her husband, two years younger than she, is hot, and is turned on by merely looking at him. She and Harry are the parents of three girls. And though she doesn't outwardly abuse the girls, she admits to herself that she doesn't like them either, as they are rivals for Harry's affection. Certainly, the studio wasn't going to a have a mother character who didn't love her kids. Rechristening her Lucy, Wald and MacDougall rewrote her as a responsible mom who fights tooth and nail for her family.

On March 9, Wald suggested several possible actresses for the role: Teresa Wright, Margaret O'Sullivan, Mercedes McCambridge and Barbara Hale. On March 20, he suggested Jane Wyman. Later that same day, he informed MacDougall that the studio tested contract star Ruth Roman in the part; two days before that, they had tested Barbara Bel Geddes.

Finally, the studio chose a sweet-faced actress borrowed from MGM who had always played "good girls," as she did so memorably opposite Van Johnson in *Thirty Seconds Over Tokyo*. On March 27, Wald wrote to Phyllis Thaxter:

> As you probably know, we tested some ten actresses for the role; and, truthfully, none of them manage to capture, as you did, (and on such short notice) some of the emotion that the character of Lucy is supposed to have.... To me the character of Lucy is a portrait of nine-tenths of the women in America. Women who daily have to face the struggle of living ... and, as they live, they hope and dream, laugh and cry, love, and are loved by children and a husband.... I feel confident that you will bring out shadings in the character that we never knew existed.

Praised by Wald, Thaxter *did* bring a degree of toughness and resolve to the role, but the woman she portrayed wasn't Hemingway's slutty Marie.

Then, on April 6, Wald wrote to Michael Curtiz, predicting that the finished film would be another *Casablanca*. Not exactly.

The film opens in the tony seafaring community of Newport Beach in Southern California, not the sleazy slum off Florida's coast. Harry Morgan (Garfield) is a combat veteran who now makes a living chartering his boat for fishing parties. It is now 1950, emphatically *not* the Depression, but Harry is still having trouble providing for his family, which includes his wife Lucy (Thaxter) and two (not three) girls (one of whom is Sherry Jackson). Garfield, the father of two girls and one boy, certainly identified. And though the actor didn't fight in the war (his heart problems made him 4-F), it's not as if he didn't want to.

MacDougall's first drafts, however, point up the dark side of Harry Morgan's war service. Surviving studio correspondence between Wald and MacDougall detail scenes where combat veteran Harry talks about his war-related nightmares and expresses his enjoyment of hunting because it gives him a chance to kill. Not wanting to deviate from the film's message of compromising one's principles for money, the scenes were discarded.

Tired of the financial struggle, Lucy insists that Harry give up the boat and move to her old man's farm. A sharpie named Hannigan (Ralph Dumke) hires Harry to take him and his gal Leona (WB contract star Patricia Neal) on a jaunt to Mexico; Hannigan abandons them without paying and a desperate Harry is forced to smuggle Chinese immigrants into the U.S. Neither Hannigan, nor Leona, were in Hemingway's novel; they are an imaginative creation of MacDougall, and apparently were such iconic figures of mystery and deceit (the self-important crook and his gal pal) that the Audie Murphy remake *The Gun Runners* builds up these characters.

The stay in Mexico forces Harry and Leona to get to know each other. It's obvious that MacDougall envisioned the blonde tart as Lucy's more lively and sleazier *doppelganger*; a classy yet naughty blonde alternative constantly tempting Harry away from his nagging, uptight wife. In the novel, Marie has no problem with Harry's dealings with crooks in order to make a buck; more realistically, especially during the Depression, many families realized that morality couldn't be served on a dinner table.

Bringing along Leona and his black pal Wesley (Latino actor Juano Hernandez) on his rendezvous to pick up the Chinese illegals, Harry suspects Mr. Sing (Victor Sen Yung) of a double-cross. Sure enough, instead of greenbacks, Sing tries to pay off Harry in slugs. During Harry's fight with Sing aboard the moving boat, Curtiz blunders badly for such a skilled filmmaker. At one point, Harry is shown fighting with his skipper's cap off, in the next shot it is back on, then it is off again. Also, Sen Yung's stunt man doesn't look a bit like him. Garfield *definitely* has a stunt man; his heart problems wouldn't have allowed for him to do his own stunts. Ultimately, Sing is shot by accident with his own gun and Harry dumps him overboard. In the novel, Harry double-crosses Sing *first* (the crook was going to drown the illegals after taking their money), strangles the Asian thug, and steals his money.

When the Chinese are picked up by the authorities, they squeal as if they were in front of an HUAC subcommittee and Harry's boat is confiscated. Lucy rips Harry a new one for getting involved with crooks, and even slams his war service, ranting on that providing for his family is "the biggest war there is and you'd better realize it!"

After the boat is repossessed by the bank, crooked middleman Duncan (Wallace Ford) gives Harry the funds to take back his boat so that he can use it to ferry four gangsters out of the country after they commit a racetrack robbery. However, Duncan, like the sleazy two-faced lawyer who sets up the Cubans' bank robbery, is double-crossed and shot dead during the holdup. The four killers are subtly named Danny, Macho, Gotch and Concho and they are played by Who's Who of B movie henchmen of the 1950s, Guy Thomajan, John Doucette, Peter Brocco and William Campbell. Rejecting Hemingway's Cuban revolutionaries, Warners returned to the tried-and-true villains they were familiar with since the days of *Little Caesar* and *The Roaring Twenties*: Gun-toting gangsters in snazzy suits and felt hats.

Infuriated by Harry's attraction to Leona, as well as his penchant for dealing with the underworld, Lucy announces she's leaving him. Harry goes on the trip anyway. However, he decides to take a couple friends along named Smith and Wesson.

When Wesley tries to warn Harry about taking the gangsters aboard, they maliciously shoot him dead (just as the Cuban Communists shoot dead the innocent Albert in the novel) and bully Harry into starting the boat. Once out on the open sea, Wesley's body is dumped overboard.

Fed up, infused with that "Now it's personal!" motivation to get back at the villains (the guiding force of movie heroes to this very day), Harry pulls the .38s from their hiding place and opens fire. Here, Curtiz and Garfield give us, without a doubt, one of the finest screen shootouts that was ever shot on American film; certainly the greatest shootout ever filmed on a claustrophobic boat set. Though badly wounded in the arm, Harry blows away the gangsters, including plugging both Gotch and gang leader Danny in the forehead.

When the Coast Guard meets the wounded skipper at the pier, he is put on a stretcher and taken into the ambulance with the now-repentant Lucy at his side. We hear that Harry's arm will have to be amputated, something that happened to the character *midway* through the novel. We also find out that Harry's execution of the gangsters will result in a big reward.

However, Curtiz' final shot is not of our wounded hero, but of Wesley's son. Sadly, the boy looks around in vain for his father, not knowing he's been shot dead and thrown into the sea. Then, as all the white characters give their attention to the wounded hero going into the ambulance, the boy is left alone. Over his lone figure, **THE END** comes up on the screen. It is one of the most heartbreaking endings to any Warner Brothers film.

Though praised by the critics for his performance in *The Breaking Point*, Garfield was about to experience the full meaning of that title within the next two years. Having portrayed little guys who battle against the Fates, the actor was about to meet a gang of bullies more dangerous than any hoodlum or fascist character he had ever faced on-screen.

On April 23, 1951, Garfield appeared before HUAC, with Frank Tavenner primarily doing the grilling. After publicly calling Communism "a tyranny that threatened the world,"[61] the actor apparently decided to keep this same basic approach before the Committee. When asked about his involvements with Communist artists in the film industry, he would either deny any involvement, or fail to remember (when he could not deny) any names the Committee might throw at him; and, whenever he could, wave his own very substantial liberal Democratic past like a flag in Tavenner's face.

Long gone were the days when he would be on a Warners set and, in order to ingratiate himself with the studio's Communist writers, say things like, "When the Revolution comes, we'll all be eating peaches and cream."[62] It was soon obvious to those around him that the politically naive actor probably didn't know what he was saying. Having forgotten the statement soon afterwards, his co-workers never realized that higher-ups at Warners quickly took note of his seemingly pro–Communist remarks.

In fact, the actor was in bed with the Communists more than one would think; his wife Roberta was a hard-line Communist. A bright, aggressive woman, Robbie was the political intellectual in the family. However, for all her smarts, Robbie couldn't stop her husband from having affairs with women who probably didn't equal her in political discourse. Despite his cheating, however, he obviously still loved Robbie and had no intention of turning *her* in to HUAC.

Red Channels, the journal that supposedly "outted" Communists in Hollywood, listed Garfield as being a contributor to various organizations the FBI listed as subversive, such as the American League for Peace (1938); the American Friends of the Chinese People (1938); the Civil Rights Congress in Detroit (1946); the Progressive Citizens of America (1947); and the kicker, the Committee to Abolish the House Committee on Un-American Activities (1947). During the late 1930s, Garfield joined these organizations to insist upon the boycott of Japanese goods, and changing government policy to assist the Chinese then under siege by Japan; the actor's involvement with the Civil Rights Congress also emphasized his concern for equal rights for all Americans. It was obvious that the actor, whose sincere altruism was not tempered by caution, gave no thought to the fact that his contributions might have been helping a conspirational, anti-democratic organization. In fact, the Communist Party was known for making the titles of the organizations they sponsored sound like legitimate charities, causing sincere-minded people to contribute to what they thought was a group genuinely helping the poor or the working class. This pernicious practice continues to this day when Islamofascists give innocent-sounding names to "charity" organizations actually funneling money to terrorist groups.

Besides his other financial contributions, HUAC couldn't help noticing Garfield's participation in a group calling for its immediate disbandment. Already this meant that any attempt at fairness from the Senators was going to be thrown out the window.

During Garfield's testimony, California Congressman Donald L. Jackson, whose jurisdiction encompassed Hollywood, even lowered himself to sophomoric insults. At one point, when Garfield mentioned that the *Daily Worker* panned his performance in Broadway's *Skipper Next to God,* Jackson rather churlishly remarked that the Committee shared its opinion. Apparently these crack investigators weren't aware that Garfield had won the Tony Award for his performance.

Despite Garfield's passionate anti–Communist statements, his evasions when pressed to name names, and his pride in his liberal views, Tavenner, Jackson and company had other ideas. They *knew* that Garfield was not a Communist, yet they still submitted transcripts of his testimony to the FBI (who *also* knew that Garfield was not a Communist) for a security clearance investigation. In fact, his political reputation was so tainted that when Garfield tried to get permission to perform for the troops in Korea in 1950, the Defense Department had actually refused him a security clearance.

As far as HUAC investigators were concerned, it was obvious that their antagonism had little to do with any alleged Communist sympathies Garfield may have had; they just wanted to "get back" at the actor for trying to outsmart them. Another reason for such vindictiveness was pure bigotry. The Committee was first called to Hollywood in 1947 by Mississippi Congressman John Rankin, one of the most anti–Semitic, racist men ever to hold a Congressional seat. This Klansman without a hood routinely baited Jewish Congressmen and, in one insane moment (presumably out of many), claimed that Communists crucified Christ. (Using the old anti–Semitic slur of the Jews' involvement in Christ's death, he was also equating them with being "Communists.") Certainly, white Christians on the left had less problems with the Committee than did Jewish or black artists; liberal actors Henry Fonda and Robert Ryan were never once subpoenaed by HUAC (Ryan had actually *started* the Committee to Abolish the House Committee on Un-American Activities!). But Garfield was a Jew from New York married to another Jew from New York whom the Committee *knew* to be a Communist. One of the Committee's major inquisitors, Richard Nixon, would later be revealed as a vicious anti–Semite when, long after leaving the White House, released tape recordings let us hear him raving against Henry Kissinger and other Jews.

Then, on June 19, less than two months after Garfield's testimony and while the FBI was "investigating" him, *He Ran All the Way* was released by United Artists. Produced by Enterprise's Bob Roberts, the production was directed by Communist John Berry and written by Communists Hugo Butler, Guy Endore and Dalton Trumbo (who was fronted by Endore). Ironically, as the political situation grew even hotter, Butler and Endore would soon find that they needed their own fronts. In fact, because of the "infamous" names involved behind the camera, many prints of the film removed Berry, Endore and Butler from the credits and, amazingly, assistant director Emmett Emerson (who apparently was not a Communist) was elevated to the position of director in the credits. Apolitical James

Wong Howe, the artist who was responsible for *Body and Soul*'s excellent photography and hand-held camera action in the ring scenes, shot the film.

Based on Sam Ross' novel, *He Ran All the Way* is a haunting film to watch, its title being a good epitaph for the final years in the life of its late star. However, Howe couldn't cover Roberts' miserly budget (much of the money came out of *Garfield's* pocket, not Comrade Roberts'). Listlessly directed by Berry, the film's sole distinction is the powerful performance by the driven man carrying the whole show,

Nick Robey is one of the urban jungle's true losers. A career hoodlum, Robey is, if we're to look at Garfield's age at the time, a 38-year-old man still living with his mom (former WB contract player Gladys George). However, this is not a Louis B. Mayer view of a loving mother and her loyal son, as the following dialogue proves:

> MRS. ROBEY: If you were a man, you'd look for a job.
> NICK ROBEY: If you were a man, I'd kick your teeth in.

Nick joins fellow sleaze Al Molin (Norman Lloyd) in the usual payroll heist at the usual factory. Predictably, they are thwarted by the plant's security officer (Republic stuntman Dale Van Sickel). During the subsequent shootout, Robey kills him.

Chased by the Man, Molin is shot, but Robey escapes. Sneaking into a community pool, Nick stashes the dough in his locker and dives in with the masses. During the swim, and to avoid a visiting cop surveying the pool for trouble, he pretends to teach plain-Jane proletariat Peggy Dobbs (Shelley Winters) how to swim. Unfortunately, after the cop disappears, Nick cruelly tells her to get lost. This is the first time we actually see a schizoid tendency in this amoral hood, and Garfield easily revives the old fire and menace he conveyed when he played Goff in *Out of the Fog*. However, the nastiness from Garfield might have been more real than suspected; according to John Berry, the actor hated working with Shelley Winters, whose prima donna ego probably raised the film's budget (and drained Garfield's already meager finances). Though Berry denies that Garfield was ill during the production

(the actor had had a "mild" heart attack two years before), the director still had stuntmen (like Dale Van Sickel) doubling for the actor during the rehearsal of strenuous scenes. Others report that Garfield tired easily and was breathless after doing the swimming scenes.

After delivering the nasty rebuff, Robey tries to charm Peggy again; the girl, obviously full of low self-esteem, ultimately accepts his company. Soon, Robey is invited to the Dobbses' cheap apartment. When police appear in the neighborhood, the paranoid Robey thinks they are after him and, pulling his gun, takes the Dobbs family hostage. Peggy, her father Fred (Wallace Ford, a year after appearing with Garfield in *The Breaking Point*), her mother (Selena Royle) and little brother Tommy (Bobby Hyatt) cannot all leave the house at once; at least one of the

EVERYMAN. John Garfield in *He Ran All the Way* (1951). It turned out to be his last film. With HUAC blacklisting him and his marriage practically over, the actor died of a heart attack in his hometown of New York City, at the age of 39.

family must be home so that the others will comply with Robey's authority and not turn him in. Though Garfield and Winters convincingly give us a sincere, even touching portrait of two losers attracted to each other, the film's whole premise is ridiculous. Like the later (and more bourgeoisie) captives in Joseph Hayes' equally ridiculous *The Desperate Hours*, the hostages' reluctance to squeal to the cops about gun-toting gangsters kidnapping members of their family is highly implausible.

However, to the film's eternal credit, Garfield the actor still comes through. Pressured by the country's reactionaries, blacklisted by the studios, smoking and drinking himself into physical oblivion, the actor still delivers a finely etched performance of a pathetic trapped soul. His Nick Robey is not too bright (kind of like Garfield), but is still very likable. A hoodlum who is not a sadist, he bandages the mom's injured hand when she cuts it on the sewing machine; he restrains himself from beating the much smaller Tommy when the kid defies him; and, in his own awkward grasping for human feelings, he loves Peggy, who is, like himself, a lonely misfit.

But Robey is also a lonely misfit with a gun. He has killed someone; if defied, he will obviously kill again. This is not a good guy. Garfield's portrait of a dysfunctional man with a strong paranoid streak is the film's sole strength. He had grown as an actor; even if he had not died and also survived the blacklist, there were no more Mickey Bordens in this actor's future. He was now too good a performer for such standard Warner Brothers tripe.

Still, Garfield had to deal with the usually vain and hysterical Winters (who, in her second autobiography *Shelley II*, claimed *not* to remember having had sex with him!). The actress wanted the film to end like Sam Ross' novel; when Robey attempts to force himself on Peggy on the living room couch, she stabs him to death. John Berry vetoed this ending because Robey would have looked like a mere rapist and lose the audience's sympathy. He also wanted Robey to force Peggy outside the apartment and downstairs for a more cinematic climax. After endless screaming arguments between Shelley, her agent and Garfield's people (aggravating the actor's heart further, no doubt), Berry finally threatened to have a female extra don a blonde wig and be shot over the shoulder to double for Winters. (Berry claimed he was even willing to do it himself.) Seeing her big, final close-up going up in smoke, Winters finally gave in. At the end, she grabs Robey's dropped gun in the lobby and, when his paranoia hits its zenith, shoots him in the stomach. Out on the street, Robey sees that Peggy actually *did* buy the getaway car he wanted and he dies in the gutter—a final good-bye to an actor whose screen persona spoke for all the nation's losers and social outcasts.

Berry had this to say about the film and the actor who made it possible:

He Ran All the Way was a helluva movie. That's one of the resentments of my life. What did I get out of that picture? Willie [William] Wyler made a similar movie about the middle class called *The Desperate Hours* later on, and it became a big thing. *He Ran All the Way* has been ignored, the actor has been ignored — except by film buffs. I think Garfield is memorable in that movie, so moving, so rich. He was as big a star as Bogart when he did that movie. Nobody knows about him any more. They wiped him out.[63]

Apparently, not everyone forgot about John Garfield. In his *New York Times* review of June 21, Bosley Crowther wrote:

John Garfield's stark performance of the fugitive who desperately contrives to save himself briefly from capture is full of startling glints from start to end. He makes a most hard and troubled creature, unused to the normal flow of life, unable to perceive the moral standards of decent people or the tentative advance of a good girl's love. And in Mr. Garfield's performance,

IV. A Revolution from Above (1946–1951)

vis-à-vis the rest of the cast, is conveyed a small measure of the irony and the pity that was in the book.

But Garfield the actor wasn't through yet. He had returned to Broadway as his Hollywood fortunes started to crumble. On March 12, he starred in a revival of Odets' *Golden Boy* at the ANTA Theater, finally playing the lead role of Bonaparte. Years later, Harold Clurman rather spitefully *still* refused to accept the fact that Garfield was right for the role.[64] Fortunately, Richard Watts, Jr., in his *New York Post* review, had another opinion: "This strikes me as one of the finest performances I've ever seen Mr. Garfield give, and it serves to remind us once more that, provided with the proper sort of role, he is one of the most brilliant and satisfying of American actors."[65]

Take that, Frank Tavenner, Donald Jackson and HUAC.

In fact, the play and Garfield were so successful that its original limited run was extended from four weeks to seven, with the actor electrifying audiences for a total run of 55 performances.

Then, on May 20, 1952, when Tavenner asked Clifford Odets "Did you ever know John Garfield to be a member of the Communist Party?" the playwright answered, "No, sir." Though standing up for Garfield may have been admirable (despite Odets' already having given the Committee several names), it was too late to help his friend: The next day, Julius Garfinkle, alias John Garfield, was dead.

In her desire to pressure Garfield to leave Hollywood and return to the Broadway stage, perhaps Roberta thought that the change of locale would effectively remove her usually errant husband from the pleasant company of some nubile young starlet. As we now know, she was wrong.

Garfield was found dead of a heart attack in the apartment of a young actress in Gramercy Park. Besides the political pressure he was under, he had separated from Robbie and had gone for over 24 hours without sleep. Immersing himself in the theater community's party scene, constantly drinking, smoking, and nervously avoiding square meals or any kind of rest, the anxious actor had just sought a little company on a lonely night. Whether he died "in the saddle" as some lurid accounts claim, no one will ever know for sure.

However, one thing was for sure. A group of arrogant men who were supposed to be our leaders took from us one of the finest American actors Broadway and Hollywood ever produced...

They were starting to drop like flies.

On May 9, Canada Lee preceded his friend to the grave by just twelve days. It's possible that even in the last 24 hours before his own death, Garfield thought of his late black friend, another socially committed artist who fought the good fight. That he would die of the same thing that killed Lee was a further irony. Both men had been hounded by HUAC, and now both would die of fatal heart attacks within two weeks of each other, and both in New York City.

Turned away by every entertainment agency, every film company, and every TV and radio station, the talented Lee was forced to work in grimy theaters on Long Island for mediocre pay which hardly covered his mounting debts. But in 1951, the actor would have his last shot on screen and show audiences that he was not the has-been character he had portrayed so convincingly in *Body and Soul*.

Based on Alan Paton's novel, the screenplay for *Cry the Beloved Country* was officially credited solely to Paton; however, he had some help from an old familiar Party member. It

VICTIMS OF APARTHEID. Sidney Poitier and Canada Lee (with unidentified extras) in church in *Cry, the Beloved Country* (1952). This moving film brought South African apartheid front and center for international audiences. However, in America, the film was actually titled *African Fury*!

was the blacklisted John Howard Lawson's last major screenplay before his pathetic script for the JD movie *The Careless Years* five years later. Produced in England by the Kordas, and directed by Lawson's frequent helmsman Zoltan Korda, *Cry the Beloved Country* continued the Korda brothers' sincere efforts to put the black experience on film before international audiences.

Ludicrously titled *African Fury* for U.S. release, the film deals with a South African minister's search for his son, as well as his sister, in racist Johannesburg (from where we are told no one ever returns!). As Stephen Kumato, Lee is supported by the up-and-coming Sidney Poitier as a sympathetic young priest. A white landowner's son, on whose land Kumato lives, is murdered by Kumato's missing son, now a criminal. Caught by the law, Kumato's son will be executed. Ironically, the tragedy brings the two fathers closer together. The landowner's son had wanted to end the poverty of the nation's blacks; after the young man's death, his father reads his son's articles and realizes how wrong his own ignorance was.

It's not known for sure whether Lawson's usual over-the-top characterizations and penchant for polemics was tempered by Paton's far more restrained approach. However, the literate script seems more like Paton's work than the work of the man who gave us *Counter-Attack* and *Blockade*. In *Cry, the Beloved Country*, it is not black or white that is evil, it is the system of apartheid that crushes one racial group, but in reality is destroying both peoples, as symbolized by the sons being taken away, all too soon, from their fathers.

For Lee, it was his swan song, a last chance to prove to everyone that HUAC and the right-wing community were robbing the world of a talented and powerful actor. Bosley Crowther said in his review of January 24, 1952, "Mr. Lee ... does a profoundly moving job in capturing the dignity, the fervor, and the humility of the old Zulu priest, especially when he is shaken by disillusion and despair."

Ridiculously, to gain permission to film in South Africa, the Kordas had to pretend that Lee and Poitier were not actors, but the director's indentured servants; otherwise, the men could not interact with each other.

As HUAC continued its assault on the Red Menace, *Cry, the Beloved Country* was a bitter reminder to Americans that there were other evils in the world that had nothing to do with those who followed the words of Marx and Lenin...

V

Breaking Eggs (1952–1958)

> One government composed of cynics is often very tolerant and human. But when fanatics are on top, there is no limit to oppression.
> — H.L. Mencken

> It is true that liberty is precious — so precious, it must be rationed.
> — Vladimir Lenin

On February 7, 1952, Twentieth Century–Fox released *Viva Zapata!* On April 10, the film's director, Elia Kazan, testified before the HUAC while the picture debuted at the Cannes Film Festival. In short order, he named those artists whom he had met and been friendly with while working for the Group Theater in the 1930s. He named Morris Carnovsky and his wife Phoebe Brand; he named bit player Tony Kraber (who recruited Kazan into the Party); and while he was at it, he named Paula Miller Strasberg, V.J. Jerome, Art Smith, and even the deceased J. Edward Bromberg, among others.

For Kazan, testifying before HUAC was the toughest thing he had ever done in his life; it was an act which, despite his many achievements, the left would make sure he never lived down. Party member Zero Mostel would contemptuously refer to him as "Loose Lips," of course neglecting to call friendly witness Jerome Robbins the same thing when the director-choreographer helped ensure his comeback in 1963 with *Fiddler on the Roof*.

Testifying before HUAC a couple years after Kazan, Tony Kraber made this famous remark when asked if he knew the director: "Is this the Kazan who signed a contract for $500,000 the day after he gave names to this committee?"[1] One can probably excuse the heated passions of a frustrated bit part actor, but not this time. For if there was an award for Best Liar of the Year, Tony Kraber would have won it. This is because Kazan had *not* signed a contract for $500,000 or any other amount shortly after he named names. In fact, because of the controversy involved in his testimony, the remaining films on Kazan's Fox contract came at a reduced salary. During that time, he and Budd Schulberg would go through hell trying to dig up investors for their *On the Waterfront* script, since the left, still a powerful force in Hollywood despite the blacklist, ensured that all doors were closed to them.

Viva Zapata! showed the director in transition. The film depicted a real-life Mexican revolutionary who resisted the corruption of Stalinism and sought to maintain the integrity of the "movement." Despite the awful miscasting of the lead role (Marlon Brando as a Latino hero) and the reduction in stature of the actor who *should* have played the part

(Anthony Quinn, who still won an Oscar as Zapata's brother), *Viva Zapata!* recalls Warner Brothers' treatment of the Mexican Revolution with *Juarez*. However, unlike the left-leaning scripts of the 1930s that showed the icons of revolution as flawless gods without a ruthless bone in their bodies, Kazan's *Viva Zapata!* (with a screenplay by John Steinbeck) showed us a Revolution gone wrong.

The temptations of power affect Zapata as well as his brother; even when he returns to his ideals, Mexican Stalinists (like Joseph Wiseman's agent provocateur) are waiting in the wings to shoot him down at the end. Kazan is saying that it isn't enough to have a Revolution from Above (Stalin's favorite line to describe his own dictatorship of the U.S.S.R.); it must serve the people's needs, not those of the men in charge.

Meanwhile, as the radical left was on the run, social commentary crept into Hollywood films from unusual directions; for instance, from the works of leftist authors from the past who were still regarded as the greats of American literature. In this manner, liberal directors like William Wyler could attack the country's social ills while cloaking the project within the aura of a classic work of American letters.

The now-dead author of one particular source novel had gone through his own tortured history since the last time he had crossed swords with Hollywood in the early 1930s…

> We have received and read the synopsis of *Sister Carrie* which [Walter] MacEwen of your staff submitted for our consideration from the standpoint of the Production Code. We regret to have to report that the story as set forth in the synopsis seems to be in violation of the Production Code because, generally speaking, it is again the "kept woman" theme, without any compensating moral values whatsoever.[2]

So wrote Joseph Breen in a letter to Jack Warner, dated October 11, 1937. At the time, the studio was already spending money on period piece sets and costuming on their Errol Flynn and Kay Francis vehicles. Never at any time an admirer of great literature (especially if the filming of it raised a production's budget), Warner promptly took a pass at bringing turn-of-the-century Chicago and New York to life on his Burbank sound stages. One of Dreiser's best-remembered novels, *Sister Carrie* certainly had a long, twisted road to travel on its way to being filmed.

In 1922, Lionel Barrymore telegrammed Dreiser and expressed interest in playing "Heirstwend" (sic) on the stage.[3] Perhaps because the actor misspelled the name of the novel's lead male character (*never* a good idea if you're hoping to impress an author whose creation you wish to play), Dreiser was not enthusiastic about responding. In the 1920s, Communist writer-producer Hy Kraft (who would later collaborate on Dreiser's screen treatment of *An American Tragedy* for Paramount) offered to dramatize the novel, and had then-playwright John Howard Lawson turn it into a play, with the projected star to be Paul Muni. In short order, Dreiser rejected both Lawson's script and Muni's casting. Though there might have been artistic reasons for this, Dreiser's attitude towards artists of a certain religious persuasion might have had something to do with the rejection; coincidentally, both Muni and Lawson were Jews.

Dreiser's novels, whenever they endeavored to portray Jewish characters, did so with vicious stereotyping straight out of the Nazi playbook (decades before Nazism was born). In one particularly loathsome portrayal, in *An American Tragedy*, when Hortense tries to bargain with the son of a haberdasher over the price of a coat she is trying to trick Clyde into buying for her, the young Jew makes it clear that a promise of her sexual favors will reduce the coat's price. In Dreiser's 1921 stage play set in a Lower East Side Jewish ghetto, *The Hand of the Potter*, Dreiser gives us an ugly portrait of a greedy Jewish landlord who still demands rent at the time of a family member's death, and depicts the family's eldest son as a rapist and sexual degenerate who assaults and murders young Christian girls. The latter stereotype was the usual excuse Russian Cossacks and Polish citizens committed pogroms on Jews at the time. The scary part of all this was that Dreiser was not a thick-headed example of Eastern European ignorance, he was an author from the American Midwest who was regarded as one of the greatest literary minds in the nation; in other words, a highly literate yet bigoted man capable of influencing a lot of intelligent as well as not-too-bright people.

To their credit, New York's Communist Party wasn't buying it. To them (at least before Stalinism settled in), anti–Semitism was emphatically *not* part of the workers' revolution; according to Marxist doctrine, anti–Semitism was an ugly distraction from the proletariats' fight against their capitalist oppressors. Wanting to ingratiate himself with Party leaders, Dreiser denied the accusations. "I have no hatred for the Jew," he cried, "and nothing to do with Hitler or fascism."[4]

The evidence proved otherwise. In the early 1930s, he accused Carl Laemmle and Universal of plagiarizing his *Jennie Gerhardt* and turning it into Fannie Hurst's *Back Street*, with the author "reasoning" that the mogul's Jewishness was the cause behind the alleged thievery. Breaking with Jewish publisher Horace Liveright (after a well-tossed cup of tea in the publisher's face in a New York hotel restaurant), Dreiser signed with Simon and Schuster in 1935. However, *this* relationship didn't last either. On May 10, 1939, he wrote to leftist author Dayton Stoddart (the author of *Prelude to Night*, which was filmed in 1948 as *Ruthless*) and had this demand: "Get me the names of non–Jewish publishers. I am thinking of changing from Simon and Schuster."[5]

Though speaking out publicly on Hitler's persecution of the Jews, Dreiser then wrote Stoddart on June 22 that the movies "are solidly Jewish.... That America should be led—the mass—by this direction is beyond all believing. In addition they are arrogant, insolent and contemptuous."

In October 1939, he expressed the fantasy that President Roosevelt was "part–Jewish" and lamented that the president's "personal animosity" was "strengthening Britain's attitude and injuring Germany in the eyes of the world. The brass!"[6] However, one does wonder about "the brass" of a man supposedly speaking out for the oppressed *only* if the oppressed are gentiles.

In 1939, Columbia Pictures expressed interest in purchasing the rights to *Sister Carrie*; however, Dreiser ultimately sold the rights to RKO for $40,000. Needless to say, the author refused to acknowledge that his great novel was going to cost a fortune to film, as RKO executive Harry Edington tried to explain in a letter dated February 5, 1940:

> [I]n breaking the story down, I found the way we want to do it ran into a million dollar budget.... I don't want to be foolish and spend the company's money on a picture ... because nobody can afford at this time to make a million dollar picture out of as intimate a story as this....
>
> If we make this story, I am determined to make it with great distinction. And when you analyze the story as to number of sets needed, the extra costumes, keeping it in period, it surprises you the amount of money that is required.[7]

Edington claimed that scenarist Dudley Nichols was also working on the story to see if he could bring it into a "sane budget."

Still, in a letter to his literary agent William C. Lengel, written two days later, Dreiser expressed enthusiasm that Ginger Rogers might be slated for the role of Carrie. Even the declining and alcoholic John Barrymore was discussed for the role of Hurstwood; however, according to the author, "he is out." Edward Arnold's name also came up for the role of Hurstwood (he had played the older man to Frances Farmer's younger woman in *Come and Get It*). Lengel himself had previously mentioned Irene Dunne for Carrie; Dreiser thought she might be too old. The agent was also hopeful that Charles Laughton, then signed with RKO, could play Hurstwood; and if not him, then Walter Connolly. Even the agent's son got into the casting business; "young Bill" suggested Frank Morgan for the role of the tragic restaurateur.

In a letter to Dreiser, dated April 19, 1940, Lengel wrote, "Half the motion picture men in New York who knew the years of plugging I did and especially the breaking down of the Hays Office, sought me out in restaurants to congratulate me on finally putting this over."[8] But Lengel was patting himself on the back a bit prematurely. Ignoring the producers' genuine concern over the story's sky-high budget, Dreiser predictably grew angry over the delay. As usual when his hopes were dashed, the author soon reverted to irrational form. His now-open anti–Semitism, as well as a growing hatred for England (which was then under Nazi attack), were pushing producers further away from the *Sister Carrie* project.

Then Dreiser topped even this controversy by publicly backing the Nazi-Soviet Pact. In 1940, he published a "factual" book on the war called *Is America Worth Saving?* This work could only be seen as the ravings of a lunatic pretending to be a great political thinker. It praised the Nazi-Soviet alliance and condemned certain forces (read that as Jewish and British) hoping to pull America into a long, drawn-out war. The book quickly disappeared from view soon after Pearl Harbor.

Dreiser never lived to see the film version of *Sister Carrie*, eventually made by his old nemesis, Paramount Pictures. One does wonder what the studio had in mind when they filmed this tale of early twentieth century romance in the days of the Cold War, with giant monsters, fears of atomic fallout, Soviet espionage and outer space films paramount (no pun intended) on moviegoers' minds.

Dreiser had finally married the long-suffering Helen Richardson in 1944; just in time as it turned out. The author died a year later, on December 28; this now made Helen the sole owner of the rights to all his novels. When Warner Brothers offered Vivien Leigh the role of Blanche DeBois in Elia Kazan's film version of *A Streetcar Named Desire*, it gave her husband Laurence Olivier the opportunity to accept William Wyler's offer to play George Hurstwood. Having already turned down the role when Wyler first offered it to him, the actor now hoped to keep the fragile Leigh company in Hollywood during filming. As part of his salary, Olivier demanded $1,000 a week in expenses from producer David O. Selznick and Paramount (not including the use of a chauffer-driven limo and a maid). The actor approved Jennifer Jones' casting as Carrie (as if he had a choice; she was now Selznick's wife). As a further incentive to Olivier's accepting the role, Helen Richardson wrote him, calling the actor the greatest dramatic intellect of his time, praising his film versions of *Hamlet* and *Henry V*, and hoping that he and Vivien would enjoy their trip to the United States. Olivier wrote her back, calling her compliments a "sweet presentiment."

Sweet presentiment or not, Dreiser's work was a brutally unsentimental portrait of love gone sour, and of romance suddenly having a dollar value rudely stamped on it in the rapidly industrialized America of the early twentieth century. In a letter to Jack Warner, dated October 11, 1937, Joseph Breen had already outlined his objections to filming the novel:

> The heroine is an immoral woman who first lives with one man without being married to him, later drops him when she meets a wealthier man, and contracts a bigamous marriage with the latter, even though she knows he is a married man. In no time throughout the story does she pay the penalty for her sins, and at the end is about to be a highly successful actress.[9]

However, Breen had some suggestions, all of which we must bear in mind if sense is to be made of the film version eventually released by Paramount nearly fifteen years after the censor wrote his letter. They were, according to Breen, an attempt to make Carrie "morally clean." These changes included:

(1) There should be no suggestion of illicit sex anywhere. The development of the love affair between Carrie and Drouet would be an honest love affair — as will be her later infatuation and marriage to Hurstwood.
(2) It was also suggested that, while the marriage between Carrie and Hurstwood would be a bigamous marriage, it would be entered into and persisted in by Carrie of complete ignorance of the real situation.

So there you have it. As the Production Code office fought tooth and nail to instill "moral values" on the script of *A Streetcar Named Desire*, the censors now used Breen's 1937 suggestions to "clean up" *Carrie*. This would make Dreiser's cutthroat "heroine" into a good girl in a way the frustrated censors would fail to make out of Blanche DuBois. With Carrie now portrayed as a virtuous heroine acceptable to American audiences, it is highly likely that, had Dreiser been alive, the Paramount film would have killed him.

Carrie Meeber (Jones), an innocent girl from the Midwest, wistfully hopes for riches, romance and excitement in some big American city. Leaving her poor working-class family, she heads for Chicago. On the train, she encounters fast-talking but morally vacuous salesman Charles Drouet (Eddie Albert). After getting a job in a factory sewing garments, Carrie injures herself on a machine and is cruelly fired and replaced by another girl. This was Dreiser's brutally honest slam at capitalism, depicting workers as literally cogs in the corporate machinery, easily replaced by another "cog."

Without money to pay the rent, our virtuous and not-too-bright heroine accepts Drouet's offer to live with him (since he's a traveling salesman, most of the time he'll be away; wink, wink). Dining with Drouet at a fancy restaurant, she meets the establishment's classy manager, George Hurstwood (Olivier). Here, the great actor's discipline and research is put to good use; he had reportedly rehearsed *everything* about the character of Hurstwood down to infinitesimal detail. He knew how to move, gesture, walk with aristocratic bearing, and even speak like an upper-crust Chicago native of 1900. He had even told Wyler to "line up" a man who could tutor him in the Chicago dialect of the times.

Though Wyler and Paramount created an opulent early 20th century atmosphere, the script itself makes little sense. Carrie is openly living with Drouet (to the anger of their neighbors), yet Wyler takes pains to show that they were *not* sleeping together; Carrie is even repelled by the salesman's kiss.

Meanwhile, in order to placate the Breen Office, the script by Ruth and Augusta Goetz shows us Hurstwood's boss, Mr. Fitzgerald (Basil Ruysdael), as a prissy old fart who spouts morality, as if he had already read the script and saw that Hurstwood was going to cheat on his grasping old crone of a wife (the faded Miriam Hopkins) with the cute, young Mrs. Selznick.

Though he has a fine home and two wonderful kids, Hurstwood hates his wife, and is very open to the attentions of the frustrated Carrie. Working late at the restaurant's office, he is about to deposit the day's profits into a safe with a special time-lock set to open the following morning. But after clumsily dropping the money, he accidentally shuts the door of the safe. It is a contrived bit of comic business more suited to Stan Laurel than the world's greatest actor.

Now armed with moolah, Hurstwood leaves his wife and family and runs off with Carrie on the midnight train to New York. However, Joseph Breen's dictates about morality haunt the film like a finger-wagging ghost. After marrying Carrie, Hurstwood neglects to inform her that he had never divorced the old battle-ax he left behind in the Windy City. Spending money like drunken sailors, however, does not work in capitalist America. With said battle-ax's private detectives on their trail, the "sinful" couple is kicked out of their swank hotel and the once-proud Hurstwood is forced to be a waiter in greasy spoons where the silverware is rusty and the service even rustier.

Forced to live in a slum, Hurstwood finds himself blacklisted from working in any restaurant (the blacklisting was an obvious comment by Wyler and the screenwriters), since he is still wanted for stealing his old boss' money. Piling it on, Mrs. Hurstwood makes sure that the marriage is not legal.

At this point, the couple find themselves arguing — an obvious Breen punishment for their sinful behavior — though Wyler actually makes them far more sympathetic than the slimy people seeking to destroy them, including the moralistic vultures who are spouting Production Code propaganda. Ultimately, Carrie leaves Hurstwood to audition for an acting job, saying that she's young and will get by, the closest the scenarists come to showing the cutthroat ambition that Dreiser instilled in the original Carrie.

Soon, Hurstwood is a homeless bum living from hand to mouth. In one controversial sequence, he is forced to sleep in a filthy flophouse (a scene from Chapter 16), where the manager kicks him back out into the street after only one night. With the Communists crowing about the poverty in capitalist nations during the Cold War, Paramount cut the scene out of its 1952 release print. (It was also considered "too depressing.") The sequence remained unseen until the studio reinserted it into their 2005 DVD release.

At the end of the film, Carrie,

PORTRAIT OF JENNIE. Jennifer Jones (aka Mrs. Selznick) is in a happy mood in this *Carrie* (1952) publicity still. In reality, her blowing take after take infuriated her leading man, Laurence Olivier.

now a major stage star. is visited outside the stage door by Hurstwood, still homeless and starving. Ignoring his shabbiness, she gladly feeds him and promises to take him back. But it is too late for him, and he tragically realizes it. After Carrie goes off to get more money to give Hurstwood, the broken man starts to leave when he idly switches on and off the dressing room's gas jet. The stark implication couldn't be clearer: Hurstwood will ultimately commit suicide, leaving Carrie to start life fresh.

Breen made it clear to Jack Warner in that 1937 letter that he disliked "the suggestion at the end that Hurstwood will commit suicide."[10] However, in 1950, with their hands full trying to make sure that Stanley Kowalski is punished for raping Blanche DuBois, this time the PCA let the implication pass. Of course, we can also assume that Hurstwood had never seen a gas jet before and, despite his misery, was just curious as to how it worked.

Regardless, the film's ending is a far cry from Dreiser's novel, where the successful and ruthlessly ambitious Carrie is riding a train and looking out the window, not realizing that she is passing the potter's grave containing the body of the man she had long ago thrown over and forgotten, George Hurstwood.

Though there were radical alterations from the book, *Carrie* is still one mean-spirited movie, as if it had channeled the personality of the real Theodore Dreiser. Instead of glorifying the kindness and good fellow spirit of Americans, with the possible exception of Carrie and Hurstwood, the film is populated by cutthroats and leeches. Though Carrie takes her licks, the film *really* lowers the boom on the dignified Hurstwood. He is belted in the face by Droeut, blackmailed by Ray Teal's sleazy detective, verbally abused by his battle-ax wife, mocked by the two-bit managers of greasy spoons (one sarcastically calls him "Rockefeller"), blackballed from employment, and finally reduced to starving in the streets (Sir Larry reportedly *did* starve himself for those final scenes); the project can plainly be called the "Let's Abuse Laurence Olivier" film. Successful and respected in his profession and with a family to be proud of (excepting his stegosaurus wife, that is), Hurstwood is an American success story, at least for the time being.

In reality, however, though it is assumed that Hurstwood is being punished for leaving his wife and family and having an affair with Carrie, according to the upwardly mobile ambitions of Cold War–era America, Hurstwood is *really* being punished for running away from capitalism. The aim of Wyler and his screenwriters is really crystal clear: We may be a rich and free nation, but reject the American dream and you'll never be able to get back on the bicycle again and start over.

Though expressing "delight" at working with his mentor's actress wife, Olivier soured on her soon enough, as we can gather from his crudely worded letter to Vivien Leigh after she departed for New Orleans for location work on *Streetcar*. Mocking the fact that Jones clearly wasn't understanding Wyler's directions, and purposely misspelling his acidly written words, Sir Larry wrote:

> I'm doing the "Caerey downt DOWNT make me live through teoo much PAIN to get ut" sequence with Jennifer really being a cunt. "I guess I downt know"—*I guess* she bloody well fucking doesn't know *anything* about *anything*. No soul, like we always said about them, dumb animals with human brains.[11]

Perhaps he had a right to slam the divine Ms. Jones for a performance that couldn't come close to his own brilliant one, but there would be a kind of poetic retribution to Sir Larry's low-blow critique of his co-star two decades later.

At least Jennifer Jones never made an *Inchon* or *The Boys from Brazil*.

When Twentieth Century–Fox released the Biblical spectacle *The Robe*, there were very few in the audience, if any that is, who realized that this paean to religious piety actually began as a work by a Communist screenwriter.

When liberal director-scenarist Philip Dunne was asked by Darryl F. Zanuck to rewrite the script to *The Robe*, Dunne wondered why no one was credited with having done the previous draft. The story behind it was a good example of the power of the blacklist, and how one scenarist ended up with a screen credit that didn't belong to him alone.

The Robe had been a bestselling novel by Lloyd C. Douglas. At first, Dunne spitefully called the book "simple-minded," then rescinded this critique by admit-

CASH AND CARRIE. Laurence Olivier as George Hurstwood on the bum and Jennifer Jones as a famous star in *Carrie* (1952). Though the Paramount film whitewashed Dreiser's cutthroat heroine, it still puts the dignified Hurstwood through the wringer.

ting, "*The Robe* is an example of the right way to dramatize the story of Jesus; obliquely, through other characters."[12]

Apparently, independent producer Frank Ross had purchased Douglas' novel in 1945 with the intention of having RKO film it. The associate producer on the project was to be Adrian Scott and the scenarist, Albert Maltz. Ross had already produced the Oscar-winning short *The House I Live In*, which used Maltz's screenplay. However, there was already dissention among the collaborators. Scott severely criticized Maltz's 272-page script. The usually sharp-witted producer of *Murder, My Sweet* immediately caught Maltz' mocking treatment of the subject matter; noting that the Communist scenarist was treating Christianity not as a way of life, but as a religion of miracles.[13] Reluctantly, Maltz was forced to write three more drafts of the script, with the final draft dated December 11, 1946, that was shortened by some seventy pages.

After the third draft, Maltz's participation in the project ended, and he would go on to do the excellent *The Naked City* at Universal-International. After the crime drama, his career was sidelined by the blacklist. A year before Cecil B. DeMille made box office gold for Paramount with *Samson and Delilah*, Ross was still having trouble getting financing for his *Robe* script.

Then in 1952, with Biblical pictures now guaranteed big box office, Ross finally obtained financing for Maltz's script from Twentieth Century–Fox. However, Zanuck reportedly told the producer, "The book is great, but I don't like the script at all. You've done it like a cheap piece of melodrama."[14] Here, the mogul was clearly accusing *Ross* of bad scriptwriting and was not aware of Maltz's previous participation in the project. However, Fox had already filmed Maltz's script of *Broken Arrow* in 1950, though the scenarist was fronted by Michael Blankfort and it was obvious even then that Zanuck was unaware of Maltz's involvement.

In his autobiography, Philip Dunne claimed that Zanuck insisted to Ross that "a rewrite by me was a condition of their agreement."[15] However, the scenarist never mentioned that Zanuck (a former screenwriter at Warners) and Ross had, according to Mel Gussow's biography of Zanuck, "wrote in broad outline a new continuity,"[16] or in other words, did their own work on the script.

In a memo to Frank Ross (with copies sent to Dunne and director Henry Koster), dated December 29, 1952, Zanuck wrote:

> Over the weekend, I once again went through the script of *The Robe*....
> It seems that sometimes we write our scripts to be *read*— rather than to be seen or heard....
> Although we have now punctuated the script with three or four good action sequences, this, nevertheless, is a talking picture. It relies mainly on the spoken word. There is no way to change that entirely, but I believe that you boys should once again go through the script page by page, word by word, and eliminate any line or speech that may be even halfway superfluous.[17]

Yet Dunne would refer to the script as "DeMille-ish" and "a typical biblical,"[18] two terms that did *not* fit with Zanuck's claims that the script "relies mainly on the spoken word." Indeed, if Dunne was disparaging the script for being DeMille-ish when he first read it, who then had put in the "three or four action sequences" Zanuck was now mentioning?

During this rewriting phase (whether by Dunne, Ross or Zanuck is uncertain), Dunne then asked Ross the $64,000 question: Who originally wrote the script? According to Dunne, the producer answered that "it was a medley of many scripts he had worked on over the years and that I could assume that he himself was the author." Declaring that he put the script "in English," Dunne also "improved some of the characterization, eliminated some of the religious hokum, interpolated some authentic Roman history, and sharpened the drama."[19]

Dunne would always claim that he didn't want to accept sole credit on the script, and was hoping that Ross would be credited. However, he was dismayed to be told by Ross that, as producer, he refused to accept *any* script credit. And so, supposedly against his will (and against the rules of his own union), Dunne was solely credited — and later praised — for the screenplay of *The Robe*.

Meanwhile, the uncredited author of the first draft of *The Robe* had his own ax to grind. As the script was going through various changes at the whims of Zanuck, Ross and Dunne, their unnamed collaborator was attacking Edward Dmytryk for being a friendly witness. Though Maltz had defended Dmytryk and Scott (meekly) during the *Cornered* controversy, and was the best man at Dmytryk's wedding, the scenarist responded to the director's testimony with something close to apoplexy. Dmytryk had just recently clarified his feelings about the Party to writer Richard English in *The Saturday Evening Post*.[20] Appalled at the Party's support of North Korea, the intrigues of Communist spies like Judith Coplan, Alger Hiss and the Rosenbergs, and the Soviets' possession of atomic weaponry, the director explained that these were his main reasons for leaving the Party. Though acknowledging that not all Communists were spies, the director said that any Communist who acts out of a "love of the Party" above all is doing something treasonable.

Having already had John Howard Lawson and Mike Gold rip him a new one for his controversial article on the Party's dictatorship over its writers, now it was Albert Maltz's turn to go schoolyard. To the editors of *The Saturday Evening Post* of May 28, 1951, Maltz called his former pal a "deliberate faker and liar" whose "present testimony about the Communist Party is false, and therefore he is a perjurer, or else, in 1947, he self-confessedly was

CROSS TO BEAR. The crucifixion scene in *The Robe* (1953). Though it was a Biblical spectacle, few knew that the screenplay was started by a Communist writer. In this scene, Richard Burton looks up at the man nailed to the cross. Could it be at Albert Maltz?

a citizen without principle, honor, or sense of public duty." Topping even this hyperbole, the author of *What Shall We Ask of Writers?* also called Dmytryk a "commodity for hire" for avoiding another prison term and wanting to resume his film career. During this tirade, Maltz neglected to mention the argument he had had with Dmytryk while the two were incarcerated at the federal prison at Mill Point, West Virginia. According to Dmytryk, Maltz claimed (after supposedly meeting with a visiting Party lawyer from New York and getting Moscow's version of events) that "the Americans and the South Koreans had invaded the North," and that "democratic" North Korea was only "striking back."

By 1953, however, the Korean War was winding down. That same year, *The Robe* opened at New York's Roxy Theater, raking in $164,000 in its first week alone.

In 1971, in his American Film Institute oral history put together with Tom Stempel, Dunne added an interesting postscript:

> [Zanuck] started telling me how much money Frank Ross had made and kept on *The Robe*. He'd kept it because he got a capital gain on the whole thing because he'd developed the project and sold it [to Fox]. Zanuck figured on this one picture Frank made and kept as much money as Zanuck had made and kept in ten years.[21]

And Albert Maltz, the man who was at least partially responsible for the success of *The Robe*, had been banished into the wilderness of the blacklisted.

Talk about needing a miracle…

> [W]e assume that you will handle with good taste, all the scenes involving the destruction of the Earth people, as well as the Martians, in such a way that no particular sequences will be excessively gruesome.[22]

In the letter quoted above, dated January 3, 1952, Paramount's Luigi Luraschi is instructed by Joseph Breen on how to make a cinematic conquest of the Earth and the destruction of its people something for the whole family.

In the early 1950s, with the blacklist in its Golden Years, Paramount decided to film H.G. Wells' classic 1898 sci-fi novel *The War of the Worlds*. However, the Surrey, England, of the late 19th century was quickly changed to the Los Angeles of the early 1950s. Needless to say, Congressional committees going after Hollywood's Communists is never once mentioned in the film. However, it's not as if Communism itself, or the fear of it, had nothing to do with the screenplay. Just as Warner Brothers' *Them!* would use the sci-fi premise of giant red ants as a euphemism for Bolshevik tyranny, so too would the Paramount film twist Wells' assault on British imperialism into an attack on 20th century Stalinists.

In Wells' novel, the author has his English narrator-hero make an impassioned plea for tolerance of the world's indigenous peoples, coupling this with an attack on colonialism. In this audacious work, Wells' narrator describes the Martians' machines as they literally goose-step their way through Surrey. In fact, their design is that of spacecraft mounted on movable stilts; this allows them to march all over the planet and fire their death rays at will. Witnessing their atrocities on the world's populace, Wells' narrator sees a dark comparison between England's colonial attitude *vis-à-vis* their "possessions" and the fact that now *they* are the victims of colonial occupiers. As our hero explains after a night hiding in the basement of a collapsed house:

> So soon as the dawn had come, I, who had talked with God, crept out of the house like a rat leaving its hiding place—a creature scarcely larger, an inferior animal, a thing that for any passing whim of our masters might be hunted and killed. Perhaps they all prayed confidently to God. Surely, if we have learned nothing else, this war has taught us pity—pity for those witless souls who have suffered our domination.

However, in just three years, as mentioned earlier, Wells' compassion for "those witless souls" would turn into a directive that "those swarms of blacks, and brown, and dirty-white, and yellow people" who do not fit into a world of the future "will have to go."

Sci-fi author Isaac Asimov had his own take on the real-life global politics of Wells' novel. In his afterword to the 1986 Signet Classic edition, Asimov wrote:

By 1898, when Wells wrote *The War of the Worlds*, European nations were supreme everywhere...

Think, then, how various non–European nations of the world, particularly those in Africa, must have felt as the 1800s drew to an end. It must have seemed to them that, for centuries, their lands had been "watched keenly and closely by intelligences greater than theirs." They must have thought that these foreigners with "intellects vast and cool and unsympathetic, regarded their lands with envious eyes, and slowly and surely drew their plans against them."

Surely to the inhabitants of the Americas, Australia, Africa and Asia, the coming of the European ships must have seemed like an invasion of Martians would seem to us today. The inhabitants had been minding their own business, doing no harm to Europeans, offering no threat, and yet suddenly they were invaded. Their land was taken over and they themselves were treated as though they were utterly without rights.

One does wonder what the Jewish Asimov might have thought of Wells' anti–Semitic writings, but he made a good point nevertheless. Not wanting to think of indigenous peoples as human beings, but instead as some kind of "cause" in which he could attack his country's imperialist policies, Wells turned the British aristocracy into creatures with long tentacles and leathery skin. Consequently, the use of British cannon fire against spears and arrows was translated into heat rays used against people whose cannons were useless.

Though the above euphemisms would not get the pompous author an invite to tea with the Royal Family, England's movers and shakers apparently didn't come to this conclusion, especially concerning Wells' not-too-subtle attack on their policies. The British public and critics saw the book as "rip-roaring adventure" (or something along those lines) and it sold well.

However, it was not as if the great socialist author didn't know where his bread was buttered. After years of speaking out against war, Wells suddenly devoted himself to the British war effort when the nation entered the First World War. He wrote anti–German pieces in the press and voiced his support for an unconditional victory over the Dirty Huns. The country's antiwar movement was outraged. In the forefront of this anger was the pacifist Fabian Society to which the author belonged; as well as one of its most vocal members, socialist playwright George

HOSTILE TAKEOVER. Ann Robinson is justifiably taken aback by the slimy green arm in the film version of H.G. Wells' *The War of the Worlds* (1953). Though she is in a state of hysteria for most of the movie, this is actually one of Ann's quieter moments.

Bernard Shaw. After reading Wells' "my country right or wrong" pronouncements, they promptly treated him like a Martian plague.

By the time producer George Pal filmed Wells' novel during the Cold War, alien treachery suddenly became Soviet aggression. In another middle finger thrust at the now-dead author, Barré Lyndon's screenplay turns Wells' violently anti–Christian sentiments on their ear. In Wells' later books like *In the Days of the Comet* and *Men Like Gods,* clergymen were portrayed as useless impediments to the author's version of a perfect world of the future. In Pal's film, however, the Catholic priest is a man of courage who sacrifices himself in the name of peace. Again, comparing the film's Martians to Soviets, we see a similarity between the extraterrestrials' treatment of humans and the Communists' treatment of perceived enemies. Certainly, when the Man of God approaches the Martian ship holding up a Bible, we are reminded of those "bleeding hearts" of the 1930s who were blinded to the evil of the Stalinist regime. And when the priest is incinerated by the Martians' death ray, we are also reminded that both Christian and Jewish clerics in Soviet-dominated territory were murdered and their churches and synagogues burned to the ground.

In the novel, Wells focuses on our hero's attempts to flee the invader and get to his wife; that is, when he's not trying to find a good hole to hide in. In the Paramount film, set in 1953, running and hiding is not seen as the American Way (as World War II and the Korean War had so recently proven). And though hero Gene Barry and heroine Ann Robinson do actually flee the carnage and attempt to hide in an old farmhouse, an episode taken from the book, a good part of the film is occupied with our military response to the invaders. Unfortunately, despite the fact that the film's military characters do have the appropriate moral strength and resolve to fight back, their weapons are

SOUND-STAGE SCARES. Gene Barry and Ann Robinson in an absurd publicity still from Paramount's *The War of the Worlds* (1953). Producer George Pal created a timeless sci-fi classic, though its subtext had a lot to do with Cold War tensions.

useless against this tentacled Green Menace (even the A-bomb). Indeed, the film becomes a euphemistic fantasy of the possibilities of a Soviet invasion of the United States, not a plea to understand the world's indigenous peoples.

"We can't beat their machines," says Professor Clayton Forrester (Barry), "we have to beat *them*!"

The doc is, of course, on the right track. Just as in the book, it is the world's germs which spell finish to the Martians' plans for world conquest. For as the Martian ships collapse and they die by the score, Sir Cedric Hardwicke's narrator explains, "After all the effort by Man had failed, it was the littlest things that God in His wisdom had put upon the Earth." (Certainly, there are those who would question the wisdom of God's putting onto the Earth biological parasites that had taken the lives of millions of people over the centuries, but hey, it worked in the film.)

At the end, having "prayed for a miracle," the world's people, singing in perfect harmony from a mountaintop, all gather to celebrate the victory of Faith over Martian-sponsored Terror.

The War of the Worlds, regarded today as a sci-fi classic, more than made back its investment on a budget of $2,000,000. In fact, in another diss to Wells, his estate was so happy with the Paramount film that it allowed George Pal to take his pick of any Wells property. Pal didn't hesitate; he chose *The Time Machine*.

Though based on Wells' socialistic tomes, the filmmaker fully realized that Martians and Morlocks added up to only one thing: Big box office.

In a report found in the FBI's file on the Hollywood Anti-Nazi League, an unnamed informant comments in an undated letter (probably written in 1940) about the organization's leader, Communist screenwriter Herbert Biberman:

> A strong personality, evidently in the grip of a fixed revolutionary idea. At the time I contacted him, Russia had already struck, and as Mr. [Martin] Dies had pointed out, there was at the time a shift in the Communist ideology as if it were being manufactured in Germany. Therefore, I could not tell whether his fixed idea was inspired by Communism or Nazism. In any case, he moves in a mental shell against which all pointed questions are blunted. He is now one of the mainsprings of the Hollywood Peace Forum.... This latter is probably a more direct substitute for the more or less defunct League. I have wondered if Biberman might not really be a Nazi working within an anti–Nazi organization.

On November 8, 1940, the Communist play *Zero Hour* debuted; it was produced by the Hollywood Theater Alliance and directed by Biberman. According to a confidential FBI summary, the play made a passionate appeal for freedom of speech, the rights of labor and, surprisingly, "to desist from the fight against Hitlerism." Three days later, Biberman delivered a speech before members of the American Peace Mobilization at Los Angeles' Embassy Auditorium. According to the FBI, after he received a standing ovation, he "was more caustic than usual in his tirades against President Roosevelt, Ambassador Kennedy, and Great Britain. He ranted against war, as usual."

During those months, both Biberman and fellow Communist Samuel Ornitz made speeches against "American imperialists." Certainly, Biberman was a man who passionately lived his life by Marxist catchphrases. The direction this took him in brought him a certain amount of screen immortality—yet it also severely limited him as an artist.

As a former theater director in New York, Biberman had directed the antiwar piece *The Man Who Reclaimed His Head* with Claude Rains (made into a film with a screenplay co-written by Samuel Ornitz). In the early 1930s, he directed the first version of the stage musical *Oklahoma* when it was a non-musical rustic drama called *Green Grow the Lilacs*. His direction emphasized the cowboys of this rural work as "the People," a phrase he would use *ad nauseam* as his involvement in the Party deepened.

Both as a playwright and director, Biberman didn't exactly set the theatrical world on fire. After becoming a B movie scenarist-director for Columbia and RKO, he impressed his bosses even *less*. In the meantime, he had married Oscar-winning actress and Party member Gale Sondergard, with the actress definitely being the more famous and better paid of the two.

He passionately defended the Nazi-Soviet Pact; this opinion would change (or perhaps be changed for him) when the Soviet Union was attacked in 1941. Now with a new crop of war movies in the offing, Biberman belatedly joined the war effort with RKO Bs like *Action in Arabia* and *The Master Race*, both in 1944.

The first film starred George Sanders in the James Bond–like role of a tough journalist out to expose the Nazis' attempts to bring the Arabs of the Mideast into their hegemony. Sanders was, of course, excellent, but the film's politics were ridiculous. Biberman promoted the fantasy that the Arab tribes ("The People," according to the director-scenarist) would rise up and fight the Germans; for instance, as depicted in the film's climax, when the tribes chase the Nazi spies into the desert and cause their Jeep to crash. Despite this rousing scene, however, Biberman totally ignored the fact that the Arabs were rabidly pro–Nazi. At the time, Arab leaders were welcomed in Germany, with several promising their Nazi hosts that they would bring the Final Solution of the Jewish people to the Mideast once the Germans kicked the British out. After the war, Arab governments would openly allow Nazi war criminals to escape justice and reside in their countries free from Allied prosecution, with many former Nazi officers helping to train Arab armies.

The Master Race dealt with a Nazi war criminal creating dissention among the Allied forces rebuilding a war-torn country. If anything, the film had an embarrassingly phony portrait of a Soviet surgeon (played by Carl Esmond), who is seen as a happy, patriotic fellow impatient to get back out to the Russian front and fight Germans. Of course, Biberman doesn't mention that Russian soldiers usually went into battle with NKVD machine-guns at their backs to ensure that there would be no retreat.

After Biberman was blacklisted and sentenced to prison along with Alvah Bessie in 1950, it would be an understatement to say that the two did not get along; the former Spanish Civil War veteran was repelled by the strident personality of his Hollywood Ten "comrade."

In the 1983 interview with Patrick McGilligan and Ken Mate for their book *Tender Comrades: A Back Story of the Hollywood Blacklist*, Bessie describes a less than harmonious relationship with his tempestuous fellow inmate, starting his reminiscence by mentioning the first time he met Biberman in New York in the 1930s. Besides lusting after Gale Sondergard ("She was gorgeous"), Bessie quickly formed his own opinion of her husband: "I didn't like him in those days on sight. He was always a pompous ass, and we used to say in Hollywood, 'Herbert is a pain in the ass, but he is our pain in the ass.'"

Starting with their sentencing in Washington, D.C., and all the way through their road trip to state prison in Texarkana, Texas, Biberman didn't shut up for one moment. According to Bessie, Biberman gave a lecture to the guards about "what our case was all about, what the American Civil War was all about, what the Russian Civil War was all about, what the French Revolution, Russian Revolution and American Revolution were all about." This history lesson was delivered while Bessie was trying to sleep.

After they became inmates, things grew testier between the two men. Soon Biberman was telling Bessie that "the men in this institution hate you," and claimed that the inmates called him a "grouch." (In the interview with McGilligan and Mate, Bessie actually refers to the Mexican inmates as "wetbacks.") However, Bessie claimed that another cellmate, a doctor arrested for peddling heroin, had told him something else:

> He said, "Alvah, the person the men hate is Herbert."
> I said, "Why?"
> He said, "He condescends to them. When we come back from the movies, he holds meetings in the hall of the cellblock, asking, "Well, fellas, how did you like the movie?" And if they don't like it, he explains to them why they should like it or why they are right to like it."

During the interview, though Bessie also refers to Biberman as "a man of great courage and great principle," the very fact that he bothered to bring up Biberman's obnoxious behavior after so many years spoke volumes.

Certainly Edward Dmytryk had his own take on Biberman's "courage" and "principle." After the director served two months in the federal prison at Mill Point, West Virginia, he decided to recant. Dmytryk's attorney, Bartley Crum, drafted a statement for him to sign insisting that he was not a Communist or fellow traveler. On the strength of this admission, he was soon offered a contract with Columbia Pictures. Then one day, Biberman showed up on his front doorstep "all smiles and sunshine"[23] asking for his help.

Biberman wanted Dmytryk to sign a petition asking for parole for the remaining eight members of the Hollywood Ten. Still considering the eight men his friends, Dmytryk agreed to sign on the condition that it would not be made public. Biberman agreed. Two days later, Dmytryk found his name splashed on the front pages of the *Hollywood Reporter* and *Variety* announcing that he had signed a petition for the parole of the remaining members of the Hollywood Ten. Shortly afterwards, a representative from Columbia called Dmytryk and said they were canceling the contract.

Besides being accused of betrayal and pomposity — from his former friends yet — Biberman soon had other fish to fry shortly after his release from Texarkana. In 1950, a strike by the International Union of Mine, Mill and Smelter Workers in New Mexico gave Biberman and two other blacklisted writers a chance to make their own film with their own point of view. Produced by Paul Jarrico (with some financing provided by the union), written by Michael Wilson, and directed by Biberman, the result of their collaboration was *Salt of the Earth*, one of the most highly overrated films ever made *anywhere*.

The Mine, Mill and Smelter Workers Union had unceremoniously been kicked out of the CIO because it was dominated by Communists, a little fact most folks seem to ignore while lavishing praise on the film decades later.

Filmed from January 20 to March 4, 1953, the film wasn't released until over a year later, on March 14, 1954, and even then in just a few American cities. Shot in Silver City and Bayard, New Mexico, *Salt of the Earth* developed a reputation as a stubborn cinematic defiance of the blacklist. Besides the film's quality, or *lack* of as the case may be, there was no denying the harassment that the production company faced while making this film.

These un–American attacks on the production had right-wing vigilantes and politicians working overtime to destroy a film that they clearly feared. The crew was attacked, sets were ruined, union projectionists refused to run the film, labs refused to edit it, and theaters refused to show it (though some eventually did). Certainly, the film's enemies, using Communist-like censorship, went about the whole thing the wrong way. Indeed, had the reactionaries paused to think about it and allowed *Salt of the Earth* to be released, and released widely, they would have realized that the film was going to die a quick death at the box office from its own laughable pretensions, poor performances and haphazard execution.

The film is a tired rendition of left-wing clichés that would be repeated, *ad nauseam*, in Jane Fonda's films of the 1970s and early 1980s. The racist bosses (though we never actually hear them spout any epithets), the callous foreman, the vicious deputies, the noble working people (who are *never* racist, crude or vicious), and the uplifting music which actually mirrors the stirring music in anti–Communist films like *Big Jim McLain* and *I Was a Communist for the FBI*, all point to a kind of cartoon-ish brainwashing in place of logical plot development.

Wilson's screenplay drowns in contrived situations concocted clearly along political lines. When the mostly Mexican workers at the zinc mines go on strike, we are told that scabs (who we never see very much of) are blocked from entering the mines by the strikers. However, when the strikers are arrested, their wives take their place on the picket lines. Tear gas is used on the women, but apparently they are protected by a force field of some kind which makes them impervious to the gas; indeed, they actually respond to the attack by beating up the deputies.

Not that these Keystone Cops don't have it coming to them. The strike leader is beaten up in the sheriff's car (the sheriff is played by Will Geer) as his wife is giving birth. This gives Biberman the opportunity to get fancy and ridiculously cut back and forth between our hero getting pummeled in the stomach and his *fro* screaming her lungs out. Why Biberman and Wilson saw a beating and the act of giving birth as physically related acts remains a mystery.

After the men are restrained from striking by the Taft-Hartley Act, their wives, who bring along their infants so *they* could also be put in the line of fire, take over the picket lines. Soon after the tear gas attack fails (of course, the women fighting back is done to stirring music) and the women are arrested, yet *more* women come out of the hills, as if on cue (one envisions Biberman waving his arms frantically) to take their place. Were these hard-working wives and mothers just spending all day up on a hill waiting for this to happen?

One thing is certain here. With the exception of the beating, the authorities seem to be portrayed as far weaker monsters in this picture than the filmmakers probably intended. During the infamous and laughable tear gas sequence, two women actually hold a deputy and one slugs him unconscious with her shoe—yet the women performing the deed are never targeted for any retribution. Later, the strikers' wives are arrested and spend their jail time loudly chanting union slogans, an act which drives the deputies crazy. *Real* psycho cops wouldn't have stood for it. For instance, no one in the jail is starved or beaten, and no one thinks to shut the women up with a fire hose or buckets of ice water. Company lackeys they may be, but these deputies are about as tough as the Teletubbies.

When the company, which owns the land, seeks to evict the workers from their cabins, the deputies are attacked by rock-throwing kids and the people merely carry their valuables back into their homes. Had the company *really* wanted to get tough, those firetrap cabins would have been burned to the ground. Also, if the company owns all the stores, why are the strikers and their families still eating? To stem the strike, the company would have denied them food and starved them out, but apparently none of the strikers or their families are suffering from hunger pangs.

Again, in the real world, the deputies would have called for backup by their scabs and turned the protest into a bloodbath. Biberman and Wilson never once try to show us the real-life goons who actually attacked the film company; instead, the authorities have to be portrayed as ineffective clowns so that the strikers can emerge triumphant. The Union was at least partially responsible for this unrealistic portrayal, censoring a scene that showed one striker as racist and another one showing a striker cheating on his wife. Apparently only a spotless image of the working man was desired by the Union, which was still Communist. In real-life, the strikers *had* won concessions from a recalcitrant management. However, by turning this actual event into a comic book version of labor strife, with clownish villains to boo and the workers' families hardly batting an eye to their sufferings, one wonders why the company villains couldn't have just as well been taken down by the Three Stooges.

Leftist artists of the 1970s (especially Jane Fonda), would certainly learn from the many mistakes of *Salt of the Earth*. When they eventually made films with elements of corporate villainy and police brutality, they made sure that *their* bad-guys weren't stopped by rock-throwing brats and women impervious to the effects of tear gas...

According to the FBI's COMPIC files, the Bureau took note of an article in the November-December 1954 *Hollywood Review*, put out by the Communist-dominated and pompously titled Southern California Council of Arts, Sciences and Professionals. In the article, the blacklisted John Howard Lawson commented on the recently released *On the Waterfront*:

> What we see on the screen is not a segment of reality; it is a total distortion.... [F]ew Americans would agree that ordinary citizens and especially the working class live and work in a climate of terror and brutality.... *On the Waterfront* should serve as a warning that it is unwise to underestimate the influences of McCarthyism in American film production or to effectively discount the effectiveness of skillfully contrived anti-democratic, anti-labor, anti-human propaganda.

On the Waterfront was anti-*human*? Even for a Communist propagandist, this was taking hysteria into a totally new direction. Kicked out of screenwriting and not able to come up with the employers that the prolific Dalton Trumbo could secretly work for, perhaps Lawson was letting his own bitter circumstances distort the facts. Certainly, his books on film history do not survive the test of time because of the author's insistence on dismissing good films made by non–Communists, yet praising *any* film made by Communists regardless of quality. Needless to say, since *On the Waterfront* was written and directed by two former Communists who named names before HUAC, any hint of fairness on Lawson's part was thrown off the roof like some *On the Waterfront* stool pigeon.

With direction by Elia Kazan and a screenplay by Budd Schulberg, *On the Waterfront* was an Oscar-winning classic which has aged well (unlike Lawson's film critiques). Rarely mentioned, however, is the participation of the man originally slated to write the project, the successful Broadway playwright whose own Communist leanings are still shrouded in mystery.

After the success of *All My Sons*, Arthur Miller claimed that he was walking around Brooklyn (at another point he said he was *bicycling* around) trying to figure out what to do with himself next. During his wanderings, Miller came to the working class neighborhood of Red Hook, which was situated on a patch of land at the western part of the borough which formed a sort of "hook" into the East River. Miller supposedly saw some interesting graffiti written in crude chalk on several sidewalks and brick walls: "*Dove Pete Panto?*" or, translated in English, "Where is Pete Panto?"

Making inquiries, the playwright found that the neighborhood was in the grip of fear, with the usually chatty residents uncharacteristically mum about what happened to the mysterious Mr. Panto. Eventually, Miller discovered (he doesn't say how) that Pietro Panto

PIER PRESSURE. Marlon Brando (with unidentified longshoremen in the background) huddles in the Hoboken cold in Elia Kazan's classic *On the Waterfront* (1954). Few knew that the director's friend, playwright Arthur Miller, was set to work on the project.

was a young, idealistic Italian dockworker fighting mob influence of the fledgling longshoremen's union in the 1930s. Predictably, he didn't live to see the 1940s. Snatched by two or three mob goons hired by Albert Anastasia, Panto was murdered on July 14, 1939, and his body dumped, where so many bodies had been dumped, in New Jersey, and then covered in quicklime. Yet another account of the murder reveals that Panto was personally strangled by notorious hit man Emanuel "Mendy" Weiss, and that he did it as a *favor* to Anastasia. (Weiss usually took his marching orders from Louis "Lepke" Buchalter, the head of Brooklyn's killer-for-hire organization, Murder Incorporated.) After placing Weiss under arrest for murder, Brooklyn Captain of Detectives Frank Bal tauntingly said to him, "Peter Panto is waiting for you."

The perpetrators of Panto's murder were revealed by former Lepke hit man Abe "Kid Twist" Reles (whose specialty was using an ice-pick) when he turned state's evidence. Though guarded by six members of Brooklyn's Finest in a sixth floor room of the Half Moon Hotel on Surf Avenue in Coney Island, Reles had somehow fallen out of an open window. A wire was crudely tied to a radiator to make it look like Reles had planned to escape by climbing down to the street. Apparently, the mob, courtesy of the NYPD, made sure he took a short-cut.

What Miller neglected to explain in his story was why anyone would still be afraid to talk a full eight years after the murder happened. Thanks to Reles, *everyone* knew what happened to Pete Panto, and the previously mentioned graffiti would have been washed off the sidewalks of Red Hook long ago. Instead, it's quite possible that the imaginative playwright took his story about the unfortunate Mr. Panto from two friends he met on the docks of Red Hook, Vincent James Longhi and Mitch Berenson. Both were Communists, and because those things sometimes overlap on the waterfront, both men were also very close to the Mob. In fact, as Miller told the story years later, after Columbia head Harry Cohn insisted that instead of mobsters, that he put *Communists* into his script about waterfront corruption, the playwright allegedly answered that he was well aware of the presence of Communists on the waterfront — *two* of them — and that he knew both men. Evidently, he was referring to Longhi and Berenson.

In fact, during the late 1940s, Miller took a long trip to Europe with Longhi, where the Marxist-mobster introduced him to Communist fans of the playwright, as well as Albert Anastasia himself, the man who allegedly ordered Panto's murder. Remember, Miller was the man who created Chris Keller in *All My Sons*, and had him declare, "You can be better! Once and for all, you can know there's a universe of people outside and you're responsible to it...." However, there is no report that the supposedly moralistic playwright denounced the Cosa Nostra mass murderer to his face or in any other way. Having been the object of a love-fest by European Marxists, as well as the guest of murderous gangsters, the playwright then returned home to write 1949's Pulitzer Prize–winning attack on the evils of capitalism, *Death of a Salesman*. Needless to say, Miller never once mentions these meetings in his self-congratulatory memoirs, *Timebends*.

In 1951, with enthusiastic support from his buddy Elia Kazan, Miller began work on a screenplay titled *The Hook*. Set on the Brooklyn waterfront, the tale concerned the efforts of a 32-year-old longshoreman named Marty Ferrara who quits when his friend is killed in a dockyard accident; to keep his family afloat, he takes a job as a bookie. Though Marty's wife is supportive, his moralistic daughter indicts him for his taking crooked money, as though the Keller family suddenly turned proletarian and was transported to Van Brunt Street. Eventually, Marty returns to the docks and tries to organize the fledgling union since the bosses are cheating the workers of overtime pay. Though fired and blackballed, his struggle to improve the conditions of the working man soon bear fruit and the union is saved.

Around the same time, however, former Communist Budd Schulberg was *also* working on a script called *Crime on the Waterfront* (though Kazan recalled the title as *The Bottom of the River*). Impressed by a series of Pulitzer Prize–winning *New York Sun* articles by a Southerner named Malcolm Johnson (Johnson won the Prize the same year as Arthur Miller), Schulberg acquired the rights to them, as well as the book Johnson later wrote based on the articles.

Unlike Miller, who gleaned from his meetings with gangsters and Communists only as much information as they wanted him to have, Schulberg actually sat in on forty meetings of the state commission investigating waterfront crime. He also got to know the longshoremen, not only in Brooklyn, but in Manhattan and Hoboken, New Jersey (Hoboken later being the setting for the Columbia film). Though Schulberg had also heard of Panto, his script reportedly deals with mostly *Irish* longshoremen and doesn't mention any gangland figure on the same level as Albert Anastasia.

Years later, Schulberg would deny ever seeing the script of *The Hook*, nor, he claimed, would he have wanted to. Certainly, Schulberg's script bears the stamp of brutal violence that Miller's does not; for outside of a couple of brawls, *The Hook* does not contain the mob murders and the palpable fear from the neighborhood residents that are prominent elements of Schulberg's work. Mob melodrama was emphatically *not* Miller's forte. Far more comfortable with distributing his characters' angst in large, whiny doses, Miller's works instead spoke to those who had problems with the system. His people always had their problems, and they hashed them out endlessly before Broadway audiences; but ultimately, it was *society* that was to blame. It caused the always-willing-to-please Willy Loman to fail; it caused two brothers to snipe at each other in *The Price*; it caused New Englanders to squeal on each other in *The Crucible*; and it allowed Joe Keller to murder pilots in *All My Sons*. Though now an ex–Communist, Schulberg's scripts seemed more down to earth, with one gangster's swing of a lead pipe conveying emotions far more distinctly than ten pages of Arthur Miller dialogue.

After Kazan and Miller brought *The Hook* to Harry Cohn, several meetings were held between the director, the playwright and the studio boss. (At a few early meetings, Kazan and Miller supposedly brought along the then-unknown Marilyn Monroe, lover to both of them, who posed as their "stenographer, Miss Bauer.") To one meeting, Cohn invited Hollywood union boss Roy Brewer. Staunchly anti–Communist (and reportedly ignorant of the gangsters in his own union), Brewer was the president of the International Alliance of Theatrical and Stage Employees (IATSE), the Hollywood moguls' officially sanctioned pro-management union. Though Kazan was unfazed by Brewer's arrogant demands, such as his appearing in a prologue to announce that unions were basically honest and gangster-free (chuckle, chuckle), Miller was plainly scared. Brewer then demanded another change: Instead of showing gangsters taking over the waterfront, the villains should be changed to Communists. (It is not known whether Brewer was glaring specifically at Miller or Kazan when he said this.) Years later, both Brewer and Kazan denied that such a demand was made, though the union boss certainly would have had no such problem accepting Marxists as the bad guys.

However, there seemed to be more to the meeting that was left unsaid. Brewer was in close contact with the FBI. It would have been highly unlikely that the union boss-management lackey didn't know of Miller's previous membership in the Communist-dominated American Labor Party; his close association with Communists in Europe and America; his wife Mary's employment at the pro–Communist magazine *Amerasia*; and that the couple had even bought their home from Philip Jaffe, greeting card manufacturer and Soviet spy. (The FBI found over 800 State Department documents in *Amerasia*'s offices, as well as in Jaffe's home.[24]) Somehow, despite Miller's shockingly close association with Party members, the playwright would still have us believe years later that he was *not* a Communist.

Maybe *The Crucible*'s falsely accused John Proctor *was* a witch after all.

Miller would later spread the lie that Harry Cohn turned thumbs down on the project because the playwright refused to have Communists as the waterfront villains (which he maintained were *not* on the docks except for the two men he met). Miller knew this would make him a hero to the left like, for instance, those slavish fans he had met years before in Europe. Instead, however, it was quite possible that the playwright was scared that Brewer and the FBI were going to reveal his past. Despite the fact that Columbia had clearly *not* cancelled the project, Miller fled back to New York the next day. In fact, Kazan was in a meeting deciding the film's budget when Miller called and told him he was withdrawing. Kazan was heartbroken; he had turned down the chance to direct the film version of *The Rose Tattoo* at Paramount so he could work with Miller on *The Hook*.

Instead of being mad, Cohn laughed off the rejection, declaring that Miller was indeed a Communist. The mogul obviously had no problem with Kazan, who was quite open about his Communist past. Still, Cohn sent Miller the famous telegram which read: "It's interesting how the minute we try to make the script pro–American you pull out. Harry Cohn."[25] Cohn would be criticized for allegedly siding with the blacklist, with this telegram as evidence of his collusion with the right. However, the Columbia president might have been closer to the truth about Miller's alleged Communism than some realized.

As mentioned before, a deal may have been struck where Miller refused to publicly criticize Kazan for testifying before HUAC if the director refrained from mentioning his friend's Communist past. It is generally accepted in later studies of the theater that Miller's plays produced during the Blacklist Years were all failures. However, *The Crucible,* which opened on January 22, 1953, played 197 performances; after debuting on September 24, 1955, *A View from the Bridge,* a one-act drama coupled with another one-act, *A Memory of Two Mondays,* played 140 performances.[26] Though not successes on a par with his two late 1940s works *All My Sons* and *Death of a Salesman,* they were not bombs either. In the decades ahead, *The Crucible* and an expanded version of *A View from the Bridge* would be revived with great success. *The Crucible* was Miller's arch comparison between the 16th century Salem witch hunts and HUAC's investigations into Communism. After hearing Miller explain the plot of *The Crucible,* Kazan's sharp-witted wife Molly promptly told him, "Those witches did not exist, Communists do."[27]

It has been mentioned, *ad nauseam,* that *On the Waterfront* was Kazan and Schulberg's justification for informing; with Miller's *The Crucible* and *A View from the Bridge* seen as retaliatory attacks on those who did inform. Indeed, with echoes of *The Hook, A View from the Bridge* is set in Red Hook, features a longshoreman protagonist, his supportive wife and, instead of a righteous daughter, a comely niece with whom he is incestuously in love with (which could also be read as Miller's damning of his loyal ex-wife in favor of the young, sexy Ms. Monroe). After informing the authorities about the presence of an illegal immigrant, he is ostracized by his neighbors and is ultimately killed at the end. One does wonder if this kind of violent retribution is what Miller felt like delivering to his former friend Kazan. Still, the code of the gangster killing a stool pigeon in *On the Waterfront* is now changed to the code of the community punishing a venomously jealous man who informed only to protect his own position (in this case, with his niece who is in love with the immigrant — or, if you will, a fat film contract with plenty of perks). Certainly, these works are clear evidence that Miller was disgusted with Kazan's testimony and used them as a condemnation of those who followed his example.

In reality, however, Kazan might have actually restrained himself from informing on the friend he had known and loved, fully aware that Arthur Miller had worn several masks down through the years in his dealings with others. He was the man whose plays were enhanced by his friend's insightful direction; he was the writer who, decades after the blacklist, continued to reinvent himself as the Man of Integrity who stood up to his supposedly false accusers; and finally, he was the husband who cheated on his wife with a beautiful film star, furthered his own celebrity by marrying her, and then tore her apart in the miserably written *After the Fall.*

In *The Price,* Miller was absolutely right when he said that we all pay a price for who we are. However, he neglected to mention that some people still think they deserve a markdown.

"In the Skouras-Adler regime, everything else [but the picture] came first. A purely political decision destroyed *Three Brave Men.*"[28] This was old Fox hand Philip Dunne writing in his autobiography on the men who replaced Darryl F. Zanuck as the production heads of Twentieth Century–Fox; as well as a barbed comment on the compromises made on the anti-blacklist film, *Three Brave Men*. However, studio files reveal that Dunne rather selectively left out his own involvement in the many compromises the production team made, and that Skouras and Adler weren't the only ones guilty of kowtowing to "purely political decisions."

Abraham Chesanow had been employed as an $1,800-a-year chart distributor in the Navy Department's Hydrographic Office since the late 1930s. During that time, one of the Roosevelt administration's New Deal policies was the building of three government-owned "planned communities." Dr. Rexford Tugwell's Resettlement Administration built a model town seven miles northeast of Washington at a cost of $14 million. Consisting of 900 dwelling units which covered a 200-acre tract in the Maryland countryside, the town was eventually named Greenbelt. Quickly, the new residents set about forming a consumer co-op to run the town's stores, started a health insurance plan, and ultimately established a local government. Abe Chasanow was instrumental in the push to establish the town. Some 57 committees were formed; instead of a central authority in the government who deemed the rules, laws were put into the books and the prices of goods and services were set only after community argument, which sometimes turned volatile.

Chasanow was married and the father of four children. Husband and wife were very involved in their new community (the Chasanow family paid $36.50 a month for a six-room row house). Then, in the late 1940s, when the government debated selling Greenbelt, Chasanow was part of an association of 1400 residents who sought to buy the town. But some 450 residents opposed the move, hoping the government wouldn't sell; the failure to sell the town would result in the continuation of rent subsidies for the residents. Against the wishes of the dissenters, in 1949, Congress authorized the town being put up for sale.

Suddenly, the Greenbelt Veteran Housing Committee, whose legal advisor was Abe

IT AIN'T MCHALE'S NAVY. Virginia Christine and Ernest Borgnine in a publicity still from the anti–Blacklist production *Three Brave Men*. The 1957 film was based on the case of Abraham Chasanow, who worked for the Navy Department for many years until he was fired as a security risk. Reportedly, anti–Semitism had something to do with the Navy's decision.

Chasanow, was being called a group of "Communist Jews" and "longhairs" by opponents of the sale. The debate was an emotional one, and the town's small Jewish community was targeted by the dissenters; at one point, the sign outside the local Jewish Community Center had "Communist" scratched in in place of Community. By the summer of 1952, the U.S. government officially sold Greenbelt, with Chasanow's association giving tenants a year whether to purchase their homes or move.

Then, in July 1953, with the town's sale practically a done deal, something was about to go horribly wrong for the one man who was known throughout the hamlet as a voice for private ownership. The Department of the Navy, for which Chasanow had been loyally working for many years, accused him of being a security risk and suspended him from his government job. It seemed that back in the 1930s Abe Chasanow had contributed to a Communist front organization supposedly helping Spanish war orphans. However, it was highly doubtful the Party would have viewed Chasanow's contribution of 50 cents as making him a major fundraiser. In 1939, seeking to become a government lawyer, Chasanow met with a left-leaning government attorney who suggested that he join the innocent-sounding National Lawyers Guild, later revealed by the FBI to be a Communist front group (Chasanow paid a dollar to join).

Some of Chasanow's neighbors were saying that he "talked like a Communist" and had "left-wing tendencies." When his case was heard by the Navy's security board, some 97 people signed affidavits in his defense, including Navy admirals and the town's cantankerous postman.

Curiously, other "security risks" were found around the same time. In one high-profile example discovered in January 1953, another Greenbelt resident was suspended from his job in the Hydrographic Office (where Chasanow had worked). The man was accused of criticizing the American Legion and advocating Bible-burning. Coincidentally, the accused was also an official at the local Greenbelt synagogue. In fact, as Chasanow's case was pending, disturbing statistics arose: Only 13 people in the Hydrographic Office were from Greenbelt, yet the five men who were suddenly suspended as security risks, coincidentally, all happened to be Jews.

At first exonerated by the Navy, Chasanow found that he still could not get his job back. Assistant Secretary of the Navy James H. Smith Jr. agreed with the Navy's Security Appeal Board, which reversed the lower boards findings of innocence. Chasanow was living a Kafkaesque nightmare. For a full 13 months, he and his large family scraped by while the Navy twiddled its collective thumbs and refused to hear his case. The Navy had no real evidence supporting its findings of disloyalty, and apparently had no intention of bringing this Jew back into government service.

That is, until publicity made the Navy back down, and back down good. Reporter Anthony Lewis, then with the long-defunct *Washington Daily News* (and later to work for the *New York Times*) won the Pulitzer Prize for a series of articles dealing with the Chasanow case. The accused man was already defended by tenacious Washington attorney Joseph Fanelli, who insisted as well that Chasanow go public with his plight. With Lewis' articles calling attention to the problem and his accusers being lambasted for their baseless charges, the Navy suddenly found a reason to reopen Chasanow's case.

Though the Navy apparently hadn't noticed during the first hearing, they now discovered that the "reliable informants" against Chasanow weren't that reliable after all; that the Navy investigators had their own agenda and misrepresented what they had originally been told; and that the attacks on the accused were probably made on the basis, not of his being an enemy of the country, but on religious bigotry (though the Navy, guilty of it themselves, didn't mention it at all, at least publicly).[29]

Belatedly, after destroying 13 months out of a man's life (and that of his family), the Department of the Navy declared Chasanow innocent. After his official exoneration, the Navy offered him a job in another department but, not surprisingly, Chasanow turned them down. He became a lawyer and a real estate broker, and eventually owned homes in Silver Springs, Maryland, and Miami. By the time he died in Atlantic City in June 1989 at the age of 78, he had carved out a full life for himself. His loyal wife had died years before, but he was survived by his only son Howard, who became a Maryland judge; three daughters, all of whom lived in the Maryland-Virginia-Washington, D.C. area; and seven grandchildren.[30]

A lot of accomplishments for a man our government had once considered a "security risk."

Philip Dunne's screenplay changed the participants' names, if not their ethnic heritages. Abraham Chasanow became Bernie Goldsmith; Joseph Fannelli became Joe DiMarco; and, in a slight concession, Abe's wife Helen Chasanow was allowed to keep her first name. In a letter to Buddy Adler, dated July 3, 1956, Fox executive Herbert Swope Jr. suggested some incredible ethnic miscasting: Irish-American James Cagney as Italian-American Joe DiMarco and WASP Henry Fonda as the Jewish Bernie Goldsmith. A possibility for the role of Assistant Secretary of the Navy John W. Rogers (aka *real* Navy Secretary James H. Smith Jr.) was British-accented contract leading man Michael Rennie.

Ultimately, Italian-American Ernest Borgnine was cast as Goldsmith for a ten-week guaranteed payment of $75,000; his *fro* was the beautiful Scandinavian-American actress Virginia Christine, signed as Helen for three and a half weeks for a total payment of $2,400; Welsh actor Ray Milland was cast as the Italian-American attorney Joe DiMarco for a ten-week guarantee of $125,000; and B actor (and one of Joan Crawford's husbands) Phillip Terry was cast as Secretary Rogers for a one-week guarantee of $1,000.[31] Other cast members were Andrew Duggan, Frank Lovejoy (wasted in a small role as a Navy officer), Nina Foch, Warren Berlinger, Joseph Wiseman, Richard Anderson, Edward Andrews and the wonderful Frank Faylen as cantankerous postman Enos Warren.

Despite Dunne's later gripe about Buddy Adler and Spyros Skouras ruining pictures like *Three Brave Men* due to "a purely political decision," the following excerpt from Dunne's August 24 letter to producer Frank McCarthy reveals how much the film's director-scenarist was a full partner in the compromises. Enclosed in his packet with the letter was the new script "that has been revised according to our recent conversations with representatives of the Navy Department."

In his letter, Dunne stated that his two main objectives were:

(1) That the published reports on which our script was based gave a distorted view of security procedures.
(2) That the Chasanow case was far from being a typical case and that under current procedures it could not happen again.
I believe that the radical changes we have made have not weakened the story in any way. Rather, I feel that this is a much stronger and more believable story, now that we have been granted a fuller understanding of the Navy point of view.

Some of Dunne's changes, after friendly meetings with Navy Department representatives, were the addition of a scene where one naval officer makes a speech stating that the botched investigation of Bernie's past was handled by investigators who were "*not* typical of employees of the FBI or ONI" (Office of Naval Intelligence).

Dunne expanded a speech by Rogers on pages 113–14, in order "to assure a favorable reception to our picture by the press.... [I]t shows that the government is in the hands of high-minded men, deeply concerned with the pressing problems of today." On page 125, "we now indicate that faulty security procedures have already been corrected" and that "the security program operates better, faster and more efficiently now than ever." Or in other words, a *new improved* Big Brother!

In early October, Fox executives ran scenes from the film (that were chosen by Dunne and Buddy Adler) for Navy officials, including Assistant Secretary of the Navy Albert Pratt. The assistant secretary apprised Swope of another major concern. In an October 8 letter to Buddy Adler, the producer wrote:

> [T]he Secretary was particularly disturbed by the performance of Phillip Terry as Assistant Secretary of the Navy Rogers. He felt that Terry's performance gave indications that Rogers was a bumbling incompetent, dependent entirely on subordinates for the information which led to his decision. Additionally, he was dismayed by Terry in the last scenes because he thought the portrayal became weak, full of pseudo-merriment and extreme happiness that he was able to reverse the decision....
>
> However, the Secretary felt that Terry did not give [Rogers] a feeling of sincerity. He strongly believed that the press conference sequence should be played with no humor, with great seriousness and, I gathered, a formal attitude of reversal rather than a warm and chuckling one.

Pratt's complaints carried a certain weight to already cowed Fox executives, which apparently included the film's activist writer-director. By the end of the letter, Swope mentions having gone over the specific points of a previous meeting "with Phil today [about] the re-casting of Rogers." Apparently, there were discussions about "making every effort to obtain Dean Jagger."

And so, Albert Pratt, Assistant Secretary of the Navy who busied himself and his vast organization with the way a Hollywood film portrayed his department, suddenly found himself treated as a casting director as well. Phillip Terry, who was to be paid $1,000 by Fox for one week's work, would be unceremoniously replaced by Oscar winner Dean Jagger, who was to be paid *$10,000* for that same one-week time frame. For the first time in its history, a Hollywood studio needlessly raised the budget of one of their productions by $9,000 because a government official didn't like the way an actor played his part.

It's not as if Dunne was asleep when this pressure was being applied. In fact, according to Fox correspondence, the director-scenarist apparently liked having his arm twisted. In the same letter quoted above, Swope uses the phrase "line changes and scene changes which were made by Phil [Dunne], *at the Navy's request*" (italics mine). In an October 8 letter to Dunne, Pratt does not give us the impression that the director was being uncooperative or rebellious at all. In fact, the cheerful Navy official begins with:

> Thank you so much for your many courtesies to us last Friday. It was a most illuminating experience for me to see some of the mechanics at work. You were most kind to ask all of my gang to cocktails for lunch. All of us enjoyed Mrs. Dunne so much and the luncheon at the studio was a rare treat.

In a reply written two days later, Dunne thanked the secretary and expressed his delight that Mrs. Pratt was able to accompany him. "I hope she enjoyed her look through the camera," chirped the former head of the Committee for the First Amendment.

However, in another letter to Assistant Secretary Pratt, dated November 9, Dunne expresses his deep gratitude that

> your people showed us during the delicate and difficult job of adjusting the picture to suit all hands. From my point of view, the most rewarding thing of all was that *I was never asked to say anything in the picture which I myself do not believe* [italics mine].... I think I can say that the picture has integrity.

Our story begins in a suburb outside Washington, D.C. Bernie Goldsmith (Ernest Borgnine), his wife Helen (Virginia Christine), and their four children are at the local I Am an American Day, an ironic beginning for a film about a man unfairly accused by his government. That night a former co-worker visits Bernie complaining that the government fired him because of an indiscretion of the past (a little foreshadowing here). In record time, Bernie is accused of being a security risk and suspended from his job, pending a hearing. Listening in on this, Bernie's rather brainless younger children tell their friends, who of course tell their folks. The angst among the family grows, and for good reason. At a town hall meeting, local upstart Jim Barron (Joseph Wiseman; underplaying for a change) asks about the accusation in front of the crowd. Soon, the whole family is treated as if they had Red Measles. Thinking themselves friendless and alone, they are surprised by the support of Pastor Steven Browning (Andrew Duggan). The pastor mentions that the Goldsmith family's rabbi is sick, so he showed up instead. Of course, Hollywood *never* showed us a realistic portrayal of a rabbi on their best day; and during the Cold War, with Jews automatically suspected of being radicals, Fox wasn't even going to try.

Soon, instead of the Kafkaesque nightmare the Chasanows had faced in real life, the Goldsmiths were going to discover that, indeed, "they have friends." And on cue from the pastor, extras come up out of the town square woodwork and put their hands on Bernie's shoulders, happily pledging support. See? The Red Scare wasn't so bad after all!

Bernie gets hold of a tough, British-sounding Italian-American lawyer named DiMarco (Ray Milland). Here, Dunne hedges his bets; DiMarco hates injustice — but he is also anti–Communist. He wouldn't be caught dead defending the Hollywood Ten — or leading some Committee for the First Amendment either.

Though the townsfolk who support Bernie as a loyal American are numerous (including the mayor, played by Edward Andrews, the villainous politico of *The Phenix City Story*), the defense has to face obstinate naval officer Lt. Mary Jane McCoy (an unusually sinister Nina Foch). However, the cute McCoy hits a brick wall when she faces an even more stubborn adversary: village postman Enos Warren (Frank Faylen). Faylen, one of *the* most underrated comic actors, puts the government pain-in-the-butt in her place with stubborn, ornery logic. The role would foreshadow his wonderful performance as the constantly griping father on TV's *The Affairs of Dobie Gillis*.

The panel votes in favor of Bernie's exoneration. Unfortunately, when he returns to the office, he finds that his security pass is still not honored. Apparently, the navy higher-ups, led by an all-too-cautious John W. Rogers (that $10,000-man himself, Dean Jagger), still have doubts about Bernie's loyalty.

Another investigation is opened, headed by Lt. Bill Horton (Richard Anderson), with astonishingly different results. They now find that the same folks who accused Bernie of Communism, never even met the man. Finally, to their eternal regret, they interview Barron, who raves on about Communists controlling "both political parties — Democrats and Republicans both," and that this all done "through Wall Street." In the original scene as written by Dunne, Barron adds another group he considers an enemy: "Communists — Zionists —

it's all the same conspiracy.... It explains how the Zionists are trying to take over the country for the Communists." In fact, on pages 135–136 of the first script draft, *every* line that has the word "Zionists" in it had been crossed out in red pen. Further down on page 136, Barron continues raving: "The lousy politicians, the one-worlders, the Zionists in Congress and in the administration. They're going to get it right where Mr. Goldsmith got it."

These lines, again, had been crossed out in red; the word "Communist," however, remains in Barron's dialogue. We can gather that the Navy, fearful of being accused of anti–Semitism (as it justifiably was during the Chasanow case), rejected anything even implying that religious bias had anything to do with their investigations, even if the epithets came from a madman like Barron.

After hearing Horton's findings, Rogers reopens the case. At the end, during a serious press conference (insisted upon by Assistant Secretary Pratt), Rogers officially clears Bernie of all charges. And instead of his wife and family, Bernie is corralled into a final photo op with DiMarco (understandable), but also *Rogers*, the man most responsible for his misery. A happy ending for all, except those poor souls unfairly accused and *never* reinstated.

In the end, the film's main theme, how those with immense loyalty to America could still be tarnished by the Communist label, especially during the Cold War, was muted considerably. The film gave our hero considerable sympathy, but it also absolved an overzealous and clearly bigoted government agency from having made some huge blunders — mistakes so serious that, instead of the accused, the agency itself should have been investigated.

And so, with Albert Pratt and his followers as unpaid script doctors, the film came and went rather quickly, having done absolutely nothing for the careers of those involved. One thing *was* certain, however: The three brave men of the title did *not* refer to Buddy Adler, Herbert Swope Jr. or Philip Dunne...

When Jack Warner appeared before HUAC in 1947, one of the six screenwriters he named as having been fired for injecting "Communist propaganda" into the studio's films was Irwin Shaw. Outraged, Shaw replied that he was not "un–American," that he never planned to overthrow the American government, that he had joined the anti-radical Authors League of America, and that he didn't have the courage any more to read bitter attacks on him in the *New Masses*.[32] Years later, when Shaw ran into Warner and Darryl Zanuck walking together on a Paris street, the author refused to shake Warner's hand.

Characteristically ignorant about the harm he'd caused, Warner reportedly said to him, "You ought to thank me for knocking you out of the movie business. Look how successful you've become since then, writing those books."[33]

Though Warner did *not* end up kicking Shaw out of the movie business, the author was able to have the first of "those books" published in 1948 — a war novel that would lead to his fame as one of the country's best young writers. A private during the war, Shaw had put his battlefield experiences to good use as he depicted the lives of three young men who became soldiers: an irresponsible Broadway playboy, a compassionate American Jew, and a skirt-chasing German ski instructor who becomes a fanatical Nazi. That year, *The Young Lions* would be rivaled only by Norman Mailer's *The Naked and the Dead* for the title of greatest novel of World War II. (Needless to say, the two writers hated each other.) On October 24, *The Young Lions* appeared in the number five slot on the *New York Times* bestseller list, with the Mailer book in the number one spot. By November 6, *The Young Lions* rose to number one, with *The Naked and the Dead* just below it. *Times* reviewer Marc Brandel declared that "reading it is a truly emotional experience."[34] William

McFee of the *New York Sun* raved that he was "moved by its art to say just how great it may be."[35]

However, other critics slammed the author for what they believed was a betrayal of working-class causes, particularly Diana Trilling in *The Nation*, who said that the characters "failed to breathe"[36]; and *Time*, which accused Shaw of succumbing to "easy fame and money."[37]

Far from succumbing to easy fame and money, Shaw wrote a sprawling novel which attacked fascist attitudes from both Germans *and* Americans. The indignities that Shaw's Jewish soldier had to withstand in the American army were a reminder of the Nazi doctrines this country was then fighting against. The intellectuals in New York's literary community, many of whom were non–Jews, and perhaps not without some jealousy, ignored Shaw's message and instead maintained that he had abandoned the ideals of the left popularized during the 1930s. However, by 1950, as he was being attacked for failing to fight for the cause, the author was having his work exploited by the extreme left outside of America.

According to an article in the *New York Herald Tribune*, dated April 23, 1950, Communist theater groups were producing two plays in Vienna that "are providing the Communists with grist for their propaganda mill." The plays were *Death of a Salesman* and *The Gentle People*. The *Tribune* reported that the Communists "and the official Soviet Army newspaper" have been using these plays to show audiences an accurate depiction of social conditions in "capitalist America."

Paranoia about one's allegiances was already on the rise. At the time, the Hollywood Ten were going to jail, the Korean War began, and it was revealed that the Rosenbergs and other Communist spies had stolen America's A-bomb secrets. In the midst of all this, anti–Communists grew concerned that the public should be able to identify all alleged or perceived enemies of the country. One of the ways they did this was to publish and distribute the pamphlet called *Red Channels*. This ridiculous document authored by a few ex–FBI agents (with the total approval and backing of J. Edgar Hoover) named several artists as alleged Communists, including, unfortunately, Shaw, the author of *The Gentle People*.

As it was, the FBI reportedly had a burgeoning file on the author that dated from 1936, the year of the production of *Bury the Dead*, and continued into the 1960s. The Bureau would take note of his authorship of the leftist *The Gentle People* as well as several of his popular magazine stories; and they followed his membership in groups with anti-fascist titles that were later revealed to be Communist-front organizations. They even kept track of his movements during the war, including his work in the Army Signal Corps that took him to England, France and North Africa. Working through military channels, the Bureau reportedly blocked his efforts to write for the Army newspaper *Stars and Stripes* (at least as a regular contributor). Ultimately, Hoover himself had referred to Shaw as a "Communist sympathizer,"[38] ignoring the author's impressive war record and proven loyalty to America.

Though known by the powers-that-be as a leftist, Shaw was no Communist (though he did work with them). However, as the FBI continued its file on the author, he made an announcement in a letter to the *New York Times* on August 20, 1950:

> I had to perform an unpleasant duty: I had to inform my agents to refuse permission to any groups or persons here and abroad to present my play, *Bury the Dead*.... It is to balk these double-tongued gentlemen [Communists] with whatever small means are at my disposal, that I have withdrawn my play. I do not wish the forlorn longings and illusions of 1935 to be used as ammunition for the likes of the killers of 1950.

The killers of 1950—and their apologists—were furious. Shaw's letter coming as it did, practically on the heels of *Red Channels* listing him as a Communist, made it look like Shaw was apologizing for his radical past. Predictably, the *Daily Worker* called him a traitor and his friends in New York's literary community voiced the opinion that he should have just ignored the Communists using his plays for anti–American propaganda. However, they continued to believe that he had sold out—especially to that land of gluttony and pap on the West Coast.

Despite Jack Warner's boast, Shaw was not quite through being a Hollywood screenwriter. He was hired by Samuel Goldwyn to write the screenplay for *I Want You*, a drama showing the effects of the Korean War on an American family. Around the same time, Shaw published *The Troubled Air*, which attacked blacklisting in TV. In the following years, the now-bestselling author would do the screenplays for *Act of Love*, *Fire Down Below* and *The Angry Age*, among others. Still, his Hollywood work would keep him far from his New York home for long periods of time, causing friction with his longtime spouse, Marion. Shaw's heavy drinking and skirt-chasing didn't help matters either. Predictably, the author almost succeeded in outdoing his arch-enemy Ernest Hemingway in boorish, infantile behavior. Then, in 1957, Hollywood decided the time was right to ask their new scenarist for the rights to his first great novel.

Actually, it looked like a two-horse race between Twentieth Century–Fox and Warner Brothers as to who would be the ones to purchase *The Young Lions*. However, to Shaw, choosing between them was a foregone conclusion from the beginning. The author had not forgotten Warner's attempt to blacklist him in 1947 and, probably with much glee, got even with the arrogant friendly witness by selling his great novel to Darryl Zanuck.

Edward Dmytryk was hired to direct. Shaw's adaptation stressed the character of the vain and cowardly Broadway big-shot who becomes a soldier, but Dmytryk was far more interested in the character of Noah, the disillusioned and persecuted Jew. Ignoring Shaw's work on the script (which infuriated Shaw), the helmsman turned the work over to veteran scenarist Edward Anhalt. However, out of the film's three young male characters to be emphasized in the screenplay, it would be the fascist role which would capture the most attention; this was due to the casting of the actor to play the part, as well as his controversial approach to the role.

It was budgeted by Zanuck at $2,000,000. Dmytryk insisted that the budget be raised. "Then," claimed Dmytryk, "by accident, I got Marlon Brando."[39] However, the casting wasn't exactly an "accident." Brando had abandoned Zanuck's laughable costume epic *The Egyptian* years before. In order not to be sued by the studio for breach of contract, he had to eat crow and appear in *The Young Lions* for a fraction of his usual salary; for this film he was paid $50,000, less than half of what he made on *On the Waterfront*. After Montgomery Clift was hired for $750,000 to play Noah, the studio again slashed the casting budget by rejecting Tony Randall for the role of Broadway playboy Michael Whitacre and replacing him with Dean Martin, who received just $25,000. The singer-comedian was on the verge of a career decline after his much-publicized split with Jerry Lewis; *The Young Lions* proved he could act, and after *Some Came Running* the following year Dino was on top again. So much for Dmytryk's claims that it was his arm-twisting the studio that got major stars involved in the project.

The film opens in the late 1930s, with kindly ski instructor Christian Diestl (Brando) about to join the German army as war clouds gather over Europe. In the United States, Jewish civilian Noah Ackerman (Clift) meets the gorgeous blonde shiksa Hope Plowman

INGLORIOUS BASTARDS. Marlon Brando (front right seat) and his men (unidentified actors) ride out to do battle with the American army in *The Young Lions* (1958). Both screenwriter Edward Anhalt and director Edward Dmytryk agreed with Brando's controversial interpretation of his role.

(played by gorgeous blonde shiksa Hope Lange) at a party and admits to falling in love with her at first sight. Wanting to marry her, the young man has to be "approved of" by her WASP father (Vaughn Taylor). "He's a Jew, papa," she admits to her father mere seconds before Noah gets off the train to meet him for the first time. Taking a long walk with Noah, old man Plowman shows the young Jew a cemetery with the family's dead gentile war veterans and admits that Noah's Jewishness has made him reach down within himself for the first time. Ultimately, the decent man approves of the marriage. However, war is soon declared and Noah joins the army.

Meanwhile, draft-dodging Broadway playboy Michael Whitacre (Martin) is *forced* to join the army to avoid jail, leaving the embrace of the beautiful Margaret Freemantle (the beautiful Barbara Rush), who had previously met Christian in Germany on the ski slopes.

In the barracks, Noah is targeted by the other men because he's a Jew, and is forced to fight all of them to prove himself. Even First Sergeant Rickett (a pre-gunfighting Lee Van Cleef) tells Noah that "this isn't some crummy tenement in the Bronx." Though severely beaten after fighting three of them (one at a time), Noah finally triumphs over the last man, winning the respect of his tormentors.

Meanwhile, Christian has been playing around with a French gal and with Gretchen Hardenberg (May Britt), the wife of fanatical Nazi officer Captain Hardenberg (Maximilian Schell). A man supposedly unchanged by war, even though he is a Nazi officer, Christian boasts that he thinks of peace "a thousand times a day." Still, while enforcing National

Socialism in the conquered nations of Europe, the rather dense Christian is unbelievably shocked that his fellow countrymen are so brutal. At one point he cries, "You cannot remake the world from the basement of a dirty little police station!"

Still later, Christian is shocked by the revelations of the concentration camps by an escaping commandant (well-played by Jewish actor Kurt Katch). Here, the Great Brando has the scene neatly stolen from him by the talented ex–Warner contract player.

When the Americans (including Noah and Michael) liberate a concentration camp, they are met by people who are now literally skin and bones. Though the studio's makeup and costume departments could not possibly come close to the living

WHEN A NAZI GIVES A LADY A TIPPERILLO... Marlon Brando and May Britt in the 1958 film version of Irwin Shaw's bestseller *The Young Lions*. The actor changed Shaw's murderous Nazi into a nice young man who didn't know about the Holocaust. Needless to say, Shaw was furious.

skeletons that actual survivors had become, it is still a powerful scene. When the town's mayor (future *Hogan's Heroes* actor John Banner) complains when a rabbi wants to hold final religious services for the dying prisoners, Lieutenant Green (an excellent Arthur Franz) threatens to have his men machine-gun any German who would interfere with the service. The comment brings praise from the passionate Noah, who realizes how much better the world would be with more men like Green.

Disillusioned with Nazism, Christian smashes his weapon and goes through the forests alone. Coming upon Michael and Noah, the Nazi officer is shot dead by Whitacre and his body rolls down a hill into a pond. Boasting he could do the stunt himself, Brando predictably dislocated his shoulder rolling down the hill (probably to the crew's applause). At the end of the film, with the war now over, Noah returns to the waiting arms of Hope.

Unfortunately, the attention of the critics and the public focused on the hammiest actor in the film. As a person, Brando literally craved attention, and he had brought much havoc to film sets with his amateurish behavior and arrogant scene-stealing tactics. Indeed, it is truly amazing that some scholars to this day still think of him as one of our greatest actors; this, despite infantile behavior and a lack of professionalism worthy of a juvenile actor in a local junior high school play.

Brando also fancied himself a great humanitarian who concerned himself with the world's social problems. However, just like his "concern" for Native-American causes, much of this behavior was proven to be the actor's own neurotic "victim fix" (a term coined by the Native-Americans he was allegedly helping), as well as the favorable publicity his activism would supposedly receive.

In the case of his performance as Nazi officer Christian Diestl, Brando rejected Shaw's depiction of the character as a likable young man who is turned into an unrepentant monster by the Nazi system. Instead, the actor favored an approach that raised eyebrows in 1958. American audiences of both theater and film had seen German soldier characters disillusioned with the Nazi system, from Clifford Odets' *Till the Day I Die* to Warners' *Hotel Berlin*. However, Brando was giving us the first *lovable* Nazi ever to appear in an American film.

During his death scene, Brando had wanted to fall down the hill and end up on a heap of barbed wire, his arms outstretched. With his tremendous ego, Brando probably thought of himself as Jesus Christ anyway, but the actor was also implying rather crudely that the Nazi was *also* murdered by "those who know not what they do." To his credit, Clift angrily threatened to walk off the picture if Brando was allowed to film the scene.

There is some controversy, not only in Brando's whitewashing of the Nazi character, but also where this interpretation might have originated. According to makeup man Philip Rhodes:

> [Brando] identified with the role because it showed the Germans as trapped in the war and what a prison Germany had been. He thought Shaw and Dmytryk made it too much in black and white, so he changed the script. There was that dichotomy throughout the picture, with Dmytryk directing it one way, Marlon playing the character his way.[40]

Apparently, believing the "good Nazi" characterization brought an innovative spark to the film, the director swooped right in to steal credit for Brando's questionable approach to the role. In his autobiography, Dmytryk claimed:

> In the novel, Christian is a reasonable man, non–Nazi, but sympathetic to many of Hitler's aims. His participation in the war brings about a moral degeneration until in the end, he is a complete Nazi, as black-hearted a villain as was ever conceived. [Edward] Anhalt and I felt that little was to be gained by keeping this characterization. Twelve years after the war, the dyed-in-the-wool Nazi heavy was a cliché, and everybody accepted the proposition that a brutal war furnished brutal opportunities for a brutal man.

Dmytryk, who had done so much to give us the image of the Nazi as a "black-hearted villain" in his own Communist-slanted films, was now accepting a fascist character as, in the movie Christian's own words, "thinking of peace a thousand times a day."

According to Brando pal and dialogue coach Carlo Fiore, the actor had told him before the beginning of the shoot how he wanted to play the role: "I'm changing the Nazi heel into a kind of tragic hero. I'm doing a complete about-face in the interpretation of the character, and it'll be a lot of work."[41]

Life magazine, picking up on Fiore's claims, reported that Brando then gave Dmytryk, Anhalt and producer Al Lichtman a *15-hour* lecture on his approach to the role, including detailed analyses of motivation and character background.[42]

Wherever the idea to portray Christian as some sort of hero (who, unbelievably, didn't know about the camps) originated, the ultimate judge of the portrayal came from its creator—and he was *not* pleased. At an interview helmed by CBS reporter David Schoenbrun while the film was still in progress, Shaw blasted Brando to his face. According to Schoenbrun, at one point:

> Brando said to Irwin, "What are you talking about, you don't know the character."
> And Irwin said, "It's my character, I gave birth to him, I created him!"
> "Nobody creates a character but an actor," Brando snapped back. "I play the role, now he exists. He is my creation."

And Irwin said, "You're a stupid actor, I'm the writer of the story, you stupid goddamn —"
And he raises his fists, they're big fists, you know. Irwin was choleric.[43]

He certainly had a right to be. As an ex-athlete and combat veteran, Shaw would have made sliced ham out of the usually overweight actor. Certainly, one must remember in the context of these arguments that during the war, Brando partied with the Broadway elite, much as *The Young Lions'* Michael Whitacre had, while men like Shaw risked their lives on the battlefield.

In later years, Brando would praise Jews for their contributions to the world of film and theater in his own questionable biography (ridiculously titled *Songs My Father Taught Me*). However, shortly after its publication, the actor criticized Jews for allegedly running Hollywood and keeping social problems out of the movies. Justifiably attacked for his anti–Semitism (especially by Jewish star Kirk Douglas), Brando was forced to retract his statements.

However, the actor's most forceful critic was his close friend Maureen Stapleton. Shortly after the film's release, she vehemently attacked him for whitewashing his role. "How could you play a Nazi like Jesus Christ?" she screamed at him. It is uncertain whether the sensitive actress had already picked up on Brando's then growing anti–Semitism, but she let him have it nevertheless: "Marlon, he's a Nazi; that's already *not* a human being! Maximilian Schell played a Nazi, you played Jesus Christ!"[44]

Having seen the Nazis' work up close, Shaw probably would have praised Stapleton for her sincere defense of his book. For in his heart, the author knew that people like Brando would never accept the truth no matter what you said to them; such as the fact that six million of his people weren't murdered by men who "thought of peace a thousand times a day..."

VI

Containment (1959–2009)

> We were morons, cretins.
> — former Communist sympathizer Yves Montand

"Oceans of tears have been shed all over the world," proclaimed California Communist Party boss William Schneidermann upon hearing the news that Josef Stalin was dead.[1] When the many deeds of the Soviet dictator were recounted, it was quite possible that there were oceans of a certain liquid involved, though that fluid might have been much redder than tears.

Stalin suffocated to death on his office couch on the morning of March 5, 1953. But official government propaganda claimed that the "Great Leader and Teacher" died of a cerebral hemorrhage. However, to this day, the specter of "medical murder" hangs over the dictator's death. Stalin was on the verge of ordering the arrests of his former number two, ex–foreign minister Vyachaslav Molotov, and NKVD (later KGB) commissar Lavrenti Beria, but by an amazing coincidence he became ill on the night of March 3. Such was the fear that this man instilled in his underlings that they were too frightened to enter his room and check to see if anything was wrong when he didn't answer repeated knocks at the door. Or maybe the conspirators purposely waited outside the room, hoping for the poison to work fast. One of those men waiting outside who allowed Stalin to choke to death on his own bile would be the next supreme leader of the U.S.S.R., Nikita Khruschev.

Back in Hollywood, anti–Communism was still popular. With the announcement of Stalin's death, the end of the Korean War, and (in another year) the ruination of Senator Joseph McCarthy, a gradual shift started; certainly not soon enough for the blacklisted artists, but a change was in the wind nevertheless. For the loyal sycophants of the Hollywood Party, however, reinstatement would be long in coming; for some, never.

John Howard Lawson's only full screenplay to be filmed for the remainder of his career, after 1951's *Cry the Beloved Country* (fully credited to Alan Paton), was a truly pathetic JD–youth problem B movie titled *The Careless Years*. It starred former child star Dean Stockwell, the tortured little boy in the antiwar drama *The Boy with Green Hair*. Dogmatic as usual, his screenplay for the Joseph E. Lewis B western *Terror in a Texas Town* had to be revised by, of all people, the blacklisted Dalton Trumbo (using the *nom de screen* Ben Parry). While still receiving payment from Kirk Douglas' Bryna Productions for work on screenplays and TV pilots, none of which were filmed, Lawson's rather creative use of pseudonyms and receiving paychecks under different names smacked of a blacklisted writer's version of a shell game.

After Lawson claimed that Bryna owed him $2,500, the company's bookkeeper, Jefferson W. Asher Jr., heatedly wrote to company executives on May 27, 1959: "We do not intend to pay James Christopher the balance of $2,500.00 under the March 15, 1959, contract until we have an explanation of the $2,500.00 paid to James Howard, who is the same person, by check number 3023 on February 3, 1959."[2]

To Lawson, the ends *always* justified the means. After Paul Jarrico and Michael Wilson wrested control of the Party from Lawson during the Blacklist Years, Jarrico spoke of the former Party enforcer. Having already referred to Lawson as "an infantile leftist," the author of *The Poseidon Adventure* commented:

> I'm sure that if Jack were told by the Soviets to criticize them, without a beat he'd have said, "Well, you know, the way the Soviets treat dissidents is really criminal." Now Lester Cole was not an intellectual and was not equipped to deal with complicated problems. But in Lawson's case, his dogmatism defeated him as an intellectual, as a person, and as an artist.[3]

Echoing this theory, former Group Theater producer Harold Clurman would remark that Lawson's involvement in the Party ruined his talent as a creative artist.

But as the years passed, none of this insight would register with the Hollywood Party's main flag-waver. In the 1970s, not long before his death from Parkinson's disease, Lawson proudly boasted to adoring leftist author Victor S. Navasky, "[I've] given a good part of my life to the struggle against thought control."[4]

That is, as long as it was implemented by someone else...

In the case of Dalton Trumbo, the scenarist would be the most famous and most admired of the Hollywood Ten because he was the one who "broke the blacklist." In reality, *Kirk Douglas* broke the blacklist, since Trumbo could hardly employ himself. To this day, however, many documentaries and plays, with a slanted approach that would have been quite at home in the Soviet cinema under Josef Stalin, portrayed the Communist screenwriter as an iconoclast and rebel; a maverick in the noble American tradition of civil dissent. Never once in these documentaries or worshipping vanity productions was Communism ever mentioned, much less anyone discussing what it meant, or whom it victimized; or that Dalton Trumbo was part of this totalitarian movement. Though Trumbo was a Communist allegedly fighting for the underdog, not one person in any of these projects mentioned his persistent love of money and pursuit of an opulent lifestyle. Certainly there were not too many struggling proletarians who typed movie scripts from their bathtub while smoking expensive cigars and consuming mug after mug of black coffee. He would win an Oscar in 1956 for a clichéd boy and his dog story (though archly turned into a boy-and-his-*bull* story) called *The Brave One*. Or rather some poor schlub named "Robert Rich" won. In fact, it didn't matter whose name he had won under. He certainly didn't win for originality; Bernard Dick unearthed information in RKO studio files that the company had a boy-and-bull story set in Mexico that they were going to film in 1941, but abandoned.[5] Did Trumbo, then signed with RKO, ever see the studio's treatment before working on his supposedly original Oscar-winning script? Anything's possible...

Nevertheless, despite the blacklist, Trumbo continued slamming the pursuit of money in his screenplays. The best of these is the wonderful *Cowboy* starring Glenn Ford. The conservative actor had one of his best roles and Jack Lemmon turned in a good serious performance (years before he stereotyped himself as a comic actor). In this film, the upright image of the cowboy is turned on its head, with the rush to get the cows to market seen as the main cause of their cutthroat behavior. Here, the Marxist screenwriter skillfully portrays a cowboy's life, not as one built on movie clichés of honor, idealism and good fellowship, but a brutally realistic view of life on the range as one of grime, sweat and dog-eat-dog competitiveness. Reflecting this attack on capitalist excess, Trumbo's *Terror in a Texas Town* screenplay gives us a hired gunman who has a greater sense of honor than his capitalist boss (a hissable Sebastian Cabot). Towards the end, after the gunman shoots his boss dead, the rich bad-guy drops to the floor with money falling on top of him as a comment on the evil of the green stuff (while the Communist screenwriter who wrote this scene always demanded a high salary for his screenplays).

Though Otto Preminger released *Exodus* (with a screenplay by Trumbo) before *Spartacus*, producer Kirk Douglas had hired Trumbo in 1958, fully intending to use Trumbo's name in the credits. However, after Douglas fired Anthony Mann, he hired Stanley Kubrick as director, a choice that eventually infuriated the pampered screenwriter.

Trumbo was incensed that the helmsman threw out much of his dialogue; long speeches were instead replaced by stunning visuals which kept up the film's pace. Used to a studio system which respected his work (as well as the fact that he didn't like a more talented artist stealing the limelight), Trumbo was clearly out of step with a new Hollywood which rejected long-winded dialogue scenes and instead paid homage to a talented auteur who impressed audiences with his style and visual flair.

Unfortunately, Trumbo's collaboration with Stanley Kubrick would reveal something far uglier than prima donna behavior. In an angry letter criticizing his director, the author of *Johnny Got His Gun* actually questioned the Jewish director's marriage to a German woman: "Did he marry her because he loved her or did he marry her because he wanted to marry a German girl in order to punish the Germans through her for what they had done to the Jews?"[6] Also problematic was the fact that Trumbo, seeing the Roman slaves as toga-clad revolutionaries, totally ignored history. Despite his claims of accurate research into the Rome of 73 B.C., he clearly whitewashed the film's principal heroes. In reality, the slave revolt failed due to the greed and hedonism of the slaves themselves. Filthy, amoral, and thoroughly degenerate, the Roman slaves of history were not the charming, passionate and sincere underdogs Trumbo envisioned, all with perfectly coiffed crew-cuts and immaculately tailored rags.

Nevertheless, Trumbo's name was back on the screen, and the industry's leftists who would glorify him years later would never mention his enmity of

CHAMPION. The great Kirk Douglas in a publicity shot for one of his best films, *Spartacus* (1960). It was he who broke the blacklist by hiring Dalton Trumbo to write the screenplay, and then billed him under his own name in the credits. However, Trumbo would clash with auteur Stanley Kubrick; the relationship brought out the worst in the screenwriter.

Stanley Kubrick, with its undercurrent of anti–Semitism and obvious professional jealousy.

Still under contract to Douglas, Trumbo scripted *The Last Sunset*. Having absolutely nothing to do with Vechel Howard's 1957 western novel, *Sundown at Crazy Horse*, Trumbo turned it into a rather perverted story of an emotionally immature cowpoke who, rejected by his ex-love, tries to romance her daughter, not realizing until the climax that the girl is actually *his* daughter as well. Though based on an earlier treatment of the book at United Artists by a writer named Eugene Frenke, the Universal western did not instill a sense of gratitude for his employment by the acerbic scenarist.

Boasting in a 1962 letter to Albert Maltz that his name on a screenplay was "a guarantee of financial success," Trumbo added, "Even that abomination, *The Last Sunset*, will not lose money, as it deserves to."[7] Apparently, the vain screenwriter forgot that Kirk Douglas and Rock Hudson were also involved in the film; though they didn't write the screenplay, they were merely *starring* in it.

However, times changed fast for the aging scenarist. His screenplays for *The Hawaiians*, *The Sandpiper* and *The Horsemen* were pathetic and overblown — the work of a writer whose characters give long speeches slamming authority figures while their audiences struggled to stay awake. (Witness Richard Burton's final monologue in *The Sandpiper*, a good substitute for Ambien.) Even his directorial debut in the film version of his own book, *Johnny Got His Gun*, inspired boredom rather than debate. "The most shattering experience of your life!"

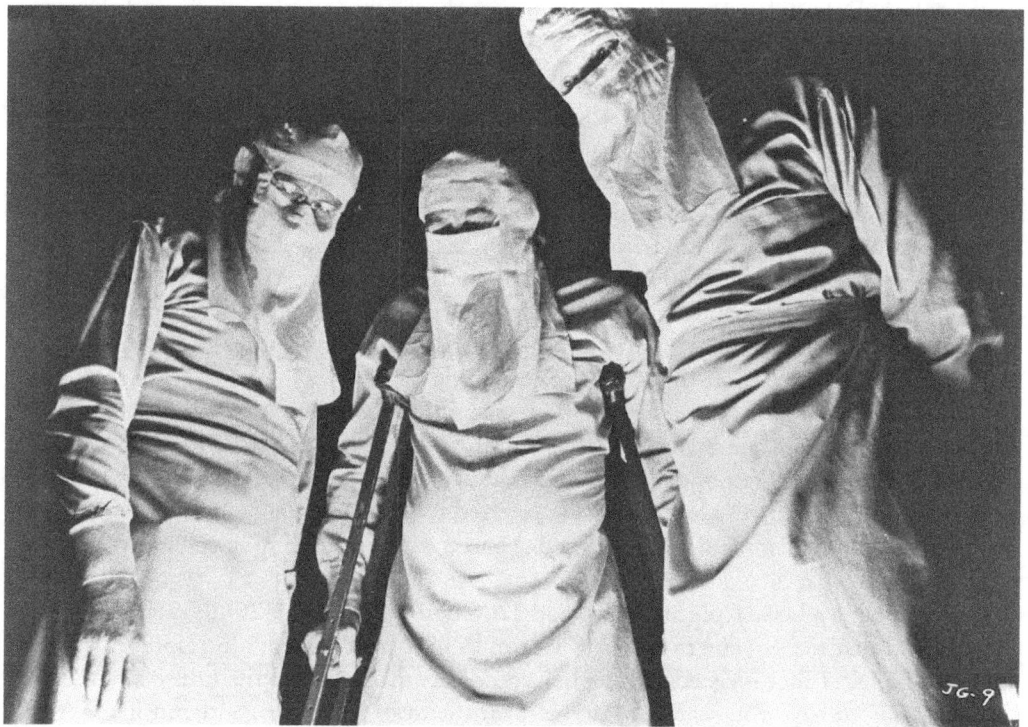

CALLING DR. HOWARD, DR. FINE, DR. HOWARD... Three masked surgeons (unidentified actors) looking down at the young man whose arms and legs they just removed in the screen version of Dalton Trumbo's novel *Johnny Got His Gun* (1971). Directing as well as doing the screenplay, Trumbo retained the pretentiousness of the book.

screamed the unsubtle tagline. Not quite. In his *New York Times* review of August 5, 1971, Roger Greenspun wrote:

> It should be obvious that *Johnny Got His Gun* is shrouded in virtue. But insistent virtue, without ideas, becomes demagoguery.... [It's] a mess of clichéd, imprecise sentimentalizing and fantasizing. On any terms that I might recognize and possibly credit, *Johnny Got His Gun* is a stultifying bad movie.

Hoping to mine youth anger against the Vietnam War, as *MASH* had, Trumbo was so in love with his own words that he failed to actually acknowledge that the youth of 1971 weren't interested in a story that was modeled on the life of Dalton Trumbo, or his sledgehammer-subtle way of presenting it. Who cared if Joe Bonham had worked in a bakery or lost his father's fishing pole in a lake when Hawkeye and Trapper John could rip away a shower curtain and reveal a naked Hot Lips?

Trumbo died in the middle of writing a new novel, *Night of the Aurichs*, a work which turns the suffering of concentration camp victims into something decidedly amoral and perverse. *Sophie's Choice* it wasn't. The truth of the matter was, with no Production Code to restrain him, Trumbo's work, always formulaic to begin with, started to descend into the world of the sleazy and degenerate.

Bernard Dick noted in his *Radical Innocence: A Critical Study of the Hollywood Ten*, "Because of his early conversion to the Left, Trumbo never associated Communism with a lack of freedom." Certainly this sentence alone, more than any tribute to him after his death, defines Dalton Trumbo, the man who supposedly cherished freedom, and the writer who kowtowed to the Party's version of it.

Lester Cole's credits were indeed few and far between after his blacklist; when he did get work, it was never under his own name. His most famous post-blacklist work was *Born Free*, an ironic title coming from a man who was still afraid to let his name appear on the screen. Few would know of his work on a TV special using Edvard Grieg's music, which starred Van Johnson and Claude Rains, *The Pied Piper of Hamelin*. Far better was his screenplay for *Operation Eichmann*, in which the non-religious Jewish screenwriter would detail the hunt for Adolf Eichmann by Israeli agents. Starring Werner Klemperer in a great performance as Eichmann, this B was released in 1962, just months after the actual Mossad kidnapping of Eichmann off the streets of Argentina.

But Cole the Stalinist never changed. In the mid–1970s, when Albert Maltz announced that he was going to donate any Soviet royalties to Alexander Solzhenitzyn and to Soviet Jewish dissidents, Cole responded in a letter that was characteristic of the man who couldn't stay at one studio for a very long time. He referred to Solzhenitsym as "that towering symbol of Czarist humanism and freedom" and accused Maltz of "aiding in the growth of neo-fascism."[8]

Not missing a beat, Cole also slammed Trumbo for his famous "Only Victims" speech and charged that the screenwriter was a "victim of his own rhetoric." In response, Trumbo wrote him a letter that insisted, "I'd rather you didn't drop around the house any more.... I'm not going to have you scare my kids to death with one of your goddamn fits."[9]

With the exception of Trumbo and Lawson, who died in the late 1970s, most of the Communist screenwriters would, to their eternal regret, live to see their arch-enemy Ronald Reagan elected president of the United States. In fact, they also lived to see this president, unapologetic in his anti–Communism, preside over the fall of the Communist Party in Eastern Europe and the breakup of the Soviet Union — an event which literally freed millions of oppressed people, the *true* masses who had suffered so long from the Dictatorship of the Proletariat.

However, in 1977, with the blacklisted now seen as heroes, it was now Lillian Hellman's turn for sainthood. Twentieth Century–Fox bought the rights to one of the stories in her memoirs, *Pentimento*. Very quickly, the studio fashioned a screenplay which made Hellman the heroine who smuggled funds to help an anti-fascist activist in occupied Europe. Titled *Julia*, the film won an Oscar for the usually hysterical Vanessa Redgrave, but the casting of the role of our playwright heroine surprised many. Instead of an actress who resembled the short, homely Hellman, Fox cast the beautiful Jane Fonda. Already infamous for her traitorous support of the Viet Cong, Hanoi Jane loved the chance to play Hellman as a brave heroine who fought injustice.

Hellman claimed that she had never seen the script that glorified her (she assumed the producers would use another name for her character); this was denied by screenwriter Alan Sergeant and Fonda herself, both of whom said that Hellman *definitely* perused the script to see how it portrayed her.

However, there were strong doubts that Hellman had ever actually met the anti-fascist heroine depicted in her memoirs. In fact, as it turned out, there was no Julia, no dangerous meetings with anti-fascists, no close gal-pal who fought for "the people," no anything. Nor had Hellman, who spent the war schmoozing with Stalinists in Moscow and writing her various projects for Hollywood and Broadway, been involved in any mission, dangerous or otherwise, against the Nazis. Even the usually antagonistic Ernest Hemingway used his

fishing boat to apprise U.S. Intelligence of any Nazi activity off the Florida coast. Hellman's FBI files never once mention her doing any intelligence work of any kind for our government, whether in the U.S. *or* in Nazi-occupied Europe.

Julia received accolades and awards, and Hellman got a standing ovation at the 1978 Academy Awards, less for her scripts than for her supposedly courageous stand against HUAC during the McCarthy era. In reality, if one is to judge from the transcripts of the hearing, her testimony before the investigators was fawning and apologetic, without a hint of defiance.

Hellman's reputation was soon going to change. Six years after *Julia*'s release, a World War II memoir appeared, written by a former member of the anti-fascist under-

HELLMAN'S MAYONNAISE. Hanoi Jane Fonda looks poised and regal as the short and homely Lillian Hellman in *Julia* (1977), supposedly based on the playwright's memoirs about the help she gave to an anti-fascist friend during the war. It turned out that she used the life of real-life heroine Muriel Gardiner Buttinger as a model for her Julia.

ground named Muriel Gardiner Buttinger. She had smuggled money to the resistance, tried to free prisoners of the Germans, and risked her life many times to keep up the fight against fascist tyranny. Like the movie Julia, she had been a daughter of privilege disowned by her wealthy pro-fascist parents. And again, like the movie Julia, Muriel had been a former medical student in Vienna. Indeed, the similarities between Muriel and Julia were too numerous to discount as mere coincidence.

Hellman was right on this score: Apparently, there *was* a heroine who did all the things the playwright said she did — and more. However, it was soon revealed that Ms. Buttinger had never even met Hellman. Indeed, as the book became a bestseller, word quickly spread in the mass media that perhaps the playwright's tale of courage and sacrifice that she experienced at the side of a brave anti-fascist heroine was actually a load of lies.

Muriel herself punctured the myth that Hellman smuggled thousands of dollars into Germany and Austria in 1937; she claimed, and several witnesses verified this, that getting currency into both nations was not a problem, as Muriel herself continued to give money to her friends through the Chase Bank all the way up to the declarations of war in 1939.[10] If this was indeed the case, this totally undercuts Hellman's claims of a dangerous mission, since it negated any reason to *smuggle* money into Germany at all

According to New York attorney Christopher Schwabacher, his father, prominent Viennese attorney Wolf Schwabacher, had known Muriel back in 1939. In fact, roving bachelor that he was, Wolf had at even shared a house with the anti–Nazi heroine.[11] Also during those years, the elder Schwabacher had done some legal work for upcoming playwright Hellman, like trying to get the Boston city elders to lift a ban on a production of *The Children's Hour*.

Meanwhile, the attorney had worked long and hard to expedite Muriel's marriage in Paris to anti-fascist Joe Buttinger so that he could come to America. Though Hellman had never met Muriel, it was soon obvious that her existence became known to the playwright when the Vienna-based Schwabacher, fully aware of Muriel's wartime mission, proudly spoke of his fellow Austrian's bravery to a select group of friends. One of these friends obviously included his client, a homely little female playwright who seethed jealously over the exploits of this brave woman — the kind of heroine she knew she could never be.[12] However, her solution was simple: Better than actually risking your life, act as if you had been rubbing elbows with those brave souls that did. In fact, the Buttingers might have also been the "inspiration" for the husband and wife anti-fascists of *Watch on the Rhine*.

The cat was out of the bag now. Not only were *Pentimento* and *Scoundrel Time*, her fabricated rewrite of the blacklist years, seen as highly inaccurate, but she would soon be attacked by another McCarthy — this time, a talented writer named Mary.

Needless to say, in the years to come, Hellman would inspire few documentaries praising her courage and self-sacrifice.

Like Trumbo, Albert Maltz also took up residence in Mexico City after his prison stay in West Virginia. Unlike Trumbo, however, Maltz did not have the connections that would hire him to work on scripts. Since the debacle on *The Robe*, Maltz scrambled for work that was clearly not there. He continued writing stories and novels, though he was forced to use pseudonyms. In fact, he was shocked that the blacklist actually extended to the publishing industry (or at least it seemed to in his case).

Then in 1960, an offer came from an unexpected direction. In the wake of Trumbo's rehabilitation, Frank Sinatra gave Maltz an offer he couldn't refuse, the chance to write a screenplay about the only American soldier in both World Wars ever executed by the Army.

The project was to be called *The Execution of Private Slovik*. Maltz had not worked with Sinatra since their Oscar-winning short *The House I Live In*, but he was well aware of the singer's then-liberal politics.

However, things were quite different in 1960. Sinatra and his Rat Pack were strenuously campaigning for Massachusetts Senator John F. Kennedy to be elected president. Actually, there was *one* member of the Pack who didn't jump on the Kennedy bandwagon: Dean Martin. The singer-comedian had no illusions about the Kennedys, and quickly saw through their callous exploitation of those they could use, including the unusually naive Sinatra.

Kennedy's people insisted that Sinatra not announce Maltz's participation in the *Slovik* project until after the New Hampshire primary — a request that Maltz wasn't happy with. Like other members of the Party, Maltz was never concerned with the cost of bad publicity on someone else's career, as long as it furthered *their* interests. This was a major reason why many liberals caught in the same bed with Communists during the Blacklist Years, eventually fled from them like the plague. Predictably, upon hearing the announcement of Maltz's participation in a project that would slam the U.S. Army, the Hearst press was furious. Newspapers across the country damned Sinatra as a commie-lover and, since he was a prominent Kennedy supporter, many questioned the young Senator's sincerity about rolling back Communism.

At first Sinatra remained defiant, a stance one would expect from the kid from Hoboken. No one was going to tell *him* who to hire. As it turned out, there *were* folks who could tell the supposedly independent singer where to go, like for instance his pals Giancana and Genovese. And there was someone else. With the singer now damned from the pulpits of the nation's churches, the cardinals of New York and Boston personally appealed to the candidate's father, the ruthless Joseph Kennedy, to step in. The cardinals threatened to hold back the Catholic vote for Kennedy if his campaign did not pressure Sinatra to fire Maltz.

Joseph Kennedy called in Sinatra. He gave him a terse, yet succinctly worded choice: "It's either Maltz or *us*."[13]

Eating a rare chunk of Humble Pie, Sinatra had to tell the press that he had made a mistake in hiring Maltz. The radical screenwriter still received the contractual payment of $75,000, though this was for doing absolutely no work. As to his unceremonial firing, Maltz wasn't even told by Sinatra, but by his underlings. The paradox couldn't be any more depressing for Maltz. Trumbo was writing screenplays for major films that were international hits, while he was still an unemployable loser damned from the pulpits of the nation's houses of worship. Even a celebrity inexorably linked with gangsters couldn't help him. His personal life didn't fare much better. A few years after the *Slovik* controversy, Margaret Maltz, his wife of 27 years, divorced him in 1964.

He plodded on. In 1967, MGM hired him to do the screenplay for his novel *Pistolero's Progress*. It was filmed as *The Last Challenge* starring conservative actor Glenn Ford. Both novel and screenplay were written under his usual pseudonym, John B. Sherry. The film was a wordy, badly paced bore, and it failed, despite Ford's usually good performance.

Then, in 1970, another conservative star gave Maltz his chance. Clint Eastwood was no commie-lover, but he recognized the value of good writers and wisely employed them for the next three decades. Universal had former Western director Budd Boetticher work on a screen story, then had Maltz do the screenplay, the first time his name was on a movie screen since another Universal film, 1948's *The Naked City*. Directed by Don Siegel, *Two Mules for Sister Sara* dealt with the Man With No Name teaming up with a nun (Shirley MacLaine) and helping revolutionaries in Mexico. Besides Maltz's plot portraying violent revolution as something positive, is his arch treatment of the nun character. Seen at first as a stuffy and pious contrast to Eastwood's laconic gunfighter, she is finally revealed to be a prostitute disguised as a nun. The screenwriter's attack on the religious establishment couldn't be any plainer, especially those clergy who condemned him during the *Private Slovik* controversy. Maltz seemed to be saying that behind every nun is a randy whore.

The following year, Universal, Eastwood and Siegel again hired Maltz; this time, his assignment was to adapt Thomas Cullinan's excellent novel *The Beguiled*. In the story of a wounded and amoral Union soldier cared for by the sexually frustrated residents of a Southern home for girls, Maltz's screenplay goes in unexpected cliché-busting directions. It was the screenwriter at his best. The soldier is not the upright young man he portrays himself to be; instead, he is selfish, exploitative, and a born liar, a charmer when it will serve his purpose. We see him twist the various females in this establishment, both young and old, white and black, around his not-so-little finger. Eastwood was excellent in this obviously *non*–Eastwood role; and one can applaud the actor for taking on such a part merely a year after his more traditional Man With No Name character in *Two Mules for Sister Sara*.

Maltz had written a happy ending for the film. However, neither star nor director liked it. Irene Kamp was hired for a rewrite, and Eastwood and Siegel had to fight their bosses at Universal to keep this new ending where the soldier is poisoned by the women. Strangely, Maltz went back to his "John B. Sherry" alias in the credits. In the next two years, he scripted just two more films, *Scalawag* for Kirk Douglas and Henry Hathaway's last pathetic film, *Hangup,* again as John B. Sherry.

Maltz died at the height of the Reagan Era in 1985. By then, the myth of unity that the CPUSA claimed for the Hollywood Ten would be exposed in the post–Blacklist years, with the "martyrs" bitterly sniping at each other over new, and in some cases emphatically *non*-radical political positions. Revelations of Soviet tyranny caused deep divisions among the former friends. Maltz would still be proud of his membership in the Party, but the claim

A MAN'S GOTTA KNOW HIS LIMITATIONS. **Clint Eastwood as the wounded Union soldier staying at the home of some frustrated Southern women in *The Beguiled* (1971). Based on Thomas Cullinan's novel, the screenplay is credited to Albert Maltz, but Eastwood and Siegel insisted on changing Maltz's happy ending. The film bombed.**

seemed to be an empty self-delusion. The knowledge of mass murders couldn't be shooed away like an annoying fly. They were not a creation of the capitalist press, and they were not the work of fascists or Trotskyites, the scapegoat of most Communist attacks.

Though Maltz was regarded as a hero by the Hollywood Left, in his last years this did not translate into concrete offers. Though a new politically correct Hollywood exists today which also sees the Communist screenwriters as heroes, Maltz's books and stories are never reprinted. His fame today (for those who still remember him, that is) is locked in with that of his comrades. He is just one of a group, not an individual. Rare copies of his books are only available for purchase on the Internet, never in bookstores.

His most famous and controversial essay was titled *What Shall We Ask of Writers?* However, the question now concerning his work is *What's the Cheapest Price I Can Get This For on e-Bay?*

The films to come out of Hollywood in the next thirty years made no bones about where they stood concerning the Blacklist Years. *The Way We Were, The Front, Guilty of Suspicion* and *One of the Hollywood Ten* were distinguished by their blatant political bias. Many of these projects were scripted by very bitter former Communists who portrayed Party members as innocent martyrs and their accusers as black-hearted villains of the old school; indeed, the HUAC investigators portrayed in these films might as well be twirling long black mustaches and tying young girls to railroad tracks. Thanks to the behind-the-scenes personnel responsible for these films, a real-life complicated situation becomes the worst of capitalist Hollywood clichés: the wholesome good-guys against the evil bad-guys, with those who support Soviet totalitarianism as heroes and those who fight tyranny being portrayed as "fascists" and "racists." These films never portrayed the efforts of sincere anti–Communists to free those trapped behind the Iron Curtain, or even once mentioned the sufferings of Eastern Europeans under Communist occupation, especially religious Jews and Christians who were systematically persecuted for who they were.

Though HUAC members were certainly no angels, in reality, neither were their enemies. The investigators and the CPUSA were mirror images of each other, though with one possible exception: HUAC didn't represent a group that excused the murders of millions of people on another continent.

As it stands, the John Howard Lawsons and Lester Coles of the Party were infuriating apologists for a political ideology that promoted freedom while in reality it practiced genocide. But they were not members of the NKVD. Nor were they spies or traitors. And, unlike the Rosenbergs, they stole no national secrets; nor did they blow up any government facilities or set fire to buildings that housed widows and orphans.

The Comintern, at Stalin's direction, knew that they couldn't exhort Americans to rise up and take over their democratically elected government in a violent revolution, an approach the Party *did* use in more politically fragile systems on the planet. But they could and did undermine American institutions by planting doubt in the minds of the American public about the very freedoms they cherished.

The Comintern's *modus operandi* was to attack America as the Big Liar, to destroy its idea of itself as a land of freedom, equality and opportunity. In the films of leftist screenwriters and performers, businesses are never secure enterprises; money corrupts or its acquisition leads to disaster; the rich are either villains or buffoons or both; and the poor and working class, especially non-whites, are emphatically *not* equal in America despite the fact that its Constitution said they were. The fact that these injustices *did* exist did not lessen the way Hollywood's Communists took advantage of the situation. In practice, the CPUSA followed the way of Bolshevism, meaning Stalin, not the precepts of freedom and equality. They were out to exploit these problems, not solve them. An example of this was during World War II when, under Stalin's direct orders, American problems were not to be attacked for the duration of the conflict. The CPUSA, while giving lip service to freedom and equality, was silent during the continued lynchings of African Americans down south, ignored the Japanese-Americans in internment camps, and allowed even more worker exploitation. After the war, when Stalin no longer needed us, the Party freely compared the nation who saved their bacon to the fascists they had just recently defeated. Predictably, Hollywood's Communist screenwriters returned to attacking the free enterprise system with a vengeance.

And, of course, there's the double standard of those who attack the rich while basking in their own material pleasures. Unlike the Communists of poorer nations, Lawson, Cole, Trumbo and the rest were loyal Party members who enjoyed a higher standard of living than they ever would have had under a Marxist system.

And there lies the paradox. The noble leftist involved in the struggle of the working class who liked his ten-room mansion and two-car garage — a situation that could only exist, ironically, in a capitalist society.

Perhaps the best example of the hypocrisy behind most revolutionary movements is a line from Paddy Chayefsky's play *The Passion of Josef D.* In a scene set in Czarist Siberia, a young Josef Stalin, then known as Djungashvili, desires the boots of his kindly Okhrana guard. When the constable's back is turned, Djungashvili suddenly stabs him to death.

However, before he can remove the dead man's boots, he turns to the audience and says:

> When a barefoot fellow tells you he is revolting against tyranny, watch out: he's only after your boots.

Chapter Notes

I. In the Red

1. John Howard Lawson in Neal Gabler, *An Empire of Their Own, New Theater*, November 1934, p. 333.
2. *Newspaper Days* by Theodore Dreiser, quoted in Mandy Merck, *Hollywood's American Tragedies: Dreiser, Eisenstein, Sternberg, Stevens*, p. 14.
3. *Ibid.*
4. Merck, *Hollywood's American Tragedies*, pp. 10–11.
5. *Ibid.*, p. 10.
6. *Ibid.*, p. 12.
7. *Ibid.*
8. *Ibid.*, p. 13.
9. *Ibid.*, p. 15.
10. Lincoln Kerstein, "James Cagney & the American Hero," *Hound & Horn*, April 1932, in Robert Sklar, *City Boys: Cagney, Bogart, Garfield*, p. 12.
11. Carlos Clarens, *Crime Movie: An Illustrated History*, p. 68.
12. Kerstein in Sklar, p. 12.
13. *The Public Enemy* file, University of Southern California, Warner Bros. Archives.
14. *Ibid.*
15. Ronald Radosh and Allis Rodash, *Red Star Over Hollywood: The Film Colony's Long Romance with the Left*.
16. *Ibid.*, p. 34.
17. *Ibid.*, p. 33.
18. *Ibid.*, p. 34.
19. *New York Times*, August 18, 1934, in Rodash and Rodash, p. 34.
20. John McCabe, *Cagney*, in Rodash and Rodash, p. 35.
21. Statement made by Dreiser, December 26, 1920, in Merck, *Hollywood's American Tragedies*, p. 18.
22. Statement made by Dreiser, April 1921, in Merck, *Hollywood's American Tragedies*, p. 19.
23. Statement made by Dreiser, December 8, 1921, in Merck, *Hollywood's American Tragedies*, p. 19.
24. Statement made by Dreiser, undated, in Merck, *Hollywood's American Tragedies*, p. 20.
25. Statement made by Dreiser, undated, in Merck, *Hollywood's American Tragedies*, p. 39.
26. W.A. Swanberg, *Dreiser*, in Friedrich, *City of Nets*, p. 253.
27. Joyce Milton, *Tramp: The Life of Charlie Chaplin*, p. 299.
28. *Ibid.*, p. 40.
29. *Ibid.*, p. 48.
30. Swanberg, *Dreiser*, in Friedrich, *City of Nets*, p. 251.
31. Josef von Sternberg, *Fun in a Chinese Laundry*, in Friedrich, *City of Nets*, p. 6.
32. Friedrich, *City of Nets*, p. 251.
33. Dreiser telegram to Samuel Hoffenstein, February 16, 1931, in Friedrich, *City of Nets*, p. 251.
34. *Ibid.*
35. Friedrich, *City of Nets*, p. 251.
36. Letter from Jesse L. Lasky to Arthur Garfield Hays and Arthur Carter Hume, June 30, 1931, found in the Theodore Dreiser Papers at the University of Pennsylvania and cited in Merck, *Hollywood's American Tragedies*, p. 84.
37. *The Daily Worker*, December 2, 1933, in Jack Salzman, *Albert Maltz*, p. 27.
38. Brooks Atkinson, *New York Times*, November 30, 1933, in Salzman, *Albert Maltz*, p. 27.
39. Lawson, "An Empire of Their Own," *New Theater*, November 1934, in Salzman, *Albert Maltz*, p. 27.
40. Quote by Paul Robeson, undated, Martin Duberman, *Paul Robeson: A Biography*.
41. Victor S. Navasky, *Naming Names*, p. 419.
42. Jeffrey Lawson quoted in Judy Kaplan and Lynn Shapiro, eds., *Red Diapers: Growing Up in the Communist Left*; quotations in Gerald Home, *The Final Victim of the Blacklist: John Howard Lawson, Dean of the Hollywood Ten*, p. 3.
43. *Ibid.*
44. Bernard F. Dick, *From Radical Innocence: A Critical Study of the Hollywood Ten*, p. 46.
45. John Howard Lawson in Neal Gabler, *An Empire of Their Own, New Theater*, November 1934, p. 333.
46. *The Emperor Jones*, Internet Movie Database, imdb.com.
47. Tom Weaver, Michael Brunas and John Brunas, *Universal Horrors: The Studio's Classic Films, 1931–1946*, p. 102.
48. David J. Skal with Jessica Rains, *Claude Rains: An Actor's Voice*, p. 69.
49. Ornitz interview with the *People's Daily World*, March 26, 1946, in Kenneth Lloyd Billingsly, *Hollywood Party: How Communism Seduced the American Film Industry in the 1930s and 1940s*, p. 147.
50. Sheila Schwartz, *The Hollywood Writers' Wars*, p. 148.

51. Duberman, *Paul Robeson*, p. 184.
52. *Ibid.*, 185.
53. *Ibid.*
54. *Ibid.*
55. *It Can't Happen Here* file, Margaret Herrick Library.
56. Mark Schorer, *Sinclair Lewis: An American Life*, p. 487.
57. Michael Meyer, *It Can't Happen Here*, p. ix.
58. *It Can't Happen Here* file, Margaret Herrick Library.
59. *Ibid.*
60. *Ibid.*
61. *Ibid.*
62. *Ibid.*
63. Schorer, *Sinclair Lewis*, p. 616.
64. *It Can't Happen Here* file, Margaret Herrick Library.
65. *Black Fury* file, University of Southern California, Warner Bros. Archives.
66. *Ibid.*
67. *Ibid.*
68. *Ibid.*
69. *Ibid.*
70. *Ibid.*
71. *Ibid.*
72. Obviously right after the film's release, *Black Fury* file at the University of Southern California, Warner Bros. Archives.
73. *Black Fury* file, University of Southern California, Warner Bros. Archives.
74. Interview with the *Observer*, July 29, 1934, in Duberman, *Paul Robeson*.
75. Interview with the *New York Amsterdam News*, October 7, 1935, in Duberman, *Paul Robeson*.
76. *London Times*, April 7, 1935, in Duberman, *Paul Robeson*.
77. Quote to interviewer from unknown periodical, 1938, in Duberman, *Paul Robeson*.
78. *The General Died at Dawn*, Margaret Herrick Library.
79. *New York Times* film review, September 3, 1936.
80. *Ibid.*
81. *The General Died at Dawn*, IMDb Trivia, imdb.com.
82. Incident related in Gabriel Miller, *Clifford Odets*, pp. 187–88.
83. *New York Times*, November 12, 1936.
84. Undated telegram from Clifford Odets to Frances Farmer; Patrick Agan, *The Decline and Fall of the Love Goddesses*, p. 20.
85. Telegram from Odets to Rainer, May 28, 1938, in Wendy Smith, *Real Life Drama: The Group Theater and America, 1931–1940*, p. 336.

II. The Old Left Hook

1. Letter from Breen to Walter Wanger, February 3, 1937, from *Blockade* file, Margaret Herrick Library.
2. From *Blockade* file, Margaret Herrick Library.
3. *Ibid.*
4. *Catholic News*[?]. *Blockade* file, Margaret Herrick Library.
5. *Ibid.*
6. Undated piece from *The Tablet*, in *Blockade* file, Margaret Herrick Library.
7. Letter from Charles Turck to Joseph Breen, July 19, 1938, in *Blockade* file, Margaret Herrick Library.
8. Letter from Breen to Turck, August 4, 1938, in *Blockade* file, Margaret Herrick Library.
9. John Howard Lawson, *Film, the Creative Process: The Search for an Audio-Visual Structure;* in *The Final Victim of the Blacklist: John Howard Lawson, Dean of the Hollywood Ten* by Gerald Horne, p. 109.
10. Lawson interview with *San Jose News*, August 11, 1966, in Horne, *John Howard Lawson: The Final Victim of the Blacklist*, p. 120.
11. Leo Frank—www.Jewishvirtuallibrary.com
12. *They Won't Forget* file, University of Southern California, Warner Bros. Archives.
13. *Ibid.*
14. *Ibid.*
15. Internet Broadway Database, 2009.
16. October 10, 1937, after the film opened all over the U.S.
17. *New York Times* film review, July 15, 1937.
18. John Cogley, *Report on Blacklisted, I-Movies*, p. 223.
19. *Ibid.*, p. 223.
20. *Dust Be My Destiny* file, University of Southern California, Warner Bros. Archives.
21. *Ibid.*
22. *Ibid.*, October 8, 1939.
23. *New York Times*, July 5, 1939.
24. *Ibid.*
25. *New York Times* theater reviews, February 16, 1939.
26. William Wright, *Lillian Hellman: The Image, the Woman*, p. 143.
27. Tallulah Bankhead, *Tallulah, My Autobiography*, p. 274.
28. Joan Mellon, *Hellman and Hammett: The Legendary Passion of Lillian Hellman and Dashiell Hammett*, p. 162.
29. Bankhead, *Tallulah: An Autobiography of Tallulah Bankhead*, pp. 274–75.
30. *Ibid.*, p. 276.
31. Lillian Hellman, *An Unfinished Woman*, p. 485; in Wright, *Lillian Hellman: The Image, the Woman*, p. 145.
32. August 2, 1940.
33. *Flowing Gold* file, University of Southern California, Warner Bros. Archives.
34. Patrick Agan, *The Rise and Fall of the Love Goddesses*, p. 22.
35. *Among the Living* file, Margaret Herrick Library, Bernard F. Dick, *Radical Innocence: a Critical Study of the Hollywood Ten*, p. 37.
36. Otto Friedrich, *City of Nets: Hollywood in the 1940s*, p. 326.
37. *The Sea Wolf* file, University of Southern California, Warner Bros. Archives.
38. *Ibid.*
39. Rudy Behlmer (editor), *Inside Warner Brothers, 1935–1951: the Battles, Brainstorms and the Bickering—From the Files of Hollywood's Greatest Studio*, p. 132.
40. *Ibid.*, pp. 132–33.

41. Internet Broadway Database, 2009.
42. Michael Shnayerson, *Irwin Shaw: A Biography*, p. 83.
43. Interview with John Anderson for the *New York Journal-American*, February 1, 1939; *Ibid.*, p. 86.
44. Interview with Harrison Carroll, "John Garfield Declares He Is in the Films to Make Good Stories," *Boston Daily Record*, March 3, 1941; Robert Nott, *He Ran All the Way: The Life of John Garfield*, p. 133.

III. Bodyguard of Lies

1. *The Remarkable Andrew* file, Margaret Herrick Library.
2. Statement made by Ring Lardner, *I'd Hate Myself in the Morning*, in Ronald Radosh and Allis Radosh, *Red Star Over Hollywood: The Film Colony's Long Romance with the Left*, p. 81.
3. *The Spectator*, June 23, 1939; David Parkinson (editor), *The Graham Greene Film Reader: Reviews, Essays, Interviews & Film Stories*, p. 304.
4. *Night and Day*, October 28, 1937, *Ibid.*, p. 234.
5. *Night and Day*, July 29, 1937, *Ibid.*, p. 210.
6. *The Novelist and the Cinema—A Personal Experience, International Film Annual*, #2, *Ibid.*, p. 443.
7. *1943: The Katyn Forest Massacre*—www.soviethistory.org.
8. *Ibid.*
9. Nora Sayre, *Running Time: Films of the Cold War*, p. 61.
10. *Mission to Moscow* file, University of Southern California, Warner Bros. Archives.
11. Howard Koch, *As Time Goes By*, p. 89; Ronald & Allis Radosh, *Red Star Over Hollywood*, p. 99.
12. *Ibid.*, p. 105; *Ibid.*
13. *Mission to Moscow* file, University of Southern California, Warner Bros. Archives.
14. *Ibid.*
15. *Action in the North Atlantic* file, University of Southern California, Warner Bros. Archives.
16. *Action in the North Atlantic*, IMDb Trivia.
17. John Howard Lawson, *Theory and Technique of Playwrighting and Screenwriting*, p. 371; Horne, *The Final Victim of the Blacklist: John Howard Lawson, Dean of the Hollywood Ten*, p. 152.
18. *Ibid.*, pp. 174–75.
19. *Ibid.*, p. 175.
20. *Background to Danger* file, University of Southern California, Warner Bros. Archives.
21. *The Daily Worker* film review, *Watch on the Rhine*, April 4, 1941; Joan Mellen, *Hellman and Hammett: The Legendary Passion of Lillian Hellman and Dashiell Hammett*, p. 173.
22. Article "*Watch on the Rhine*" by Alvah Bessie in *New Masses*, April 15, 1941; *Ibid.*, p. 173.
23. *Ibid.*, pp. 105–08.
24. Alexander Stephens, *Communazis: The FBI Surveillance of German Émigré Writers*, p. 103.
25. Unknown author.
26. Joan Mellen, *Hellman and Hammett: The Legendary Passion of Lillian Hellman and Dashiell Hammett*, p. 174.
27. *Watch on the Rhine* file, University of Southern California, Warner Bros. Archives.
28. William Wright, *Lillian Hellman: The Image, the Woman*, p. 167.
29. Joan Mellen, *Hellman and Hammett: The Legendary Passion of Lillian Hellman and Dashiell Hammett*, p. 195.
30. *Northern Pursuit* file, University of Southern California, Warner Bros. Archives.
31. *None Shall Escape* file, Margaret Herrick Library.
32. *Objective, Burma!* file, University of Southern California, Warner Bros. Archives.
33. Bernard F. Dick, *Radical Innocence: A Critical Study of the Hollywood Ten*, p. 41.
34. Robert Sklar, *City Boys: Cagney, Bogart, Garfield*, p. 156 (box office for *Johnny Come Lately* was $2.4 million) and p. 159 (*Blood on the Sun* made $1,000,000 more than that).
35. *Pride of the Marines* file, University of Southern California, Warner Bros. Archives.

IV. A Revolution from Above

1. Ronald and Allis Radosh, *Red Star Over Hollywood: The Film Colony's Long Romance with the Left*, p. 119.
2. *Ibid.*
3. Ronald Reagan, with Richard C. Hubler, *Where's The Rest of Me?*, p. 197.
4. *Ibid.*, p. 192.
5. *Ibid.*, p. 197.
6. *Ibid.*, p. 197.
7. Om and Phil Kuntz (editors). *The Sinatra Files: The Life of an American Icon Under Government Surveillance*, p. 42.
8. *Ibid.*, p. 43.
9. Lawson's article "Return to the 'Free World'" in *Masses and Mainstream*, undated, 1951; Gerald Horne, *The Final Victim of the Blacklist: John Howard Lawson, Dean of the Hollywood Ten*, p. 215.
10. Kenneth Lloyd Billingsley, *Hollywood Party: How Communism Seduced the American Film Industry in the 1930s and 1940 by Kenneth Lloyd Billingsly*; Appendix 1, pp. 290–98.
11. *The Daily Worker*, February 12, 1946; *Ibid.*, Appendix 2, pp. 299–300.
12. *Ibid.*
13. *The New Masses*, March 12, 1946; Radosh, *Red Star Over Hollywood*, p. 128.
15. "Art and politics" by Howard Fast, in *New Masses*, February 26, 1946; *Ibid.*, p. 128.
16. From the testimony of Leopold Atlas before HUAC, March 12, 1953; *Ibid.*, p. 129.
17. Theater review, unknown author.
18. Film reviews, unknown author.
19. Marion Meade, *Dorothy Parker: What Fresh Hell Is This?*, pp. 331–38.
20. *Smash-Up: The Story of a Woman* file, Margaret Herrick Library.
21. Interview with Marsha Hunt, Patrick McGilligan and Paul Buhle, *Tender Comrades: A Back Story of the Hollywood Blacklist*, p. 311.
22. Gerald Horne, *John Howard Lawson: The Final Victim of the Blacklist*, p. 166.

23. Letter from Joseph I. Breen to Walter Wanger, April 17, 1946, *Smash-Up: The Story of a Woman* file, Margaret Herrick Library.
24. *Ibid.*
25. Bob Herzberg, *The FBI & the Movies: A History of the Bureau on Screen and Behind the Scenes in Hollywood*, p. 143.
26. Film review, unknown author, *Smash-Up: The Story of a Woman* file, Margaret Herrick Library.
27. Bernard F. Dick, *Radical Innocence: A Critical Study of the Hollywood Ten*, p. 129.
28. February 19, 1947, *Ibid.*, p. 129.
29. Edward Dmytryk, *It's a Hell of a Life, But Not a Bad Living*, pp. 168–69.
30. Mona Z. Smith, *Becoming Something: The Story of Canada Lee*, pp. 149–50.
31. Copies of this "passionate statement of innocence" were sent to various New York editors. It appeared in full in the *Daily Compass* on June 20, 1949, and in an edited version in the *New York Herald Tribune* on June 22; *Ibid.*, p. 285.
32. Richard Schickel, *Elia Kazan: A Biography*, p. 150.
33. FBI file on Paul and Eslanda Robeson.
34. *Ibid.*
35. Article from March 20, 1949, *Los Angeles Times*, in FBI file on Paul and Eslanda Robeson.
36. Paul Buhle and Dave Wagner, *A Very Dangerous Citizen: Abraham Lincoln Polansky and the Hollywood Left*, p. 117.
37. Interview with Paul Buhle and Dave Wagner in Los Angeles, 1997, edited by Patrick McGilligan and Paul Buhle, *Tender Comrade: A Backstory of the Hollywood Blacklist*, p. 486.
38. Stanley Kramer with Thomas M. Coffey, *A Mad, Mad, Mad, Mad World, A Life in Hollywood*, p. 34.
39. *Ibid.*, p. 38.
40. *Ibid.*, p. 39.
41. Philip Dunne, *Take Two: A Life in Movies and Politics*, p. 98.
42. *Ibid.*, p. 98.
43. Mel Gussow, *Don't Say Yes Until I Finish Talking: A Biography of Darryl F. Zanuck*, p. 139.
44. Richard Schickel, *Elia Kazan: A Biography*, p. 206.
45. *Pinky* file, USC School of Cinema & TV.
46. *Ibid.*
47. *Ibid.*
48. Jeff Young (editor), *Elia Kazan: The Master Director Discusses His Films, Interviews*, p. 56.
49. Philip Dunne, *Take Two: A Life in Movies and Politics*, p. 62.
50. Robert Sklar, *City Boys: Cagney, Bogart, Garfield*, p. 214.
51. *The Lawless* file, Margaret Herrick Library.
52. David Caute, *Joseph Losey: A Revenge on Life*.
53. Article in StarSpeak, Kirk Crivello, *Fallen Angels: The Glamorous Lives and Tragic Deaths of Hollywood's Doomed Beauties*, pp. 12–13.
54. *The Lawless* file, Margaret Herrick Library.
55. Marshall Fine, *Bloody Sam: The Life and Films of Sam Peckinpah*, p. 37.
56. IMDb, Ernest Hemingway.
57. Quote from Truman Capote, undated, James Charlton (editors), *Fighting Words: Writers Lambaste Other Writers—from Aristotle to Anne Rice*, p. 104.
58. Boze Hadleigh (editor), *Hollywood Babble-On: Stars Gossip About Other Stars*, p. 190.
59. *The Breaking Point* file, University of Southern California, Warner Bros. Archives.
60. *Ibid.*
61. Garfield's testimony before HUAC, April 23, 1951, Frank Tavenner doing the questioning; Robert Nott, *He Ran All the Way: The Life of John Garfield*, p. 273.
62. *Ibid.*
63. Interview with Patrick McGilligan, 1995; editors, McGilligan and Buhle, *Tender Comrades: Backstory of the Hollywood Blacklist*, pp. 73–74.
64. Robert Sklar, *City Boys: Cagney, Bogart, Garfield*, p. 223.
65. Undated *New York Post* review, *Ibid.*, p. 223.

V. Breaking Eggs

1. Richard Schickel, *Elia Kazan: A Biography*, p. 273.
2. University of Pennsylvania Library website. www.library.upenn.edu/collections/rbm/Dreiser
3. *Ibid.*
4. Article "Dreiser Denies He Is Anti-Semitic" in *New Masses*, April 30, 1935; Donald Pizer, *American Naturalism and the Jews: Garland, Norris, Dreiser, Wharton and Catha*, p. 45.
5. *Ibid.*, p. 47.
6. Letter from Dreiser to H.L. Mencken, October 13, 1939, *Ibid.*, p. 47.
7. University of Pennsylvania Library website.
8. *Ibid.*
9. *Ibid.*
10. *Ibid.*
11. Terry Coleman, Olivier, p. 223.
12. Philip Dunne, *Take Two: A Life in Movies and Politics*, p. 253.
13. Bernard F. Dick, *Radical Innocence: A Critical Study of the Hollywood Ten*, p. 95.
14. Undated quote from Darryl F. Zanuck; Mel Gussow, *Don't Say Yes Until I Finish Talking: A Biography of Darryl F. Zanuck*, p. 163.
15. Philip Dunne, *Take Two: A Life in Movies and Politics*, p. 254.
16. *Ibid.*, p. 163.
17. *The Robe* file, USC School of Cinema & TV.
18. Philip Dunne, *Take Two*, p. 254.
19. *Ibid.*, p. 254.
20. *Saturday Evening Post*, May 19, 1951; Edward Dmytryk, *It's A Hell of a Life, But Not a Bad Living by Edward Dmytryk*, p. 146.
21. Rudy Behlmer (editor), *Memos from Darryl F. Zanuck: The Golden Years at Twentieth Century–Fox*, p. 260.
22. *The War of the Worlds* file, Margaret Herrick Library.
23. Edward Dmytryk, *It's A Hell of a Life, But Not a Bad Living*, p. 144.
24. Richard Schickel, *Elia Kazan: A Biography*, pp. 221–35.
25. Arthur Miller, *Timebends*, p. 308; Richard Schickel, *Elia Kazan: A Biography*, p. 233.
26. Internet Broadway Database.

27. Richard Schickel, *Elia Kazan: A Biography*, p. 449.
28. Philip Dunne, *Take Two: A Life in Movies and Politics*, p. 383.
29. *Time*, May 10, 1954, The Administration: The Greenbelt Mystery.
30. *New York Times*, June 14, 1989, Obituaries.
31. *Three Brave Men* file, USC School of Cinema & TV.
32. Michael Shnayerson, *Irwin Shaw: A Biography*, p. 162.
33. Article "What I've Learned About Being a Man" by Irwin Shaw, *Playboy*, January 1984; *Ibid.*, p. 162.
34. *New York Times* book reviews, October 3, 1948; *Ibid.*, p. 172.
35. *New York Sun* book reviews, October 1, 1948; *Ibid.*, p. 172.
36. *The Nation*, October 9, 1948; *Ibid.*, p. 172.
37. *Time* book reviews, October 11, 1948, *Ibid.*, p. 172.
38. Herbert Mitgang, *Dangerous Dossiers: Exposing the Secret War Against America's Greatest Authors*, p. 125.
39. Edward Dmytryk, *It's A Hell of a Life, But Not a Bad Living*, p. 101.
40. Peter Manso, *Brando: The Biography*, pp. 449–50.
41. Undated quote from Philip Rhodes; Carlo Fiore, Bud, P. 203; *Ibid.*, p. 450.
42. Undated quote from Marlon Brando; *Ibid.*, p. 250.
43. Michael Shnayerson, *Irwin Shaw: A Biography*, pp. 252–53.
44. Peter Manso, *Brando: The Biography*, p. 466.

VI. Containment

1. Stephen Schwartz, *From East to West*, Kenneth Lloyd Billingsley, *Hollywood Party: How Communism Seduced the American Film Industry in the 1930s and 1940s*, p. 250.
2. Letter to Edward Lewis, June 8, 1959, found in Kirk Douglas Papers, Box 11; Bernard F. Dick, *Radical Innocence: A Critical Study of the Hollywood Ten*.
3. Nancy Lynn Schwartz, completed by Sheila Schwartz, *Hollywood Writers' Wars*, p. 153.
4. Victor S. Navasky, *Naming Names*, p. 419.
5. Bernard F. Dick, *Radical Innocence: A Critical Study of the Hollywood Ten*, pp. 206–07.
6. *Ibid.*, p. 209.
7. Helen Manfull (editor), *Additional Dialogue: Letters of Dalton Trumbo, 1942–1962*, p. 556.
8. Letter from Lester Cole to Albert Maltz, November 15, 1977, Ronald Radosh and Allis Radosh, *Red Star Over Hollywood: The Film Colony's Long Romance with the Left*, p. 232.
9. Lester Cole, *Hollywood Red*, p. 432.
10. William Wright, *Lillian Hellman: The Image, the Woman*, pp. 368–76.
11. *Ibid.*, pp. 370–71.
12. Joan Mellen, *Hellman and Hammett: The Legendary Passion of Lillian Hellman and Dashiell Hammett*, pp. 447–48; and William Wright, *Lillian Hellman: The Image, the Woman*, pp. 370–71.
13. Shawn Levy, *Rat Pack Confidential*, p. 159; and Lawrence J. Quirk and William Schoell, *The Rat Pack: Neon Nights with the Kings of Cool* by Lawrence J. Quirk and William Schoell, pp. 150–51.

Bibliography

Books

Agan, Patrick. *The Decline and Fall of the Love Goddesses.* Los Angeles: Pinnacle Books, 1979.

Ambler, Eric. *Background to Danger.* New York: Alfred A. Knopf, 1943.

Arnold, William. *Frances Farmer: Shadowland.* New York: McGraw-Hill, 1978.

Bankhead, Tallulah. *Tallulah: My Autobiography.* New York: Dell Publishing, 1942.

Barzman, Norma. *The Red and the Blacklist: The Intimate Memoir of a Hollywood Expatriate.* New York: Thunder's Mouth Press/Nation Books, 2003.

Behlmer, Rudy. *Behind the Scenes: The Making of.* Hollywood: Samuel French Trade, 1982.

_____, ed. *Inside Warner Brothers: 1935–1951.* New York: Simon & Schuster, 1985.

_____. *Memos from Darryl F. Zanuck.* New York: Grove Press, 1993.

Bentley, Eric, ed. *Thirty Years of Treason: Excerpts from Hearings Before the House Un-American Activities Committee, 1938–1968.* New York: Viking Press, 1971.

Bergman, Andrew. *We're in the Money: Depression America and Its Films.* Chicago: Ivan R. Dee Publishing, 1971.

Billingsley, Kenneth Lloyd. *Hollywood Party: How Communism Seduced the American Film Industry in the 1930s and 1940s.* Rocklin, CA: Forum, a division of Prima Publishing, 1998.

Brooks, Richard. *The Brick Foxhole.* New York: Harper & Brothers, 1945.

Buhle, Paul, and Dave Wagner. *Blacklisted: The Film Lover's Guide to the Hollywood Blacklist.* New York: Palgrave Macmillan, 2003.

_____. *A Very Dangerous Citizen: Abraham Lincoln and the Hollywood Left.* Berkeley and Los Angeles: University of California Press, 2001.

Caute, David. *Joseph Losey: A Revenge on Life.* New York: Faber & Faber, 1996.

Clarens, Carlos. *Crime Movies: An Illustrated History.* New York: W.W. Norton, 1980.

Cogley, John. *Report on Blacklisting: Movies.* New York: Fund for the Republic, 1956.

Cole, Lester. *Hollywood Red: The Autobiography of Lester Cole.* Palo Alto, CA: Ramparts Press, 1981.

Coleman, Terry. *Olivier.* New York: Henry Holt, 2005.

Cooper, Matthew. *The Nazi War Against Soviet Partisans: 1941–1944.* New York: Stein & Day, 1979.

Coren, Michael. *The Invisible Man: The Life and Liberties of H.G. Wells.* New York: Macmillan, 1993.

Corliss, Richard, ed. *The Hollywood Screenwriters.* New York: Avon Books, 1970, 1971, 1972.

Crivello, Kirk. *Fallen Angels.* New York: Citadel Press, 1988.

Dalin, David G., and John F. Rothman. *Icon of Evil: Hitler's Mufti and the Rise of Radical Islam.* New York: Random House, 2008.

Dean, Phillip Hayes. *Paul Robeson.* New York: Marian Searchinger Associates, 1978.

Deane, Pamala S. *James Edwards: African-American Hollywood Icon.* Jefferson, NC: McFarland, 2010.

DeJonge, Alex. *Stalin and the Shaping of the Soviet Union.* New York: William Morrow, 1986.

Dick, Bernard F. *Hellman in Hollywood.* East Brunswick, NJ: Fairleigh Dickinson University Press, 1982.

_____. *Radical Innocence: A Critical Study of the Hollywood Ten.* Lexington, KY: University of Kentucky Press, 1989.

_____. *The Star-Spangled Screen: The American World War II Film.* Lexington, KY: University Press of Kentucky, 1985.

Diggins, John Patrick. *The Rise and Fall of the American Left.* New York: W.W. Norton, 1992.

Dmytryk, Edward. *It's a Hell of a Life, But Not a Bad Living.* New York: Times Books, 1978.

Doherty, Thomas. *Hollywood's Censor: Joseph I. Breen & the Production Code Administration.* New York: Columbia University Press, 2007.

Douglas, Kirk. *The Ragman's Son.* New York: Simon & Schuster, 1988.

Druxman, Michael B. *Paul Muni: His Life and Films.* Cranbury, NJ: A.S. Barnes, 1974.

Duberman, Martin. *Paul Robeson.* New York: Alfred A. Knopf, 1988.

Dunne, Philip. *Take Two: A Life in Movies and Politics.* New York: Limelight Editions, 1980.

Dziak, John J. *Chekistry: A History of the KGB.* New York: Ballantine Books, 1988.

Ehrlich, Scott. *Paul Robeson: Athlete, Actor, Singer, Activist.* New York: Chelsea House, 1988.

Eyman, Scott. *Print the Legend: The Life and Times of John Ford.* Baltimore: John Hopkins University Press, 1999.

Fine, Marshall. *Bloody Sam: The Life and Times of Sam Peckinpah.* New York: Donald L. Fine, 1991.

Friedrich, Otto. *Before the Deluge.* New York: HarperCollins, 1972.

_____. *City of Nets: A Portrait of Hollywood in the 1940s.* New York: Harper & Row, 1986.

Gabler, Neal. *An Empire of Their Own: How the Jews Invented Hollywood.* New York: Doubleday, 1988.

_____. *Winchell: Gossip, Power and the Culture of Celebrity.* New York: Vintage Books, a division of Random House, 1994.

Gansberg, Alan L. *Little Caesar: A Biography of Edward G. Robinson.* Lanham, MD: Scarecrow Press, 2004.

Gussow, Mel. *Don't Say Yes Until I Finish Talking: A Biography of Darryl F. Zanuck.* New York: Doubleday, 1971.

Hanson, Peter. *Dalton Trumbo: Hollywood Rebel.* Jefferson, NC: McFarland, 2001.

Haynes, John Earl, and Harvey Klehr. *In Denial: Historians, Communism and Espionage.* San Francisco: Encounter Books, 2003.

Hemingway, Ernest. *To Have and Have Not.* New York: Scribner's, 1937.

Herzberg, Bob. *The FBI and the Movies: A History of the Bureau on Screen and Behind the Scenes in Hollywood.* Jefferson, NC: McFarland, 2007.

Holzer, Henry Mark, and Erika Holzer. *Aid and Comfort: Jane Fonda in North Vietnam.* Jefferson, NC: McFarland, 2002.

Horne, Gerald. *The Final Victim of the Blacklist: John Howard Lawson, Dean of the Hollywood Ten.* Berkeley: University of California Press, 2006.

Hoyt, Edwin P. *Paul Robeson: The American Othello.* Cleveland-New York: World Publishing, 1967.

Jarlett, Franklin. *Robert Ryan: A Biography & Critical Filmography.* Jefferson, NC: McFarland, 1990.

Jensen, Geoffrey. *Franco: Soldier, Commander, Dictator.* Washington, DC: Potomac Books, 2005.

Kavieff, Paul R. *The Life and Times of Louis Buchalter.* Fort Lee, NJ: Barricade Books, 2006.

Kingsley, Sidney, and Arthur Koestler. *Darkness at Noon.* New York: Random House, 1951.

Koch, Howard. *As Time Goes By: Memoirs of a Writer.* New York: Houghton Mifflin, Harcourt, 1979.

Koch, Stephen. *The Breaking Point: Hemingway, Dos Passos, and the Murder of Jose Roble.* New York: Counterpoint, a division of Perseus Books Group, 2005.

_____. *Double Lives: Spies and Writers in the Secret Soviet War of Ideas Against the West.* New York: Free Press, a division of Macmillan Press, 1994.

Kramer, Stanley, with Thomas L. Coffey. *A Mad, Mad, Mad, Mad World: A Life in Hollywood.* New York: Harcourt Brace, 1997.

Kuntz, Tom, and Phil Kuntz, eds. *The Sinatra Files: The Secret FBI Dossiers.* New York: Three Rivers Press, 2000.

Lawrence, Jerome. *Actor: The Life and Times of Paul Muni.* New York: Samuel French, 1974.

Levy, Shawn. *Rat Pack Confidential.* New York: Broadway Books, 1998.

Lewis, Sinclair, and Michael Meyer, introduction. *It Can't Happen Here.* New York: Signet Classics, 1935; introduction, 2005.

Lukacs, John. *June 1941: Hitler and Stalin.* New Haven, CT: Yale University Press, 2006.

Manfull, Helen, ed. *Additional Dialogue: Letters of Dalton Trumbo, 1942–1962.* New York: M. Evans, 1970.

Manso, Peter. *Brando: A Biography.* New York: Hyperion Books, 1994.

McGilligan, Patrick, and Paul Buhle. *Tender Comrades: A Backstory of the Hollywood Blacklist.* New York: St. Martin's Press, 1997.

McGrath, Patrick. *John Garfield: The Illustrated Career in Films and on Stage.* Jefferson, NC: McFarland, 1993.

McLellen, Diane. *The Girls: Sapphoes in Hollywood.* New York: St. Martin's Press, 2000.

Meade, Marion. *Dorothy Parker: What Fresh Hell Is This?* New York: Penguin Books, 1987.

Mellen, Joan. *Hellman and Hammett: The Legendary Passion of Lillian Hellman and Dashiell Hammett.* New York: HarperCollins, 1996.

Merck, Mandy. *Hollywood's American Tragedies: Dreiser, Eisenstein, Sternberg, Stevens.* Oxford, England: Berg Publishers, 2007.

Meyers, Jeffrey. *Bogart: A Life in Hollywood.* New York: Houghton Mifflin, 1997.

Miller, Gabriel. *Clifford Odets.* New York: Continuum Publishing, 1989.

Milton, Joyce. *Tramp: The Life of Charlie Chaplin.* New York: De Capo Press, 1996.

Mitgang, Herbert. *Dangerous Dossiers: Exposing the Secret War Against America's Greatest Authors.* New York: Donald I. Fine, 1988.

Morella, Joe, and Edward Z. Epstein. *Rebels: The Rebel Hero in Films.* New York: Citadel Press, 1971.

Moynahan, Brian. *Comrades: 1917 — Russia in Revolution.* New York: Little, Brown, 1992.

_____. *The Russian Century: A History of the Last Hundred Years.* New York: Random House, 1994.

Navasky, Victor. *Naming Names.* New York: Penguin Books, 1980.

Nott, Robert. *He Ran All The Way: The Life of John Garfield.* New York: Limelight Editions, 2003.

O'Reilly, Kenneth. *Hoover and the Un-Americans: The FBI, HUAC and the Red Menace.* Philadelphia: Temple University Press, 1983.

Packard, Jerrold. *Neither Friend Nor Foe: The European Neutrals in World War II.* New York: Macmillan, 1992.

Parkinson, David, ed. *The Graham Greene Film Reader: Reviews Essays, Interviews & Film Stories.* New York: Applause Theater Books, 1995.

Paul, Allen. *Katyn: The Untold Story of Stalin's Polish Massacre.* New York: Scribner's, 1991.

Pizer, Donald. *American Naturalism and the Jews: Garland, Norris, Dreiser, Wharton and Cather.* Urbana and Chicago, IL: University of Illinois Press, 2008.

Quirk, Lawrence, and William Schoell. *The Rat Pack: Neon Nights with the Kings of Cool.* New York: HarperCollins, 1998.

Radosh, Allis, and Ronald Radosh. *Red Star Over Hollywood: The Film Colony's Long Romance with the Left.* San Francisco: Encounter Books, 2006.

Radosh, Ronald. *Commies: A Journey Through the Old Left, the New Left and the Leftover Left.* San Francisco: Encounter Books, 2001.

Radosh, Ronald, Mary R. Habeck and Grigory Sevostianov, eds. *Spain Betrayed: The Soviet Union in the Spanish Civil War*. New Haven, CT: Yale University Press, 2001.

Rapoport, Louis. *Stalin's War Against the Jews: The Doctor's Plot and the Soviet Solution*. New York: Free Press, 1990.

Reagan, Ronald, and Richard C. Hubler. *Where's the Rest of Me?* New York: Dell Publishing, 1965.

Roberts, Randy, and James S. Olson. *John Wayne: American American*. Free Press, 1995.

Robertson, James C. *The Casablanca Man: The Cinema of Michael Curtiz*. London, U.K.: Routledge Publishing, 1993.

Robins, Natalie. *Alien Ink: The FBI's War on Freedom of Expression*. New Brunswick, NJ: Rutgers University Press, 1992.

Robinson, Edward G., and Leonard Spiegleglass. *All My Yesterdays*. New York: Hawthorn Books, 1974.

Salzman, Jack. *Albert Maltz*. Boston: G.K. Hall, 1978.

Sayre, Nora. *Running Time: Films of the Cold War*. New York: Dial Press, 1982.

Schickel, Richard. *Elia Kazan*. New York: HarperCollins, 2005.

Schorer, Mark. *Sinclair Lewis: An American Life*. New York: McGraw-Hill, 1961.

Schulberg, Budd. *What Makes Sammy Run?* New York: Random House, 1941.

Schwartz, Harry. *Eastern Europe in the Soviet Shadow*. New York: John Day, 1973.

Schwartz, Nancy Lynn. Completed by Sheila Schwartz. *The Hollywood Writers' Wars*. New York: Alfred A. Knopf, 1982.

Shelden, Michael. *Graham Greene: The Enemy Within*. New York: Random House, 1994.

Shnayerson, Michael. *Irwin Shaw: A Biography*. New York: Putnam's, 1989.

Sibley, Katherine A. S. *Red Spies in America: Stolen Secrets and the Dawn of the Cold War*. Lawrence, KS: University Press of Kansas, 2004.

Skal, David, and Jessica Rains. *Claude Rains: An Actor's Voice*. Lexington, KY: University Press of Kentucky, 2008.

Sklar, Robert. *City Boys: Cagney, Bogart, Garfield*. Princeton, NJ: Princeton University Press, 1992.

Smith, Mona Z. *Becoming Something: The Story of Canada Lee*. New York: Farrar, Straus & Giroux, 2004.

Smith, Wendy. *Real Life Drama: The Group Theater and America, 1931–1940*. New York: Alfred A. Knopf, 1990.

Stephan, Alexander. *Communazis: FBI Surveillance of German Émigré Writers*. New Haven, CT: Yale University Press, 2000.

Streeter, Michael. *Franco*. London: Haus Publishing, 2005.

Trumbo, Dalton. *Johnny Got His Gun*. New York: Lippicott Publishing, 1939.

Turnbull, Andrew, ed. *The Letters of F. Scott Fitzgerald*. New York: Scribner's, 1963.

Vaksberg, Arkady. *Stalin's Prosecutor* (aka *The Prosecutor and the Prey: Vishinsky and the 1930s Moscow Show Trials*). New York: Weidenfeld & Nicolson, 1990.

Volkman, Ernest, and Blaine Baggett. *Secret Intelligence: The Inside Story of America's Espionage Empire*. New York: Doubleday, 1989.

von Sternberg, Josef. *Fun in a Chinese Laundry: An Autobiography*. New York: Collier Books, 1966.

Walsh, Raoul. *Each Man in His Time*. New York: Farrar, Straus & Giroux, 1974.

Weaver, Tom, Michael Brunas and John Brunas. *Universal Horrors, The Studio's Classic Films, 1931–1946*. Jefferson, NC: McFarland, 2007.

Wright, William. *Lillian Hellman: The Image, the Woman*. New York: Ballantine Books, 1986.

Young, Jeff. *Kazan: The Master Director Discusses His Films*. New York: Newmarket Press, 1999.

Youngkin, Stephen D. *The Lost One: A Life of Peter Lorre*. Lexington, KY: University Press of Kentucky, 2005.

Internet Sources

Adamick, Paula. "*Enemy of the People: Paul Robeson and Communism*," Catholic Insight, www.catholicinsight.com, December 1, 2001.

"Burma in World War II," http://worldwar2database.com/html/burma.htm

Dunn, J.R. "Hollywood's Red Decade," http://www.americanthinker.com/2007/11/hollywoods_red_decade.html

FBI: Electronic Reading Room-files on celebrities, www.foia.fbi.gov/famous.htm

Internet Broadway Database, www.ibdb.com

Internet Movie Database, www.imbd.com

"Is the Soviet Union Islam's Best Friend?," http://www.rand.org/pubs/papers/P6529/

"Leo Frank," http://www.jewishvirtuallibrary.org/jsource/anti-semitism/frank.html

"The Lynching of Leo Frank," www.ajhs.org

"1943: Katyn Forest Massacre," http://www.soviethistory.org/index.php?page=subject&SubjectID=1943katyn&Year=1943

Stefan Heym Archives-Cambridge University Library, www.lib.cam.ac.uk/MS

The New York Times film review archives, www.nytimes.com/ref/movies/reviews/index

"Theodore Dreiser and Hollywood," University of Pennsylvania-Special Collections, www.library.upenn.edu/collections/rbm/Dresier

TIME, www.time.com

"Warsaw Uprising 1944," www.warsawuprising.com/katyn.htm

"The World at War — Poland Timeline 1918–52," www.worldatwar.net

Index

Act of Love 263
Action in Arabia 248
Action in the North Atlantic 125–129, 189
Adler, Buddy 255, 256, 259, 261
Adler, Luther 3, 61, 182
Adobe Walls 117
Afraid to Talk 23
After the Fall 198
Aherne, Brian 44
Albert, Eddie 109, 191, 238
Algiers 70
All My Sons (film) 200–201
All My Sons (play) 25–26, 197–199, 253, 254
All the King's Men 207
The Amazing Dr. Clitterhouse 103
Ambler, Eric 130, 131–132
An American Tragedy (book) 10, 14–15
An American Tragedy (film) 15–17, 18
An American Tragedy (play) 16, 235
Among the Living 100–101
Anastasia, Albert 5, 232
Anders, Rudolph 166
Anderson, Richard 258, 260
Andrews, Dana 147
Andrews, Edward 258, 260
The Angry Age 263
Anhalt, Edward 263, 266
Anticipations 21
Armstrong, Robert 167
Arnold, Edward 59, 60, 105, 237
Arthur, Jean 32
Asimov, Isaac 244–245
Ataturk, Gamel 133
Atlas, Leopold 186
Atwill, Lionel 34
Awake and Sing 49, 82

Bacall, Lauren 126, 221
Back Street (novel) 236
Background to Danger (film) 132–135
Background to Danger (novel) 130–132
Bacon, Lloyd 125
Badlands of Dakota 100
Ball, Lucille 87, 88, 90

Bankhead, Tallulah 95, 96, 97
Banks, Leslie 52
Banner, John 265
Bardette, Trevor 76
Barnes, Howard 77
Barrie, Wendy 88
Barrier, Edgar 181
Barry, Don "Red" 79
Barry, Gene 246, 247
Barrymore, John 82, 236
Barrymore, Lionel 236
Bart, Jean 32–33
Barzman, Ben 167, 216
Barzman, Norma 167
Batista, Fulgencia 5, 57, 213
Baxter, Anne 147, 150
Beaumont, Hugh 168
Beer and Blood 11
Begley, Ed 198
The Beguiled (film) 276
The Beguiled (novel) 276
Behind the Rising Sun 156, 168
Bendix, William 136
Bennett, Joan 34
Bentley, Eric 26
Bercovicci, Conrad 186
Beria, Lavrenti 118, 268
Bern, Paul 215
Berry, John 228, 229, 230
Bessie, Alvah 63, 64, 123–124, 140, 152, 153, 161, 164, 185–186, 221, 248–249
Bey, Turhan 134
Bezzerides, A.I. 126
Biberman, Abner 98
Biberman, Herbert 32, 33, 247–249, 250
The Big Knife (film) 215
The Big Knife (play) 213–215
Bishop, Julie 127, 152, 153
Black Fury 43, 47–48
The Black Pit 24
Blackwell's Island 83
Blockade 65–70
Blyth, Ann 141
Blood on the Sun 166–170
Body and Soul 74, 85, 195–197, 231
Bogart, Humphrey 75, 105, 109, 125, 126, 128, 221
Bohnen, Roman 108, 166

Boles, John 79
Border Flight 59
Bordertown 44
Borgnine, Ernest 256, 258
Bottoms, Timothy 93
Bowman, Lee 191, 192
Brand, Max 143
Brando, Marlon 234, 252, 263, 265–268
The Brave One 269
The Breaking Point 221–227
Brecht, Bertold 32, 135, 157
Breen, Joseph I. 4–5, 33, 37, 40–41, 43–44, 46–48, 565–66, 67–69, 127–128, 132–133, 146, 153–154, 191, 219, 235, 237–238, 244
Brennan, Walter 59, 147
Brewer, Roy 254
The Brick Foxhole 193–195
Bride of Frankenstein 33
Bridges, Lloyd 208
Bright, John 10–13, 123
Britt, May 264
Brocco, Peter 236
Brodie, Steve 194
Broken Arrow 241
Bromberg, J. Edward 3, 212, 234
Brooks, Louise 221
Brooks, Richard 193–195
Browder, Earl 167, 173–174
Brown, Grace 9–10
Brown, Rowland 10
Bryant, Nana 79
Buchalter, Louis "Lepke" 252
Buckley, Harold 80
Buckner, Robert 120–122, 124
Buhle, Paul 182–183, 190, 206
The Bulwark 9
Burnett, W.R. 117, 118, 126, 132
Bury the Dead 107, 108, 262
Butler, Frank 136–137, 138
Butler, Hugo 228
Buttinger, Joe 141, 274
Buttinger, Muriel Gardiner 5, 141, 274

Cabot, Bruce 79
Cabot, Sebastian 270
Cady, Jerome 87, 90

Index

Cagney, James 10–14, 86, 93, 166, 168, 169–170, 222, 258
The Caine Mutiny (film) 160
Calleia, Joseph 90
Cameron, Rod 113
Campbell, William 224, 225
Canova, Judy 188
Cantor, Eddie 31
Capone, Al 11
The Careless Years 232, 268
Carey, Macdonald 216, 217, 218
Carillo, Leo 66, 67
Carnovsky, Morris 3, 181, 234
Caroll, Richard 89
Carradine, John 90
Carrie (1952) 238–240
Carroll, Madeline 54, 66, 69–70
Caruso, Anthony 144
Castle on the Hudson 87
Chandler, Raymond 179, 180
Chaplin, Charles 15, 215
Chapman, Marguerite 165, 166
Chasanow, Abraham 256–258
Chayefsky, Paddy 278
The Children's Hour (play) 95, 144
China's Little Devils 35
Chodorov, Edward 123–124
Christians, Mady 3, 141, 143, 156, 157, 200
Christine, Virginia 256, 258
Churchill, Winston 112, 113, 186
City for Conquest 105
Clark, Colbert 101
Clark, Dane 126, 171
Clash by Night (play) 62
Clift, Montgomery 187, 188, 195, 263–264
Cloak and Dagger 182–183
Clurman, Harold 3, 49, 61, 65, 107, 199
Cobb, Lee J. 3, 50, 108
Cohen, Morris "Two-Gun" 5, 55, 56
Cohn, Harry 5, 155–156, 177, 254–255
Cole, Lester 78–81, 91–92, 100–101, 136–139, 154–156, 161–162, 166–167, 272
Collinge, Patricia 156
Come and Get It (book) 57
Come and Get It (film) 57, 59, 143
Commandos Strike at Dawn 165
Confessions of a Nazi Spy 103, 114
Conroy, Frank 95, 200
Conried, Hans 136
Conway, Morgan 79
Cook, Donald 12
Cook, Elisha, Jr. 22, 76
Cooper, Gary 53, 54, 56, 165
Cooper, Matthew 147
Copeland, Aaron 148
Coren, Michael 20–21
Corey, Jeff 209
Corliss, Richard 159
Cornered 179–184, 184
Coulouris, George 141, 144, 146
Counselor-at-Law (play) 42, 44, 46, 82

Counter-Attack 45, 165–166
The Country Girl (play) 61
Cowboy 269
Crain, Jeanne 210, 211, 212
Crawford, Joan 3
Crehan, Joseph 46
Crosby, Bing 59, 190
Crosby, Dixie 190
Crossfire 193, 195
Crowther, Bosley 98, 99, 112, 151, 158–159, 192, 209, 230–231, 233
The Crucible (play) 198, 254
Cry, the Beloved Country (film) 53, 231–233, 268
Cry, the Beloved Country (novel) 231
Cullinan, Thomas 276
Curtis, Nathaniel 169
Curtiz, Michael 47, 48, 81, 82, 107, 120, 222, 224–226, 227

Daniell, Henry 145
Dantine, Helmut 152
Darwell, Jane 156
Darkness at Noon (novel) 179, 180
Darkness at Noon (play) 49
DaSilva, Howard 175
Dassin, Jules 200
Daves, Delmer 170, 171
Davies, Joseph P. 120–123
Davis, Bette 75, 98, 143, 144, 170
Davis, Joan 188
Davis, Sammy, Jr. 31, 176
Day, Doris 192
Dean, Phillip Hayes 36–37
Death in the Deep South 72–73
Death of a Salesman (play) 198, 254, 262
DeCamp, Rosemary 168
de Cordova, Arturo 136
DeHavilland, Olivia 86, 99, 215
Dekker, Albert 60, 101, 102
DeMille, Cecil B. 28, 78, 241, 242
Destination: Tokyo 170
DeSylva, Buddy 137, 139
Dewey, Thomas 75
Dick, Bernard F. 28, 139, 155, 169, 272
Dickson, Gloria 76
Dies, Martin 13
Dieterle, William 65, 68, 188
Dietrich, Marlene 16, 140, 141
Digges, Dudley 31, 187–188
Dingle, Charles 195
Distant Drums 165
Dix, Richard 33
Dmytryk, Edward 145, 156–159, 160, 179–180, 193–195, 242, 243, 263
Dr. Jekyll and Mr. Hyde (novel) 20
Donlevy, Brian 113
Doorway to Hell 10
Dorsey, Hugh 71, 72
Dosier, William 180
Dos Passos, John 27
Doucette, John 226
Douglas, Kirk 195, 222, 267, 268, 270, 271

Douglas, Lloyd C. 241
Dreiser, Sara 8, 9
Dreiser, Theodore 5, 7–10, 13, 14–18, 39, 235–238, 240
Duberman, Martin 202
DuBois, W.E.B. 26
Duff, Howard 200
Duggan, Andrew 258, 260
Dumbrille, Douglas 98
Dunne, Philip 5, 210, 211–212, 241–242, 255–256
Duryea, Dan 60, 95
Dust Be My Destiny (film) 82–86, 196
Dust Be My Destiny (novel) 82
Dynamite 28

East of the River 87
Eastwood, Clint 275, 276
Ebb Tide (film) 58, 60
Edmond, Carl 191, 248
Edwards, James 4, 208–209
The Egyptian 263
Eisenstein, Sergei 15–17
Elmer Gantry (novel) 38
Emery, John 113, 167
The Emperor Jones (film) 24, 26, 29–32
The Emperor Jones (play) 24, 25, 36
Endore, Guy 228
Entwhistle, Peg 33
Erdman, Richard 162
Evans, Madge 79
Exclusive 59–60
The Execution of Private Slovik 275
Exodus 270

Farmer, Frances 3, 4, 57–60, 61, 98, 99, 100–101, 103, 144
Farrell, James T. 185
Farrow, John 87, 90, 91
Fast, Howard 186
Faylen, Frank 75, 258, 260
Feffer, Itzak 202
Ferber, Edna 59
Fiddler on the Roof (play) 234
The Fifth Column 99
The Fighting 69th 93
Finkel, Abem 42, 47, 103
Finkel, Ruth 42
Fiore, Carlo 266
Fire Down Below 263
First Men in the Moon (silent film) 19
Fitzgerald, Barry 60, 106, 200
Fitzgerald, F. Scott 28–29
Fitzgerald, Geraldine 28, 106, 144, 145
Five Came Back 87–88, 89–91
Fix, Paul 206
The Fixer (book) 27
A Flag Is Born 45
Flowing Gold 87, 100
Flynn, Errol 143, 152, 153, 162, 163, 222, 235
Foch, Nina 258, 260
Focus 198

Fonda, Henry 66, 67, 68, 69, 228, 258
Fonda, Jane 251, 273
Fong, Benson 159
Force of Evil 206–207
Ford, Francis 98
Ford, Glenn 269, 275
Ford, Henry 47, 117
Ford, John 210, 211
Ford, Wallace 168, 226, 229
Foreman, Carl 208–209
Fort, Garrett 101, 166
Four Daughters 81, 92
The Four Horsemen of the Apocalypse (1922) 9
Francis, Kay 235
Franco, Francisco 5, 63–64, 65, 70
Frank, Leo 71–72, 73, 77
Franz, Arthur 265
Frawley, William 54
From Here to Eternity (film) 177
Frye, Dwight 79
Fuller, Samuel 177–178
Fung, Willie 79
Fury 218

Gable, Clark 3, 180
Gabriel in the White House 41
Garfield, John 3, 4, 61, 81–84, 86–87, 99–100, 105–107, 109–110, 170–172, 175, 195–197, 213–216, 221, 227–231
Gargan, William 45
The General Died at Dawn ix, 53–56, 57
Genovese, Vito 275
The Gentle People 61, 207, 209, 262
Gershwyn, Ira 148
Gillette, Chester 9–10
Gillis, Jackson 80
Gilpen, Charles 25–26
Glassmon, Kubec 10–11
Goebbels, Joseph 21, 118, 148
Gold, Mike 28, 185–186
Golden Boy (play) 60–61, 62, 82, 199
Goldwyn, Samuel 57, 97, 147, 151
The Good Earth (film) 44
Gough, Lloyd 196
Granger, Farley 147
Grant, Cary 60, 130, 170
Grayson, Betty 61
Greed 16
Greene, Graham 5, 22, 114–117, 118
Greene, Ward 72–73, 76, 77
Greenstreet, Sydney 134
Griffith, D.W. 15
Gruber, Frank 152
A Gun for Sale 114, 115–117
A Guy Named Joe 157, 160

Hale, Alan, Sr. 85, 126
Hale, Richard 155
Hall, Jon 98
Hall, Mordaunt 18
Hall, Porter 54

Hammett, Dashiell 95–96, 142–143, 144, 145, 186, 187
The Hands of the Potter 235, 236
Hardwicke, Sir Cedric 247
Harlow, Jean 215
Harriman, Averill 119
Harriman, Catherine 119
Haskin, Byron 126
Hathaway, Henry 200, 276
Hayden, Sterling 218
Hayward, Susan 101, 102, 189, 190, 191, 192
Hays, Will 4, 37, 40, 42
He Ran All the Way (film) 215, 228–230
He Ran All the Way (novel) 229, 230
Hearst, William Randolph 39, 60, 124, 164, 169
Hecht, Ben 180
Heisler, Stuart 101, 192
Hellinger, Mark 86, 200
Hellman, Lillian 5, 95–97, 139–140, 141–147, 186–189, 273–274
Hemingway, Ernest 5, 99, 216, 221, 223–224
Hernandez, Juano 196, 223, 226
Heydrich, Reinhard 136
Heym, Stefan 135–136
Heywood, DuBose 29
High Sierra (film) 109
High Sierra (novel) 117
Highway to Hell 33–34
Hitchcock, Alfred 197
Hitler, Adolf 2, 5, 19, 35, 39, 64, 65, 68, 106, 112
Hoffenstein, Samuel 16–17
Holden, William 113, 175
Holmes, Phillips 18
Home of the Brave (film) 208, 209, 212
Home of the Brave (play) 207–208
Homolka, Oscar 136
Hoover, J. Edgar 177, 197, 205, 262
Hopkins, Miriam 238
Hopper, Hedda 202–203, 204, 214–215
Horne, Gerald 126, 192
Horne, Lena 211
Hostages (film) 136–139
Hostages (novel) 136
Hotel Berlin 266
The House I Live In (film) 177–179, 241
The House I Live In (song) 177
The House on 92nd Street 200
Howard, Sidney 39, 40
Howard, Vechel 271
Howe, James Wong 228–229
Hoyt, John 218
Hudson's Bay 271
Hull, Henry 162, 163
Hunt, Marsha 93, 190–191
Hunter, Kim 156
Hurst, Fannie 81, 236
Hussey, Ruth 156, 157
Huston, John 213

Huston, Walter 120, 121, 147–148, 149

I Am a Fugitive from a Chain Gang 33, 44, 72
I Am the Law 103
I Want You 263
I Was a Communist for the FBI 191, 250
If I Had a Million 79
Imitation of Life (film, 1934) 34
In the Days of the Comet 246
Indiana Jones and the Kingdom of the Crystal Skull 1
Invasion of the Body Snatchers Film (1956) 220
The Invisible Man (film) 19, 20, 21, 33, 34
The Invisible Man (novel) 20–21
The Invisible Man Returns 106
Island of Dr. Moreau (novel) 18
Island of Lost Souls 18, 19
It Can't Happen Here x, 37, 39–42

Jackson, Donald L. 228, 231
Jackson, Sherry 225
Jaffe, Sam 108
Jagger, Dean 147, 259
Jarrico, Paul 249, 269
Jenkins, Allen 90
Jennie Gephardt 18, 236
Jolson, Al 75
The Jolson Story 166
Johnny Got His Gun (film) 93, 157, 271–272
Johnny Got His Gun (novel) 92–95, 159
Johnny Got His Gun (radio play) 93
Johnson, Malcom 253
Johnson, Van 159, 160, 225
Jones, Gordon 101
Jones, James Earl 36
Jones, Jennifer 237, 238, 239, 240–241
Joslyn, Allyn 75
Juarez 44, 82
The Juggler 195
Julia 273, 274

Kandel, Abem 75
Katch, Kurt 134, 145, 265
Katz, Otto 5, 64, 136, 140–141
Kazan, Elia 3, 5, 49–50, 105, 108, 193, 198–200, 210–212, 234, 251, 253, 254
Kearney, Joseph 16
Kelly, Nancy 213
Kennedy, Arthur 198
Kennedy, John F. 275
Kennedy, Joseph 275
Kenyatta, Jomo 53
Kerensky, Alexander 1
Khrushchev, Nikita 268
Kingsley, Sidney 49
Kirov, Sergei 19
Kirstein, Lincoln 10, 12
Kitty Foyle 156

292　Index

Klemperer, Werner 272
Knowles, Patrick 90
Knox, Alexander 106, 154
Koch, Howard 120–121, 122
Koch, Stephen 127
Koestler, Arthur 49, 179
Korda, Alexander 51, 52–53, 232, 233
Korda, Zoltan 51, 52–53, 165, 232, 233
Kosleck, Martin 148, 149, 151
Kraft, Hy 17, 235
Kramer, Stanley 195, 208, 209
Kruger, Otto 76, 82
Kubrick, Stanley 270–271

Ladd, Alan 115, 117, 175
Laemmle, Carl 21, 336
Lamarr, Hedy 70
Lancaster, Burt 200, 201, 222
Lane, Priscilla 81, 83, 84, 85–86
Lange, Hope 264
Lardner, Ring 182
Larue, Jack 181
The Last Challenge 275
The Last Mile (play) 180
The Last Sunset 271
Laughton, Charles 19
Laurents, Arthur 207, 208
The Lawless ix, 216–220
Lawrence, Jerome 42, 43
Lawrence, Marc 74
Lawson, John Howard 3, 5, 23–24, 26–29, 57, 65–66, 126, 165, 182, 189–192, 231–232, 268–269
Lederer, Francis 114
Lee, Canada 4, 196–197, 205, 210, 231–233
Lee, Robert E. (author) 43
Leigh, Vivien 237, 240
Lenin, Vladimir Ulyanov 2, 5, 92, 234
LeRoy, Mervyn 72, 73, 74, 77, 103, 159–160
Lewis, Sinclair ix, 5, 18, 37–38
Leyda, Jay 120, 121, 122
The Life of Emile Zola 45, 115
Lifeboat 197
Little Caesar (novel) 117
The Little Foxes (film) 97–98
The Little Foxes (play) 95–96, 97–98
Litvak, Anatole 109, 110
Litvinov, Maxim 120
Liveright, Horace 236
Lockhart, Gene 79, 98, 152
Lorre, Peter 132, 134
Losey, Joseph 216, 218–219
Lost Boundaries 210, 212
The Lost Weekend (film) 191
Love, Montague 113
Lovejoy, Frank 258, 260
Loy, Myrna 33
Luce, Claire Booth 50
Lukas, Paul 114, 136, 141, 143, 144
Lundigan, William 210, 211

Lupino, Ida 106, 109, 110, 174
Lynn, Jeffrey 81

MacArthur, Charles 180
MacDonald, Kenneth 195
MacDougall, Ranald 161, 162, 164, 222–223, 224, 225
MacLaine, Barton 46, 74
MacMurray, Fred 59
MacPherson, Jeanne 28
Macready, George 166
Maguire, Dorothy 193
Maibaum, Richard 74
Mailer, Norman 261
Mainwaring, Daniel 216, 217, 220
Malamud, Bernard 27
Malden, Karl 108, 199–200
The Maltese Falcon (film) 134
The Maltese Falcon (novel) 142
Maltz, Albert 5, 22–24, 117, 118, 170–172, 177, 178–179, 183–186, 200–201, 241, 244, 272, 274–277
The Man Who Reclaimed His Head (film) 34–35, 248
The Man Who Reclaimed His Head (play) 32–33, 248
Mankiewicz, Herman 180
Mann, Erika 141
Mann, Thomas 141
Manpower 134
Mara Maru 222
Margin for Error (play) 50
Marked Woman 75
Marlow, Brian 100
Marshall, Brenda 106, 134
Marshall, Gen. George C. 169
Marshall, Tully 117
Martin, Dean 263, 264, 275
Martin, Marian 79
Massen, Osa 134
Massey, Raymond 105, 125, 126, 143
The Master Race 248
Mate, Ken 13, 248
Mayer, Louis B. 40, 215
McCarey, Leo 13
McCarthy, Mary 274
McCauley, Richard 109
McGilligan, Patrick 13, 190, 248
McLaglen, Victor 98, 105
McMahon, Aline 111
Mellen, Joan 139, 142, 151
Men in White (play) 49
Men Like Gods 246
Meridyth, Beth 28
Merrill, General Frank A. 161
Merry-Go-Round 22–23, 184
Michoels, Solomon 202
Middleton, Charles 33
Milestone, Lewis 53, 54–55, 147, 151
Milland, Ray 60, 258, 260
Miller, Arthur 5, 188–189, 197–200, 251, 252–253, 254–255
Miller, Marvin 79, 167
Mission to Moscow (book) 120
Mission to Moscow (film) 120–124

Mitchell, Thomas 111
Mola, General Emile 63, 64
Molotov, Vyachalev 5, 87, 120, 129, 268
Monroe, Marilyn 198, 254, 255
Morgan, Ralph 59
Morley, Karen 45
Morris, Chester 87, 88, 90
Mostel, Zero 234
Moynihan, Brian 128–129
Muni, Paul 4, 42–45, 46, 47, 82, 103, 165, 235
Munzenberg, Willi 5, 64, 140, 141
Murder My Sweet 179
Murphy, Dudley 29, 30
Mussolini, Benito 64, 65, 68
My Dream Is Yours 192

Naish, J. Carrol 46
The Naked City (film) 200–201, 241
The Naked City (TV show) 200
Navasky, Victor 269
Neal, Patricia 225
Nichols, Dudley 211
Night of the Quarter Moon 209
Nixon, Richard M. 228
Nolan, Lloyd 58, 59, 60, 105
None Shall Escape 154–155
Norris, Edward 75
The North Star 147–151
Northern Pursuit 152–154
Nott, Robert 175, 214
Novello, Ivor 16, 17
Nugent, Frank 56–57, 87, 90, 91

Objective Burma 161–165
O'Brien, Pat 13
Obringer, Roy 44, 122, 143, 144
Odets, Clifford 3, 5, 49–51, 53–54, 56–59, 213, 214, 215, 231
Odlum, Jerome 82–83
The Old and the New 15
Olivier, Sir Laurence 237, 238–239, 240, 241
On the Waterfront 234, 251
O'Neill, Eugene 24, 25, 26
O'Neill, Henry 34, 47
Operation Eichmann 272
Ornitz, Samuel 33–35
Our Blushing Brides 28
Out of the Fog 111–112, 229

Pal, George 246, 247
Palance, Jack 215
Panto, Pete 251–252
Parker, Alan 190, 193
Parker, Dorothy 5, 140, 189–191
Parker, Eleanor 170, 172
Parks, Larry 166
Passion of Josef D. 278
Paton, Alan 231–232
Patrick, Lee 220
Paul Robeson (play) 36–37
Paxton, John 180, 181, 195
Peace on Earth 22
The Pearl (novel) 98
Peck, Gregory 193

Peckinpah, Sam 220
Pentimento 273
Peron, Juan 181
Pevney, Joseph 197, 207
Phagan, Mary 71–72
Picon, Molly 116
Pine, William 216, 217, 218
Pinky 210–212
Pistolero's Progress 275
Poitier, Sidney 209, 232, 233
Polansky, Abraham 197, 206, 207
Pope Pius XI 68
Powell, Dick 180, 181
Pratt, Albert 259, 260
Prelude to Night 236
The Price 198, 254, 255
Price, Vincent 106
Pride of the Marines 170–172
The Public Enemy 10–13

Qualen, John 46, 111
Quality 211
Quinn, Anthony 105, 234

Raft, George 105, 109, 132, 134
Rainer, Luise 61–62, 136, 137, 138
Rains, Claude 21, 32, 33, 34, 75, 81
Rankin, John 228
Reagan, Pres. Ronald 146, 175–176, 272–273, 276
Reed, Walter 218
Reid, Carl Benton 95, 147
Reles, Abe "Kid Twist" 252–253
The Remarkable Andrew (film) 113–114, 157
The Remarkable Andrew (novel) 113
Revere, Anne 85, 196
Rhythm on the Range 59
Rice, Elmer 42
Richards, Ann 187
Richardson, Helen 8, 9, 237
Riddle, Nelson 177
Ride a Crooked Mile 60
Ridgely, John 152
Risdon, Elizabeth 90
Robbins, Jerome 234
The Robe (film) 242, 243, 244, 274
The Robe (novel) 241
Roberts, Bob 228
Roberts, Roy 206
Robeson, Eslanda 35–36, 37
Robeson, Paul 4, 24–26, 29–32, 35, 37, 51–53, 201–206
Robeson, Paul, Jr. 32
Robinson, Ann 245, 246
Robinson, Edward G. 103, 104, 105, 114, 200
Rogers, Ginger 156, 157, 158, 159, 206, 236
Rogers, Leila 158, 206
Roosevelt, Eleanor 195
Roosevelt, Pres. Franklin Delano 35, 41, 120, 139, 164
Ross, Frank 177, 241, 242, 244
Ross, Sam 229, 230
Rossen, Robert 5, 74–75, 77, 82, 85, 103, 104, 106, 107, 109, 196, 207
Ruggles, Charlie 59
Rush, Barbara 218, 264
Russell, Gail 216, 217–218, 219
Ruthless 236
Ryan, Robert 156, 157, 194, 208, 228

Salome, Where She Danced 60
Salt of the Earth 249–251
Samson and Delilah 241
Sanders of the River (film) 51–54
Sanders of the River (novel) 51–52, 53
The Sandpiper 271
Sands, Johnny 218
Sayre, Nora 127
Schary, Dore 217
Schell, Maximilian 264, 267
Schickel, Richard 188, 198
Schmid, Al 170, 171, 172
Schneidermann, William 13, 268
Schorer, Mark 39
Schulberg, B.P. 16, 27
Schulberg, Budd 16, 27, 139, 183, 234, 251, 253–254
Scott, Adrian 179, 180, 182, 183, 193, 195, 241
Scoundrel Time 274
The Sea Wolf (film) 103, 104–107, 180
The Sea Wolf (novel) 103–104
The Searching Wind (film) 187–188
The Searching Wind (play) 186–187
Selznick, David O. 103, 237
Sen Yung, Victor 226
Shalako (film) 156
Shannon, David 186
Shaw, George Bernard 22, 245–246
Shaw, Irwin 5, 107–109, 145, 195, 261–263
Shayne, Robert 191
She Done Him Wrong 13
Shek, Chiang-Kai 55, 161, 169
Sheridan, Ann 99
Sheriff, R.C. 20, 21
Shostakovich, Dmitri 202
Shumlin, Herman 96, 97, 140, 142, 144, 146, 187
Sidney, Sylvia 61, 111, 167, 187, 188
Siegel, Don 275, 276
Siegel, Sol 137
Silver Lode 60
Sinatra, Frank 175–177, 178, 275
Sinners in Paradise 77, 79–80, 91
Sister Act (novel) 81
Sister Carrie 9, 18, 235–237
Sklar, George 22, 23, 24
Skipper Next to God 228
Slayton, Governor Frank 71–72
Slezak, Walter 60, 196
Smart Money 13
Smashup: The Story of a Woman 70, 189–193
Smith, C. Aubrey 90
Sorell, Herb 174

South of Pago Pago 98–99
The Spanish Earth 97, 141
Spartacus 270
Stalin, Josef 2, 5, 19, 35, 64, 112, 120, 129, 147, 173, 186, 235, 268, 278
Stapleton, Maureen 267
A Star Is Born (1937) 189, 190, 192
Steffens, Lincoln 12–13, 14
Steinbeck, John 98, 235
Steiner, Max 145
Stevenson, Robert Louis 20
Stillwell, General Joseph 162
Stoddart, Dayton 236
Stone, Milburn 79
The Story of Louis Pasteur 115
A Streetcar Named Desire (film) 237, 238, 240
Strong, Leonard 167
Success at Any Price 28
Success Story 28, 184
Sumner, Cid Ricketts 211
Sundown at Crazy Horse 271
Sutter's Gold 16
Swope, Herbert, Jr. 256, 258, 261

Tales of Manhattan 201
Tamiroff, Akim 53–54, 60
Tavenner, Frank 227, 228, 231
Taylor, Kent 87, 88, 90
Taylor, Vaughn 264
Teal, Ray 154, 240
Tender Comrades 89, 156–159
Terror in a Texas Town 268, 270
Terry, Phillip 258, 259
Thaxter, Phyllis 160, 225
Them! 244
They Won't Forget 72–73, 75–77
The Thief of Baghdad 53
The Thin Man (novel) 142
Thirteen Women 33
Thirty Seconds Over Tokyo 89, 159–160
This Gun for Hire 24, 114, 117–118
Thomas, William 216, 217, 218
Thompson, Dorothy 18, 38–39, 123
Three Brave Men ix, 255–256, 258–261
Till the Day I Die 49–50, 266
The Time Machine (film) 247
The Time Machine (novel) 19, 247
To Have and Have Not (film) 221
To Have and Have Not (novel) 220–221
Toast of New York, the 60
Tobias, George 108, 162
Too Many Parents 59
Tracy, Spencer 159, 160, 180
Travers, Henry 155
Trotsky, Leon 122
The Troubled Air 263
Trumbo, Dalton 28, 35, 87–88, 90, 92–95, 112, 113, 156–159, 269–272
Tucker's People 206
Tully, Tom 152
Turner, Lana 73, 75

Tuttle, Frank 117, 118, 136, 138
Two Mules for Sister Sara 275–276

Uncertain Glory 143
Under My Skin 216

Valentino, Rudolph 9
Van Cleef, Lee 264
Van Sickel, Dale 229, 230
Van Zandt, Phil 166
Verboten 178
A View from the Bridge 198, 255
Vishinsky, Andrei 122–123
Viva Zapata! 234–235
The Voice of Stephen Wilder 216
Von Ribbentrop, Joachim 87, 122
Von Sternberg, Joseph 16, 17, 18
Von Stroheim, Erich 16, 148, 149, 151

Wagner, Dave 182–183, 206
Wald, Jerry 109, 164, 170, 222, 225
Wald, Mavis 200
Walker, May. James 22
Walker, Robert 159, 160
Wallace, Edgar 51, 52–53
Wallach, Eli 177
Wallis, Hal 83, 85–86, 104, 105, 134, 142, 187

Walsh, Raoul 126, 134, 152, 161, 162
Wanger, Walter 65, 68, 70, 189
The War of the Worlds (film) ix, 126, 244–247
The War of the Worlds (novel) 244–247
The War of the World (radio show) 20
Warner, Jack L. 5, 13–14, 42, 46–47, 48, 109, 120, 123, 124, 125, 164, 235, 261
Washington, Fredi 30
Watch on the Rhine (film) 141–145, 150, 184, 186
Watch on the Rhine (play) 139–140, 184
Waters, Ethel 211
Watson, Lucille 141
Wayne, John 177, 222
We Were Strangers 213
We Will Never Die 45
Weisel, Elie 155
Weiss, Emanuel "Mendy" 5, 252
Welles, Orson 20
Wellman, William 12
Wells, H.G. 5, 15, 19–22, 244–245, 246, 247
West, Nathanael 87, 89

Wexley, John 103–104, 180, 182, 183
Whale, James 20, 21, 79, 80–81, 91
What Makes Sammy Run 27, 183
Whitney, Peter 126
Wilde, Cornel 105
Wilson, Michael 249, 250, 269
Winter, Ella 12–13, 14
Winters, Shelley 215, 229, 230
Wiseman, Joseph 235, 258
Withers, Jane 147
Woods, Donald 144
Woods, Eddie 13
The World Changes 42
World Premiere 100
Wray, Fay 61
Wright, Teresa 98
Wright, William 97, 157, 187
Wyler, William 235, 238, 239

Yankee Doodle Dandy 14, 129
Yiddle with a Fiddle 116
Young, Robert 187, 188
The Young Lions (film) 145, 195, 263–267
The Young Lions (novel) 261–262

Zanuck, Darryl F. 5, 11, 13, 193, 210, 211, 212, 241, 242, 261, 263

www.ingramcontent.com/pod-product-compliance
Lightning Source LLC
Chambersburg PA
CBHW081541300426
44116CB00015B/2712